Human Society

Christine Hambling and Pauline Matthews

Second Edition

Macmillan Education

First published 1974
Reprinted 1975, 1976 (twice)
Second edition 1979
Reprinted 1980

Published by
MACMILLAN EDUCATION LTD
Houndmills Basingstoke Hampshire RG21 2XS
and London
Associated companies in Delhi Dublin
Hong Kong Johannesburg Lagos Melbourne
New York Singapore and Tokyo

Printed in Hong Kong

Contents

Acknowledgements

The author and publishers wish to thank the following for permission to use photographs:

Cover: John Hillelson Agency, Aerofilms.

Associated Press pp. 86, 129; Barnaby's pp. 145 lower, 171; Anne Bolt pp. 196 top, 200, 201; B.I.T. p. 36 top; British Tourist Authority pp. 50 lower, 170 lower, 188, 189, 193, 205, 212, 213; British Hovercraft Corp. p. 69 top; B.B.C. p. 74; Brooke Bond Oxo Limited p. 179; Canadian Information Service pp. 13 right, 148 lower, 149 top, 150 left; J. Allan Cash 17, 49, 108, 147, 148 top, 150 right, 194, 206; Camera Press 66, 240, 241, 242, 243, 244, 251 top; Canadian High Commission pp. 10, 11; Central Office of Information pp. 69 lower, 165 right, 204, 231; Country Commission pp. 172, 173, 255; Commissioner of Police pp. 207, 210; Douglas Dickens p. 192; Mary Evans Picture Library pp. 35, 39, 51, 55 top, 57 right, 72, 85, 91, 119 lower, 166, 208; *Evening Gazette*, Middlesbrough p. 71 top; Finnish Embassy pp. 18, 19; F.A.O. pp. 50 top, 62, 63, 276; Ghana Information Service p. 175 lower; *Guardian* p. 121; Ann Hibbard p. 197; International Labour Office pp. 41 top right, 43, 78 lower, 79; I.L.E.A. p. 123 lower; Japanese Information Centre p. 196; Keystone pp. 40, 41 lower, 55 lower; Graham Keen pp. 97, 119 top; John Laing Ltd p. 219 lower; L.C.C. Photo Library p. 110; National Film Board of Canada p. 10; National Parks Commission p. 230 top; Observer – Transworld pp. 14, 15; Popperfoto pp. 6, 7, 12, 13, 28, 41 top left, 67, 73, 93, 101, 107, 113, 122, 127 top, 145 top, 146, 151, 152, 153, 159, 160, 162, 163, 198, 232, 233, 251 lower, 262, 267 lower, 279; Picturepoint pp. 22, 23, 246; Royal Danish Ministry for Foreign Affairs pp. 149 lower, 154; Radio Times Hulton Picture Library pp. 237, 239, 247, 250; Service de Presse et D'Info des Communantes Européennes p. 47; Shelter pp. 57 left, 165 left, 216, 221, 223, 224, 225, 230 lower; Society for Cultural Relations with the U.S.S.R. pp. 143, 144; South African Railways pp. 87 lower, 168 lower; Syndication International p. 263; Taylor Woodrow Services Ltd p. 219; T.U.C. pp. 37 top, 71 lower; U.N.E.S.C.O. pp. 25, 44 lower, 48, 275; U.N.I.C.E.F. pp. 168 top, 190 left, 220, 264, 278, 279; Unigate p. 77; United Nations pp. 87 top, 90, 271; U.S.I.S. p. 267; Vanderstock pp. 36, 37, 44, 45, 49, 89, 94, 95, 109, 111, 126, 127, 134, 135, 142, 143, 170, 190, 208; W.H.O. pp. 76, 157, 195, 258, 260, 273, 274, 278; Wellcome Museum p. 123; World Bank Group pp. 277, 278; A. & C. Black Limited p. 166 lower.

The authors and publishers wish to thank the following, who have kindly given permission for the use of copyright material:

Cambridge University Press, for a table from *The Affluent Worker: Political Attitudes and Behaviour* by Goldthorpe *et al;* David & Charles Ltd, for extract from *Land & Leisure* by Patmore; Granada Publishing Ltd, for a table from *The British Political Elite* by W. L. Guttsman; Harper & Row Pub. Inc., for extract adapted and condensed from *Wolf Child and Human Child* by Arnold Gesell Copyright © 1940, 1941 by Arnold Gesell, by Permission of Harper & Row Pub. Inc.; Her Majesty's Stationery Office for a table from *Britain: An Official Handbook 1971;* Laurence Pollinger Ltd, (on behalf of William Morrow and Co. Inc.) and Penguin Books Ltd, for extract from *Coming of Age in Samoa* by Margaret Mead; Longman Group Ltd, for a table from *Population* by Kelsall; Macdonald & Co. (Publishers) Ltd, for extract adapted and condensed from *Man in Society* by Douglas *et al,* copyright © 1964 by Macdonald & Co.; Macmillan Publishing Co. Inc., for extract from *Human Society* by K. Davis copyright © 1948, 1949 by Macmillan Publishing Co. Inc.; Routledge and Kegan Paul Ltd, for a table from *How People Vote* by M. Benny, A. P. Gray and R. H. Pear.

The publishers have made every effort to trace the copyright-holders but if they have inadvertently overlooked any, they will be pleased to make the necessary arrangement at the first opportunity.

Thanks are due to Brian Matthews for his constant help and encouragement; and to Charles Matthews, friends and colleagues at Sydenham School and in the Association for the Teaching of the Social Sciences for their useful criticisms.

Introduction

What is Social Science?

We live in a complicated society and it is not easy to understand the way that different parts of it work. There are millions of people doing different jobs, with different ideas and attitudes, and all wanting different things. There is a variety of skills to be learned and many machines to operate. The pace of life becomes quicker and quicker, especially as science and technology are developing all the time.

A *social* scientist has to try and explain what is happening to peoples' lives just as a *natural* scientist tries to explain what is happening in the world of nature. Both kinds of scientist are always collecting information but one collects it about *people* whilst the other collects information about natural *things*. The next step after collecting information is to put it into some kind of order. Finally the social scientist has to try and describe the facts he has collected and to explain them. Natural scientists who study physics, chemistry and biology have been using this kind of collecting–ordering–explaining method for many years, but social scientists did not really begin to do this until the end of last century and therefore *social* science is a very young form of science. While it is growing fast, it still has a lot to learn.

One of the largest problems facing social scientists is that they have feelings towards the groups of people they are studying, and they have to be particularly careful to realise what their feelings are and to try not to let their feelings interfere with their work. They must be extra careful not to bend the facts to fit with their own hopes and fears and interests.

Social scientists can take a special interest in different parts of their work. Some are particularly interested in studying societies where there is no written language and where the people lead a very simple way of life. These scientists have a technical name – ANTHROPOLOGISTS. Others are particularly interested in wealth and trade and the way in which scarce goods are spread around. These scientists are called ECONOMISTS. Others are particularly interested in the way the human mind works and thinks and reasons. These scientists are called PSYCHOLOGISTS. Others are particularly interested in complicated societies like Britain and they are called SOCIOLOGISTS.

All of these scientists are studying one special part of the social life of human beings, and working together they can pool their information to help us understand more about man and the groups he belongs to.

1 Pre-Industrial Societies

Human Society

In the early Stone Age, before about 8000 B.C., people lived in small groups, probably consisting of about twenty members, all part of the same family. The main concern of these groups was simply to survive, and they lived very hard lives, never knowing for certain that the group would be alive and well the next year, the next month or even the next week. In order to live, they had a few basic requirements; they needed food and drink, and some kind of shelter. Depending on the climate, they might also have needed clothing.

In many ways the life of early man was very similar to that of intelligent animals such as the apes. Apes live in family groups, get their food in the same way as the earliest man, and make very simple nests or shelters out of twigs and grass. But in a very important way, early man differed from the apes; whereas each ape in a family group has to find its own food (except when very young), early man was able, because he was more intelligent, to organise his group so that certain members did some jobs, and others did different jobs. The advantage of this is obvious; if you spend all your time on many different tasks, you cannot become as skilled at any of them as if you concentrate most of your time on one only. By spending most of your time doing one job you learn to do it better and more efficiently. The system of splitting up work so that one man does one job and another does a different one, is called the DIVISION OF LABOUR. Some animal societies have a division of labour too; bees and ants are organised so that groups specialise in different tasks, though all co-operate in the same overall plan. In the case of some other animals, including man, tasks are shared out according to sex and age. Unlike other animals, however, man is able to change the division of labour if there is a reason for doing so. Man recognises that some individuals, irrespective of whether they are men or women, young or old, have certain abilities and are fitted to perform certain tasks. The division of labour among humans is therefore never as rigid and inflexible as it is among animals. Man has control over his SOCIAL ORGANISATION.

Man also has control over his physical surroundings, to a greater or lesser extent. To get enough food and warmth for his family, early man devised ways of changing his physical surroundings; he used tools to make fire, weapons, clothing and shelter. No animal has ever made even the simplest tool, although apes have come very close by using stones as implements.

Men have control over the other people around them. All human groups – families, groups of friends, workmates – have ways of influencing the members of the group. There may be rules, as there are in a school or a youth club, or there may be laws laid down by a national parliament. Very often it is just a matter of what is or is not 'done'. A group of school friends may simply understand that they must support each other: no one needs to put it in writing. Animal societies do not have this kind of social control. Animals have ways of laying down rules, but although they can communicate with each other, they have nothing so complicated as language. Without language men would not be able to express their ideas and beliefs, even to themselves.

Man is creative. Early societies have left evidence of great artistic ability in the form of cave paintings. Men expressed their feelings by painting, dancing, and making objects out of wood, clay and stone. Sometimes people used their art to try and make things happen: some dances were intended to bring rain; by painting a buffalo the artist may have hoped to become a successful hunter.

By making tools, by using ritual, religion, magic and art to influence future events man shows that he is unique among animals. He has the ability to think ahead, to plan for the future. He may plan for the next day by laying in an extra store of food, or he may plan for the winter by building a strong house. He may plan for death and the after-life by building a tomb and making gifts to the gods. Man believes that he can change the course of events by doing the right things now, and this is perhaps the most important way in which human society differs from animal society; human society is capable of change.

Hunters and Gatherers

The men of the Stone Age had to spend most of their time providing the absolute necessities of life. They got their food by hunting wild animals and by fishing, and by gathering wild berries, fruit, fungi and honey. They did not know how to grow their own food and they did not yet have domesticated animals, so they had to rely entirely on what they could find around them and on their own skill in collecting or hunting food. Hunters and gatherers, as people who live this kind of life are called, had a very simple division of labour. They split the two main jobs – hunting and gathering – so that the men did one, and women did the other. Thus a boy would become a skilled hunter, and a girl would have to learn from her mother and other female relatives how to find the most juicy and edible roots and berries.

Some people today live in a similar way to early Stone Age men, e.g. (1) the Pygmies of the Congo and South-East Asia, (2) the Indians of the Amazon, and (3) the Bushmen of the Kalahari desert. The Australian Aborigines and the Eskimos of Greenland and Alaska also used to live like this.

We are going to look at two of these societies in more detail. We shall see what kind of family

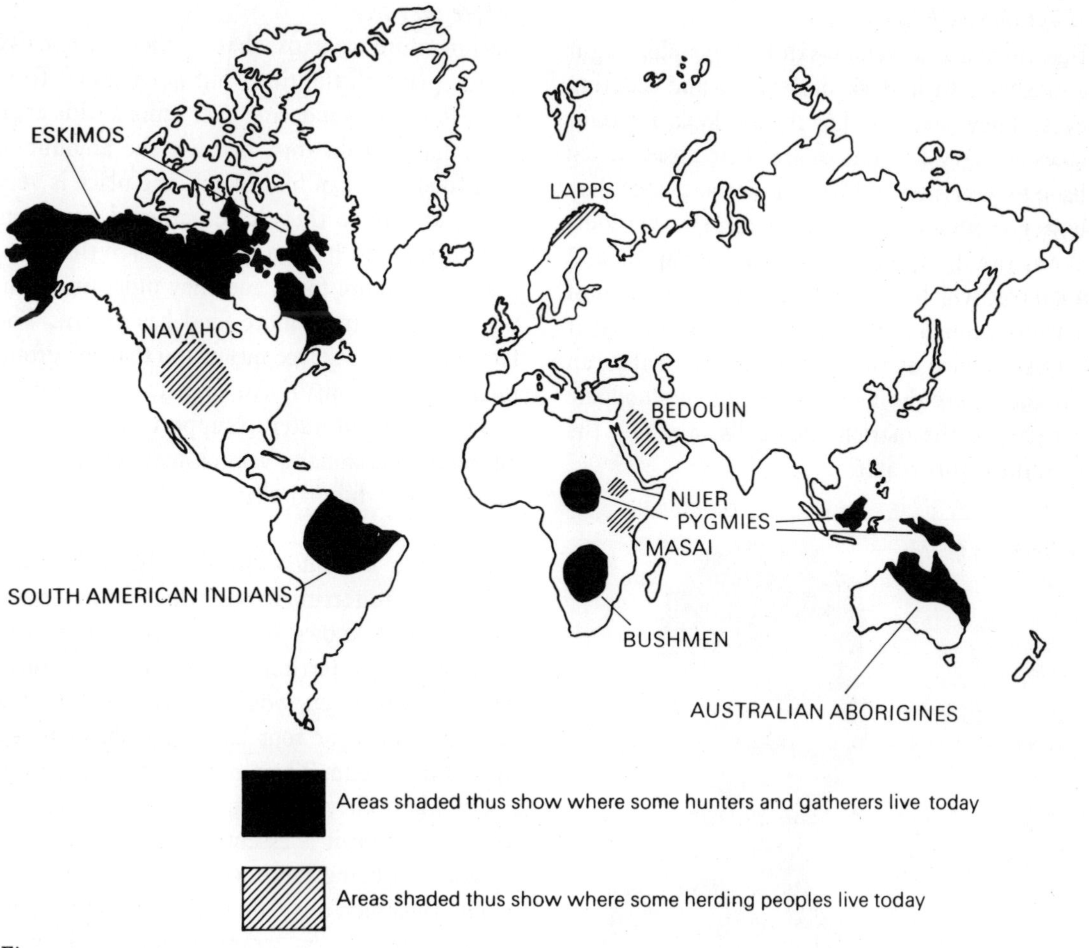

Figure 1

life, work, religion and education exist in a very simple society.

THE BUSHMEN OF THE KALAHARI DESERT

The Kalahari desert is a vast area of dry bush land in South West Africa and western Botswana. For most of the year, from March to December, there is little or no rain; the sun is fierce and the ground is dusty. The only growing things are low bushes and spiky grass full of thistles and thorns, and the very occasional baobab tree. Baobab trees are enormous, up to two hundred feet high and thirty feet across the base, and in summer they bear a dry pear-shaped fruit which the Bushmen eat.

Rain falls between December and March, and is often torrential, drenching the dry and dusty earth. Then all the grass turns green and the trees and plants flower, while the earth turns to mud, but in March the drought starts again, and slowly the bush dries up for the next nine months.

The Bushmen live in family groups in the Kalahari desert, and have a way of life which is entirely ruled by the harsh dry conditions of the area.

What they look like

Bushmen are a yellow-skinned people, slight and short, with dark curly hair and slanting eyes. They have a rather Asiatic look, for their faces are very flat and so are their noses. They have to wear skin and leather clothes, since they have no cotton or wool; men wear a leather loin-cloth, and the women a small leather apron and a KAROSS, which is a cape made from the skin of a whole animal and tied at the waist so that it forms a pouch at the back where the baby can sit, and where the mother can put the food she collects, or the ostrich egg-shells in which the Bushmen store water.

A Bushman hunter.

Where they live

Bushmen are NOMADS, that is, they do not live in one place all the time, but move about from place to place, wandering over quite a wide area. They have to do this, because the amount of wild food they can find in any one place is very small, and once they have gathered the roots and berries and hunted the animals in that area, there is no more food, and they must move on, not returning until more food has grown. The fact that food is scarce means too that the group must be kept small. An area cannot provide enough food and water to support a large group, although occasionally groups may get together for a short while so that friends and relatives may meet.

Although Bushmen are nomads, each group has a definite territory over which it may roam and which it knows very well. No group may trespass on the territory of another, for otherwise the Bushmen would never know that a particular bush or root had not been gathered by another group. They might travel for days to a spot where they remember there being a good supply of food; it is essential that they can rely on the food being there when they arrive.

The Bushmen travel on foot, carrying all their possessions – tools, weapons, pots and ornaments – with them. Although they never own very much, this can amount to a large bundle, but the Bushmen are used to walking and can cover the ground at four or five miles an hour, even though they are heavily laden.

Work

The work of the Bushmen is almost entirely concerned with getting food. When they are not actually out looking for food, they may be making tools and weapons, or skinning animals and cooking them. Their tools and weapons are sometimes made of metal, for although the Bushmen do not know how to make metal themselves, they sometimes get it from neighbouring peoples, trading it for the things they have made.

Below is a list of some of the jobs that may be done by men and by women:

Men

Hunt animals like the gemsbok, eland and wildebeest.
Make weapons, such as arrows with poisoned tips.
Make tools and equipment such as string out of grass fibres.
Collect honey by climbing trees and smoking out the bees.
Skin and clean an animal so every bit is used for something, food, clothing or equipment.

Women

Make the hut out of grass and twigs.
Collect roots and berries and melons in a kaross, with the help of a digging stick.
Care for the children, nursing and carrying them until they are three or four years old.
Gather firewood and make fires.
Make beads and ornaments for all the family.

To be good at their work, Bushmen have to be very careful and observant, so as not to miss clues which may point to food.

Here are two extracts from *The Harmless People*, in which Elizabeth Marshall Thompson describes a woman and a man at work:

Keeping her eyes on the ground, Twikwe noticed a tiny crack in the sand. She scooped at it with the point of her digging stick, tipped out a truffle, and picked it up almost without stopping. As we walked on she broke it in half, put half in her kaross, and offered half to me. I ate it. It was light brown and had a delicious salty flavour. Truffles grow an inch or so below the hard-surfaced ground and have no leaf or stalk nor vine to show where they are, only the tiny crack made by the truffle swelling, which the Bushmen notice.

A man has to be just as observant to be a successful hunter.

Short Kwi was famous as a hunter. He often killed more game in a year than many other men kill in their lives, a great hunter among a hunting people. The other Bushmen told stories about him – about the time he had killed four wildebeests in a herd of many, about the time he had killed an eland, a wildebeest and a wild pig all in one day. It was his technique of hunting to be relentless in his pursuit; therefore, if he shot an animal and suspected others to be in the vicinity he would let the wounded animal run where it would while he hunted on and shot another, and another, and when all were as good as dead he would rest, then return to pick up the trail of the one he felt would die soonest. He almost never lost an animal, for his eyes were sharp and he could follow a cold trail over hard ground and even over stones; he could tell from fallen leaves whether the wind or passing feet had disarranged them; and the meat that resulted from his prolific hunting was never wasted, for he would bring other hunters to help him dry it, then carry it off to a werf somewhere to share with the others.

A family of Bushmen. The mother will carry her child around with her when she goes looking for food, until he is three or four years old.

One of the most important pieces of equipment for the Bushmen is the ostrich egg-shell. They use these for storing water; when there is plenty of water, they fill as many egg-shells as possible, and bury them in the sand until there is a drought, making quite sure they know where they have left them. Any tool or equipment which helps men do their work more easily is called CAPITAL EQUIPMENT. In our society capital equipment may be complicated tools or expensive machinery. The capital equipment of the Bushmen, such as ostrich eggshells and digging sticks, is much simpler, but just as important to their work.

The family

Figure 2 is a family tree showing how the members of a group of Bushmen might be related to one another.

This family tree includes only the daughters of the family, an unmarried son, and the son who is leader of the group. This does not include the youngest generation, for obviously the little children live with their parents whether they are boys or girls. But when the children grow up and get married the boys usually go and live with their wives' families while the girls and their husbands continue to live at home. After a couple have been married some time, however, they can decide whether to stay with the wife's family or whether to move and live with the husband's family. Can you think of a reason why the girl's parents would be very glad to have another young man to live in the family?

Boys may not get married until they have hunted and killed their first wild animal, so if a man never learns to hunt successfully he may never have a family of his own. Unless he is a competent hunter, a man cannot support a family, and he would just be putting an added burden on the whole community.

Boys and girls learn the skills they will need to equip them for adult life from the other members of their families. They are not taught in the way that children in Britain are taught in school, but pick up what they must know by helping, by making mistakes and learning how not to make the same mistake the next time. From quite an early age they are expected to collect firewood, and small animals and insects for food, and they will have been taken with their mothers on expeditions into the bush, to gather roots and berries, ever since they were babies.

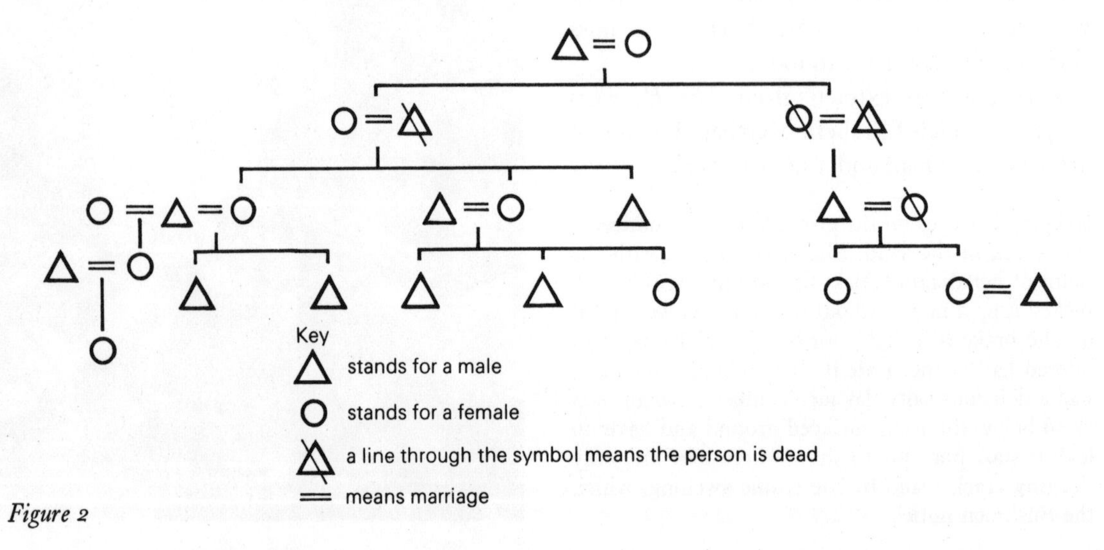

Figure 2

By his early teens, a Bushman boy must already be a good hunter.

Belief

Bushmen children do not only learn how to stay alive, they learn too about the spirits which live in the bush country and which help or harm Bushmen in their efforts to survive.

Bushmen believe that there are three gods. In the east lives the great god whose name is Gao Na, which means Big Man. He makes the spirits of the dead out of his medicine smoke, and some medicine men (who are people with special powers to heal others) say they have seen him.

Bushmen use their spirits and gods to explain things for which we in Britain would give scientific explanations. People cannot go through life without any understanding of the things that happen to them. We all need to be able to guess at what is going to happen, and so we invent ideas on the basis of what we already know and which fit the events of our everyday lives. The scientist can base his ideas on the experiments and experiences of the thousands of scientists who have worked before him. The Bushman's theories about the world cannot be tested like this and also they are not affected by the ideas of so many other people, because Bushman society is very small and has little contact with other societies.

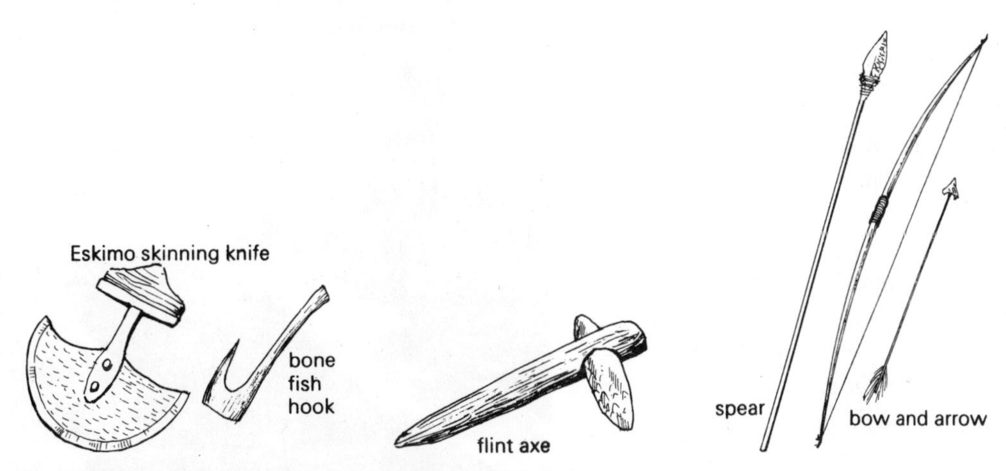

Figure 3 Tools and weapons used by hunters and gatherers at different times and in different places.

An Eskimo draws in a seal at Pelly Bay.

THE ESKIMOS

The Arctic region includes the Northern parts of the mainland of Canada, Alaska and Siberia, and many islands in the Arctic ocean. The North Pole is in the middle of a sea of ice surrounded by land. For most of the year it is winter but during the very brief summer flowers grow in profusion, transforming the landscape. The only animals which can survive are those adapted to the freezing conditions. Seals, arctic foxes, polar bears and fish survive the harsh winters. Caribou (similar to reindeer), walruses and many birds migrate south during winter, returning to the Tundra in the summer. Burrowing animals cannot exist at all because the ground is not suitable, and animals which hibernate cannot exist because the summer is not long enough for them to store up enough fat to last through the winter. The humans who live in the Arctic are called *Eskimos*.

An Eskimo hunter with a harpoon beside a kayak and a sealskin tent, looking out over Pelly Bay, Canada.

Way of life

Until the twentieth century the Eskimos lived a similar way of life to Stone Age people. They made fire by friction, hunted with spears and bows and arrows, made their tools from bone, horn and driftwood, burned seal oil for lighting, and used skins for clothing. Today this is all changing and the changes will be discussed in detail in a later chapter. The present chapter is concerned with the old way of life based on hunting.

The old way of life

In conditions such as the Eskimos lived, the main concern was survival. Every day involved a hunt for food or a battle against the weather. Although the Bushmen live in a very different climate from the Eskimos they share the concern for survival and resemble the old Eskimos strongly in this way. The Arctic has a yearly cycle of long hard winter and short summer. This cycle determines the movements of the caribou, and the availability of fish, seals, foxes and walruses for food and for furs. Upon this cycle the whole survival and hence social life of the Eskimos was based. Work was not for money to provide food and the necessities and luxuries of life, as in Britain, but to provide the basic essentials of life: food and warmth. For the Bushmen warmth is provided by the climate. The Eskimos had to provide their own warmth and therefore to make clothes and housing to withstand the climate.

Life during the winter – the Eskimos of Pelly Bay

During the winter seals were the main source of food. They also provided fat for cooking, lighting and warmth, and skins for clothing. Seals do not migrate, but instead stay in the Arctic during winter, living in the sea beneath the thinner ice and coming up to breathing holes occasionally. During these brief appearances at the holes, seals could be speared.

Silhouette of an Eskimo hunter standing beside a seal breathing hole. This man holds a rifle but the traditional way would have been to spear fish at holes of this type.

If an Eskimo were out hunting alone he would find it a difficult task to watch all the holes at the same time. If he watched the wrong hole he and his family might starve. Suppose, however, that he had brothers or grown-up sons to help him. They could each watch a different hole and one would be sure to catch something. The men could then share their catch and no one would be hungry. This kind of co-operation was used in many areas including Pelly Bay in Northern Canada, and many seal-sharing partnerships existed. Such a group of men formed part of an EXTENDED FAMILY. The extended family also included grandparents, aunts, uncles and cousins.

An extended family by the cache where food was stored out of the reach of wild animals. This photograph was taken many years ago in Alaska. Very few Eskimos live or dress like this nowadays.

In Britain today many people live near their extended family and some have members of their extended family living in the same house. The Eskimos of Pelly Bay lived near their extended family in the winter because they needed to co-operate in order to survive. In the summer however they separated into smaller groups to fend for themselves because 'the living was easier'.

Eskimo life in the summer

Figure 4 shows an Eskimo boy called Mossessee with his close family in the summer. He is with his father, his mother and his two sisters. This close family is called by a special name – a NUCLEAR FAMILY. The word 'nucleus' means 'in the centre' and these are Mossessee's nearest or 'central' relatives. Most people in Britain today live with their nuclear family which has only two generations in it.

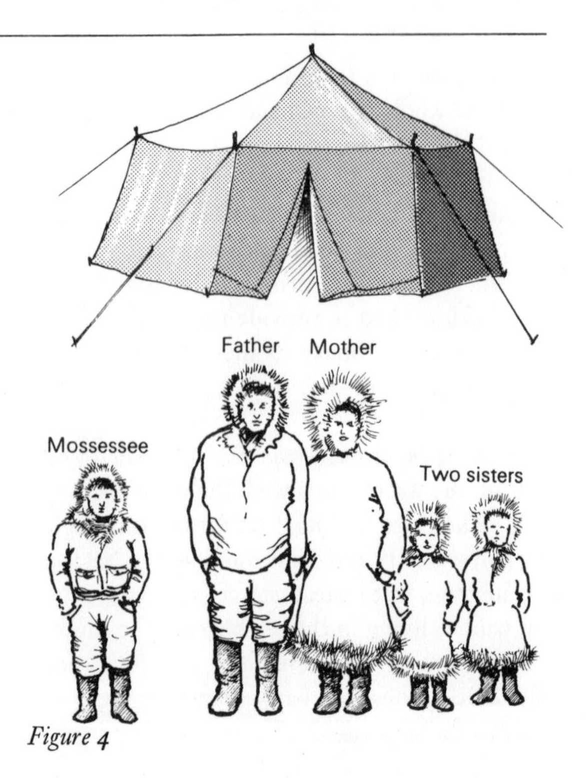

Figure 4

The traditional way of life. An Eskimo family beside their igloo about to feast on seal meat.

Ceremonial drum dance igloo, Tuktoyaktuk, Canada.

In the spring the caribou would return from the warmer lands in the south in readiness for the summer. Now the living was easier. A man no longer needed his relatives to help him out. His relatives were somewhere else fending for themselves, only to be re-united in the harsh conditions of the next winter. The nuclear family would live in a tent made of caribou skin. As the caribou returned they would follow a traditional trail and would be closely watched by the Eskimos who would wait for a chance to spear and capture them. The caribou had to slow down to swim across rivers and this was a good place for Eskimos to lie in wait. The diagram below shows the nuclear family and the extended family linked together.

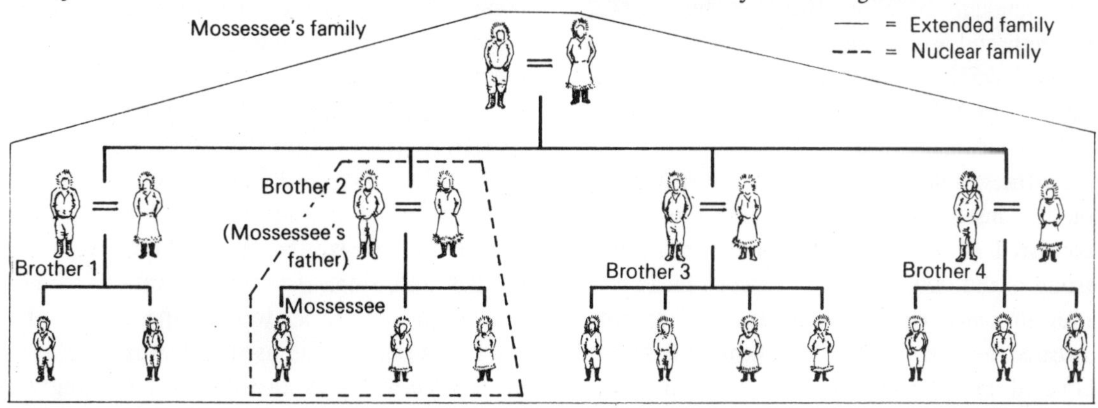

Figure 5

Traditional Eskimo art showed scenes from everyday life. Behind the caribou is a cairn of stones built by the Eskimos to scare the caribou to where they could be caught. Caribou are short-sighted and think that the cairns are men.

Within the family, Eskimos divided up their work according to men's work, women's work and children's work. Men hunted and built igloos and tents. Women made clothes from the hides and pelts, making patterned garments by using varying shades of fur with a great degree of skill. The holes pierced in the hides were just large enough to allow the thin bone needle through and when the garment became wet it swelled slightly, so that the hole was completely blocked by the sinew thread, making a waterproof seam.

In the winter, clothes were worn with the fur on the inside for extra warmth. The clothes consisted of a large fur anorak and leather trousers and boots. They were worn fairly loose even in winter to allow ventilation. If a person sweated too much then he might find himself covered in ice when he cooled down and in danger of losing his life. Women also did the cooking and cut up the carcasses, cleaning the skins and making the skins soft by chewing them. Women made the skin boats and covers for the canoes called kayaks, while men made the tent poles and the frame for the kayak. Children learned the tasks which they would perform when adults, e.g. the girls made small bone dolls and dressed them with scraps of fur.

The flesh of the caribou was used for food for the Eskimo's family and dogs, and as bait for fox traps. The hides had no commercial value so each hunter kept only those he needed.

The hides were dried and used for clothing, tent-making in the summer, and lining snow houses in the winter. Bones were used for needles and sinew for thread, antlers formed brakes on sledges as well as the handles for snow knives. Fat was used in lamps with moss for a wick and was also used for cooking the food.

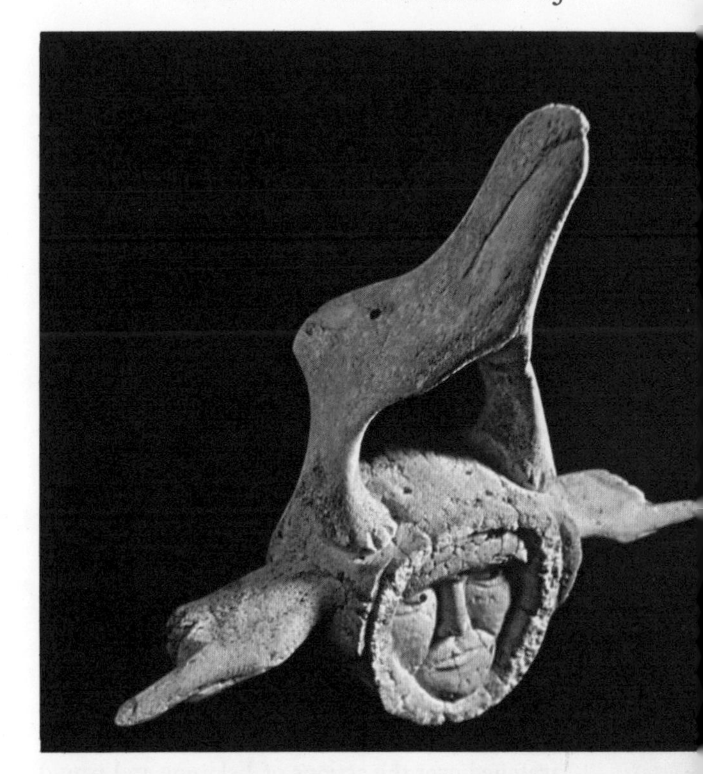

Eskimos had to use the few materials around them in their art. Bone was always available and was often used for carvings such as these.

The changing way of life

One of the changes which had a great effect on Eskimos' life was the introduction of guns. The main and more recent changes will be mentioned later on, but guns have been available to Eskimos for a long time.

Eskimos would have to obtain the guns from somewhere, and pay for them in some way. The main way of paying where there is no money is by exchanging things.

Eskimos needed guns, knives with sharp metal blades to replace knives made of stone and bone, rope to tie sledges and fix tents and cooking pots.

Many of the furs obtained from arctic animals were popular for coats and other clothes among people in cities. Seal pelts, fox, arctic squirrel and other furs were among the popular ones. By a system of exchanging furs for the goods they required, at trading posts, Eskimos managed to accumulate new tools and utensils. This system is known as BARTER.

However there are some problems involved with a system like this. For example, how would an Eskimo exchange a whole seal skin for a half a gun if that was what a whole seal skin was thought to be worth? What would an Eskimo do if no one liked his skins and he had nothing else to swop? How would the man at the trading centre work out the exact price of each skin an Eskimo brought in? How would an Eskimo save for the future if his skins were too large and bulky to be stored?

In other societies people tried in the past to solve these problems by inventing simple kinds of money. Sometimes sea shells would be used, or coloured stones. Eventually people hit on the idea of using small pieces of metal, and later notes were used too. Money is useful because it can be divided up into little pieces (not like a seal fur or a gun). It can be stored easily so saving is possible; it can be carried around, and it can be used to compare one thing with another and so exact prices are possible.

However, in the old way of life Eskimos had no money, so they had to be content with barter until their way of life began to change.

Religion

The difficult conditions for survival and the need for humans everywhere to explain the life around them both had an effect on Eskimo beliefs. Eskimos were sometimes said not to believe anything but rather to fear everything. There were so many things to fear in the Eskimo environment; there were wild animals which could kill, blizzards which prevented hunting and harmed those out facing them, storms, cracking ice which might cause danger to the traveller, and always the bitter cold outside the igloo. Eskimos explained their environment by three main spirits:

Nuliajuk was a girl spirit believed to be an orphan cast out to the cold by the Eskimos. She then took revenge by her power over the animals, especially the seals, for she could make them escape during hunting and she was greatly feared.

Tatket was the spirit of the moon who watched over the actions of Eskimos and would help Nuliajuk to take revenge if bad deeds were done.

Narsuk was the spirit of storms who would help Nuliajuk and Tatket by conjuring up blizzards and ice to make life and hunting very dangerous. To help themselves appease the angry spirits Eskimos had a priest or *Angatok* who could go into a trance and communicate with the spirits. If an Eskimo knew he had done wrong he would often confess to the Angatok and this made courts of law or other formal ways of dealing with criminals unnecessary. The power of the Angatok and the pressure of the whole community weighed upon a guilty person's mind until his guilt was too much for him and he revealed his wrong action.

As well as believing in the spirits, Eskimo life was surrounded by many superstitions and taboos which regulated people's behaviour.

Many people in Britain will not walk under ladders, and they throw salt over their shoulder if they spill it, to prevent bad luck. This is very similar to some of the taboos which Eskimos had. Eskimos believed that all animals had spirits and that the offended spirits would cause animals to avoid hunters if people broke the rules concerning them. When a seal carcass was brought into a house, women had to stop sewing at once, and before the seal could be skinned the dead animal – or its spirit – was given a drink of water. Reindeer meat and seal or walrus meat could not be eaten on the same day, nor could they be stored together. Women might not begin work on the winter deerskin clothes until the reindeer hunting season was ended.

Herding – A more secure way of life

The way of life of hunters and gatherers is a very risky one. Since they have to rely on wild animals and plants for food, they can never be very certain how much food there will be next week, or indeed whether there will be any food at all. After about 8000 B.C. men began to develop ways of making their food supply more reliable; they took the first steps in changing their environment to suit their needs. Men had already used tame dogs in hunting and now they began to domesticate other animals, such as cattle, sheep, goats and pigs for food, and horses, oxen and camels for transport. In Mesopotamia the first dairy farming began, and sheep's wool began to be used for clothing.

The most important effect of this development was to ensure that people got more food and had a more permanent supply of food. Men were no longer living from day to day. This meant that men's lives became less difficult, more stable and more secure. Because there was more food to go round, they could live in bigger groups than hunters and gatherers. Some societies today live almost entirely on their herds. These people are NOMADS, constantly on the move, because their animals need grazing and water, and cannot stay long in one place. Since cattle are very easily stolen, these peoples are often engaged in raids on other herds, and in fights with other herding peoples.

Examples of herding peoples today (although there are others) are:

the Navahos of North America who herd sheep and goats;
the Lapps of Scandinavia who herd reindeer;
the Bedouin of Arabia who herd camels;
the Nuer and Masai tribes of East Africa who herd cattle.

No one knows for certain how the Lapps originated. They are not like other European people in Scandinavia; on average the Lapps are much shorter. Neither are they Mongoloid people like the Eskimos, for although most are dark, about a quarter have fair hair and blue eyes.

THE REINDEER-HERDING LAPPS

The Eskimos are not the only people to inhabit the far north. The Lapps also live in the Arctic, in the region of the North Cape of Norway, in northern Sweden and Finland, and in the Kola Peninsula of the USSR. These people lead a way of life that was common when most of Europe was covered by the Great Glacier, and they live in conditions similar to those which must have existed during the Ice Age. The Lapps have, of course, been affected by the developments in the rest of Europe; many have given up the traditional way of life, and even those who still follow the herdsman's way of life have adopted some modern methods and acquired modern equipment. Nowadays there are about 100,000 Lapps herding 440,000 reindeer.

As with the Eskimos, the life of the Lapps is very strongly affected by the changing seasons. In winter the temperature is usually below minus 10° centigrade and can fall much lower; for a month or two there is no sunlight at all, although there is twilight for part of the day. The Lapps face the constant dangers of blizzards and wolves, fuel shortage and famine. The gloom of winter is in utter contrast to the lightness and brightness of summer. In most of the Lapp territory, the sun circles the tundra continuously for a period of at least two weeks, and sometimes more than two months. The snow and ice melt and in their place flowers and grass spring up on the plains and the slopes of the mountains.

How they live

Lapp shelter has to be portable, so the traditional dwelling is a tent made out of reindeer skin, shaped like a cone with poles to hold up the skin. At the top there is a hole through which the smoke escapes, and this is about two or three feet across. Even though the Lapps sometimes make a more permanent house, in the same shape but covered with earth, their houses are not nearly so efficient as those of the Eskimos. At night the temperature is almost as low inside as it is outside, and since this might be as low as minus 50 °C, even the skin coverings are not enough to keep the people warm. Apart from being cold, it is also very smoky. If the smoke hole is closed to keep out the cold, the tent very soon fills with smoke, and even when the hole is open the people have to sit on the floor where the air is freshest. The floor is covered with twigs of birch, so it is dry enough to sleep on.

Again, because they are nomads, the Lapps have very few possessions. They keep their utensils in a 'travel box', and apart from this the only piece of furniture will be the cradle which hangs from the ceiling. While they are travelling, the people often eat only cold food, and although in summer they manage to get some vegetables and berries, on the whole they eat only meat, which they store out of the dogs' reach, hanging from a tripod of forked poles.

The boat-shaped sledges are pulled by reindeer along a well-defined track.

Great skill is needed in looking after the herd. In this picture a visitor to the Lapps is examining the reindeer.

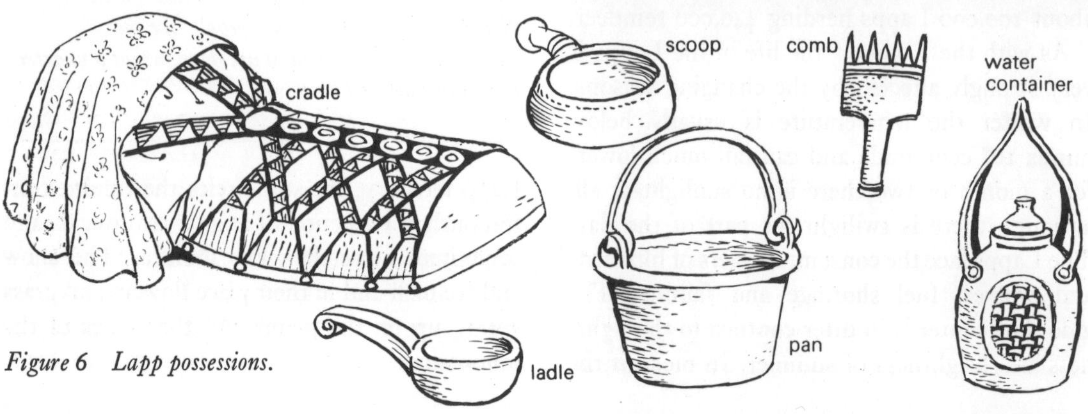

Figure 6 Lapp possessions.

Lapp children learn to look after the herd from a very early age. One important skill they must master is that of lassoing the reindeer, for the herds of different families often get mixed up.

The Lapps keep the few tools they need for cleaning skins, sewing, cooking and so on in their travel box.

Language

The Lapps have their own language, which is like Finnish and other languages of northern Europe and north-western Asia. There are three dialects which are so different that one Lapp sometimes cannot understand another. People's language develops so that it fits the needs of their everyday life. Where English has just one word for reindeer, the Lapps have very many different words. Each herdsman needs to be able to distinguish his reindeer from those of other people, so he has different names for his animals, based on their sex, age, colour and the shape of their antlers. A reindeer is called by a different word every year for the first seven years of its life. There are over fifty terms which describe the antlers, and another fifty which describe colour. In this way, the Lapps have a very highly specialised vocabulary related to their occupation and way of life. A different herding people – say the Bedouin or the Nuer – will have a similarly specialised vocabulary, but one which relates to the particular animals – in this case the camel and cow – which they herd.

The pattern of work

Lapps live in a group or CLAN of two to six families, which is called a SITA. The clan is led by the father who owns the biggest herd, and each individual family needs at least 300 reindeer to survive, killing about 40 to 50 each year for food. This means that the herd of the whole clan will usually be over a thousand, or even two thousand. To drive and protect so large a herd requires very great discipline and organisation.

On the move, the Lapps and their reindeer form a V. At the head of the herd, the leader of the sita moves on skis, carrying a decorated staff which represents his authority over the whole herd. Beside him moves the lead deer, which has been trained from calfhood to lead the herd. Without the skill and knowledge of these two figures, the sita and herd would disintegrate. The survival of the whole community depends on them.

Behind the lead deer and head of the clan the rest of the herd follow. First come a number of reindeer in single file, carrying packs and babies, with men skiing beside them. The heavier baggage is carried on sledges shaped like a boat and pulled by reindeer, all tied nose to tail. Women and babies ride on some sledges, while other small children are allowed to ride on reindeer. At the very rear of the herd, men and dogs work hard to keep the stragglers from straying too far.

The Lapps make long journeys four times a year, between seasons. After spending winter on the lowlands, the clan leaves the shelter of the forests and climbs to the lower slopes of the mountains. Here the cows have their calves. Then in June, the winter equipment is left behind, and the clan moves higher, away from the heat and flies, to the upper mountain regions. These areas may be a hundred and fifty miles away from the wintering districts. The autumn camps are the same as the spring camps. In November the snow is deep enough for travelling by sledge to be possible, and the journey from the mountain slopes to the lowlands takes place. Animals are killed during the late autumn and winter, partly because it is possible to preserve meat in cold weather and partly because the animal skins are thicker at this time. The size of the herd makes organisation essential. In earlier times, herds tended to be smaller and were managed by more men. Today, with fewer men and larger herds, the whole operation becomes much more complicated, and for this reason, it is necessary for the Lapps to have leaders, both of the herd and of the sita, who have the skill and authority to manage the rank and file.

Ritual and belief

The weather is vitally important to the men who herd the reindeer, and because of this, the Lapps have developed all kinds of rituals which they believe help them to control and predict the weather. These rituals are very ancient, and although many have died out, some remain still: Lapps in different areas believed in different spirits, but usually the spirits were connected with nature and the weather, such as sun, wind and water. The Thunder God was one important being, and the Earth Mother another. She would look after every childbirth, and had powers to heal. The Lapps had three ways of accounting for illness: (1) if illness was sent by the gods, it could not be cured and the person would die; (2) if it was sent by an individual such as a sorcerer, it might be cured, (3) ordinary sickness was not fatal, and could be cured by potions made out of vegetables. Charms or amulets such as the teeth of a bear or reindeer were also used to ward off sickness. In these ways, the Lapps of the olden days worked out their own explanations for the events of their everyday lives, and evolved ways of controlling them.

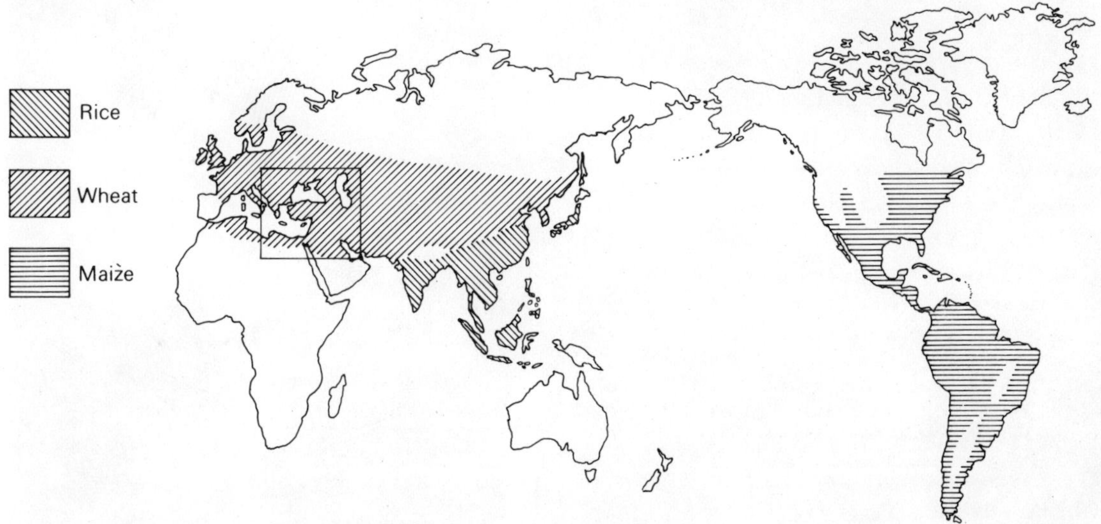

Figure 7 *By A.D. 1500 cereals were cultivated in the areas shaded above.* *Figure 8* *In the 'fertile crescent' (the shaded area below) the cultivation of wild barley and wheat began as long ago as 5500 B.C.*

Agricultural societies

THE IMPORTANCE OF AGRICULTURE

At about the same time that men began to herd animals for their own use, another revolution was taking place in certain fertile parts of the world. Men were learning to grow their own food. They noted the effect of the seasons on the growth of wild grasses – wild barley and oats – and gradually learnt to control that growth.

The invention of food cultivation had a very important effect upon the development of society. The fact that men could grow their own food meant that their supply of food was much more certain and reliable, and therefore they were more secure. It meant too that they could produce more food than before – that there was more to go round – and this in turn meant that no longer did each man have to be mainly concerned with his own supply of food. Instead some people could concentrate on other tasks – making pots, weaving cloth, building houses and so on. For the first time, people existed who did not actually produce food for themselves.

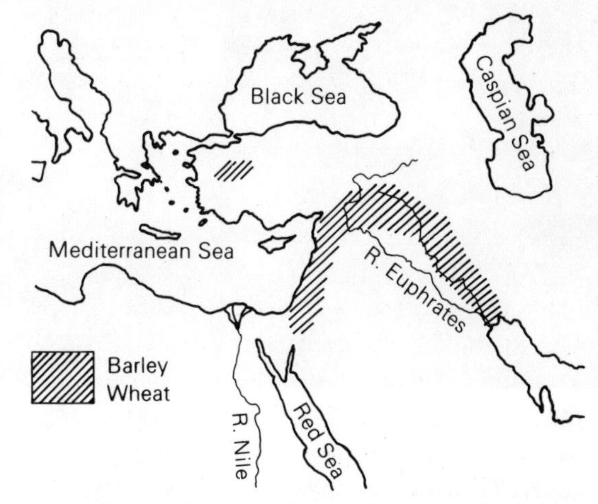

Societies also grew bigger because there was enough food to support more people. As they no longer had to move around from place to place searching for food, they could lead a much more settled life in one area. Villages grew up where there were not only groups of farmers producing food for the whole community, but where there were also potters and weavers and other people with special skills, who sold their goods in return for food and other goods. When these people began to congregate in the same place, then towns and cities began to develop.

The Aztecs usually built their temples in the form of a stone pyramid. Stone is expensive, and large buildings require a lot of labour and materials; the size of a building gives you an indication of the wealth and scale of a society. The terrace at the foot of the steps is approximately one hundred feet long.

Because the people living in towns concentrated on making *things* rather than food, they were called manufacturers; the industries they worked in were very small since most of the people were needed to grow food, and the machinery that they used was simple and could easily be put in the room of a house. So the weaver would own his own loom, and the potter his wheel and kiln, and their families would help them in their work.

As the towns developed and grew larger, there arose a need for people to organise them and the surrounding countryside. So towns and cities became centres of GOVERNMENT and were the places where law officers and judges would come to settle disputes or to try offenders. Schools and churches or temples would also be built there, and some of the people living in the cities were teachers and priests. These people were part of an even smaller group who not only did not produce their own food, but did not make anything either. They concentrated on producing services for the others.

THE AZTEC CIVILISATION

It is difficult to find a society still existing which is at this particular stage of development – in this half-way house between the simple societies we have looked at so far and the complex industrial society in which we live. There are many 'developing countries' in the world today, but few are growing without the help of another more complex society. Britain, the USA, China and the USSR, as well as many other industrialised countries, give money and technological aid to developing countries so that they can jump the 'in-between' stages of growth. With help, they can speed up the pace of their development and achieve a standard of living closer to that of industrial societies without going through the same slow process of change.

We can get some idea of the intermediate stage if we study a society which no longer exists but of which we have evidence through the findings of archæologists and historians. There are a number of such societies, which based their economies on agriculture and succeeded in producing a large enough surplus of food to support a city. We could look at the ancient civilisations of the middle east – Egypt and Sumer – or those of the far east – China and India. This section is about yet another civilisation, however, which flourished from the fourteenth to the sixteenth century A.D., that of the Mexican Aztecs.

In the fourteenth century the Aztecs were just one of a number of small tribes wandering the isthmus of Central America. This area had previously been dominated by more advanced societies such as the Maya and the Toltecs, but it was only with the coming of the Aztecs that the whole of Central America from the dry plains in the north to the steaming jungles of the isthmus itself came under the power of one government.

A statue of the Rain God in Mexico-Tenochtitlan. Because agriculture was the most important activity of the Aztecs, the Rain God held a special place among the Aztec gods.

The very size of the area they controlled, and the sheer numbers of people involved, meant that the Aztecs had to work out a very much more complicated system of government than was needed in a small-scale society. That government had to be based in a centre for the

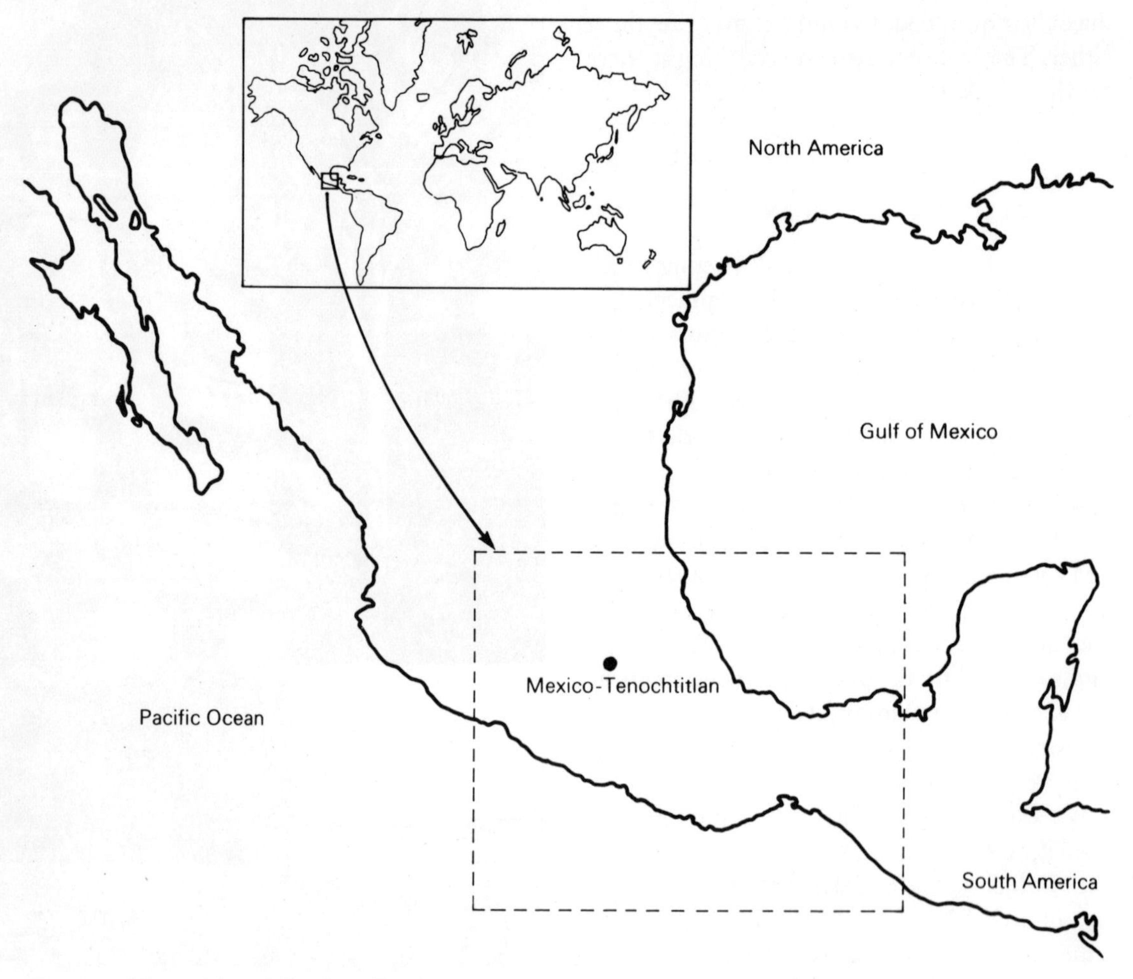

Figure 9 The position of the Aztec Empire.

whole society. The centre was the CAPITAL or chief city of Mexico-Tenochtitlan. Between the early fourteenth century when they founded Mexico-Tenochtitlan and the early sixteenth century when they were conquered and destroyed by the Spanish invaders, the Aztecs built up a society which was very complex. Not only did they create great buildings – temples and palaces – but they also developed a number of SOCIAL INSTITUTIONS which they needed to control their society. They had courts of law to administer justice, and officials to collect taxes and to organise trade and industry. They also had a system of writing which enabled them to keep accounts of their past history and files of their present affairs. Much of what we know about the Aztecs we have learnt from their own records. The rest we have gained from Spanish historians, for in 1517 Mexico was invaded by the armies of Spain which eventually crushed the Aztec civilisation.

Here is a description of what one Spaniard, Bernal Diaz del Castillo, saw when he entered the city of Mexico-Tenochtitlan:

The Maya were able to build temples such as this one, called the Temple of Quotations, while the Aztecs were no more than a wandering tribe.

. . . We saw the three causeways that lead into Mexico – the causeway of Iztapalapan, by which we were later to flee, on the night of our great defeat . . . and that of Tepeyacac. We saw the aqueduct that comes from Chapultepec to supply the town with sweet water, and at intervals along the three causeways the bridges which let the water flow from one part of the lake to another. We saw a multitude of boats upon the great lake, some coming with provisions, some going off loaded with merchandise . . . and we saw temples and oratories shaped like towers and bastions, all shining white, a wonderful thing to behold. And we saw the terraced houses, and along the causeways other towers and chapels that looked like fortresses. So, having gazed at all this and reflected upon it, we turned our eyes to the great market-place and the host of people down there who were buying and selling; the hum and murmur of their voices could have been heard for more than a league. And among us were soldiers who had been in many parts of the world, at Constantinople, all over Italy, and at Rome; and they said they had never seen a market so well ordered, so large and so crowded with people.

Government

The Aztec empire consisted of about forty provinces, and contained people of many different tribes. The main task of the provinces was to raise taxes for the emperor in Mexico-Tenochtitlan, and, to make this possible, an official of the emperor lived in each provincial capital. Every complex society needs a group of officials whose sole job is to make sure that the decisions of the government are carried out. This particular official was only concerned with collecting the emperor's taxes; he had no other powers or duties. So on the whole, the provinces were able to keep themselves to themselves and had a fair measure of independent self-government. Some kept their own chiefs on condition that they paid taxes, although others had to accept the chiefs appointed by Mexico. In all cases the provinces were independent of the capital so long as they paid up on time, supplied a number of soldiers for the army, and sent their most important cases to the Mexican law-courts. A system of government such as this, in which the country is made up of several provinces which come under the control of a central authority for certain purposes, such as taxation, war and justice, is generally known as a FEDERAL system.

Social groups

The Aztec people were divided into groups according to the jobs they did. At the bottom of the social scale were the *slaves*. These people were not citizens; they were a kind of possession and were owned by their masters. Male slaves worked as farm-labourers, porters, or servants, while female slaves spun, wove cloth, sewed or mended clothes in the master's house. Slaves were not paid for their work, but were given food, shelter and clothing similar to that of an ordinary citizen. They could marry free citizens and own goods, money and houses. They might even buy their freedom or be freed on the death of their master, so a slave need never lose the hope of becoming a free citizen.

Next to the slaves came the vast mass of ordinary free people who were *farmers*. These people would own their houses and have a plot of land to cultivate for as long as they lived. Their children would go to the local school, and when the authorities handed out food and clothing, they were entitled to their share.

Life was simple but not uncomfortable for this group of people. Their one-roomed huts with a central fireplace would be furnished with a wooden bench, a woven mat for a bed and some boxes and baskets in which clothes and tools would be kept. The bed clothes were made of cotton and would be worn as cloaks during the day by the man. Women wore capes rather like the modern Mexican poncho and skirts which wrapped over and came down just below the knee. Working women wore sandals but wealthier people went barefoot; to go without shoes showed that a woman never had to do the sort of heavy work which involved walking long distances. Men wore sandals, however much money they had; for whatever their position or STATUS in society, they were likely to travel and their feet would need protection against the rough paths.

As well as being farmers, some men were also specialist *craftsmen* who might be invited to work for noblemen or in the temples. While they were doing these special jobs they would be given food and shelter but might not be allowed to live with their families. When the job was over they could return to their homes with the valuable presents they had received in pay, in recognition of the fact that while carrying out these special tasks they could not produce food for their families.

There was also a separate class of people for whom being a craftsman was a full-time job. These men tended to live in certain parts of the towns, and formed special organisations or

Figure 10 *Aztec warriors wore very elaborate armour and carried very simple weapons. At the fall of the Empire they still did not use the wheel, any kind of pack animal, or iron, and they were just beginning to use bronze.*

GUILDS according to their craft. There were guilds of goldsmiths, jewellers, quarrymen and featherworkers. Some men worked directly for the emperor in his palace or for the nobility in their houses, whilst others worked at home, turning feathers and jewels which they received from traders and nobles into jewellery and ornaments. Each workshop consisted of the man and his family, his wife and children helping him with his work.

In spite of their tremendous technical ability, and the vast size of their empire, the Aztecs used neither the wheel nor any kind of beast of burden. They had no carts, carriages, horses or mules. The only link between the towns was therefore an earthen path which had to be wide enough to allow two people carrying loads on their backs to pass each other. Goods were carried from one town to another by long caravans of human porters organised by a class of travelling *merchants*. These merchants transported not only goods, but also news and information from one place to another. They were thus the most important means of communication between the different parts of the empire.

At the very top of the social pyramid stood the ruling class consisting of *nobles*, *priests* and *officials*. As we have seen, the vast majority of Aztecs were food-producers, and it was recognised that this was the most important task that had to be performed. Without the farmers, the rest of the society could not survive, and so even the great nobles who normally did no labouring work would cultivate a little piece of land on special occasions out of respect for the gods of the earth. Usually, however, the chiefs obtained their food from the farmers in their area, and in return agreed to protect their rights. If the need arose, it was the job of the chief to organise the local men into a small army to defend their area. Every Aztec man had at one time or another to undergo a period of military training.

All the members of the ruling class (the priests, warriors, officials, judges and magistrates) depended on the emperor for their power; they were the servants of the state. The priests were also the servants of the gods, but because the emperor was also the high priest, they also came under his control. One of the main differences between the government of an early civilisation and that of a modern complex society lies in the fact that in a society such as the Aztec, the king or emperor combined all the most important jobs. Not only was he the lawmaker and chief magistrate, but was in addition the high priest and commander-in-chief of the army. As a society becomes more complex, however, all these posts can no longer be filled by one person, for no single man could have the time, energy or skill to perform all necessary tasks properly. Here again, therefore, we see that with greater complexity comes a greater division of labour. The job of government itself is split up among many individuals and groups in an industrial society, instead of being concentrated in the hands of one ruler.

A wooden mask covered with turquoise mosaic. Masks like this were probably used in religious ceremonies. Very few are left today, because the Aztecs hid them from the Spanish invaders, and no one knows what happened to them.

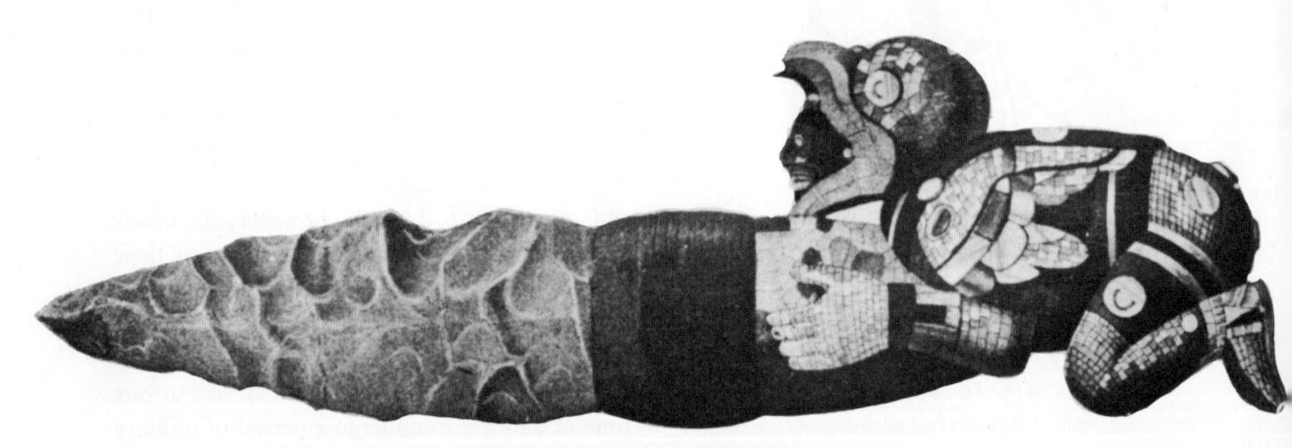

This knife would have been used for human sacrifice at special religious ceremonies.

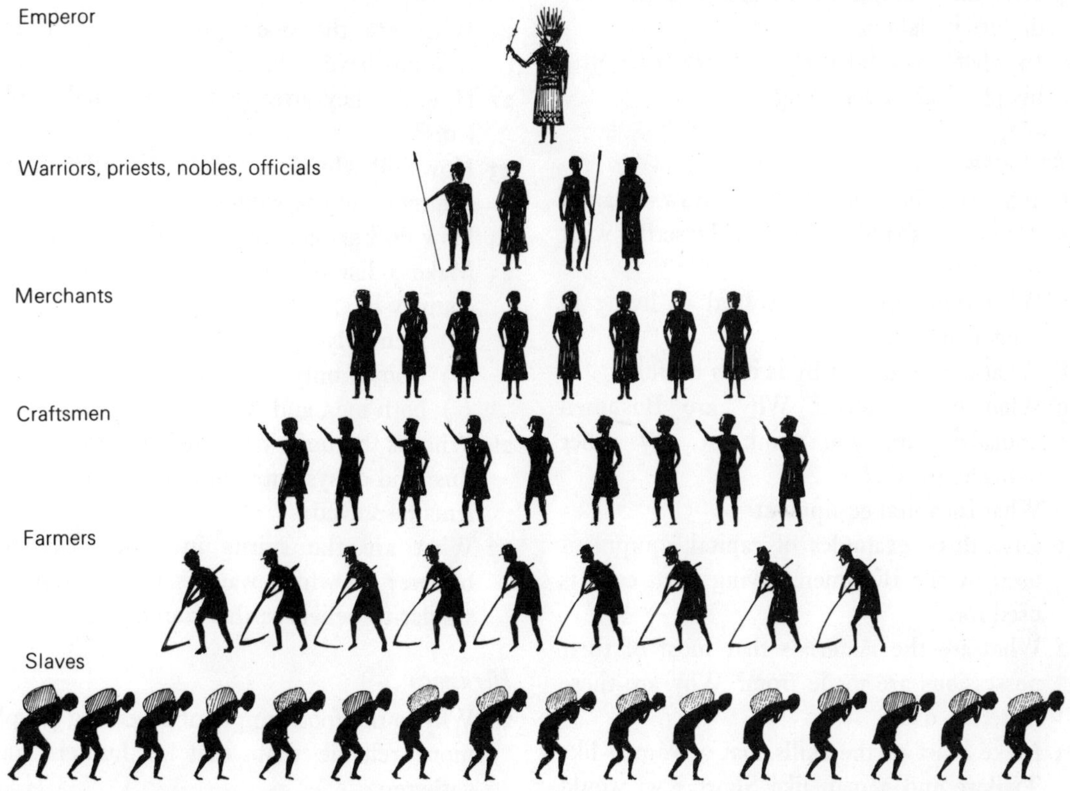

Figure 11 Aztec society was layered or stratified *into social classes, each having certain rights and duties.*

Social stratification

All societies are divided into different groups to a greater or lesser extent. The society of the traditional Indian village is divided in a highly rigid manner into different castes. The Aztecs had a looser system of social classes; people tended to remain in the same class as their families, but it was possible for an individual to earn enough money or to become sufficiently well-educated to enable him to move into a higher class. We call any system by which people are put into different groups, whether caste or class, whether on the grounds of birth, occupation, education or social standing, a system of SOCIAL STRATIFICATION.

Stratification means an arrangement in layers, so if we can imagine the society divided up into layers or STRATA with one layer of people considered higher or better in some sense than another, we can say that the society is stratified. As we shall see, the way in which an industrial society is stratified is rather more complicated than the fairly simple caste and class systems of the Indian village and the Aztec empire.

READING AND UNDERSTANDING

Early Man

1 What were the basic needs of men living in the early Stone Age?
2 In what ways was the earliest human society similar to that of the apes?
3 What is meant by the division of labour?

4 Give an example of an insect group that divides its labour.
5 In what ways did early man try to control his physical surroundings?

The Bushmen

6 Where do the Bushmen live? Draw a map of Africa and shade in the area. Describe what sort of area it is.
7 What difficulties are involved in living in such a climate?
8 What is a kaross? Why is it so useful?
9 What is a nomad? Why are Bushmen nomads? Can you think of any other nomadic people?
10 What is capital equipment?
11 Give three examples of capital equipment used by the Bushmen, saying what each is used for.
12 What are the materials that most of their possessions are made from? Why are these materials used?
13 Make a list of the skills that a woman like Twikwe and a man like Short Kwi would have acquired.
14 How big, roughly, would a Bushman family be? In what ways does the size and membership of a Bushman family differ from the size and membership of your own family?
15 Where do young married couples go to live when they first get married? Where may they live later on?
16 What must a boy do before he may get married? What is the reason for this custom?
17 What do Bushman children have to learn, and how do they learn?
18 Describe some of the beliefs held by the Bushmen.
19 Why are their beliefs so necessary to the Bushmen?
20 Why are the ideas and beliefs of the Bushmen not tested in the same way as the theories of the scientist in our society?

The Eskimos

21 What are the main problems which the Eskimos have to face?
22 How do they attempt to solve these problems?
23 How and why does family life differ in the summer and the winter?
24 How do Eskimos divide up their work?
25 Make a list of jobs that are done in this country by
(*a*) men only
(*b*) women only
(*c*) both men and women.
26 What is 'barter'? What are the problems of this kind of system? How could these problems be solved?
27 What are the spirits in which Eskimos believe? In which ways is Eskimo religion similar to beliefs in this country?

Herdsmen

28 Why is the food supply of a herding people more reliable than that of hunters and gatherers?
29 Who live in bigger groups, herdsmen or hunters and gatherers? Why is this so?
30 Why are herdsmen nomads?
31 Why is it important for herdsmen to be good at fighting?

The Lapps

32 Describe the physical environment of the Lapps. What especial dangers are faced by the Lapps?
33 What do the Lapps look like?
34 Draw a picture of a Lapp tent and describe what it must be like to live in such a home.
35 What are the main possessions of the Lapps? What are they made of?
36 What is a sita?
37 Make a plan showing how a Lapp clan organises the drive from one region to

another. Show who leads the herd and where the animals and rest of the clan are positioned.

38 What symbol of authority is carried by the leader of the sita?

39 What rituals were traditionally practised by the Lapps?

40 What were the spirits generally connected with? Can you give an explanation for this?

Agriculture

41 What effect did the first agricultural revolution have on the size of farming societies?

42 How did the agricultural revolution make possible the establishment of villages and towns?

43 What is a manufacturer? What did the early manufacturers make? Why were early industries small?

The Aztecs

44 When did the Aztec civilisation flourish?

45 What was the capital of the Aztecs? What was special about where the capital was situated?

46 How many provinces existed in the Aztec empire, and what did the provinces owe to the emperor?

47 What is a federal system of government?

48 What does the word 'stratification' mean?

49 Which jobs did the emperor do?

50 Make a list of the jobs done by each group in Aztec society. Which group had the greatest amount of responsibility? Which groups had the greatest wealth? Which groups had the greatest power over the rest of society?

POINTS FOR FURTHER DISCUSSION

1 How does the division of labour work in your home and your school?

2 Do animals exercise social control over other animals?

3 Why is it so important that the Bushmen have a definite territory which they recognise as their own? What might be the effect on the Bushmen if another society came to live in their territory?

4 Why is the Bushmen group so small? How might the way of life have changed to allow the group to get larger?

5 How many of the skills of the Bushmen are normally acquired by people living in a complex society?

6 What would a Bushman have to learn in order to live in a city in Britain?

7 Bushman children do not go to school. Why do you go to school?

8 Should young couples in Britain have to prove that they can support themselves and a family before being allowed to marry?

9 In what ways do the Bushmen's beliefs explain the world around them?

10 Do people in Britain have beliefs and myths about the weather and sickness? What are the beliefs of people in a complex society about?

11 Among the members of your class, how many live with or very near to their extended families?

12 Do you think that many families today divide work into men's work and women's work?

13 Law among the Eskimos is very different from law in Britain. What do you think are some of the main differences?

14 How superstitious are you and your friends?

15 Why is organisation so essential in order to move a herd?

16 What connection is there between the size of a group and the amount of organisation required? What conclusions can you draw about the amount of organisation needed in a complex society?

17 Can you think of any symbols of authority used in present-day Britain? What do the symbols show?
18 Why was the first agricultural revolution essential for the existence of manufacturers and people producing services?
19 How would the early industries compare with industries in Britain today with regard to size, equipment, ownership and skills of workers?

PROJECT WORK

1 *The environment*
Draw a map of the world showing where present-day hunters and gatherers live. Find out what the climate is like in these areas. What animals do the people hunt and what other food is available? Are the societies truly 'Stone Age', or are metals used as well? If metals are used, how are they obtained?

2 *Myths*
Find out more about the myths of hunting and gathering societies. How do the myths illustrate the effect of the environment on the people? Are the gods or spirits friendly or unfriendly? Are they kind, strict, just or moody? Does the world appear as a good or a bad place to live in? What is the point of the myths?

3 *Beliefs*
Re-read the sections on the beliefs of the Bushmen and Eskimos. Then look up these Biblical references: Exodus, chapter 3, 13–14; Genesis, chapter 3, 8; 1 Samuel, chapter 19, 20–24; Genesis, chapter 37, 5–8; Mark, chapter 5, 1–13; 2 Kings, chapter 5, 27. What similarities can you find in the aspects of Hebrew religion described in the Bible and the aspects of Bushman and Eskimo religion mentioned in this book? Can you think of any reason for these similarities?

4 *Art*
Find out more about the art of hunters and gatherers. Does it take the form of paintings or carvings? What materials are used? What are the subjects of the art (e.g. animals, people, trees)? Is the art an expression of feeling and creativity? Does it have some practical purpose?

5 *Children*
Describe the life of a boy or girl brought up in a hunting and gathering society. Who looks after the children when they are small? What skills do they have to learn, and how? What values and rules are they taught? What ceremonies do the young people have to undergo and why?

6 *Government*
Find out about the government of another early agricultural society such as England in the twelfth and thirteenth centuries, or Egypt in about 2000 B.C. What similarities can you find in the way these societies were ruled? Who were the most important people in the society, and how did they exercise their power?

7 *Stratification*
What is the connection between the scale of the Aztec society and its system of social stratification? Is it sensible to talk of Bushmen or Lapp society being stratified?

8 *Cities*
Compare plans of several early cities, for example, medieval European cities with Greek and Roman cities. What are the most important buildings marked? What do the plans tell you about:
(*a*) the scale of the society
(*b*) the types of job done by the members of the society

(*c*) the technical skill of the engineers and builders
(*d*) the wealth of different groups in the society?

9 *Slaves*
Compare the lives of slaves in the Aztec, Egyptian and Roman civilisations and the southern states of America at the beginning of the nineteenth century. What rights, if any, did the slaves have? Could they ever obtain their freedom? Were they mainly foreigners? What were their main occupations? Why did these societies have such large numbers of slaves?

10 *Agriculture*
Study the methods of cultivation used in any early agricultural society. Why did the society settle in that particular area? What crops were grown? What capital equipment was used by the farmers? How was food distributed? What trading went on, and what was used for currency?

USEFUL BOOKS FOR PUPILS

Bleeker, S. *The Eskimo* (Dobson 1960)
Bleeker, S. *The Masai* (Dobson 1960)
Bleeker, S. *The Navaho* (Dobson 1961)
Boer, F. *Igloos and Totem Poles* (Butterworth 1959)
Hurman, A. *As Others See Us* (Edward Arnold 1977)
Huxley, F. *People of the World in Colour* (Blandford 1964)
Mead, M. *People and Places* (Blackie 1964)
Land and People: packs of teaching material produced by the Royal Anthropological Institute and ILEA (Blackwell 1978)
World History Themes: study packs on Africa, India, China, available to teachers from the Learning Resources Centre, Kennington, London SE11

USEFUL BOOKS FOR TEACHERS

'Anthropology for the Classroom', *Social Science Teacher* (vol. 3, no. 1 1973)
Balikci, A. *The Netsilik Eskimos* (Natural History Press, New York 1970)
Barnett, A. *The Human Species* (Penguin 1968)
Burland, C. *The Mythology of the Americas* (Hamlyn 1970)
Cole, S. *Races of Man* (British Museum 1963)
Corcoran, D. et al. *Why People Live in Societies* (Open University Press, Course D100 1–5 1971)
Marshall Thomas, E. *The Harmless People* (Penguin 1969)
Percival, T. *Anthropology on the Box* (Film and Song, November 1970)
Royal Anthropological Institute, *Guide to Resource Material*
Vaillant, G. *The Aztecs of Mexico* (Penguin, 1965)
Woodburn, J. *Hunters and Gatherers – The Hadza* (British Museum 1970)

FILMS

Lost World of the Kalahari (6 parts); 30 mins each; Central Film Library
The Hadza; 40 mins; ILEA 2069
The Alaskan Eskimos; 27 mins; ILEA 31
Boy of Botswana; 17 mins; ILEA 2217
What is Anthropology?; 20 mins; EAV 78TF003 (a slide/tape set)
Caribou Hunters (Cree and Chippewa Indians); 18 mins; Central Film Library
Lapland; 30 mins; ILEA 602
Nomads of the Jungle (Malayan hunters and gatherers); 20 mins; ILEA 1096
Man the Creator (Indian Village); 12 mins; Concord Films Council
Land of the Long Day; 38 mins; Central Film Library C.434

See also the series of anthropological films made for *Man: A Course of Study* – one of the USA Social Studies Projects. These are now available from the British Film Institute.

2 The Economy of Complex Societies

As we have seen, there are a number of stages in the process by which the simplest society, that of the hunters and gathering peoples, may develop into a more complex society. New ways of producing food must be learnt so that there can be greater control of the environment and way of life. The societies of the Bushmen, Eskimos and Lapps are obviously very different from twentieth-century Britain. But what is the crucial factor that makes them so different?

It is in the SCALE or size of the society that the important difference lies. Simple societies are organised on a small scale and consist of a few people whose lives are governed very much by the climate and geography of the area where they live. A complex society consists of millions of people performing many different tasks, with considerable scientific knowledge about themselves and their environment, and therefore with much more control over that environment.

In order to make the affairs of the complex society run smoothly there needs to be very detailed organisation of every aspect of people's everyday lives. More rules are needed, more decisions have to be taken; people are no longer entirely governed by the seasons or the weather, but are controlled by man-made laws and rules. The size of the Aztec empire meant that officials were necessary to organise other people's lives for them. Yet by present-day standards, the Aztec society was small. Much more organisation is needed in Britain today to avoid our being overtaken by disorder and chaos.

Every area of our lives is governed by rules, whether written down in the form of laws or simply understood as part of the customary way of doing things. It is the job of the social scientist to study the patterns of our behaviour, both as individuals and in groups, and to try to explain these patterns. Perhaps too he must try to predict what we will do in the future and suggest ways in which we can usefully change our methods of going about things.

This medieval German picture shows all the family working in their own home.

One area of activity the social scientist will study concerns the way in which we produce goods and services – that is, the way in which we make things and do things for other people – and how we share out the wealth of our society. This aspect of a society's activity is known as the ECONOMY. This word is made up of two Greek words meaning 'household' and 'law'. Just as each household has to work out ways of earning money, spending some of it and saving some of it, so the society as a whole has to do much the same thing, except that it has to consider not only the organisation of production and trade within the society, but also trade with other societies. The economist will study the economy of a society or a number of societies, and try to pick out patterns in the events that occur. From these patterns he can make general statements about things that have happened and are likely to happen, which may be useful not only to that particular society but to other societies with similar economies as well.

Industrial society

An industrial economy is one in which goods are no longer manufactured in houses or cottages by individual craftsmen and their families by means of small hand-operated machines, but instead are made by many people working in factories with large, power-operated machines. That is, manufacturing is no longer a small-scale operation, but a large-scale complex operation. The process by which a society changes from a small-scale method of production to a large-scale one is known as the process of INDUSTRIALISATION.

French fishermen bring in the day's salmon catch.

The Industrial Revolution

Britain was the first society to begin industrialisation, and the process speeded up in the nineteenth century. Because the upheavals caused by industrialisation were so immense and had such far-reaching effects, this period of British history is known as the Industrial Revolution. The first steps towards the mechanisation of industry took place in the field of textiles, but other industries including transport soon followed by introducing revolutionary new equipment.

Before the industrial revolution, a revolution had taken place in agriculture. New ideas on crop rotation and animal farming had been introduced, as well as new kinds of agricultural machinery. This development meant that more food could be produced by fewer people, and so large numbers of agricultural labourers were released for work in the new factories. Here again we find an AGRICULTURAL SURPLUS allowing a greater production of goods and services.

Sectors of employment

The jobs that people do in any society can be divided into types or SECTORS.

The number of people working in offices has grown enormously since the nineteenth century.

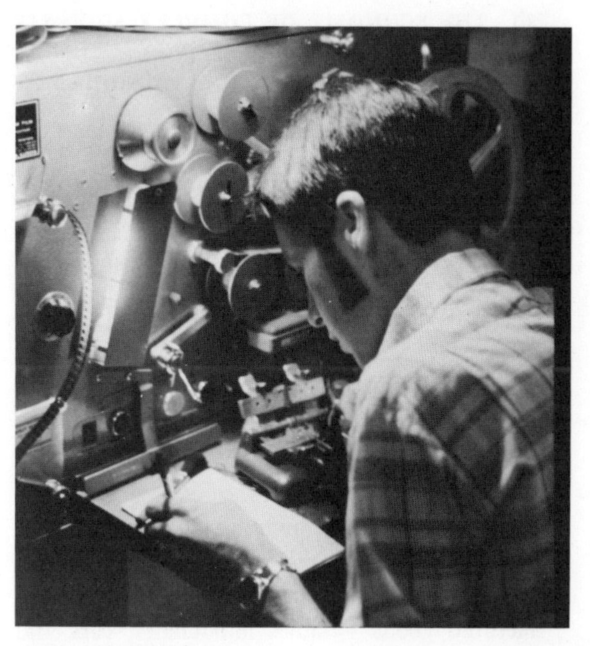

A film projectionist.

One of the most essential members of an industrial society.

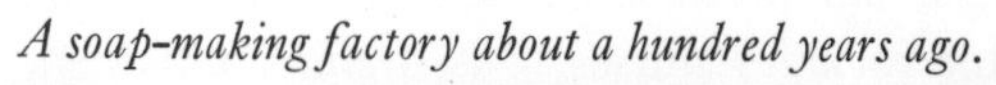

A soap-making factory about a hundred years ago.

There are three main sectors of employment:

WORK WITH NATURAL RESOURCES

This includes work on the land or at sea, and in mining, quarrying and forestry. It is called the *primary* (first) sector since before we can do anything else at all, we must grow enough food to live, and produce the raw materials like wood, metal and coal to enable us to go on and make other things.

MANUFACTURING WORK

The *secondary* sector includes jobs where people are using the raw materials produced by the workers in the primary sector to make manufactured goods – tables and chairs, cars and television sets, shoes, ships and sealing-wax, and all the other millions of things that we use every day.

SERVICES

In the *tertiary* (third) sector, people do not make things, but produce services for others. This sector includes nurses, bus drivers, milkmen, shop assistants, garage mechanics and teachers.

In a complex society like ours, most people work in the secondary and tertiary sectors. This is because we in Britain get much of our food and raw materials from other countries, and in return sell the goods we have manufactured. Even in a complex society which produces a great deal of food or raw materials, this does not necessarily mean that there are many people working in the primary sector. The machinery used on farms and in the mines of such countries is so advanced that a very few people can be used to produce a great deal. The total number of people working in a society is known as the LABOUR FORCE. The proportion of the labour force working in the different sectors of employment varies according to the scale and size of the society.

Urbanisation

Before the Industrial Revolution, most people in Britain lived in country districts. This was because by far the largest part of the labour force worked in the primary sector of employment, especially in agriculture. The introduction of factories and large-scale machinery into the manufacturing sector changed the picture a great deal, however. More people were needed to work in the new factories, and by the middle of the nineteenth century, the picture would have changed from this:

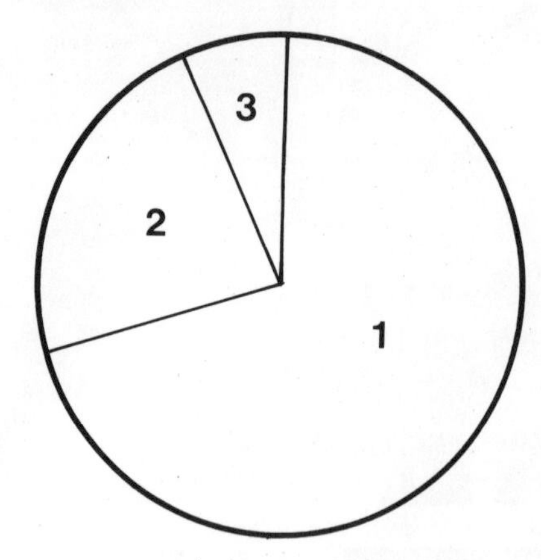

mid 18th century

Figure 12

to this:

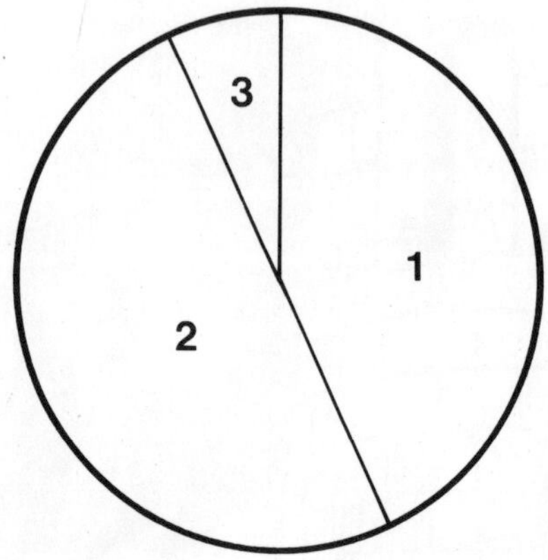

3
2
1

mid 19th century

Figure 13

Nowadays very few people in Britain work on farms or in the other primary industries like mining and fishing, and the picture looks more like this:

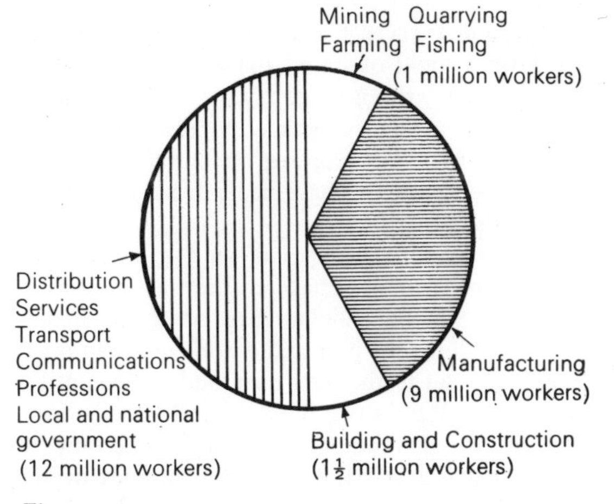

Figure 14

People who work in the secondary and tertiary sectors have to live in or near towns, so that the growth of these sectors of employment has been accompanied by the growth of towns. When large numbers of people move from the countryside into the towns and cities, which is an inevitable part of the process of developing from a small-scale to a large-scale society, this is called URBANISATION. URBAN means 'of the town', just as RURAL means 'of the country'. These diagrams show how urbanisation has taken place in Britain since 1801:

To cope with large numbers of workers moving into the towns, houses were quickly and cheaply built, creating slums, some of which still stand.

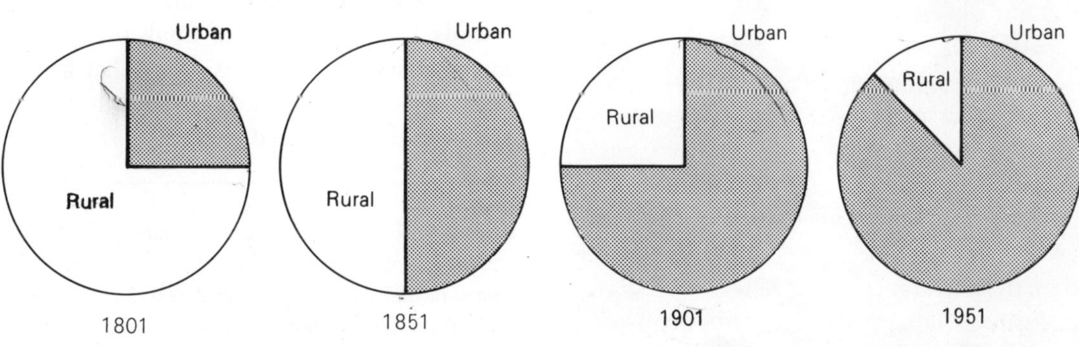

Figure 15 Location of population.

The division of labour

In the factories the workers are split up into groups, each doing a different task or set of tasks. In a simple society a craftsman such as a potter would be responsible for all the work of making a pot. He would have to prepare the clay, mould it into the right shape, paint or glaze it and fire it. In a factory all the work is divided into stages, each completed by a different set of workers, so that no one person or group sees the article through from start to finish. Thus there is greater division of labour within the factory. How many advantages can you think of in organising work in this way? Can you think of any disadvantages? Here is a factory worker's description of his normal day's work:

On the line

We go in at seven-thirty. To get to our shop you go down a flight of stairs, and at the top of them someone has written HAPPY VALLEY. It is part of an enormous factory with a population of eight thousand. We start working on our line at about eight o'clock, after we have had a drink of tea and a look at the papers.

There are nine benches down the line, a man standing at each. We make all the tractor parts in our shop. On our line we panel-beat the hoods, each man doing his part of the work and then man-handling it on to the next man, and so on, until it gets to me. We do two hundred and sixty hoods a day, and it only takes me two minutes to do my bit of it, though I was timed for ten minutes by the time-study man. When there aren't hoods enough to make up our two hundred and sixty a day we 'borrow' from the next day – and then forget the next day that we have borrowed them . . .

There are nine men all told who work on our line, and each one is a character, an individual in his own right. My work comes to me in a completely automatic way, in the gestures of an automaton. With a rag wrapped round my eyes I could still do it, and could do dozens before I realised that I had done any at all. But underneath this my mind never stops working. It lives by itself. Some call it dreaming, and if so, I am dreaming all day long, five days a week.

From *Work*, Vol. 1, edited by Ronald Fraser (Penguin).

How would you sum up this man's attitude towards his work? Do you think that he gets much satisfaction from his job? What are the kinds of work which give the greatest satisfaction to the individual worker?

In industrial societies there are still many jobs which are rarely done by women. Traditional jobs for women include looking after children and fashion modelling. Mending the road and driving a bus are less usual.

Asti
Gancia

Both these pictures show part of the manufacturing sector – but on very different scales.

In an industrial society there is also greater division of labour in the society as a whole. Whereas Eskimo girls or boys would have little or no choice as to the work they would do as adults, children in a complex society are faced with many possibilities. Often the choice of occupation is made when we are still at school, when we decide whether to stay on beyond the compulsory school-leaving age and make up our minds which course to follow. We may have to learn special skills to do our chosen job, so that other people without these skills cannot help us in our work. Extreme specialisation and division of labour within a society may mean that we cannot all do each other's jobs, so we have to go on doing the same jobs for the rest of our lives, unless we are prepared to undergo some kind of re-training. It also means that we can concentrate on becoming good at one particular thing. On the other hand, it may be argued that although a skilled tool cutter will cut more tools if he does nothing else all day, he would have a more varied and interesting life if he could have two or more jobs. It may be that complex societies have chosen to sacrifice variety and individuality in return for increased production through specialisation.

Mass production

The capital equipment used in the factories is power-operated and built on a much larger scale than the hand-operated tools, and this means that more goods may be produced by the same number of workers. Because much of the shape and design of the goods depends on the machine, and because so many goods are being produced at the same time, we say that the goods are being MASS PRODUCED. Mass production means that

1 The costs of production will eventually go down because fewer workers are necessary.
2 Because the goods can be produced more cheaply, they can be bought by more people, whose standard of living will therefore rise.

but

3 The goods are all alike and lack variety, so people's range of choice may be limited.

Some people claim that because the things we buy are mass produced we are becoming a mass produced society; we all tend to think alike, look alike and behave in the same way. It is said that people have not so much individuality as in former times. Does this seem to you to be a true picture of our society? If it is , do you feel that it is more important that we each preserve our individuality than that we make more goods available to everybody in our society?

A traditional style of shopping centre.

Trade

We have already seen that if a man specialises in a particular job, he can increase his output. In a simple agricultural society a man with a gift for making pots would gradually spend more and more of his time as a potter, exchanging his products for the farmer's food or the weaver's cloth. Trade started in the form of BARTER (see page 15) but, as this became too complicated, money was invented to make it easier.

Not only individuals, but whole communities and countries benefit from specialising in the production of particular goods and services, as long as they can find another community who will buy them and sell different products in return. Early cities existed by selling manufactured goods to rural areas and buying food in exchange.

Maize is an important primary product of Mexico today, just as it was five hundred years ago at the time of the Aztecs.

In this modern shopping centre we need to ask who owns these shops and who will benefit most from the sale of goods in such shops.

We can see the same idea working today in international trade, that is, trade among countries. Britain is a small island with a large population and a high level of skill in technology and industry. There is not a great deal of space to grow food, and there are not many large deposits of minerals or metals. It is sensible for Britain to buy food from countries where the natural conditions are suitable for large-scale agricultural production, and to buy metals, wood and so on from countries rich in raw materials.

Countries which are important in the PRIMARY SECTOR (see page 38) are called PRIMARY PRODUCERS. Some examples of primary producers are

Barbados
Canada
Chile
New Zealand
Nigeria

What are the PRIMARY PRODUCTS of each of these countries?

EXPORTS AND IMPORTS

Goods and services which are sold abroad are called EXPORTS. Goods and services which are bought abroad are called IMPORTS. The income Britain earns from selling exports abroad increases the wealth of the country. This income can be used to buy imports from other countries. We cannot spend more abroad than we earn, however. If we try to import more than we export, we run into trouble and have to start borrowing from other countries. The money we pay out for imports must equal the money we earn in exports. This is called the BALANCE OF PAYMENTS.

THE BRITISH BALANCE OF PAYMENTS

During the last twenty years Britain has had great difficulty in keeping her imports and exports balanced. Very often imports have been greater than exports, and then Britain has had a balance of payments DEFICIT, and has had to borrow money from other countries.

If a country is selling more than it is buying, it has a balance of payments SURPLUS. This is just as bad from the international point of view as a deficit for, in the long run it is bound to put other countries into difficulties.

Country A is obviously in surplus, while country B is in deficit. We should not blame B entirely, however. Unless A agrees to buy more from B, there is very little B can do, apart from reducing its imports.

Some countries are continually in balance of payments difficulties. A poor country with a large population such as India cannot produce enough food for its own use, let alone produce a surplus which it can export. Unless it does manage to export to other countries it cannot afford to buy the food it needs. It cannot improve its industries by importing capital equipment. It is caught in a vicious circle from which it cannot escape unaided.

FREE TRADE *versus* PROTECTION

One way in which a government can encourage people to buy home-produced rather than foreign goods is by putting a TARIFF on imports. A tariff is a sum of money charged on certain goods coming into the country. Naturally this puts the price of the imports up, and makes home-produced goods relatively cheaper. When the government puts a tariff on imports it does so partly to PROTECT the home industries.

Another form of PROTECTION is the EXPORT SUBSIDY. In this case the government gives money to the home industry to enable it to sell its goods abroad at a lower price.

These practices are frowned upon by most countries, for they can lead to a 'beggar-my-neighbour' situation. Each country may end up trying to protect its industries with export subsidies or tariff walls, and these are bound to restrict trade. If one country sets up a tariff against the goods of another country, foreign governments may well try to get their own back by doing likewise. In the long run, no one is any better off. So most countries agree that except in very special circumstances these policies should be banned, and that there should be FREE TRADE.

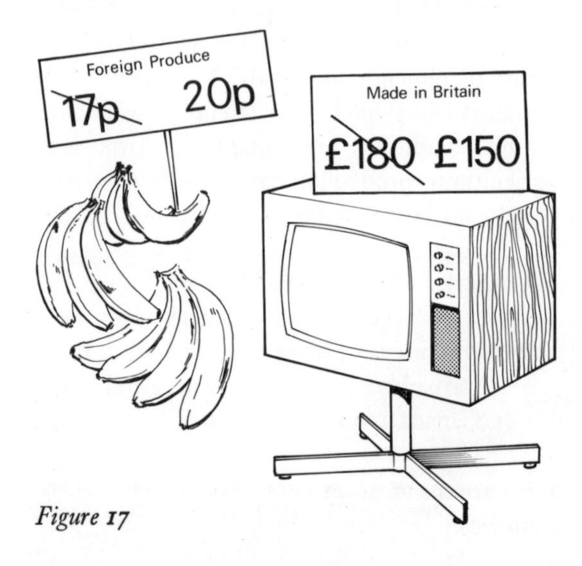

Figure 17

Figure 18

One of the advantages of a customs union is that traffic between two countries need not be held up at the frontier.

THE COMMON MARKET

Sometimes a group of countries decides to get together and remove the trade barriers amongst themselves, while keeping a common tariff on the goods of countries outside the group. Trade is free within the group, but trade is not free with countries outside the group.

The European Economic Community (EEC), sometimes known as the Common Market, is this sort of organisation. Goods, labour and capital may move freely within the community, but countries outside the EEC find it very difficult to sell their goods to countries within the EEC. Some people argue that the EEC is a club of rich countries bent only on making themselves richer. Poor countries are prevented from trading with these rich countries. Supporters of the EEC say, on the other hand, that there are special agreements with poor countries which enable them to trade with the countries of the Common Market. Whichever argument you support, it is still true that common markets and other kinds of customs unions restrict the amount of free trade that can go on, and reduce the benefits of specialisation for the world as a whole.

What counts as rich or poor within a country depends on the general standard of living in that country. In many developing countries today, the owner of a bicycle is relatively well off.

The national income

The money that the individual citizens of a country earn in one year can be added together to form an idea of the wealth of the whole country – the NATIONAL INCOME. Another way of looking at the same thing is to measure the amount that is produced in one year, and this is called the NATIONAL PRODUCT. By looking at the size of the national product in two different years, we can see if the country is getting richer and, if so, at what rate.

When the national income or national product is getting bigger from year to year, we say that the country is experiencing ECONOMIC GROWTH. A great deal of effort and energy is spent by economists in working out how Britain's economic growth can be improved, and in comparing Britain's performance with that of other countries. Britain has been growing rather slowly in recent years in comparison with some other countries.

SHARING THE WEALTH

It is not enough to look at the size of the national income in working out how wealthy a country is, however. The standard of living of the citizens depends on several major factors; first, the size of the population affects the size of the income received by the individual. If the population rises, in order for people to keep the same standard of living, the national income must rise in proportion. Secondly, although the national income may rise from year to year, the effect of price rises must also be taken into account. In recent years the value of money has fallen because Britain is suffering from INFLATION – the problem of persistently rising prices. So again, the country's national income must rise faster than prices if its standard of living is to improve.

Thirdly, we must look at the way in which the national income is shared out or *distributed*. Is it shared out fairly equally so that everyone enjoys roughly the same standard of living, or are there a few individuals who receive a very large share, leaving the rest of the country very poor? Studies have been carried out which compare the distribution of the nation's wealth in three periods: before the First World War, between the wars, and after the Second World War. They suggest that great inequalities in the way national income is shared out have remained.

One such study has estimated that

1 *Before* 1914
1% of adults owned two-thirds of the wealth
2% owned the next one-sixth
and 97% owned the remaining one-sixth

2 *Between* 1919 *and* 1938
2% of adults owned two-thirds of the wealth
5% owned the next one-sixth
and 93% owned the remaining one-sixth

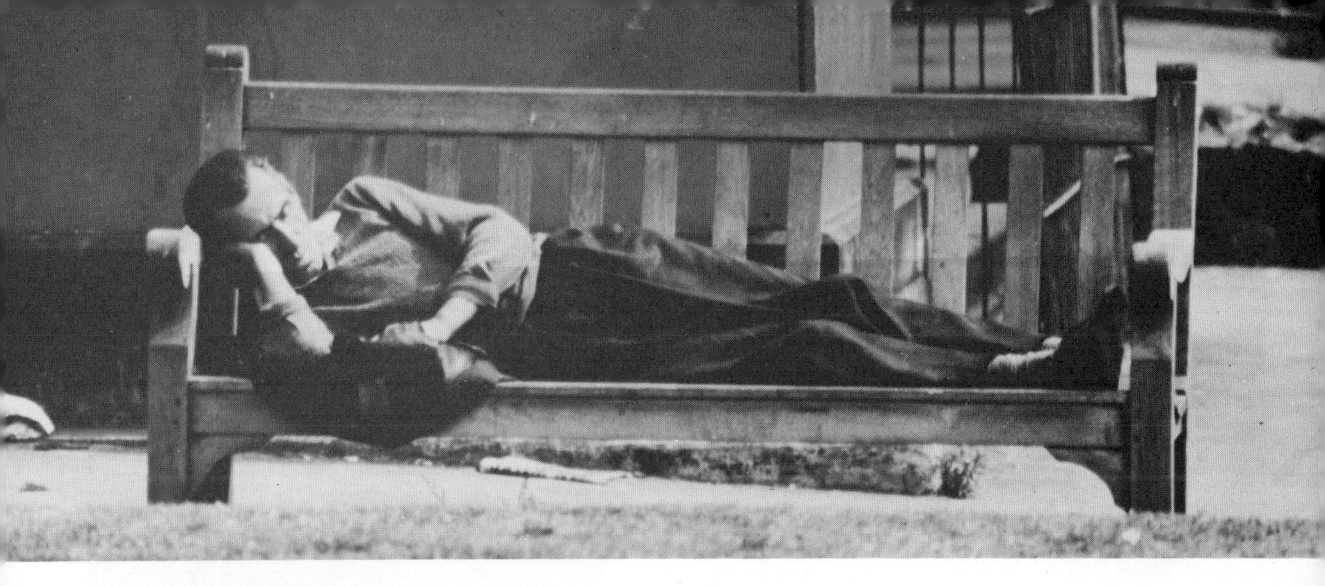

It is clear that in Britain today a great gap still divides the rich from the poor.

3 *After* 1945
3% of adults owned two-thirds of the wealth
7% owned the next one-sixth
and 90% owned the remaining one-sixth.

So, although the position has been made slightly more equal, according to this study enormous differences in wealth existed even in the postwar period.

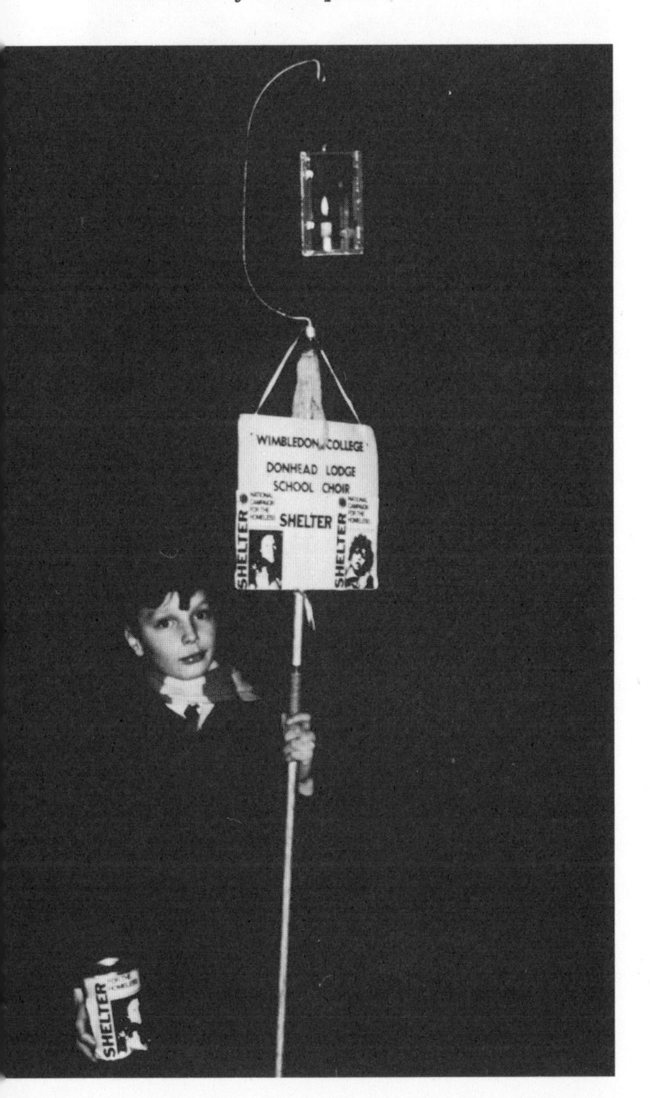

TAXATION

The amount an individual earns or receives in profits from investments or interest on savings is not the amount he has available for spending. He has to pay tax on his income. It is argued that the great inequalities between high and low incomes have been reduced through taxation. This is through Britain's system of PROGRESSIVE income tax, which means that the more you earn, the more you pay in proportion to the whole of your income.

Ordering food, Mexican-style and British-style.

Income tax

The amount of income tax you pay depends on the size of your income. The rich are more able to contribute to the services provided by the country than the poor. Income tax is a DIRECT tax because people pay it directly from their earnings.

Every so often the local tax office sends each worker a tax return form on which he makes a claim for tax relief and states whether he has any income additional to his normal wage. Most people pay their tax through the Pay-As-You-Earn scheme (PAYE), in which case the employer is told how much income tax must be paid, and deducts that amount each week or month from the worker's earnings.

Everyone is allowed a certain amount free from tax; this is called a *personal allowance*. The amount of this depends on his financial responsibilities. A married man with children or someone taking care of an elderly or sick relative, gets a higher personal allowance than a single person with no dependants.

After this, the worker's earnings are taxed at a higher and higher rate, the more he earns, so that someone with a very high salary may actually receive less than he pays in tax. Someone with a very low salary, on the other hand would pay very little, if any, of his income in tax.

A single person
or married woman – £675 tax free

For helping a
dependent relative – up to £100 tax free
(£145 if claimant is a single woman)

A married man – £955 tax free

plus £240 – £305 for each child,
depending on age

Figure 19
Source: *F WA Guide to Social Services 1976* (figures for 1975–6)

A Punch *cartoon of 1894. People have always complained of high taxes.*

Lemon-Squash.
WILLIAM HARCOURT (the Barman). "Wonder if I can squeeze any more out of HIM?"

Indirect taxes

The merit of direct taxes like income tax is that the amount paid depends on ability to pay. INDIRECT taxes do not have this advantage. PURCHASE TAX is an example of an indirect tax; a certain percentage of the price paid for many kinds of goods is taken by the government in tax. Just what percentage is taken depends on the rate fixed for that type of article; luxury goods are taxed at a higher rate than essentials. But whether a man is a millionaire or an old-age pensioner, the amount of purchase tax he pays on an article is the same. EXCISE DUTY payable on petrol, tobacco and alcoholic drink is another kind of indirect tax.

The government has now introduced a new kind of indirect tax to replace the old purchase tax. The new tax is called Value Added Tax, usually abbreviated to VAT. Although the changeover from the old system has been costly and initially perhaps confusing, the government believes that in the long run VAT will prove a fairer and easier system to work. A further advantage of VAT is that in adopting it Britain has come into line with other Common Market countries.

	Tax due	Tax sent to authorities
Stage 1 Textile manufacturer imports raw cotton with a value of 50p	10% of 50p = 5p	5p
Stage 2 Shirtmaker buys finished cotton from textile manufacturer for £1·00 + 10p tax	10% of £1·00 = 10p This is paid to the textile manufacturer. He keeps 5p to pay himself back the tax paid at Stage 1 and sends	5p
Stage 3 Shopkeeper buys shirt from shirtmaker for £2·50 + 25p tax	10% of £2·50 = 25p This is paid to the shirtmaker. She keeps 10p to pay herself back the tax paid at Stage 2 and sends	15p
Stage 4 Customer buys shirt from shopkeeper for £4·00 + 40p tax	10% of £4·00 = 40p This is paid to the shopkeeper. He keeps 25p to pay himself back the tax paid at Stage 3 and sends	15p
The Exchequer will receive in total 10% of £4·00		40p

This total tax of 40p is eventually paid by the customer, but in the meantime the Exchequer has had the use of the money paid in tax at the earlier stages.

The general principle behind VAT is that it is a sales or turnover tax, which is collected in instalments. At each stage in the production chain the manufacturer pays part of the tax due on the article he is producing according to the value added by him. As part of this chain, the retailer and customer also pay part of the tax. The chart above shows how a value added tax of 10% might be levied on a shirt which cost £4 before the customer paid tax.

RATES

So far we have only considered taxes levied (taken) by the national government. There is another kind of tax which many consider unfair, but for a different reason, and which is levied not by the national government, but by the local authority. This is a kind of tax on houses and buildings, and is known as the RATES. Every house, flat, shop, factory or other building is assessed by the Board of Inland Revenue and given a RATEABLE VALUE according to how old it is, how big it is, whether it has certain amenities such as a bathroom, inside lavatory, garage and its own front door, and in what kind of neighbourhood it is situated. The householder who occupies the house or flat is then required to pay a sum each year (usually in two half-yearly payments) to the local authority. How much he pays depends on the rateable value of his house, and on the rate charged by the local authority. If the rateable value of his house is £100 a year, and the rate charged is fifty pence in the pound, the householder will pay fifty pence for each of the pounds that his house is valued at; in this case, then, the householder will pay £50 a year in rates.

The rates are used by the local authority to pay for services provided for the local community. Education is the biggest single item paid for out of the rates.

The system of obtaining money through the rates has been criticised a good deal. There is

Figure 20 Public spending.

a) *Pattern of spending*

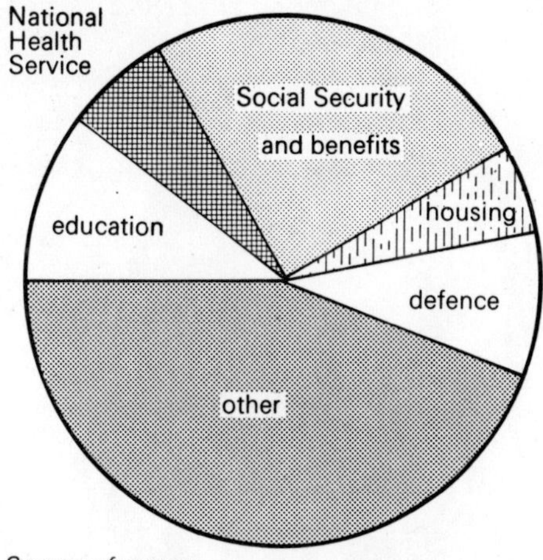

b) *Source of money*

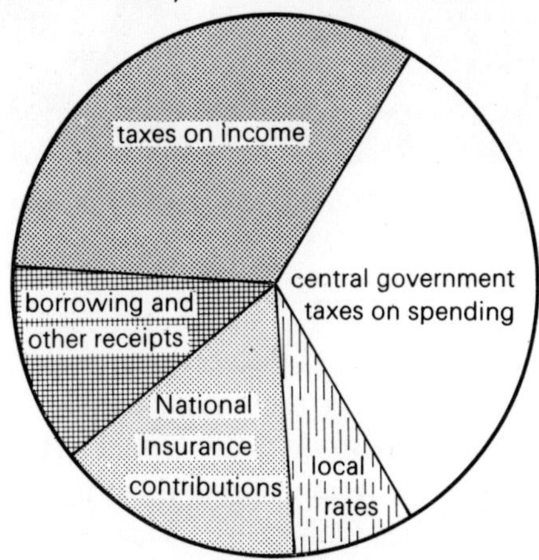

c) *Who spends the money?*

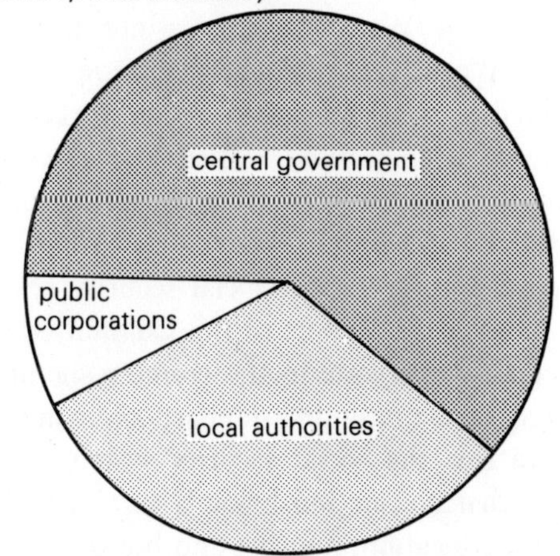

relief from payment of rates for people on very low incomes, but if a man improves his home by putting in a bathroom, or adding a garage, he is penalised since he will then have to pay higher rates. There are many people who use the amenities of an area who do not pay rates directly; for example, young people out at work who are living with their parents, or people coming into the area every day to work, although living in another district. This last argument applies with especial force to central London.

How the local authority may spend £1.00 of the rates

40p	education
11p	police and fire services
10p	housing
7p	clinics
6p	roads
5p	refuse collection and disposal
4p	parks
3p	libraries
14p	other services
£1.00	

NATIONAL INSURANCE

There is another regular deduction that is made from a man's earnings. This is his NATIONAL INSURANCE contribution. Every week employers and employees pay a sum into the compulsory state insurance scheme which entitles every worker with a certain number of contributions to his or her credit to the following benefits:

Unemployment benefit, for those out of work and unable to find another suitable job

Sickness benefit

Maternity benefit

Widows' benefit

Guardians' allowance, provided for orphans

Death grants to help with burial or cremation

Retirement pensions for men over sixty-five and women over sixty

Mining has one of the highest accident rates of any occupation in Britain. People who have accidents at work may be eligible to claim industrial injury benefit.

War pensions to people disabled, widowed or orphaned during the world wars

Industrial injury benefits paid to those who have an accident at work.

CHILD BENEFIT ALLOWANCES are now paid for each child in the family. These are not dependent on contributions to national insurance, and neither are SUPPLEMENTARY BENEFITS, which are extra payments made to people who for one reason or another cannot manage on the standard insurance benefits. People who have not stamped their weekly card and therefore are not entitled to national insurance benefits may receive supplementary benefits if they can prove their financial need.

National insurance and supplementary benefits are part of the system of SOCIAL SECURITY. The idea that the community as a whole should take responsibility for those in need is hardly new; the last resort of the very poor in the nineteenth century was the workhouse, but these institutions were made as unpleasant as possible to deter people from entering them unless they were desperate. Old-age pensions and a state insurance scheme were introduced before the First World War, but it was not until the Second World War that a *comprehensive* system, intended to cover all citizens, was worked out. In 1941 a committee, called the Beveridge Committee since it was under the chairmanship of William Beveridge, was set up to look into ways of starting such a social security system, and in 1942 the Report of the Committee suggested that everyone in the country should be assured of a minimum standard of living. To achieve this the social security system should ensure that no one fell below a certain level of income, education, housing and health services.

Once in the workhouse, the only hope lay in life after death.

Under the welfare state, the visit to the baby clinic has become part of every mother's routine.

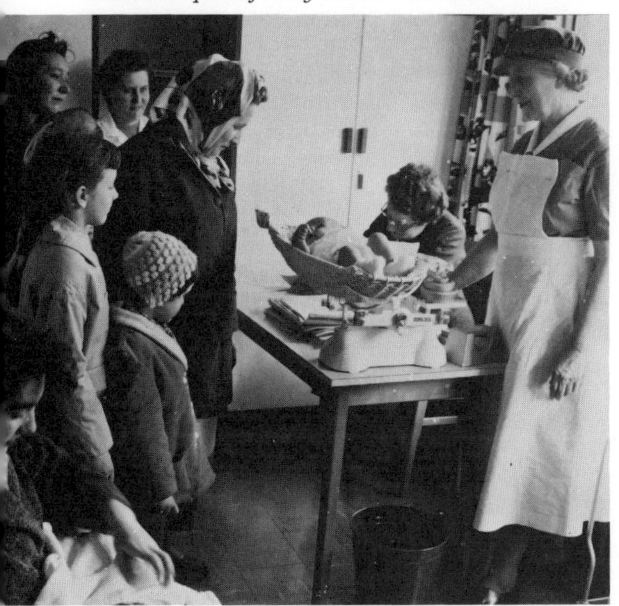

Acts of Parliament were passed in the years 1946 to 1948 which made the recommendations of the Beveridge Committee law.

The aim of the social security system was to provide everyone with an acceptable standard of living 'from the cradle to the grave'. During the 1950s it was generally believed that the Acts passed in the late 1940s had succeeded in virtually wiping out poverty in the UK. Phrases like the 'affluent society' have been used to describe Britain today, suggesting that hunger, bad housing and acute poverty are things of the past. In 1960 a study was carried out by two sociologists, Brian Able-Smith and Peter Townsend, which showed that such a belief is seriously mistaken. This study claimed that instead of fewer people living in poverty, between 1953 and 1960 the number had actually grown, from 7·8 per cent of the population to 14·2 per cent.

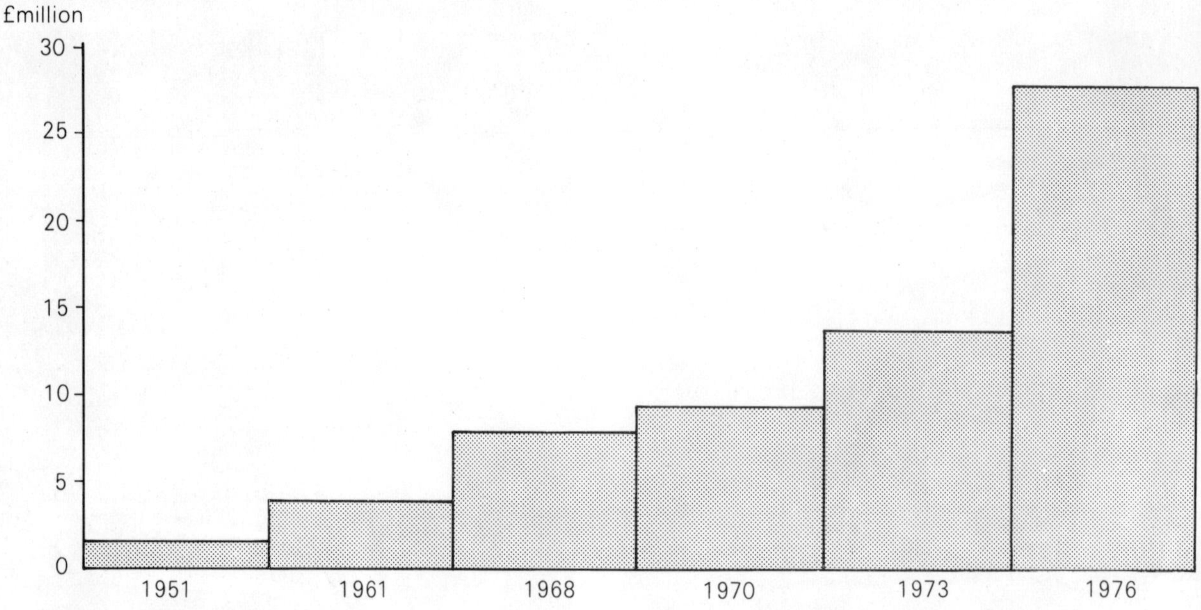

Figure 21 *The cost of the Social Services 1951–76, years ending 31 March.* Source: *Annual Abstract 1976.*

There were seven and a half million people in 1960 for whom the welfare state had not provided the solution.

In 1968 Britain spent roughly two and a half times as much on the Social Services as she did in 1958. Yet, as the table below indicates, the *share* of all public expenditure which goes to the Social Services has not increased.

Share of total public expenditure given to Social Services, 1958–1975

	1958	1968	1974	1975
Housing	4·9%	5·8%	9·5%	7·9%
Education	9·4%	11·4%	11·7%	12·5%
National Health Service	8·7%	8·8%	11·5%	12·3%
Social Security	16·2%	17·5%	16·4%	16·4%
Total	39·2%	43·5%	56·5%	49·1%

Source: *Social Trends*, CSO

POVERTY IN THE TWENTIETH CENTURY

What is meant by 'poverty' in the 1960s and 1970s? From 1966 to 1968 a study was made by a group of sociologists at Nottingham University of a district in Nottingham called St Ann's. Nearly forty per cent of the community were found to be living in poverty. This is how Ken Coates and Richard Silburn in their book, *Poverty: the Forgotten Englishmen*, describe the children growing up in this area:

> They are not well developed. They are on average smaller and less hardy than the middle-class kids from the suburbs. They don't win at the inter-school games. They lack stamina, fall ill easily and are often absent from school. Every epidemic which hits the city booms in St. Ann's. The school health service reports that fresh starters are often in need of attention for complaints which would ordinarily have been under care for some time. . . . They are not starving, but they frequently suffer from ill-balanced diets. Some of them come to school without breakfasts, either because mother went off to work before them, or perhaps because the family got up late. A third of them get free school meals as against a thirtieth of the children on the housing estate.

Who are the poor? The sociological studies of poverty have shown that there are five main groups of people who are most likely to be living 'below the poverty line'. In 1960 there were:

In the 1890s relief for the poor came largely from the charity of the rich. But even under the welfare state, millions today still live in poverty.

three million people in families where the head of the family earned a low wage or had several children, or both

two and a half million old age pensioners

three-quarters of a million in fatherless families

three-quarters of a million in families with one parent disabled or sick

half a million in families with the father out of work.

READING AND UNDERSTANDING

1. Rewrite this sentence in your own words: 'Simple societies are organised on a small scale – complex societies are organised on a much larger scale.'
2. Why are people in complex societies less influenced by the weather than the members of Bushmen or Eskimo society?
3. What difference does industrialisation make to the scale and type of organisation of manufacturing industry?

4 Why was a revolution in agricultural methods essential to the Industrial Revolution in Britain in the nineteenth century?
5 What are the three main sectors of employment? Which sector is largest in a simple and in a complex society? Explain the difference.
6 What does the word 'urbanisation' mean?
7 What does figure 15 tell you about the numbers of people working on farms in 1801 and 1901?
8 How many people work in the factory described in the passage 'On the Line'? How many men work on the writer's line? What are the men making? What is an AUTOMATON? What is MASS PRODUCTION?
9 Fill in the gaps with words from the list below. Some of the words occur twice in the passage.

If two countries —— in the —— of different —— and services, each can benefit from —— ——with the other. Goods and services sold abroad are called ——; goods and services bought abroad are called ——. It is important that —— should equal ——. If —— are greater than ——, the country will have a balance of payments deficit. If —— are greater than ——, there will be a balance of payments surplus. A deficit means that the country has to —— from other countries. A surplus means that other countries are being forced into a difficult position because the over-successful country is —— gold and currency reserves in a miserly fashion.

Goods and services can only be exchanged without hindrance if there is —— trade. Sometimes a country tries to —— its own industry by giving export ——, or by putting up import ——. When several countries join together to put up a common barrier against the rest of the world, while removing restrictions on trade with each other, this is known as a —— ——. One such union is the —— —— ——.

MISSING WORDS: free, hoarding, goods, protect, borrow, subsidies, trade, imports, common, European, tariffs, exports, Community, production, market, specialise, Economic.

10 How do economists measure the growth of an economy?
11 What is the difference between direct and indirect taxation?
12 In what way is income tax *progressive*?
13 What does PAYE stand for?
14 Draw the houses in figure 22 below. Make a list of the factors the local authority would have taken into account when assessing their rateable values.
15 What entitles a worker to national insurance benefits?
16 If a worker is not entitled to national insurance benefit, what help may he receive from the state?
17 What is meant by 'a comprehensive system of social security'?
18 Look at figure 21. By how much did the cost of social services rise between 1951 and

Figure 22

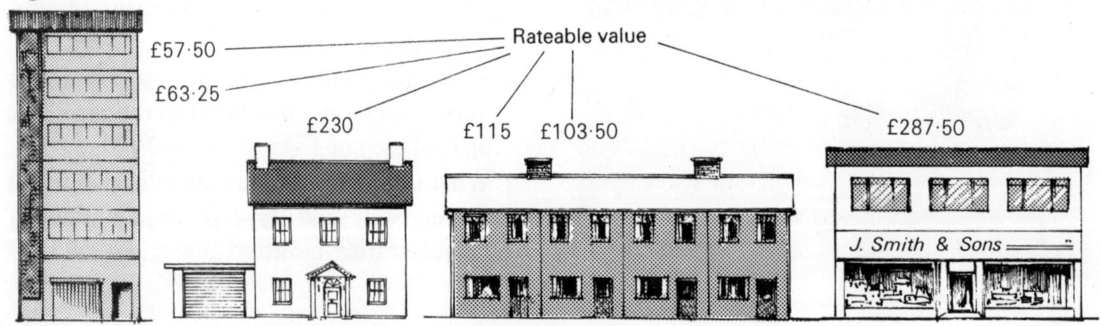

1976? Did the rise mean that everyone was receiving more and better social services in 1977?

19 How did poverty affect the physical development of the children of St Ann's?

20 What may tell the school authorities that a child comes from a poor family?

21 Why do children living in poverty often eat an ill-balanced diet? How may this affect their health?

POINTS FOR FURTHER DISCUSSION

1 What are some of the jobs an economist might do?

2 Do a survey of the members of your group. How many are hoping to work in the primary sector of employment, how many in the secondary sector and how many in the tertiary sector?

3 Here are two diagrams which represent the labour force of a large-scale and a small-scale society. They are divided into three according to the proportion of the labour force working in each sector of employment:

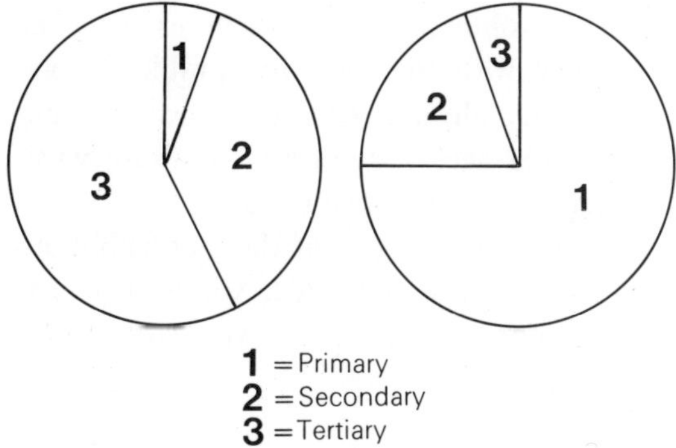

Figure 23

Which diagram represents a large-scale society, and which a small-scale society?
Can you explain *why* the diagrams are so different?

4 What are the advantages and disadvantages of mass production? Do the advantages outweigh the disadvantages, in your opinion?

5 If you wanted to judge how rich a country is, what facts would you have to know about it?

6 Why is the system of rates often criticised? Do you agree with the criticisms?

7 Can you think of any new ways by which the government might raise money to pay for essential services?

8 What do you understand by 'the affluent society'? What other countries are affluent? Is everybody in Britain affluent?

9 Poor people usually have considerable problems in addition to the problem of low income. What are the main problems faced by these people? How can these problems be overcome?

PROJECT WORK

1 When you switch on the light at night-time, you change your environment. Give as many examples as you can of ways in which complex societies can control their physical environment by using their scientific knowledge.

2 Take a daily newspaper and cut out all the articles concerned with the economy. Sort them into groups according to the subject they deal with, for example, productivity or exports and imports. What proportion of the paper is devoted to the economy? (You can work this out by measuring the column inches.) How many articles are straight reports on events or economic figures and how many are commentaries which express the writer's own opinion? What seem to be the most important issues to do with the economy at the moment? How do different newspapers differ in their treatment of economic affairs?

3 Make a list of jobs which are performed in each sector of employment in Britain today. How many of these jobs would have been performed two hundred years ago? Can you think of any jobs which would have been done in the eighteenth century which are no longer in existence?

4 What skills or qualifications are required for the following jobs – doctor, bus driver, store manager, teacher, park attendant, hairdresser? Put them in order according to the number of qualifications needed. Find out what is roughly the average pay of each. Is the job requiring the highest qualifications the most highly paid? Which seems to be the most and which the least pleasant job to do? Are people doing unpleasant jobs paid highly? Should they be, in your opinion?

5 What factors limit a person's choice of job in Britain today?

6 Find out what are the main items Britain buys and sells abroad. What are *invisible exports*? How important are invisible exports to Britain's balance of payments?

7 Which are Britain's main competitors in the world market? Which of these are most successful in competing against British goods? What makes these countries so successful? Are there any lessons which Britain can learn from her competitors?

8 Which countries belong to the EEC? How is the EEC governed? What are the main areas of agreement among EEC countries, and in what ways has co-operation between the EEC members most helped the countries concerned?

9 Find out how much of the retail price of the following goods is excise duty or purchase tax: bottle of whisky; twenty cigarettes; a new car; a gallon of petrol; a record. Any make or brand will do. Why does the government choose to tax these particular goods and not, say, bread or apples?

10 Look up the population and national income statistics for any developing country. What is the size of the national income per head of the population? What steps are being taken to raise the level of economic growth (*a*) by the country itself, and (*b*) with aid from other countries, or from international organisations?

11 What are the present old-age pensions for single people and for married couples? Work out what you think would be the average weekly budget of an old-age pensioner. Is the pension adequate?

12 Find out what benefit a worker may receive if he has an accident at work. What must he do in order to claim benefit? What may he claim when he is no longer entitled to benefit?

13 What is the cost of the weekly stamp paid by a man and a woman over the age of eighteen? What contribution does the employer pay? What may a married woman worker pay?
You can find out most of the answers to questions 11, 12 and 13 from the local office of the Ministry of Health & Social Security.

14 What voluntary organisations exist to help people with the following problems: poor housing, physical handicap, mental handicap, old age, widows and destitute wives, destitute or orphaned children?
Do a project on one of these organisations. Find out how it started, where it gets its money from, and exactly what sort of work it does.

USEFUL BOOKS FOR PUPILS

Barr, J. *Standards of Living* (Penguin 1969)
Burkitt, A. *Focus on Health* (Nelson 1973)
Cootes, R. V. *The Making of the Welfare State* (Longman 1966)

Corina, M. *Pile It High, Sell It Cheap – the career of Sir Jack Cohen* (Weidenfeld & Nicolson 1971)
CSV *The Elderly in Society* (Community Service Volunteers 1975)
Dickson, M. & A. *Count Us In* (Dobson 1967)
Garrett, J. *Visual Economics* (Evans 1966)
Leigh, F. *Growing Old* (Checkpoint series 7) (Edward Arnold 1976)
Longman's Secondary History Packs (1975): *The First Industrial Revolution; Social Problems Arising from the Industrial Revolution*; *Social Welfare*
Marsh, J. *The Welfare State* (Harrap 1976)
Martin, I. *Workhouse to Welfare* (Penguin 1971)
Moss, P. *History Alive* Books 3 and 4 (Hart-Davis Education 1974)
Nobbs, J. *Social Economics* (McGraw-Hill 1971)
Sawyer, R. & White, J. *Care and Community* (Ginn 1971)
Schools Council/Nuffield Humanities Project *Poverty* (Heinemann 1970)
Sidey, P. S. *The Welfare State* (Macmillan Nation Today series 1967)
Stuttard, C. G. *Problems at Work* (Ginn 1970)
Thomas, M. W. *Focus on the EEC* (Nelson 1973)
Whittaker, D. *The Social Services* (Longman 1976)

Pamphlets on the following can be obtained from Holmes McDougall Ltd (1973):

Old Age
Young People
Health and Hospitals

USEFUL BOOKS FOR TEACHERS

Abel-Smith, B. & Townsend, P. *The Poor and the Poorest* (Bell 1965)
Beynon, H. *Working for Ford* (Penguin 1973)
Beynon, H. & Nichols, T. *Living with Capitalism* (Routledge & Kegan Paul 1977)
Braverman, H. *Labour and Monopoly Capital* (Monthly Review 1975)
Central Office of Information *Social Services in Britain* (HMSO 1970)
CIS Crisis Series *Cutting the Welfare State* (1975)
CIS Report 7 *Your Money and Your Life* (1974)
Coates, K. & Silburn, R. *Poverty: The Forgotten Englishmen* (Penguin 1970)
Family Welfare Association *Guide to the Social Services* (revised annually)
Field, F. *Low Pay* (Armour Books 1974)
Fraser, R. *Work*, vols I & II (Penguin 1968)
Illich, I. *Medical Nemesis* (Calder 1976)
Marsh, D. C. *Changing Social Conditions in England & Wales, 1871–1961* (Routledge & Kegan Paul 1965)
Ollman, B. *Alienation* (Cambridge University Press 1973)
Toynbee, P. *A Working Life* (Penguin 1971)
Urry, J. & Wakeford, J. *Power in Britain* (Heinemann Education 1973)
Willmott, P. *A Consumer's Guide to the Social Services* (Penguin 1967)

The DHSS will supply free of charge, in whatever quantities you require, every pamphlet they print about benefits.

FILMS

The Quiet Revolution (industrialisation in Sweden); 20 mins; Guild Sound & Vision Ltd
Industries of Japan; 18 mins (free); Guild Sound and Vision Ltd
Industrial Revolution in England; 25 mins; ILEA 1620
China's Industrial Revolution; 14 mins; ILEA 2056
Yugoslav Village; 9 mins; ILEA 1463
One + one + one (large-scale industry); 29 mins (free); Sound Services
European Community; 18 mins (free); Guild Sound & Vision Ltd
Continent Without Frontiers; 37 mins (free); Guild Sound & Vision Ltd
A Fable (international co-operation); 17 mins (free); Guild Sound & Vision Ltd
Born Losers; 30 mins; Granada TV *World in Action*; Concord Film Services
St Ann's; 45 mins; Concord Film Services and ILEA 563
Hospital 1922; 47 mins; ILEA 2305

The following films are available from the Slide Centre Ltd:

Population, Health, Education AUC/114
Trade Union History AUC/117
Foreign Trade RGB/258
The Social Services AUC/146

3 The Organisation of Production

In a pre-industrial society like that of the Aztecs, or in Britain before the Industrial Revolution, each worker could have his own capital equipment. The weaver would keep his loom in his cottage, and the peasant farmer would own his plough and scythe. With industrialisation the capital equipment becomes mechanised, and it is much more expensive to start up in production. Buying a combine harvester is very different from buying a wooden plough. Individual workers simply cannot afford to buy large-scale machinery even if they have somewhere to put it and the skill to work it. So in an industrial society the organisation of production cannot be left to each worker by himself.

In complex societies two major solutions to the problem of how to organise production have emerged. The first is that used in capitalist societies, and the second is that of the soviet economies.

These peasants working in the Andes live in a pre-industrial society. They do not own the land, but are probably working with their own tools.

The capitalist economy

In a capitalist economy (such as existed in Britain in the nineteenth and early twentieth centuries) production is organised so that the capital equipment is bought and owned by rich individuals who then pay workers to come and operate the machinery. These owners of capital equipment are known as CAPITALISTS. In a truly capitalist economy the capitalists not only own the factories, mines and so on, but actually run them too. Their job would be to estimate how many machines and workers are needed, how much they will be able to sell, and how much they can pay their workers. From the money they get for selling their goods, they have to pay for new or replacement equipment, and cover other costs such as rent and rates for the factory buildings, the power to run the machinery, and wages to pay the workers. The money they keep for themselves is their pay for organising the factory and their reward for risking their money in the first place.

In most capitalist societies, however, this pattern of production is now rare. There are hardly any small factories which can be owned and run by a single individual or family. Nowadays it is much more likely that the capital equipment will be owned jointly by many people, each of whom has a share in the enterprise and a share in its profits. These people are called SHAREHOLDERS. In this case the firm or COMPANY is run by a board of directors whose job it is to represent the shareholders. One of the directors will be the managing director, and he is the man who actually takes responsibility for organising the firm. He will be paid a salary for this job, and will probably own shares in the company as well. He will have a number of other managers working under him who are also paid salaries, and who run different aspects of the business – sales, personnel, production and so on.

STOCKS AND SHARES

The kind of firm described above is known as a JOINT-STOCK COMPANY because its capital equipment or stock is owned jointly by a number of people. When people buy a share of a company's capital equipment they are said to be INVESTING in the company, and they are known as investors. There are several ways in which investors can go about buying stocks and shares. The majority get the help of their bank managers who advise them on what shares they should buy. Others go straight to a specialist in stocks and shares, called a stockbroker. This is someone who makes his living out of buying and selling shares on behalf of his clients, and in return receives a fixed commission.

Stocks and shares are bought and sold at the Stock Exchange, a market dealing in company and government finance. If there were no Stock Exchange it would be very difficult for individuals to get in touch with firms and impossible for firms to borrow money from individuals.

SAVINGS AND INVESTMENT

There are about twenty-two million people owning investments in Britain today, but only about two-and-a-half million of these invest directly through the Stock Exchange. The rest are INDIRECT INVESTORS. When people pay regularly into life assurance and pension schemes, or contribute to the funds of trade unions and friendly societies, their money is used to buy investments on behalf of the contributors. Similarly when an individual saves money in a bank, the bank invests this money, usually in a very safe government concern, and with the profits they make on their investments, the banks are able to pay out interest on the savings of their clients.

In this way people's savings are put to good use, by helping firms to put in more capital equipment and to expand production. No investment and therefore no growth in production would be possible unless people were prepared to save. But savers must put their money into a bank or similar institution, or invest directly for their savings to be any use; hoarding money in a piggy bank or under the floor boards gives no help to firms who want to borrow.

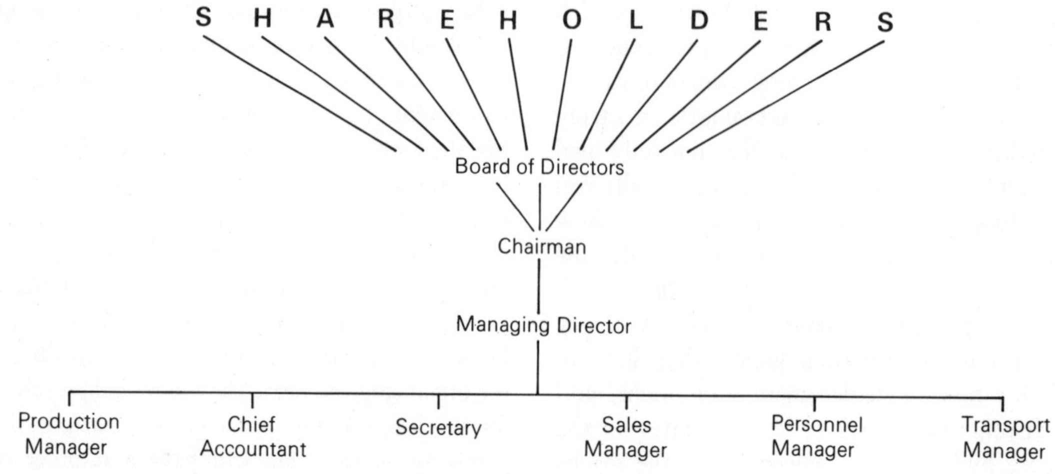

Figure 24 Organisation of a joint-stock company.

The Stock Exchange, London. On the pillar is a notice board showing current share prices.

BANKS

What are the services provided by banks, and what are the different types of bank in Britain?

The main purposes of a bank are to enable people to keep their money safely: to lend money to individuals and to firms: and to allow people to write cheques to settle their debts without using cash, and so make paying bills easier and safer.

COMMERCIAL BANKS such as the National Westminster and Barclays are the biggest banks. They have a head office, probably in London, and thousands of local branches spread all over the country. Two kinds of account are available at a commercial bank, and many people have both kinds. A CURRENT ACCOUNT is used as a way of paying bills. Once the initial deposit of money has been made, the client is given a cheque book and he may write cheques for any sum up to the amount he has deposited. He can pay cheques other people have given him into his current account, and many people have their salaries paid directly into their bank accounts. The other kind of account is the DEPOSIT ACCOUNT, and is used mainly by people who want to save money in return for interest. No cheque book is issued with this account, and if the client wants to withdraw his money he must usually give a week's notice. This is to encourage people to leave their money in their deposit account for a long period, so that the bank can invest it without fear that the saver will want to withdraw it quickly.

TRUSTEE SAVINGS BANKS were started in the nineteenth century to help people with just a little money to save. Interest is paid on savings, and sometimes withdrawal notice has to be given.

It is also possible to save through the NATIONAL SAVINGS BANK which is operated by the Post Office. Withdrawals may be made on demand up to a limited sum, but a little time elapses before larger amounts can be withdrawn. A small rate of interest is paid on an ordinary account, but a higher rate is paid on the special investment account, and so notice has to be given if withdrawals have to be made from the investment account.

The Soviet economy

The first country to develop this method of organising its production was the Union of Soviet Socialist Republics (USSR). Other countries strongly influenced by the USSR, such as East Germany, Poland, Hungary and Czechoslovakia, are also organised in this way.

One of the basic differences between a capitalist and a soviet economy is that instead of individuals owning and controlling the means of production (factories, farms, mines and so on) and keeping the profits from these enterprises, all the capital equipment is owned and controlled by the government. Communists believe that the profits from industry and agriculture should be used for the benefit of all the people in the country, so that although managers are appointed to direct farms and factories, they are simply employees of the government like everyone else, and have no private financial interest in the firm.

Collective farming is common in most Communist countries. These people on a Chinese Commune are harvesting the early rice crop at the same time as planting the later crop.

COLLECTIVE FARMS

Farming in the USSR is a COLLECTIVE operation. During the 1930s the Soviet government forced individual peasants who often owned very small patches of land to pool their land and machinery to form much larger farms. It is possible to organise production much more efficiently on large farms, and the extra food thus produced could go to feed the growing numbers of factory workers in the cities. Machinery and fertiliser were provided by the state. The government laid down the crop each farm should produce and production targets were set for each area. Similar targets were set for workers in factories and mines; workers who exceeded these production targets were rewarded, sometimes with money, sometimes with medals, but a production manager whose factory or farm failed to reach the target could be penalised, even by dismissal.

CENTRAL CONTROL

In a communist economy, therefore, the government has control of production. Not only does the State lay down what should be produced and how, it also sets the wages that shall be paid to the workers and the prices that shall be charged in the shops because these are also owned by the State. Some advantages of central control are said to be:

(*a*) The government can decide what needs to be produced for the good of the country as a whole. It can decide, for example, that it is better to make tractors so that everyone will eventually get more food, rather than luxury cars for a small number of the very rich.

(*b*) The profits from industry and agriculture can be used to buy more capital equipment so that production can be increased; or they can be used to build more schools and hospitals and provide better welfare services for the country;

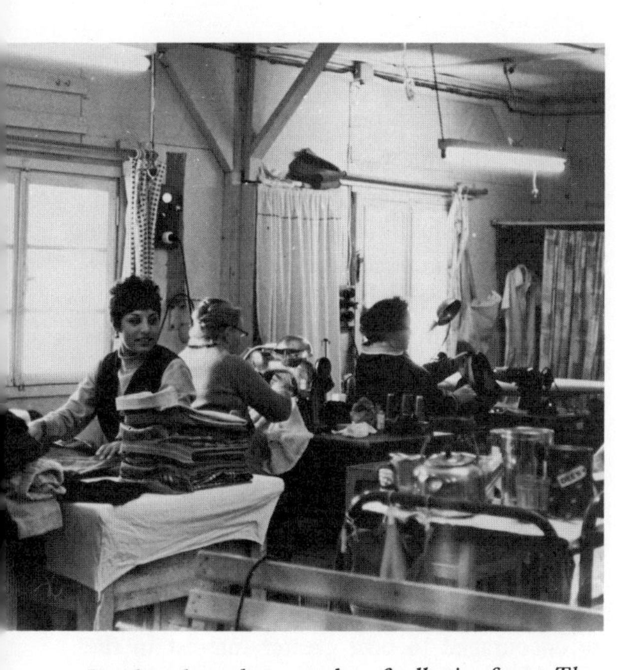

Israel too has a large number of collective farms. The members share not only the farm work, but also work together in the kitchens, nursery, laundry and sewing room.

or they can be used to pay the workers higher wages. In a capitalist economy, the profits are paid to the people who invested in the firm in the first place, and therefore they may simply end up by making the rich people richer.

(*c*) Because all wages and prices are controlled by the State, no group of workers can force up their wages by striking or by putting prices up.

(*d*) Because the firms are owned by the State, the workers may feel that they are working for the good of the country and therefore for themselves rather than for an individual employer. They may, then, be prepared to put more effort into their work.

There are disadvantages, however, too.

(*a*) It is a very difficult task to estimate just how much of a commodity is needed by the whole economy at any particular time, especially when the needs change from year to year. In

deciding how much steel to produce the government economists must take into account the DEMAND for steel of all the industries using it. These industries may be expanding their own output of things like cars, railway lines, knives, forks and machinery. If the economists make a mistake – and this is very easily done – all these different industries will be affected, and there will be shortages not only of steel, but of all the goods that are made of steel. It is a tremendously difficult job to estimate just how much of all goods and services will be needed.

(*b*) People who disagree with central control say that because the managers of firms have no financial interest in the firm (they do not own shares in the firm), they do not work so hard because they lack the INCENTIVE to work hard. On the other hand, the managers know that they will not be promoted, and may even lose their jobs, if they do not do their best.

(*c*) Although central control allows the government to decide what the country needs, this may not be the same as what the people in the country *want*. The amount of choice of things to buy will be smaller if the government decides to concentrate on building roads and houses rather than on making cosmetics and television sets. The people *may* decide to sacrifice luxury goods in return for more useful things, but unless the government is responsible to the people in a truly democratic manner, central control can take away freedom of choice. In the USSR production of luxury goods like cars and washing machines has always taken second place to production of machinery and capital equipment. This may be sensible in the long run, but is it what the people want?

STATE CAPITALISM OR WORKERS' CONTROL?

Although in a communist economy the means of production are owned by the State and therefore by the people, the amount of control that the ordinary worker has over the farm or factory where he works is just as small as in a capitalist economy. So the soviet type of production system has been described as no more than 'State capitalism'. Many would say that the State behaves in exactly the same way as the capitalists in a capitalist economy.

In some communist countries such as Yugoslavia, however, an attempt has been made to give the workers more say in the running of the enterprise where they are employed. Workers' councils have been set up, and decisions on production, investment, wages and marketing are made by the councils, or at least in discussion with them. In this way true democracy can enter the work situation, and ordinary people are encouraged to take greater interest in the place where, after all, they spend much of their waking hours.

The mixed economy

Britain today does not have a truly capitalist economy, but neither does the government have complete control over economic affairs. Britain operates what is sometimes called a MIXED ECONOMY. This means that although much of industry is in the hands of private companies, some organisations are owned and controlled by the state. Examples are, British Rail, and the gas, electricity and coal mining industries. These industries have been NATIONALISED, that is, they are owned and controlled by the government.

Why does the government own these industries and not others? There are various arguments in favour of the nationalisation of certain kinds of enterprises.

(*a*) Organisations like the railways run more efficiently if they are controlled by one board of management.

Public transport is one of the nationalised industries that few people want to see in private hands.

(*b*) Some industries, such as the coal industry, need to be kept going for the sake of the whole economy, and yet are not profitable enough for private investors to want to risk their money in them.

(*c*) The general public needs to be confident that there will always be a supply of gas and electricity, and the government can ensure this.

(*d*) The aircraft industry needs a great deal of money invested in it if Britain is to keep abreast of other countries, so the government supports it for reasons of national prestige.

(*e*) The basic industries – transport, coal and steel – on which other industries depend, should be planned so that the whole economy, rather than just a small section, benefits and only the government can do this overall planning.

INTERFERENCE OR INTERVENTION

The same arguments have been put forward against nationalisation as against central control:

(1) Nationalisation interferes with the freedom of the individual.

(2) Managers have no incentive to put their best into their work.

(3) If there is only one organisation producing, say, coal, there is no competition with other firms to increase output and reduce prices. (This argument also applies, of course, to very large private firms or MONOPOLIES.)

The opponents of nationalised industries, government grants to private industry, and government encouragement of firms wanting to set up in areas of high unemployment (the DEVELOPMENT DISTRICTS like north-east England, Northern Ireland and Scotland) say that this interference allows inefficient firms to carry on in business and reduces healthy competition between firms. Supporters say that the government is not interfering but *intervening* to prevent hardships arising from low wages and unemployment.

UNEMPLOYMENT

Since the Second World War it has been generally accepted that the government should try to keep the level of unemployment below $1\frac{1}{2}\%$. Economists have worked out that an unemployment figure at roughly this level accounts for the people who are moving between jobs, or have just left school. Also included are the people who will never be able to have a permanent job because of some special disability.

There are various reasons why unemployment rises above the $1\frac{1}{2}\%$ level. A whole industry might be in decline because of falling demand for its product. Areas which rely mainly on the ship-building, coal-mining and textile industries for employment have a higher-than-average number of people out of work. The government can help these areas by encouraging new firms to build factories there in return for grants of money or loans at low rates of interest. Special training centres may be set up to enable former miners or ship-builders to learn new skills.

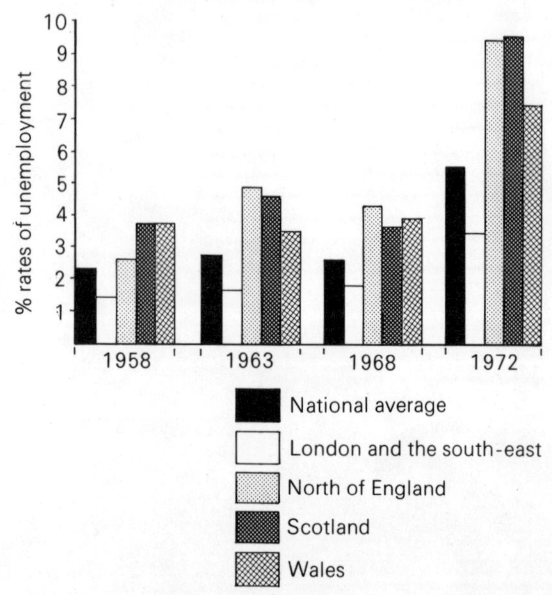

Figure 25 Regional unemployment in Great Britain, 1958, 1963, 1968 and 1972.

Unemployment was so widespread and so severe in the 1930s that many of those who remember it feel that unemployment is one of the worst evils that can occur in industrial society.

Employers were so afraid of the early trade unions that Parliament passed laws banning unions. Anyone caught breaking these laws was liable to be sent to prison, or transported to the colonies.

CAUTION.

HEREAS it has been represented to us from several quarters, that mischievous
designing Persons have been for some time past, endeavouring to induce, and
e induced, many Labourers in various Parishes in this County, to attend Meet-
, and to enter into Illegal Societies or Unions, to which they bind themselves
unlawful oaths, administered secretly by Persons concealed, who artfully
eive the ignorant and unwary,—WE, the undersigned Justices think it our duty
give this PUBLIC NOTICE and CAUTION, that all Persons may know the
ger they incur by entering into such Societies.

ANY PERSON who shall become a Member of such a Society, or take any Oath, or assent to any Test or
laration not authorized by Law—

Any Person who shall administer, or be present at, or consenting to the administering or taking any Unlawful
, or who shall cause such Oath to be administered, although not actually present at the time—

Any Person who shall not reveal or discover any Illegal Oath which may have been administered, or any Illegal
done or to be done—

ny Person who shall induce, or endeavour to persuade any other Person to become a Member of such Societies,

WILL BECOME

Guilty of Felony,

AND BE LIABLE TO BE

Transported for Seven Years.

ANY PERSON who shall be compelled to take such an Oath, unless he shall declare the same within four
s, together with the whole of what he shall know touching the same, will be liable to the same Penalty.

Any Person who shall directly or indirectly maintain correspondence or intercourse with such Society, will be
emed Guilty of an Unlawful Combination and Confederacy, and on Conviction before one Justice, on the Oath of
e Witness, be liable to a Penalty of TWENTY POUNDS, or to be committed to the Common Gaol or House
Correction, for THREE CALENDAR MONTHS; or if proceeded against by Indictment, may be CON-
ICTED OF FELONY, and be TRANSPORTED FOR SEVEN YEARS.

Any Person who shall knowingly permit any Meeting of any such Society to be held in any House, Building,
other Place, shall for the first offence be liable to the Penalty of FIVE POUNDS; and for every other offence
mmitted after Conviction, be deemed Guilty of such Unlawful Combination and Confederacy, and on Conviction
efore one Justice, on the Oath of one Witness, be liable to a Penalty of TWENTY POUNDS, or to Commit-
ent to the Common Gaol or House of Correction, FOR THREE CALENDAR MONTHS; or if proceeded
gainst by Indictment may be

CONVICTED OF FELONY,

And Transported for SEVEN YEARS.

OUNTY OF DORSET.
Dorchester Division.

February 22d. 18[illegible]

C. B. WOLLASTON,
JAMES FRAMPTON,
WILLIAM ENGLAND,
THOS. DADE,
JNO. MORTON COLSON,

HENRY FRAMPTON,
RICHD. TUCKER STEWARD,
WILLIAM R. CHURCHILL,
AUGUSTUS FOSTER.

G. CLARK, PRINTER, CORNHILL, DORCHESTER

Companies may have to dismiss workers if there is a temporary fall in demand for their products. Some firms may decide not to buy any more machinery for a while. So some workers in the machine-tool industries become REDUNDANT. They no longer earn as much as they did when they were at work, and may have to put off buying a new car or television set. They may have to do without a holiday this year, and their cut in earnings may be so great that they can only afford the barest essentials. In this way, demand for all kinds of products from cars to airline tickets may fall, leading to further redundancies in yet more industries. The government can help here too. It can encourage people to keep up their normal level of spending by cutting taxation. Higher unemployment benefits may also help to prevent demand from falling to a disastrously low level.

Industrial relations in Britain

In the middle of the last century an individual worker had no say over the amount of money he should be paid, or over his working conditions. Hours, wages, holidays (if any) and conditions in the mines, factories and farms were completely at the whim of the employers, and as a result many people, including women and children, worked in appalling conditions for very little money.

Matters were improved somewhat by government legislation; Factory Acts were passed laying down the maximum number of hours to be worked, and inspectors were employed to make sure that safety regulations were enforced. But still relations between employers and their employees were very one-sided; the employers were rich and powerful and, although they were not all exploiters of labour, their attitude towards their employees was conditioned by the times in which they lived. They saw no reason to pay wages higher than the barest minimum required to keep body and soul together – SUBSISTENCE wages.

TRADE UNIONS

It was only when workers began to act collectively – to band together in trade unions – that power between employers and employees became more evenly balanced.

In this passage, Joseph Arch tells of the very beginning of the National Agricultural Labourers' Union:

> The day was February 7th 1872. It was a very wet morning, and I was making a box. My wife came in to see me and said, 'Joe, here's three men come to see you. What for, I don't know.' But I knew fast enough. In walked the three; they turned out to be labourers from over Wellesbourne way. I stopped work, and we had a talk. They said they had come to ask me to hold a meeting at Wellesbourne that evening. They wanted to get the men together, and start a Union, directly. I told them that, if they did form a Union, they would have to fight hard for it, and they would have to suffer a great deal; both they and their families. They said the labourers were prepared both to fight and to suffer. Things could not be worse; wages were so low, and provisions so dear, that nothing but downright starvation lay before them unless the farmers could be made to raise their wages. . . .
>
> When I reached Wellesbourne, lo, and behold, it was as lively as a swarm of bees in June. We settled that I should address the meeting under the old chestnut tree; and I expected to find some thirty or forty of the principal men there. What then was my surprise to see not a few tens, but many hundreds of labourers assembled; there were nearly two thousand of them. The news that I was going to speak that

Even in 1871 children were employed in factories such as this brickyard.

night had been spread about: and so the men had come in from all the villages round within a radius of ten miles. Not a circular had been sent out, nor a handbill printed, but from cottage to cottage, and from farm to farm the word had been passed on; and here were the labourers gathered together in their hundreds. Wellesbourne village was there, every man in it; and they had come from Moreton and Locksley and Charlecote and Hampton Lucy, and from Barford, to hear what I had to say to them. By this time night had fallen pitch dark; but the men found bean poles and hung lanterns on them, and we could see well enough. It was an extraordinary sight, and I shall never forget it, not to my dying day. I mounted an old pig-stool, and in the flickering light of the lanterns I saw the earnest upturned faces of these poor brothers of mine – faces gaunt with hunger and pinched with want – all looking towards me and ready to listen to the words that would fall from my lips. . . . We passed a resolution to form a Union then and there, and the names of the men could not be taken down fast enough; we enrolled between two and three hundred members that night. It was a brave start, and before we parted it was arranged that there should be another meeting at the same place in a fortnight's time. I knew now that a fire had been kindled which would catch on, and spread, and run abroad like sparks in stubble; and I felt certain that this night we had set light to a beacon, which would prove a rallying point for the agricultural labourers throughout the country.

Today over ten million people belong to nearly 600 unions, although most belong to one of the eight largest, each of which has more than a quarter of a million members. Unions exist to look after their members' interests in many ways. In addition to trying to improve pay, working conditions, holidays, apprenticeship, overtime and redundancy payments, some also pay out sickness and accident benefit, unemployment and strike pay, and pensions. They run educational courses through the post and at Ruskin College, the Trades Union college at Oxford. Unionists also take an active part in many aspects of national affairs, advising the government on matters which affect all working people.

The Trades Union Congress

Nearly all trade unions are members of the Trades Union Congress (TUC). This meets for a week, once a year, to discuss matters affecting all unions and to decide on a joint policy for all unions which are members of the TUC. At the Congress, delegates from the different unions elect a General Council to carry on the work of the TUC on a full-time basis.

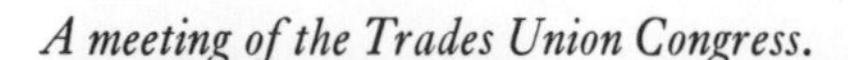

A meeting of the Trades Union Congress.

The shop steward's job is to deal with matters on the shop floor. He is probably the union official the workers know and trust most.

Types of union

(*a*) *General unions.* These unions represent many kinds of workers, and are the largest unions. The two biggest, the Transport and General Workers' Union, and the General and Municipal Workers' Union include clerical and industrial workers in practically every sector of the economy.

(*b*) *Industrial unions.* Industrial unions such as the Union of Post Office Workers and the National Union of Mineworkers represent the workers in a particular industry, whatever the job they do in the industry.

(*c*) *Craft unions.* These unions tend to be the smallest since they represent skilled craftsmen such as printers, plumbers and so on. Some unions have tried to become more effective by amalgamating with other unions, but there are still some very small craft unions, such as the Jewish Bakers, with only two dozen or so members.

Union organisation

The local branch of the union is the place where individual members can meet and have their say in union policy. The branch also elects union officers who will put forward the members' views to the district or national organisation. Probably the most important man at the local level, however, is not the branch official, but the SHOP STEWARD, who represents the workers in a particular section of a firm. With the trend towards larger and larger unions, many workers feel out of touch with the district or area officials, and consider that the shop steward is the man who, as a worker on the same shop floor as themselves, understands their grievances and problems best. He is always around if a problem arises, and it is often he who makes the decision, in consultation with his fellow-workers, whether to take action on a particular problem.

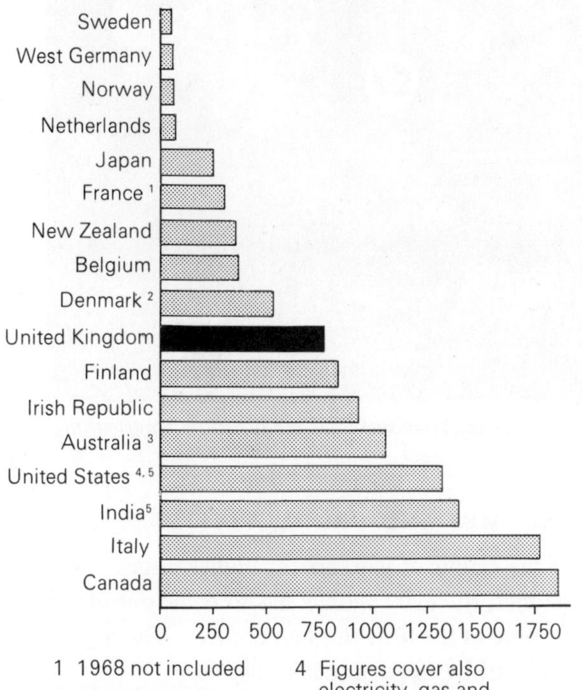

Figure 26 Industrial disputes – a comparison of seventeen countries

Source: *Department of Employment Gazette* November 1976

EMPLOYERS' ORGANISATIONS

Not only have the workers banded together to negotiate with employers over matters such as wage rates and hours of work, but the employers themselves have also formed groups, such as the Confederation of Shipbuilding & Engineering Employers. The working conditions of most workers today are therefore decided by a process of COLLECTIVE BARGAINING between on the one side the trade union, and on the other, the employers' association.

Factors of production

Three things are necessary before production of goods can take place: there must be land and raw materials, labour and capital equipment. Without any one of these *factors of production* no goods would be produced. A carpenter can do nothing without wood, a workshop and tools; the poorest peasant cannot grow food without seed, a plot of land and simple equipment such as a plough or a hoe. Very large productive enterprises such as ship-building yards, steel works and electronic component manufacturers may use thousands of workers, tons of raw material and highly technical or heavy machinery. The quantity of output produced depends on the combinations and kinds of factors of production involved. Two men can plough a field more quickly than one. A man with a tractor will plough a field more quickly than a man with a horse. A field which is properly fertilised gives a bigger crop than a neglected field.

Mechanisation increases productivity in agriculture.

When a man succeeds in producing more in a given time than he did before, he has become more PRODUCTIVE. Another way of putting this is to say that his PRODUCTIVITY has gone up. The tractor driver's productivity is higher than that of the man with the horse because he is using better capital equipment. One man may have higher productivity than another because he works harder, or because he is physically stronger, or because he is more skilled. If each worker improves his productivity, either through his own efforts, or through being given better tools and training, the total amount produced by the factory or the farm (OUTPUT) will increase.

INCOMES AND PRODUCTIVITY

If the claims of workers for higher wages are to be met, the extra money has to come out of the income of the firm employing them. The money received by the firm has to pay for:

(*a*) the cost of raw materials, power, rent and so on
(*b*) the cost of investing in new or replacement machinery
(*c*) wages for the workers
and (*d*) dividends paid to shareholders.

One way of giving more to the workers would be to take money away from (*a*), (*b*) or (*d*). But to do this may damage the firm, since it obviously needs enough machinery and materials to go on producing, and if lower dividends are paid to shareholders they may take their money out of the firm.

More could be paid to the workers without damage, however, if the firm's output could be increased. Income would go up if productivity were to rise, and higher wages could be paid out of the increased income. Some firms have made productivity agreements with their workers, promising to pay them higher wages if they manage to produce more.

In the past, productivity and output have not risen as fast as the incomes of workers and managers. One result of this tendency for incomes to go up without a corresponding rise in output is that prices rise in order to fill the gap, and when this happens, the country is said to be suffering from INFLATION – a tendency for prices to keep on rising.

Index numbers help us to see percentage changes more clearly than if we try to compare the money figures for incomes and output. An index of 150 represents an increase of 50 per cent over the base year.

The Retail Price Index is a good example of the use of index numbers.

Here are the figures for:

(a) Base year 1962

1962	July 1971	July 1972	July 1973
100	155·2	164·2	179·7
	July 1974	July 1975	July 1976
	210·4	265·6	299·8

Source: Daily Telegraph Information Service

(b) Base year 1970

1970	1973	1974	1975	1976	1977
100	126·7	147·0	182·5	211·4	233·1

Source: *OECD Main Economic Indicators*, August 1977

Figure 27

The next chart shows how a graph could be made from one of these sets of figures.

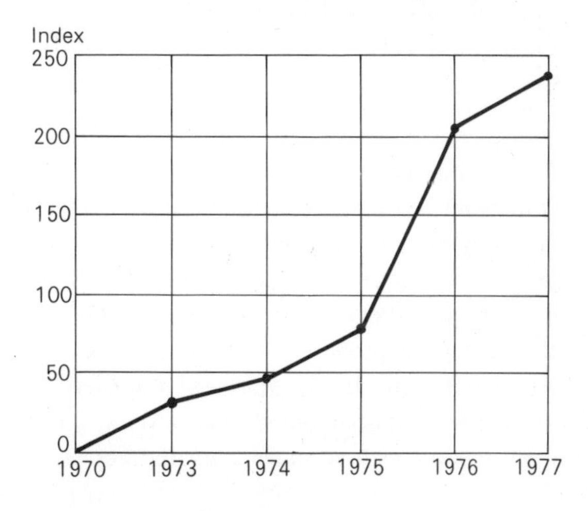

Figure 28 Index of retail prices 1970–77

Inflation: Britain compared with other industrial countries

	1970	1973	1974	1975	1976	1977 (May)
West Germany	100 (base year)	118·8	127·1	134·7	140·8	146·5
France	100	119·9	136·3	152·2	166·8	181·1
Belgium	100	117·7	132·6	149·5	163·2	173·9
Italy	100	122·4	146·2	171·3	199·6	235·7
United Kingdom	100	126·7	147·0	182·5	211·4	243·8
Japan	100	124·5	153·4	171·4	187·5	202·3 (April)
United States	100	114·4	127·0	138·6	132·6	155·3

Source: *OECD Economic Indicators* July 1977

AUTOMATION

A machine is highly AUTOMATED if it can do a lot of work on its own without needing much attention. An automatic washing machine is one which soaks, washes, rinses and dries clothes at the press of a button or turn of a dial. When a factory is automated most repetitive jobs are done by machines, and the workers are mainly occupied in supervisory jobs, like occasionally pushing a button, or watching a television screen that shows whether the machines are working properly. In a complex society new machines are always being invented and it is likely that AUTOMATION will increase in the future.

Results of automation

One result of increased mechanisation is that a machine-minder takes little responsibility for the end product of his work. Not only may his work require very little mental and physical effort, but he probably feels no personal involvement in it. In the words of the German sociologist and economist Karl Marx, 'The worker becomes a stranger from the object he

In an automated factory, workers are needed to repair and service machinery rather than to operate it.

This work may be slow, but is it worse than machine-minding?

The development of computers has relieved office workers of much boring paper work. But computers have to be programmed, and often this work is just as dull.

has made, and this estrangement is called alienation.' ALIENATION is not just felt by machine-operators in factories; clerical workers and others may also feel this basic dissatisfaction with their work. This is how a clerk in Ronald Fraser's book *Work* (volume 1) describes his work: 'The basic fact remains . . . that in common with other jobs I've had, it has no value as work. It is drudgery done in congenial surroundings. You feel dispensable, interim: automation will take it over one day, the sooner the better. You are there for the money, no other reason. You begrudge the time.'

Automation in factories today extends the meaninglessness of machine-minding. Fewer workers control or even understand the jobs they spend their days doing. Less and less skill or knowledge is gained through being at work. Instead hopes are being turned to the possibility that higher output can be produced by fewer workers with more machines. People begin to hope for a shorter working day. Writers such as Aldous Huxley in *Brave New World* have carried this suggestion very far and painted a picture of a future life in which all time is leisure time and there is no work at all. During this century the official working week has been reduced for most workers from about sixty hours a week to around forty hours. But the average statistics hide the fact that many workers depend on long hours of overtime to take home

Pubs are places where people can recuperate after a hard day's work. Are we going to need facilities for more active, creative leisure pursuits in the future?

Figure 29 Average working hours.

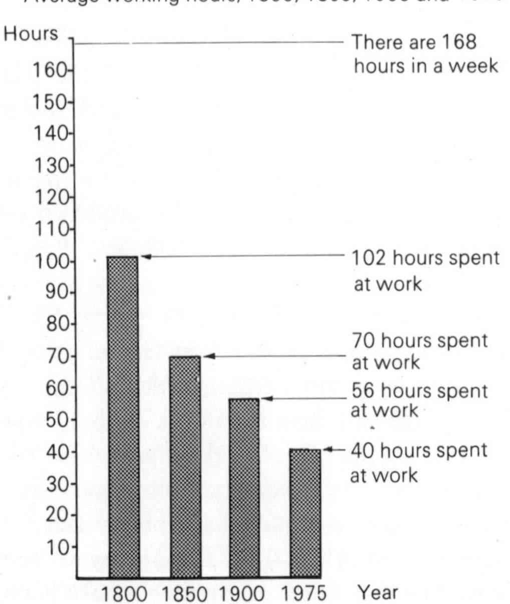

a satisfactory wage. It has been suggested that by the end of the 1980s most people will not start working until their middle twenties, and will probably finish in their middle fifties. Even during their working life they would have about three free days a week. Is this a rosy picture of the future? Do we have to stop working to begin to enjoy ourselves or could we change the nature of work so that it becomes a source of satisfaction?

THE AGE OF LEISURE

'It's boredom that's the trouble.' How often this has been said in explanation of anti-social or delinquent behaviour. We have come to accept that young people in their teens may get into trouble with the police if no leisure facilities are provided in their areas. How much greater the problem will be if not only young people but the whole of society reacts to an increase in spare time in a bored and destructive way. Some writers are so pessimistic as to talk in terms of the *problem* of 'the Leisure Age'. Dennis Gabor in his book *Inventing the Future* starts, 'Our civilisation faces three great dangers. The first is destruction by nuclear war. The second is being crippled by over-population, and the third is the Age of Leisure.'

What kind of leisure?

How our society copes with the problem of more spare time depends largely on how we plan now for the Age of Leisure. Should we, for instance, concentrate to a much greater extent on educating school children in the use of their leisure, instead of putting so much emphasis on learning skills for work? If automation requires less physical effort of workers, we possibly need to change the pattern of our leisure activities from those which simply provide us with rest and recuperation after a tiring day's work to activities in which we are more creative. The worker in an automated factory may spend all day on his own, watching his machine. What is he likely to need, in compensation, after work? Have most areas in Britain the facilities to deal with the problem of more leisure? What needs to be done now?

READING AND UNDERSTANDING

1 Who owns the capital equipment in (*a*) a simple society; (*b*) a capitalist society?
2 What role does the capitalist play, and what is his reward?
3 Why did joint-stock companies come into existence?
4 What are the functions of the Stock Exchange?
5 What is an *indirect investment*?
6 Explain the difference between saving and hoarding. Which is the more economically useful?
7 Who owns the capital equipment in a soviet economy?
8 What are the economic advantages of collective farming over peasant farming?
9 What is meant by *central control* of the economy?
10 What does the word *incentive* mean?
11 What is a *mixed economy*?
12 What is a *monopoly*?
13 Why were employers in the nineteenth century able to exploit their workers?
14 What difference did collective action by the workers make?
15 What made the farmworkers in the Wellesbourne district so desperate to form a union?
16 What are some of the functions of the TUC?
17 Which is the smallest and which the largest type of union?
18 What difficulties may arise from small size unions and what from very large size?
19 What is a shop steward?
20 What does the term *collective bargaining* mean?
21 Look at figure 26
   (*a*) Which country lost most days through industrial disputes in the period 1966–1975?
   (*b*) Which country lost fewest days in 1966–1975?
   (*c*) Which countries had a worse record than the UK for the period?
22 What factors of production go into the making of a loaf of bread?
23 What do we mean by *automation*?
24 What did Marx mean by the word *alienation*? What effect may greater mechanisation have on workers' alienation?
25 Did the clerk in the passage from Fraser's *Work* think that higher automation would be a good thing? What reasons did he give for his opinion?
26 What has happened to average working hours since 1800?

POINTS FOR FURTHER DISCUSSION

1 Can you think of any industry other than the aircraft industry which the government might support for reasons of national prestige?
2 Why does the coal industry need to be maintained, even though it is unprofitable for private investors?
3 In what ways may a worker's productivity be increased? Why is it necessary for productivity to rise if incomes are to rise over a long period? What may happen if incomes rise faster than productivity and output?
4 What problems may be presented by the introduction of shorter working hours? Can you think of any solutions to these problems?

PROJECT WORK

1. Different methods of saving through National Savings are mentioned on p. 65. Find out from the Post Office and Trustee Savings banks what are the advantages and disadvantages of each method of saving.
2. Pupils often have to bring money to school to pay for school journeys, visits to museums, tickets for the school play, and new uniform. Large sums of money are always at risk. What advantages would a school banking system have? Can you work out how a school bank would operate?
3. Find out all you can about life on a collective farm in Russia. Compare this with collective farms in other countries, for example a Chinese commune, or an Israeli kibbutz. Do workers on a collective farm feel more involved in their work than people working for a privately-owned organisation? What is family life on a collective farm like?
4. What attempts have been made to set up workers' control in Britain? Find out more about co-operative and co-ownership schemes. Note whether the introduction of such schemes has led to higher or lower productivity, and whether the workers themselves are happy with the working of such an enterprise.
5. Choose one nationalised industry and think of reasons why it was taken over by the government. When was it nationalised? Does it seem to be more efficiently run today than before nationalisation? What do you think would be the effect if control were to pass back into the hands of private companies?
6. Figure 25 shows rates of unemployment in different parts of Britain in the 1960s. What are the areas of highest unemployment? What are the major industries in these areas? Why are these areas so badly hit?
7. What is the present level of unemployment in the country as a whole? Is it above $1\frac{1}{2}$ per cent? If so, is the government taking steps to remedy the situation? You can find out much of this information by reading the newspapers and by listening to the news on television and radio.
8. Find out what these trade union terms mean: demarcation dispute; strike; picket; blackleg; lockout; closed shop.
9. Unions find it difficult to organise support in these occupations: shop work, farm work, hotel work, and occupations where most workers are women. What do you think are the reasons for this?
10. When prices continue to rise fast, workers try to maintain their standard of living. What methods can they use? Which groups in society are particularly hit by inflation? How can the government protect these groups?
11. Make a list of suitable leisure-time occupations of people engaged in the following jobs: shop assistant; farmer; bank clerk; machine-operator.
    Work out for each how the non-working hours would be filled, and then say why you have chosen these particular leisure activities.
12. Find out about the introduction of automated machinery in a particular factory or industry. How did this affect the numbers of people employed? What union regulations were set up? What are the pay and working conditions of the workers in the automated plant like, in comparison with the pay and working conditions of people in non-automated parts of the industry? How did automation affect output and productivity?

USEFUL BOOKS FOR PUPILS

Cootes, R. J. *Trade Unions* (Longman, Oliver & Boyd 1975)
Davies, B. & Herder D. *Production and Trade* (Social Science series) (Longman 1975)
Finn, E. *Talking About Unions* (Wayland 1976)
Gard, E. *British Trade Unions* (Methuen 1970)
Garrett, J. *Visual Economics* (Evans 1966)
Macdonald, Countries series (1974):
China
USA
Soviet Union
Nobbs, J. *Social Economics* (McGraw-Hill 1971)
Sommer, P. *Commercial Life* (Harrap 1972)
Thomas, M. W. *Managing Your Money* (Nelson 1975)
TUC *The History of the Trade Unions 1868–1968*

USEFUL BOOKS FOR TEACHERS

Braverman, H. *Labour and Monopoly Capital* (Monthly Press 1974)
Brittan, S. *Steering the Economy* (Penguin 1971)
CIS Crisis series *Who's Next for the Chop?*
CIS Reports:
Courtaulds, Inside Out (1974)
Unilever's World (1975)
Where Is Lucas Going? (1975)
Cockburn, A. & Blackburn, R. *The Incompatibles* (Penguin 1967)
Hyman, R. *Marxism and the Sociology of Trade Unionism* (Pluto Press 1971)
Lane, T. *The Union Makes Us Strong* (Arrow Books 1974)
Nove, A. *The Soviet Economy* (Minerva 1961)
Nyerere, J. *Freedom and Development* (Oxford University Press 1974)
Nyerere, J. *Freedom and Socialism* (Oxford University Press 1969)
Nyerere, J. *On Socialism* (Oxford University Press 1970)
Open University *The European Economic Community: Economics and Agriculture* (Open University Press, Course P933 5–6 1973)
Open University *The European Economic Community: History and Institutions* (Open University Press, Course P933 1–2 1973)
Parker, S. R. *The Sociology of Industry* (Allen & Unwin 1967)
Parkes, S. *The Future of Work and Leisure* (Paladin 1972)
Smigel, E. *Work and Leisure* (College and University Press 1963)
Wagner, L. et al. *Nationalized Industries* (Open University Press, Course P203 4 1972)

FILMS

Journey to Sarawak (agricultural co-operatives); 20 mins; Concord Films Council
Giye Us the Works (industrial relations); 25 mins; Concord Films Council
What About the Workers – are they to blame?; 50 mins; Concord Films Council
This is the North-East; 29 mins (free); Central Film Library
The Bargain (cartoon on banking); 10 mins (free); Central Film Library
The Bank of England at Work; 34 mins (free); Central Film Library
The Curious History of Money; 16 mins (free); Central Film Library
My Word is My Bond (the Stock Exchange); 27 mins (free); Guild Sound & Vision Ltd
The Sure Thing (insurance); 14 mins (free); Guild Sound & Vision Ltd

The following films are available from the Slide Centre:

Money and Banking AUC/140
Public Finance AUC/144

NB The Curious History of Money has pamphlets to accompany it, available on request from Barclays Bank Ltd.

4 Political Life

What is politics about?

We have seen that as the first societies developed from the very small hunting and gathering, herding and farming communities into larger societies, towns and cities grew up where people lived by producing manufactured goods and services. In a very small-scale society there is no need for a special group of people to make the rules and to see that the rules are kept, although there is likely to be someone – usually an older man – to whom the rest may turn for help and guidance. He will make the basic decisions, such as when to pack up and move on. In a large-scale society, however, decisions are more complex and more numerous. It is no longer merely a question of deciding whether to travel to this winter camp or that, or whether to move now or to wait one week longer. There are more people, doing more jobs, and there is bound to be a need for more rules. (See Chapter 7.)

This is seen clearly if we look at rules about property. RULES OF PROPERTY – rules about who owns what – vary in different societies. Bushmen own no property except for a few simple tools and weapons, a digging stick, a kaross, a bow or a spear. No Bushman would ever steal such possessions from another, and there is no need for rules about stealing. You might say that there is no such thing as stealing. The word 'thief' has no meaning in a society which has no CONCEPT – no general idea – of property. To most large-scale societies the concept of property is important. It is basic to our way of life that we own things as individuals – houses, shoes, pencils and rubber bands, and as members of groups – hospitals, street lights, fishing rights. Because people in complex societies possess different amounts of wealth, do different jobs and have different ideas and beliefs, their interests often clash, and conflict arises. Disagreement among individuals and groups becomes more likely the larger the scale of the

The crown and sceptre of the medieval king were symbols of his authority. They were the outward sign that he had the right to rule.

society, and the need for more rules is therefore greater.

The necessity for laws and the enforcement of laws poses a problem; who shall make the laws and make sure that they are carried out? This is the central question of politics. The word POLITICS comes from a Greek word *polis*, meaning *city*. Certain ancient Greek cities, Athens, for example, drew up their laws by bringing all citizens, *polites*, together in an assembly, where they could argue questions out amongst themselves. The decision or POLICY with which the majority agreed was adopted as the decision for everybody, and because all citizens had participated in the process of coming to that decision, it was something that was accepted by everybody.

Any political system has not only to provide the means by which laws can be made, but to ensure that most people support the system. In the Greek city-state all citizens took part in the government (women and slaves were not citizens and so took no part), and so most consented to the decisions. Sometimes, however, the people who make the rules, the rulers, do not have the support of the majority, and so, instead of simply relying on the people's consent, they have to resort to other means to enforce laws. The most obvious method is to use physical force, or the threat of violence. A ruler who is backed by physical strength can make the people obey his will if there are no others who can match his strength.

Political leaders may rely on other kinds of power to make people do what they want. If the people believe that the ruler is specially chosen (though not by them) to lead the country, they may give him their support. When people believe that it is right for a ruler to have power over them, then he is said to have AUTHORITY. The medieval kings of Europe were supposedly chosen by God; they held power by reason of a DIVINE RIGHT, and anyone who disobeyed the king was going against the will of God. It was the religious and moral duty of the people to support the king, who was really a kind of intermediary, passing on God's orders to the people. Ruler-priests rely on the same kind of authority.

Occasionally a leader emerges who is able to win the people to his side through the sheer force of his personality. He can exercise such a powerful hold over people, whether they are individuals or in a crowd, that he is able to make them do what he wants. Lenin, one of the leaders of the Russian Revolution, is described as possessing this kind of authority. Although he was not a tall man, he had great presence, and his eyes had a compelling, almost hypnotic quality which enabled him to hold crowds spellbound.

Lenin. This photograph was taken in Petrograd, now called Leningrad, in January 1918.

The German sociologist, Max Weber, who lived from 1864 to 1920, has classified the different types of authority. He called the gift of commanding loyalty and obedience through force of personality CHARISMA. The charismatic leader is accepted by the people because they have faith in him personally. One problem of this kind of domination, however, is that the group or society may break up when the leader dies, unless another charismatic personality replaces him, or unless some other kind of authority can be used instead of charisma.

Medieval kings of Europe held TRADITIONAL authority. The king ruled because his father ruled before him, and *his* father before that. They inherited their position as king, and their subjects obeyed out of a personal loyalty and respect.

The third kind of authority Weber distinguished was LEGAL authority. People obey the rules because they believe they were drawn up according to the correct legal procedure. The ruler too has been put into authority according to the correct procedure, whether through appointment or through election. He can only act according to the rules; he is far more limited in what he may or may not do than is the charismatic leader who can more or less do as he pleases, or the traditional leader. The governments of most large-scale societies have this kind of legal authority. There are definite procedures to be followed when we have an election in Britain, and for a government to be accepted it must have followed the rules.

In the last resort, the success of a political system depends on how well it works. If the system is successful in welding people together into a society, in resolving conflicts and arguments, if it ensures that the necessary rules are made and kept, and if the people, for whatever reason, are persuaded that the government can protect them from threats from another society, the system will continue. When the system fails to do these things, the time eventually comes when it is replaced by another.

Government in a simple society

A simple society needs fewer rules than a complex society, but any group needs some organisation. How does a society which has no king, no courts of law and no police force organise itself?

Generally the answer is to be found in the KINSHIP SYSTEM. We have already seen that simple societies are organised along family lines. A group of Bushmen or Eskimo will probably consist of no more than one extended family. A Lapp clan is made up of several extended families, and a Nuer tribe also includes people who, though not of the same family, are nevertheless distantly related. Among simple societies, then, a man's friends are his kinsfolk, his relatives. His enemies are outside the group; they

The judges of the International Court of Justice at The Hague (in the Netherlands) have the legal authority to decide on issues between countries. Their special robes are the symbol of their authority.

In Bushmen society important decisions are made by the elders of the family. This Bushman shows his special position in the group by the skin, beads and decorated cap he is wearing.

are the people who are not related to him. The people who take decisions for the tribe or clan are the elders or heads of the families. These are the men of wisdom and strength of character, and they are obeyed because of their high position within the kinship system.

There are two other reasons why the decisions are likely to be respected. In the first place, the decisions are usually connected with natural events, the harvest, moving the herd, and so on. These decisions have been made many times before. The elders are rarely confronted with a new situation and so they can rely on tradition and their own experience to tell them what is best. Because what they decide will not vary much from year to year, no one questions it.

In the second place, the leaders of simple societies are often believed to have religion on their side, just as God supposedly supported the medieval European kings. So they can appeal to the gods, and play on people's fear of the supernatural to back up their authority.

Conflicts within the tribe are often avoided by the fact that a man is unlikely to view himself only as a member of a family. His AGE-GROUP is almost as important to him. Boys of the same age play together and are prepared for initiation together. When they are old enough they may form the fighting unit which defends the tribe against outside aggression. Later on still, some of the members of the age group will be the elders of the tribe. Because the age group cuts across family groupings, individuals within the family will have close friends in several other families, and this helps to prevent quarrels between families. When quarrels do arise, they have a greater chance of being settled peacefully.

Figure 30 The two most important groups for a boy in a simple society are his family and his age group.

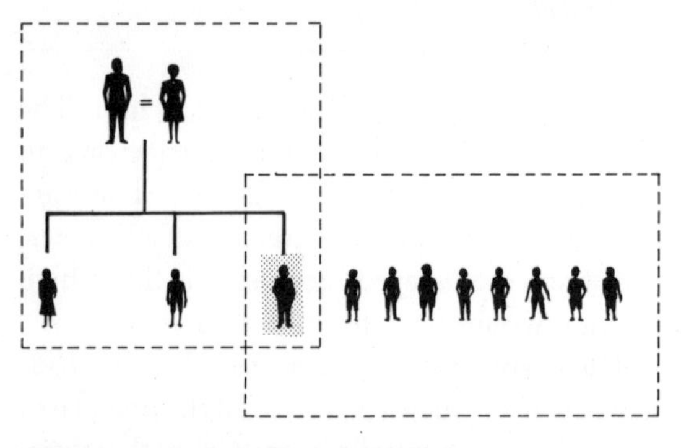

The existence of members of a single age group in many families means that arguments can be avoided, and disputes can be resolved, in a friendly manner rather than by resorting to fighting.

The State

Once a society is big enough to support cities it can be described as a STATE. When in Britain we talk about 'the State', we generally mean the government. We do not mean a particular political party which happens to be in power now, but the whole system of prime minister, members of Parliament, civil servants and judges, which is always there, whether the individual minister or judge changes or not. We talk about the Queen as Head of State, and about the opening of Parliament as a State occasion. The word *State* suggests permanence; we expect it to last unless something disastrous like a civil war occurs. It also suggests that there are people who are citizens of the State. (Compare the word *citizen* and the word *city*.) In some sense citizens belong to the State. If I go abroad, unless I go through the complicated procedure of changing my nationality, I am still a British citizen. We cannot change our citizenship simply by moving from one State to another.

A State is self-governing. Territories in Africa, America and Asia which were taken over and colonised by European States have since become States themselves. They have achieved STATEHOOD through becoming independent. A State has definite boundaries. Within the boundaries the government of the State has authority. Once you cross the boundary you pass into the territory of another State, and the new State may have a different set of laws which you must obey.

The State fights your battles for you. If you have a disagreement with your neighbour because he dumps his rubbish in your back garden, the way to resolve this is not to have a fight and see who wins. You may take him to court where an employee of the State, the judge, will decide who is right. If he decides in your favour and your neighbour still empties his dustbin over your wall, the *State* may use force to make him obey.

SIMPLE STATES

The Aztec civilisation was a simple State, and so were the countries of medieval Europe. In a

The power of the state lies in the armed forces. In which of these pictures is the power more real *and in which is the power more* symbolic?

simple State the jobs that the State has to do are all controlled by one man, the ruler of the State. He must be

commander–in–chief of the army
chief magistrate, who settles disputes
high priest (or in some sense a religious leader)
chief law-maker.

Naturally the rulers of simple states can delegate jobs to chosen officials; any king would have a general to head his army and a chief justice to head his law courts. But the final responsibility would lie with the king himself. He would personally conduct major battles, and would act as a kind of final court of appeal in the case of very sticky legal problems. Personal control by one man of all the major areas of State activity is only possible when the State is small. As it grows larger and has more people doing more jobs in larger towns and factories, it is no longer possible for one man to head the State. The jobs of law-making, law-giving and law-enforcing must be split up; there must be division of labour here as everywhere else.

The General Assembly of the United Nations is guided by the Security Council, a much smaller group of representatives from various nations. The United Nations makes rules which its members agree to obey, governing such matters as international trade. Without an international police force, however, it is not always possible to make sure that members obey the rules.

COMPLEX STATES

A complex State, then, is one in which the main tasks of government have been divided among several groups or individuals.

(*a*) Laws must be made. This is usually done in an assembly or parliament of representatives. The assembly is probably guided in its decisions by a smaller council of ministers, consisting of the important men and women in the government. The assembly is known as the LEGISLATURE because it legislates (makes laws) on behalf of the people.

(*b*) The laws must be administered. If a law is passed that all traffic must flow on the right instead of on the left side of the road, the law does not put itself in practice. The people do not wake up one day and happily drive to work on the other side of the road as if they had been doing it all their lives. There would be accidents, and a lot of drivers would lose their way, if only because the road signs would be in all the wrong places, and the traffic lights facing the wrong way.

Somebody has to be responsible for putting the laws into effect, and making sure that they are applied fairly and in the manner intended. Every state has to have a body of officials called the ADMINISTRATION or BUREAUCRACY. These people are appointed and are paid employees just like any other workers. They have to be completely impartial in the way they treat people. It would be a very corrupt administration which accepted bribes in return for stretching the law in someone's favour.

(*c*) Sometimes the laws need interpretation. Not every law is so clearly set down that no one is in any doubt as to its meaning. People often dispute who has the rights of a certain case. There may be an argument as to whether this law or that should be applied here. The task of interpreting the laws and settling disputes lies

The Chamber of the House of Commons has changed very little since this picture was made in 1834. Although the Chamber was badly damaged during the Second World War, it was rebuilt in almost the same style after the war. Despite the overcrowded conditions, MPs preferred to keep the intimate character of the old Chamber.

with the JUDICIARY. The judiciary is the body of judges, who, like the bureaucrats, are appointed officials. Like the legislature and the bureaucracy the judiciary is always there; it does not matter if an individual judge dies or retires, for he can be replaced, and the work of the judiciary must go on whatever happens.

We are now going to look in turn at the different branches of government in Britain in greater detail.

The legislature

As we have seen, this is the law-making body within the political system. In Britain the legislature is Parliament. Parliament is divided into two parts, the House of Lords and the House of Commons. This division dates from the middle ages when Parliament was no more than an advisory body to the king. The king would consult Parliament if he wished, but he need not necessarily do so, although kings who persistently ignored the chief lords and nobles – the next most powerful men to himself – tended to run into trouble. It is true of any political leader that he cannot afford to override his most influential advisers too often. In medieval England the lords were clearly distinguishable from the common people. They were men of very great wealth, and controlled whole counties. There was no question of lords and commons sitting together, and the views of a commoner would never carry the same weight as those of a noble. So parliament was divided into two Houses, the upper and the lower, and for a long time the role of the Commons was simply to agree (and occasionally to refuse) to grant the king sums of money, gained through taxation, to finance wars or the building of new castles in England.

Today the balance of power between the two Houses has altered. The industrial revolution accelerated the decline of the power of the nobles, whose money was mainly tied up in agriculture. With the rise of industry came a new group of men, the capitalists, who owned and ran the factories, mills, mines and shipyards. These people were among the richest men in the country, yet their political power was not equal to their financial power. Gradually the importance of the House of Commons increased as the manufacturers came to dominate the scene.

At the same time, urbanisation involved the migration of many workers from the country to the expanding towns. But most members of the House of Commons had previously been elected by people living in the country. The new towns found themselves very much under-represented, with only one MP to many thousands of people, while deserted areas of countryside had one member for half-a-dozen electors.

From the beginning of the nineteenth century suggestions were put forward as to how the House of Commons could be reformed. Many land owners strongly resisted the pressure to change which came from industrialists, town-dwellers and other reformers; they saw that the power they had to influence elections in rural areas by bribing or threatening their tenants would dwindle away, and for a long time they were successful. A reform of the Commons in 1832 did much to remove corruption in elections, but it was not until 1867 that the townspeople were given a better share of representation, and even then only men with a certain amount of property could vote. UNIVERSAL SUFFRAGE, the right of all people to vote, came for men, and for women aged thirty and over, in 1918. In 1928 women were finally accepted as electors on the same terms as men, and allowed to vote at the age of twenty-one, and the voting age for all was lowered to eighteen in 1969.

Over the same period, the power of the House of Lords declined. It came to be an accepted principle that the elected representatives of the people should have a greater say in political decisions than peers who hold their position because of their birth only. In 1911 and 1949 Acts of Parliament were passed with the effect that the House of Lords today is little more than a debating chamber. Effective decision-making has passed entirely to the lower House, for although the Lords can delay the passing of a measure, they cannot dismiss it altogether. There are now also LIFE PEERS – men and women who have been given titles for life in return for services to the country, so the members of the House of Lords are now from more varied social backgrounds.

THE HOUSE OF COMMONS

The Commons today consists of six hundred and thirty members, who are elected once every five years or sooner, if the Prime Minister decides to go to the country before the five years are up, at a general election. If in the meantime a member dies or retires, a by-election is held so that no seat is ever vacant for more than a short time.

Members of Parliament

Members of Parliament are elected to represent a CONSTITUENCY. A constituency is a geographical area, and the country is so divided up that there are roughly the same number of people in each constituency. If the areas were unequal in voting population, some people's votes would effectively be worth more than others'. The theory is that the MP looks after the interests of his constituents, serving them in the way he thinks best. So an MP from a mining constituency, where most of the electors

The Houses of Parliament, from Parliament Square.

are miners and their families, would take a prominent part in discussions on new laws relating to working conditions down the mines. An MP from an area threatened by a new motorway is expected to ask questions about the route, and if his constituents oppose the plan, to try to get the route changed.

Almost anyone can stand as a candidate for parliament; exceptions are peers (who sit in the House of Lords), people in prison, and people certified insane. The usual way to get yourself elected is to persuade one of the political parties to adopt you as a candidate. You can try to go it alone, but there are definite advantages in being the official candidate of a party. There are laws preventing candidates from spending too much on elections (why?), but even so, it is an expensive business. Not only must the candidate put down a £150 deposit which he forfeits if he fails to get a certain proportion of the votes cast in his constituency, but he must also spend money on advertising and hiring halls for meetings. He needs helpers who will canvass for him, and he may have to take time off from work. Very few private individuals can afford the time and money to promote a successful campaign. If they are the official Labour, Liberal or Conservative Party candidates, however, expenses will be paid out of party funds, and the campaign may be arranged by a full-time professional party agent. It is hardly surprising that seats are almost inevitably won by the candidate from one of the major parties.

THE POLITICAL PARTIES

The three main parties in Britain are organised at two levels, the mass party level and the parliamentary party level.

(a) *The mass party*

In each constituency the people who regularly support the main parties in Westminster form a local branch of the party. These are ordinary men and women who give up their time to take an interest in political affairs, and whose main function is to canvass voters at election time by going round knocking on doors, trying to persuade people to vote for their candidate. Every year an annual conference is held, usually at a big seaside resort, to which all branches send delegates. The delegates discuss the policies which they feel the party should adopt, and make recommendations to the party leaders. In practice, however, although the leaders must listen to what the conference has to say, policies are almost invariably decided without reference to the mass parties. Decisions are made by the leaders themselves, and the rank and file of the parties have very little real power.

(b) *The parliamentary party*

This is the organisation at Westminster. Elected members of Parliament are members of the parliamentary party, which is headed by the party leader. The leader is an MP who has played an important role in party affairs for some time, and whom the other MPs have elected. If the party wins a general election, it is this man who is invited by the Queen to form a government, and so he becomes Prime Minister. He appoints other prominent MPs as ministers with responsibility for the various areas of government activity such as employment, the environment, health and social security and so on, and some of these Ministers form the Cabinet. Other MPs are appointed as Whips. It is their job to make sure that ordinary MPs are in the House of Commons when they are needed and that they vote according to the leader's direction.

The fact that MPs are required to 'toe the party line' makes them less able to carry out the wishes of their own constituencies. If the Cabinet decides on a policy which conflicts with the interests of his constituents or with the MP's own views, he has a very difficult decision to make. If he votes against the government and according to his conscience, he may be expelled from the party and this is almost bound to mean the end of his political career. If he votes with the government he may be accused of being a 'yes-man', and of neglecting his duty to his constituents. It is here that the theory that the MP is primarily the representative of his constituents breaks down. In theory each constituency chooses the best man to represent it; in

At Speakers' Corner in London anyone who wants to, can stand up and state his political beliefs. On a fine Sunday, crowds will gather to listen and argue with the speakers.

Although smaller political parties exist, on both the left and the right wing, they rarely get enough support to win a seat in Parliament.

practice, however, voters choose not between candidates, but between the parties backing the candidates. Electors are coming more and more to see their vote as cast not for Smith or Jones, but for the leaders of the main parties. The party leaders are much more important than individual candidates at the general election; interest in the results centres not on who has won any particular seat, but on which party has won this seat, and therefore on how large the parliamentary majority of one party will be.

Party policies

The political parties are associated with certain IDEOLOGIES – ideas about which policies are best. These ideologies are sometimes described as right-wing or left-wing. This can best be understood if you imagine the political parties situated on a line; parties left of centre have some things in common, and parties right of centre have some things in common.

Communist Party — Labour — Liberal — Conservative — National Socialist

The parties at the extreme ends have been included as examples only; there is a British Communist Party, but it is not nearly so large as the Labour, Liberal or Conservative parties, and there are other small, extreme left-wing parties which would have done equally well as examples. The National Socialist Party had a misleading name, for Socialism is usually associated with the left although this party was on the right. This is a historical example; the National Socialists, or Nazis, were the political party which came to power in Germany in the 1930s under the leadership of Adolf Hitler.

The basic ideologies of the right and left are difficult to sum up simply. In making the ideas easy to understand one tends to distort them or exaggerate them. Here, however, are some of the differences:

(i) The Conservative Party wants to *conserve* or keep things as they are. This party is associated with a tradition of government by a small group of well-educated, wealthy land-owning families who derive the bulk of their support from the middle classes and from agricultural areas, although a large number of working class people also vote Conservative.

The Conservative Party believes that the individual should be given freedom to make his own way in the world, to work when, as and how he pleases. Although the Conservatives have come to accept that the State must provide for the poor, the old and the sick, the idea of State intervention to rescue the individual is against Conservative principles. If an industry is about to collapse, it should be allowed to do so. Only when the natural forces in society and the economy are allowed to work themselves through, without State interference, will a balance be achieved. If people are put out of work because a firm has gone bankrupt, they must be left to find other jobs, if necessary in other parts of the country.

A very important word in Conservative ideology is *competition*. 'Fair play and let the best man win' might be a Conservative motto.

(ii) The Labour Party developed as the party of the under-represented working man in the late nineteenth and early twentieth centuries. It is traditionally associated with trying to improve the share in national prosperity, and the say in national affairs, of the mass of working people.

The Labour Party opposes Conservative thinking on competition; the contest can never be fair because some people start off with special advantages. Rich people may buy a better education, and have money to back their commercial schemes. Healthy people have all their faculties and can stand up for themselves better than the sick and handicapped. Children with two parents and a happy home have an obvious advantage over abandoned and orphaned children. The State cannot remove all these differences, but it can do a lot to help, by providing free education, better facilities for the sick, and better housing and community environments for the socially deprived. If a factory is faced with closure, the Labour Party would be more inclined to prevent this happening, on the grounds that in the long run more harm will be done to the economy and to society by allowing people to lose their jobs than will be done by using public money to prop up an inefficient enterprise. The State must manage the economy because, in a world where free competition is hindered by inequality, a situation of perfect balance in which there are no people out of work, no factories lying idle or operating inefficiently, the national income is growing at a satisfactory rate, and exports and imports are just equal, will never be achieved without State intervention.

A key Labour word, therefore, is *equality*. This does not mean that everybody should receive exactly the same treatment, or be expected to do exactly the same things as everyone else. It means that everybody should have an equal opportunity to do the best they can, and that people should not be treated differently on the irrelevant grounds of wealth, class, sex, colour or religion.

Neither of these two parties consists entirely of individuals who think exactly alike. Nor do the Conservatives reject equality or Labour reject the idea of competition. These are differences of emphasis, rather than radically opposing views. In fact, both parties have their own right and left wings, made up of people with more extreme views, and somewhere in the centre are people who could be members of either party since their views overlap to a great extent. There are other people who take a left-wing stand on some subjects, and a right-wing stand on others. You might ask why people in the

The Easter March by supporters of the Campaign for Nuclear Disarmament has become a regular event. Pressure groups may gain publicity through this kind of demonstration, but this method is not necessarily the most effective in getting what they want.

centre do not ally themselves with the Liberals since they would seem to have more in common with that party.

One reason why liberal-minded people do not join the Liberal Party would certainly be that as things have stood for the last thirty years, candidates have a much better chance of being elected if they are members of one of the two larger parties. To see why this is so, we have to examine the electoral system (see page 98).

Pressure groups

Members of the main political parties hold a wide variety of views on many issues. No one party can be counted on to give its whole-hearted support to any particular cause. Neither can people always expect their MP to protect their interests, for in the last resort, the loyalty of the MP is likely to be to the party leadership, and there are very few who are prepared to commit political suicide by voting against the party line. There are many groups of people, however, who have an overwhelming interest in a particular cause, and who want to see the government take action on an issue, although they are in no way seeking to take an active part in government themselves. Such groups are known as PRESSURE GROUPS, or sometimes as INTEREST GROUPS. They are concerned to bring pressure to bear on the government over a particular issue, and they are a group of people who share the same interest.

Some pressure groups exist permanently, putting their case forward when something comes up which affects them. The Royal Society for the Prevention of Accidents keeps a watchful eye on government measures for road safety, and sometimes mounts its own campaigns to make people more careful. The Lord's Day Observance Society is constantly trying to get laws passed banning certain activities on Sundays. Trade Unions are another kind of permanent interest group. The government often finds these groups very useful in drawing up new policies, and meetings are held to which representatives of the groups are invited in order that they may put their point of view. This is one way in which the government can take account of public opinion.

Other groups are purely temporary, formed for a limited and specific purpose, and disbanded when that purpose has been fulfilled. The controversy over the siting of the third London airport provides a good example of temporary pressure groups at work. The original site chosen was Stanstead, but the opponents of this choice, including the residents of Stanstead, formed themselves into such a powerful pressure group that the decision was reversed, and the government appointed a Special Commission to propose another site.

The methods used by the groups vary. They may try to form a special connection with an MP whom they can count upon to put their case in Parliament. (The trade unions have used this method with particular success.) They may try to win over a number of MPs during a campaign by writing to them or by going along to Westminster to talk to them personally. Some groups are invited to help the government draw up new measures, and so do not have to make the same kind of effort. Groups may try to influence the government through public opinion. Some manage to get the press on their side, and a newspaper may print an article putting their case. A television programme may be centred on their grievance. Or they may try to gain publicity by demonstrating in large numbers in the streets or outside the Houses of Parliament.

THE ELECTORAL SYSTEM IN BRITAIN

The ELECTORAL SYSTEM determines the kind of elections we hold, and lays down the rules and procedures to be followed. There are many types of electoral system, each with different voting rules. The type we have in Britain is called the SIMPLE MAJORITY system. All this means is that in a contest between two or three candidates for a seat in Parliament, the one who polls the most votes wins the seat. This appears perfectly fair, yet this system has led to what most people would consider to be very unfair results, and there are many people who would like to see the system changed.

In the first place, it is quite possible for a party to have a majority in the House of Commons, and therefore to form the government, even though most people have voted against it. Imagine a constituency in which the results were as follows:

Smith (Con)	9,000
Jones (Lab)	7,500
Bates (Lib)	3,500
Total	20,000

Smith is clearly the winner, and yet he has polled only 9,000 votes, while Jones and Bates together have 11,000. Smith has therefore been elected on a MINORITY VOTE. It is a common complaint by Labour against the Liberals that all the Liberal candidate succeeds in doing is splitting the Labour vote, and thus ensuring that the Conservative wins.

If a similar result occurred in enough constituencies, the Conservative Party would be in power, although most people in the country opposed it. The two major parties generally manage to balance each other out since both have enough constituencies in which they have more supporters than either of the other two parties. The Liberal Party is not in so fortunate a position, however; there are about three million Liberal voters in the country and yet they rarely win more than half a dozen seats in Parliament. This is because they are spread out among many constituencies. If they were all concentrated in about a hundred constituencies, they would probably win ten times as many seats.

This is not the worst criticism, however. It is actually possible for a party to be elected even though another party has polled more votes. This happened in 1951 when the Conservatives were elected, even though more people voted Labour. To see how this can happen we have to imagine several constituencies:

Newtown		*Westbury*		*Upper Woodville*	
Long (Con)	8,000	Evans (Con)	3,000	Harris (Con)	9,000
Scott (Lab)	6,000	Jackson (Lab)	15,000	White (Lab)	8,000
Rogers (Lib)	6,000	Robbins (Lib)	2,000	Berry (Lib)	3,000
	20,000		20,000		20,000

Southchurch		*Thorndown*	
Brown (Con)	7,500	Thompson (Con)	6,000
Martin (Lab)	6,500	Thornton (Lab)	12,000
McDougall (Lib)	6,000	Merrick (Lib)	2,000
	20,000		20,000

1 Which candidate won in each constituency?
2 Which party won most seats overall?
3 How many votes did each party poll?

The critics of the simple majority system say that Britain should adopt one of the electoral systems used on the Continent. Most European countries have a system of PROPORTIONAL REPRESENTATION. There are many variations of this system, but all are concerned to give fair shares to the parties by ensuring that the number of seats they win is more or less *proportional* to the number of votes they poll. So, if a party wins one-fifth of the votes, it would get one-fifth of the seats.

Opponents of proportional representation say that it encourages politics to be unstable. It helps small parties to continue to exist in a way that the simple majority system does not. We have seen what difficulties the Liberal Party has in winning even half a dozen seats, and the smaller parties have in recent years failed to win any seats at all in the British Parliament. If the votes are more evenly distributed among a number of smaller parties, there is a likelihood that no one will have an overall majority in Parliament. In order to form a government, the party with the most seats would have to join forces with another party. This sort of government is known as a COALITION. Some countries are permanently governed by groups of parties working in coalition, and do not necessarily experience political instability. Other countries, on the other hand, have found it difficult to keep the same coalition going for more than a few months at a time. After a short period of working together, the governing parties have an argument, the coalition collapses and a new government has to be formed. If the parties cannot come to an agreement, there may even have to be a new general election.

Consider the following two cases. The first result is quite possible under the simple majority system:

1

Party	*Number of seats in parliament*
Conservatives	300
Labour	295
Liberal	10

(*a*) Does any party have an overall majority?
(*b*) Which party is in power?
(*c*) What difficulties might that party have in staying in power?
(*d*) What alternative government is possible?

The second situation represents a possible result under a system of proportional representation:

2

Party	*Number of seats in parliament*
Conservative (R)	310
Labour (L)	250
Liberal (L)	50
National Front (R)	10
British Communist Party (L)	20
Socialist Party of Great Britain (L)	10

(*a*) Which party would first be invited to take office?
(*b*) The parties marked R are right of centre, those marked L, left of centre. Who have more seats, the left or the right wingers?
(*c*) How would you expect the parties to vote, left wing or right wing, and what effect would this have on the government?
(*d*) What would happen if the Liberals swapped sides?
(*e*) What do you suppose is the long-term effect on a country if it has a change of government every few months?

Supporters of proportional representation, on the other hand, say that places like Tasmania have operated a system of proportional representation for many years and still have only two parties. They also point to the countries in Western Europe, such as Ireland (Eire) and Western Germany, which have a number of parties, and usually have a coalition government, without any corresponding political instability. More things make a country unstable, they say, than the simple fact of having a coalition government.

Why do you suppose that the supporters of proportional representation have had so little sympathy from the two main parties in Britain?

Democracy and Totalitarianism

The legislative system we have in Britain is one which is based on very ancient ideas. One of these ideas is that the citizens of a state should have some say in policy-making. This is a *democratic* ideal. The word DEMOCRACY comes from two Greek words meaning government and people. There are a lot of words to do with government which end with *-cracy*. Can you think of any? What do they mean?

The particular idea we have of democracy in this country was influenced to a great extent by thinkers in the eighteenth century. According to the eighteenth-century democratic ideal, the best policies for the country would emerge if only the people themselves were allowed to decide the issues. In the early Greek city-state, the citizens were few enough to meet in one assembly. In eighteenth-century England this was hardly possible, for the population was far too large. So the political philosophers (as the people who wrote about the theory of politics were called) wrote about a way in which the people could still decide issues, even though they could not all meet in a single assembly. Instead they would elect representatives who would assemble in order to carry out the will of the people. The job of the representative was to speak about the wishes of the people who had elected him, to act as their mouthpiece.

A very brief glance at the British system of government will show that it does not fit this democratic ideal. Once elected, MPs do not always do what they promised they would do before the election. They follow the party line, and the party line is determined not by the mass members, the rank and file, but by the party leaders.

Because we clearly do not have 'government by the people' in the eighteenth century sense, does this mean that Britain is not a democracy? Most of us would be unwilling to say this; we like to think that we have some control over our governments, and it would be a very serious charge indeed if we were to claim that our elections are nothing but an elaborate farce designed to trick us into believing that we have power where we have none.

One answer to this charge is that the eighteenth-century idea of democracy is not the only one, and that it is in fact as unrealistic under today's conditions as the Greek ideal of a single assembly of citizens was then. The scale and complexity of our society make it impossible that we, the electorate, should make final decisions on political issues. Very often we have only the most elementary understanding of the problems confronting the politicians. We need experts in all fields of knowledge to explain to us the case for and against many political issues. Just as the growth of industrial society has led to the greater division of labour in the field of production, here too, in the field of politics, there is a need for specialists, professional politicians whose *job* it is to understand and make wise political decisions. The age of the amateur is over; we expect a high level of skill and performance in every field, and we cannot afford to make mistakes in our political decisions any more than we can afford to support blunders in industrial production.

How far should people go in trying to influence government policy? In a totalitarian state there is very little freedom to say what you think, and demonstrations are not usually allowed.

In our society democracy is a word used in politics to show that we have the chance to choose between competing teams of experts, the politicians, who are committed only to following broad principles of policy. The teams have different long-term aims and basically different ways of achieving them. The most voters can do is to refuse to re-elect a team next time. Outside politics there is not much democracy. Most people do not have the chance to control their work situation, even though they spend a great deal of their lives at work.

Because democracy is one of those words which is always used to express a favourable meaning, most states are anxious to describe themselves as democracies, even though they may allow no freedom of choice whatever. In some countries elections are held to preserve the appearance of democracy, but the rulers make sure by one means or another that the result always works out in their favour. They can do this by tampering with the voting papers, giving out false results, or only allowing their own supporters to stand. In some states even the assassination of the opposing candidate is not unknown.

Sometimes the name TOTALITARIAN is given to societies in which only one political party is

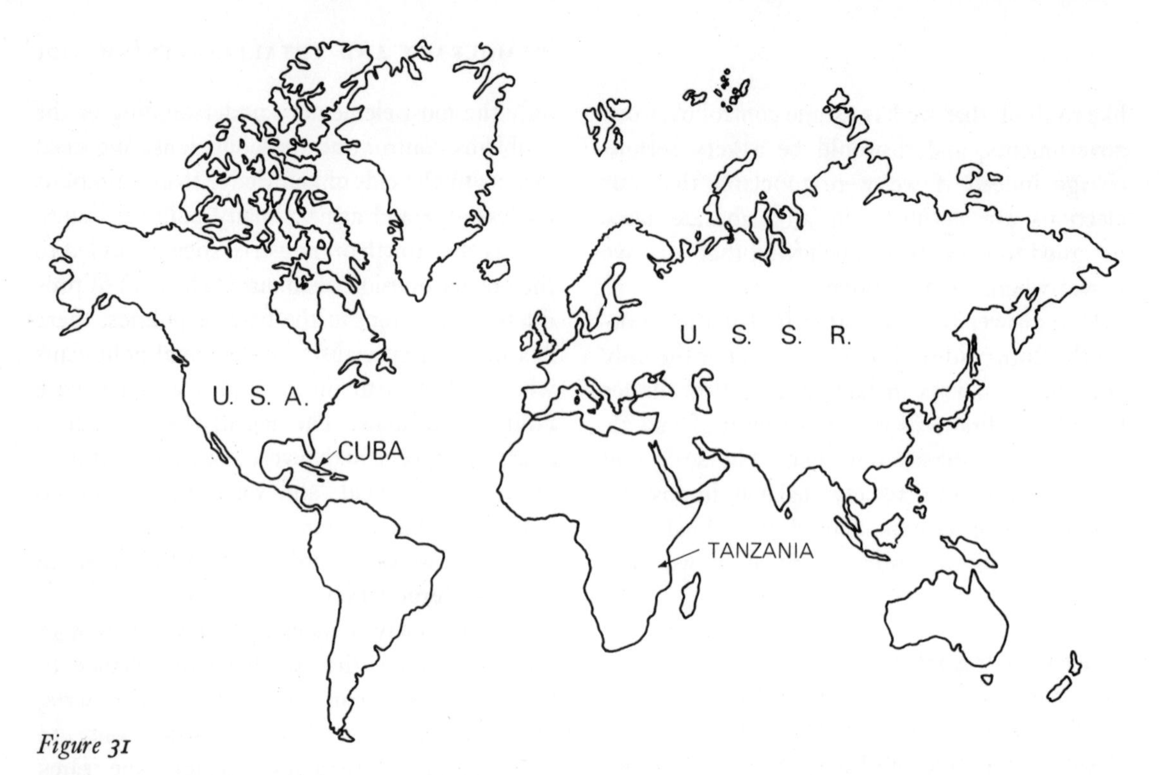

Figure 31

allowed to exist. Not all present-day societies which have only one party can be described as TOTALITARIAN. We have to consider what kind of control people have over their work situation and who gets the profit from their work. Modern Tanzania has a one-party political system but there are many socialist villages in which the village-dwellers co-operate and make democratic decisions about production. Examples of modern totalitarian states are Germany under the Nazis during the 1930s and 1940s; Spain under the ruling Falangist party until General Franco's death in 1975, and the USSR now where the only party is the Communist party. We shall now look in more detail at the USSR.

THE GOVERNMENT OF THE USSR

One of the first things to remember about the USSR is that it is made up of a number of separate Republics, in much the same way as the USA is made up of many separate States. The people living in the eastern Republics are not only racially different from those in the south and the west, but have very different traditions and customs. They speak different languages, eat different foods, and have as little in common as, say, a Tibetan and an Australian.

Secondly, it must be remembered that until the Russian Revolution in 1917, Russia was a pre-industrial country. Most people worked on the land, lived at or below subsistence level, and owed feudal allegiance to the local landowner and the Tsar. The aim of the revolutionary leaders was to bring the new Union of Soviet Socialist Republics into the twentieth century as fast as possible, by industrialising at a rapid rate. This involved taking measures to increase agricultural and industrial output, which affected vast numbers of people in a very drastic way. You may think that the government was justified in taking these measures because you agree that the USSR needed to industrialise quickly. Or you may think that the *end* (industrialisation leading to a higher standard of living in the very long run) did not justify the *means* (collectivisation of agriculture and forced labour). It is difficult to see how a virtually medieval empire, shattered by the First World War and the civil war which accompanied the Revolution, could have transformed itself into a modern industrial state without very definite direction by the government. The history of the newly emerging African states would seem to suggest that a democratic form of government is not suitable for a country undergoing rapid social and economic change, for there too, totalitarian systems of government have developed.

The early Revolutionary leaders of the Soviet Union needed a means of
(*a*) holding the country together
(*b*) communicating with the people
(*c*) ensuring that their orders were carried out.

The tool they used was the Communist Party. Every town and village had its party committee which took orders from the committee on the next level – the area or district committee. These in turn were responsible to the committee at Republic level which was under directions from the Central Committee in Moscow. The structure of the party has remained much the same ever since, and the party organisation still extends throughout the Soviet Union, at every level of existence.

The Communist Party is far more than a political party in the sense of the word that we understand in Britain. It does far more than simply draw people together for the purpose of expressing their political ideas. It works in some ways like churches do in parts of Britain; it organises all kinds of social activities for workers, housewives and children. It runs holiday camps and hotels. It plays an important part in education, mainly political education. The branches which are organised for children and young people – the Young Pioneers and the Komsomol – are like Sunday School, the Scouts, and the Youth Club all rolled into one. Through them children are given instruction in the ideas of Karl Marx and Lenin, on which the political and economic systems of the USSR are based. Pioneer Palaces have been built in many large towns and cities where children can go and take part in all kinds of activities. These buildings are very often superbly equipped with sporting, drama, art and craft facilities, libraries and music rooms. With such lavish provision for their leisure, no child living near to a Pioneer Palace could ever complain, as young people in Britain are constantly complaining, 'I'm bored – there's nothing to do.'

The members of the Central Committee of the Communist Party are the most powerful men in the Soviet Union. In the fifty or so years since the Revolution, the Central Committee has sometimes been dominated by one man, occasionally by more than one. These men are never elected in any formal way, however. They emerge as leaders after some kind of power struggle within the Kremlin. Western observers find it difficult to work out exactly what takes place, since the Russians keep these developments very secret. Various phrases are used to show that there has been a change in membership of the ruling group. When it is announced that a leader is ill, or has left the capital for a prolonged holiday, this is usually interpreted as meaning that he has fallen from power.

The leaders of the Soviet Union use the Communist Party as a one-way channel of communication. Through the party committees at every level they control every aspect of political and economic life. Look at the section on *central control* of the economy for a more detailed explanation of this. The Party is not the same as the formal structure of the government, however, although it *does* have effective control over the whole country. There is a legislature, bureaucracy and judiciary existing alongside the Party organisation, although quite separate from it.

The legislature consists of a system of councils or SOVIETS, which form a pattern similar to that of the party committees. Each village and town has a soviet, and on the next level each district and area has a more important soviet. There is a supreme soviet for each republic and finally the Supreme Soviet of the USSR which meets in Moscow.

The members of the soviets are elected, but until recently the elections have been almost completely meaningless. In the days of Stalin's regime (1929–1956) it was normal for officials to publish absurd results which claimed that an abnormally high proportion of the electorate had actually voted, and that everyone had voted for a supporter of Stalin. It is only recently, and still very rarely, that voters have been given any choice of candidate, and even when there is a choice, both contenders would naturally be good party members.

The party also controls all newspapers and radio and television networks. *Pravda* is the official party newspaper, and this gives a lead to other newspapers as to the line they should take. Journalists and writers have to be very careful about what they say in articles, for they must on no account contradict the party line. Through this *total* control over the mass media, the party leaders can very easily present their policies in as favourable a light as possible to the mass of the people, and since no organised opposition is allowed, the policies are never seriously questioned by most people.

It is impossible to say whether the Soviet Union will develop into a more 'open' society as it achieves its goal of reaching the same standard of living as western countries. Tight control of the economy may be relaxed as production of consumer goods – cars, televisions, clothes, varied food and so on – increases. People who have tried to criticise the government policy have, however, been sentenced to long terms in prison or labour camps, and the move in 1968 by Czechoslovakia to allow greater freedom of thought and political participation met a violent reaction in the form of invasion and occupation by the Red Army.

The bureaucracy

The task of the bureaucracy is to see that policies are carried out. Even in a simple state it is necessary to have a bureaucracy. The Aztec Emperor employed officials to travel round the provinces and collect his taxes, while other officials stayed behind in Mexico-Tenochtitlan to receive and count the money. One of the most early developed bureaucracies was that of ancient China, where to be a MANDARIN, an official of a certain grade, was an honour. Officials were chosen by written examination, and their careers were carefully structured so that they started at the foot of the ladder, and if they were good at their job, they gradually progressed to the top.

Larger and more complex states require larger and more developed bureaucracies. The size of the bureaucracy depends not only on the size of the country, however, but also on how much government activity there is. The British government today is involved in far more activities than it was before the Second World War. The growth of the Welfare State, the increase in the numbers of schools, and the government's involvement in economic affairs led to the establishment of new ministries in the years after the war, and large numbers of people were employed in putting the new measures into action. Today more people work in the Civil Service (the British bureaucracy) than in any other single occupation in this country. There are even more Civil Servants than there are teachers.

Max Weber wrote about bureaucracy, and his theories have had a great influence on the way later sociologists have studied organisations in general. Weber said that there were certain features of bureaucracies which could be found in many large-scale organisations, including schools, hospitals, factories, trade unions and big offices. All these organisations are controlled in a way similar to the Civil Service. He listed the characteristics of a bureaucracy as follows:

(*a*) It does not *make* policy, but carries out the policies made by others. In a school this means that the teachers and pupils are following courses and pursuing aims that have been set for them by people outside the school such as the school governors, the local education authority and the government.

(*b*) The officials are chosen by tests and examinations, and cannot be appointed simply because they know 'the right people' or in return for money or other favours. They need paper qualifications to prove that they are suitable.

(*c*) The officials must always act according to the rules of the organisation and they must be utterly fair. They must not show any favouritism towards particular people.

(*d*) There is a high level of division of labour. Some officials do certain jobs, while others specialise in different jobs. In secondary schools the staff do not all teach the same subjects. They are divided into departments, each of which is responsible for a subject or group of subjects, history, modern languages, science, English and so on.

(*e*) The officials form a HIERARCHY. This means that some officials are in a higher position than others. In a school, some pupils are made captains or prefects. The staff have authority over all the pupils, but certain members of staff, heads of houses or departments, hold a senior position to the other teachers. In overall authority, at the top of the hierarchy, are the head and deputy.

(*f*) The jobs of the officials are very secure. Some workers are threatened with dismissal or redundancy because their firm or factory is about to close. The government of a country is very unlikely to go out of business (unless there is a revolution), and it is rare for a school, hospital or trade union to close down. It may be hard to get a job as an official to start with, since qualifications are demanded. However, once a person has the job he is not likely to lose it. Because officials feel secure in their jobs, they are supposed to be more honest and incorruptible, since they are less tempted to try and make money or get promotion by illegal means.

(*g*) There are records and files kept on the work done. This means that if one official leaves, his work can be carried on without interruption by a replacement, who has only to look in the files to find out what has been achieved so far.

If we study the British Civil Service, we can see how well it fits into Weber's idea of a bureaucracy.

(*a*) The Civil Service does not make policy, but carries out the policies of Parliament. Each major government department or ministry is headed by a member of the Cabinet, who is known as the Minister, or sometimes as the Secretary of State. The permanent officials are there to serve the Minister, and not to put into action ideas of their own. In practice, however, the Minister is very much at the mercy of his civil servants. His knowledge of a situation will depend to a large extent on what they tell him, and he is bound to be highly influenced by their ideas and suggestions. They, after all, have spent the whole of their working lives dealing with education, employment or whatever their ministry is concerned with, whereas the Minister, before he became a member of the Cabinet, was probably only an ordinary MP without the same expert knowledge. Some politicians move from one ministry to another in a matter of months; they cannot be expected to know all about everything.

(*b*) Civil Servants are divided into grades according to the type of work they do. The most senior grades work closely with the Minister, answering his questions, advising him on policy matters and writing official papers. Recruitment to these grades may be through an examination, and it is usual for the officials to have a university degree as well. Lower down the scale, the executive officers are not concerned with advising the Minister on matters of policy, but with putting policy into practice. They too need qualifications – usually A levels, and some executive officers have university degrees too. The routine work of correspondence and filing is done by clerical officers.

(*c*) Civil servants have to be completely fair in their dealings with the public. An income-tax inspector who charged a lower rate for his friends would be totally unacceptable to government and people alike. Not all countries succeed in maintaining a civil service as fair as the British Civil Service, and occasionally we read of trials of officials in other countries on charges of bribery and corruption.

(*d*) The division of work among the different grades has already been described. Each ministry specialises in a broad field, and within the ministry there are further divisions which are concerned with particular areas. Within the Department of Trade and Industry, therefore, there is a division which deals with the coal industry, another concerned with electricity supply, yet a third with the gas industry, and so on.

(*e*) A civil servant's career is carefully mapped out so that after a certain number of years' service he can expect promotion and a salary rise. To some extent in the lower ranks, and to a large extent in the upper ranks, promotion depends on MERIT; the official has to show that he has worked well and possesses a good understanding of his job. But to be confident of continuous employment and a steady income, all he has to do is to be competent at his job; he does not have to prove himself outstandingly good at it.

(*f*) Anyone who has ever applied for social security benefit will know that forms have to be filled in to complete even the simplest task. There are rules and procedures for every action an official takes, and nearly all of these are recorded in files. This is essential for the continued smooth running of the Civil Service, but has led to a frequent charge against officials that they are 'petty bureaucrats' concerned with nothing but 'red tape'. There is certainly a permanent danger in any bureaucratic organisation that officials may lose sight of their goals, and become bogged down or even obsessed with the routine matters of filling in the appropriate forms and keeping the files up to date.

The judiciary

You can find a detailed description of the work of the law courts in the chapter on Social Control. In this section we are going to look at the different types of law in Britain in order to see what the role of the judiciary is in interpreting the laws.

STATUTE LAW AND COMMON LAW

Statute laws are laws that are written into the statute book. They are the laws that parliament has created, and start life as a Bill in either the House of Lords or the House of Commons. The chart on page 204 shows how a Bill progresses through Parliament to become law. If the law is not clearly set out, or if the wording is confusing, the judge faced with applying the law to a particular case will have to interpret it as he thinks fit. Some laws, however, are so ancient, that they have never actually been written down. These laws are part of common law, and

A group of newly appointed judges outside the House of Lords. What are the symbols *of their office or position?*

are so basic that we in this country just accept them as part of our rights. For example, we take it for granted that if we buy a new car it will be delivered complete with wheels and an engine. We do not have to sign an agreement with the dealer to this effect because any judge would uphold our claim that under common law a salesman should not be allowed to cheat in this manner.

CODED LAW AND CASE LAW

Some countries have a *code* of all the laws that have ever been passed. A code in this context means that the laws have been set down in a list, and when a judge is in doubt as to what the law is in a certain case, he can refer to the code to tell him what to do.

Britain does not have a code of law. British judges are given great responsibility in interpreting the law, and when a judge is in doubt, instead of referring to the code, he looks to see if there has been a similar case before. If there has been such a case, he bases his judgement on that PRECEDENT; he tries to follow the same course as the judge in the earlier case. This means that when there is no precedent, the judge is in a very responsible position. He knows that his judgement in this test case will influence the way in which all similar cases are judged in the future. Britain, then, uses a system of case law.

Local affairs

So far we have considered government at a national level. In most complex societies, however, the local community of town, village or city has responsibility for dealing with some questions of purely local interest.

In Britain, the structure of local government is rather similar to the structure of the national government. There is a legislature in the form of the local council, which is elected by the people in the district. Often the council is divided along party political lines, and political party ideas are entering more and more into discussions about local government affairs.

The laws which are passed by the local council are not as important as the national laws passed by Parliament. They are called BY-LAWS and deal with relatively unimportant matters, such as the hours between which cars may be parked in the High Street, or whether bicycles may be ridden in the park. At the entrance to public gardens there is usually a notice setting out the by-laws relating to use of the gardens.

The local authority provides a variety of services. Housing, the police, the ambulance service and recreational facilities such as London's Hayward Gallery (below) are organised on a local basis.

There is also a separate bureaucracy for the local authority. Local government officials are there to carry out the services provided by the local council, and are quite separate from the Civil Service, although they work in a very similar way. On the whole the work of the local authority is not concerned with vital policy issues, since these are generally decided by the national government for the country as a whole.

Very large local authorities, on the other hand, such as the Greater London Council, employ many thousands of officials on tasks every bit as complex as those concerning the majority of civil servants. The GLC occupies an enormous building facing the Houses of Parliament and the directors of the different departments within the GLC are individuals of similar standing to senior Civil Servants in the ministries across the river.

Occasionally important policy decisions are left to the wishes of the local authority. The most important service provided at the local level is the Education Service. A large proportion of the money available to local authorities is spent on education, and although the national government can bring pressure to bear on how that money is spent, on the whole it does not do so, with the result that the local council is left with a great responsibility.

The controversy over the introduction of comprehensive education shows how difficult it is to draw a hard and fast line between national and local government. Until 1969 local authorities had been left free to provide what type of schools they wished, within the limits of the 1944 Education Act. This Act set down the basic duty of the local authority to provide free compulsory education up to the age of fifteen, and for further education to be available to those who would benefit from it. So the local councils could set up comprehensive schools if they wished, or they could keep the more traditional grammar, secondary modern and technical schools. Look at the section on Education for a more detailed description of the 'tripartite system'. In 1969, the Labour government, which had for some time supported the principle of comprehensive education, decided to carry out a policy of comprehensive schools for the whole country. The only way in which it could *force* the local authorities to set up comprehensive schools was by passing a new Education Act to replace the 1944 Act. This it was unwilling to do. It would have taken a long time, and would have made a later change in policy impossible without yet another Act, since in order to be effective, it would have had to be very detailed about the kind of schools to be provided. The big advantage of the 1944 Act was that it was not at all detailed and so was much more flexible.

Instead of passing a new law, therefore, the government tried to bring pressure to bear on

The decision on whether to build comprehensive schools is made by the local education authority. Because it is a local *decision, the type of schools provided varies considerably from area to area. Do you think this is a fair system?*

the local authorities in another way. Some of the money spent by local authorities comes from the rates, but this is not nearly enough to meet their needs, so the national government provides them with a great deal more. In 1969, the Secretary of State for Education and Science sent a letter or CIRCULAR to all local authorities in which he *asked* them to submit plans for turning all their secondary schools into comprehensive schools. If they failed to do this by a certain date, the letter went on, there would be no more money forthcoming from the central government.

This had the local authorities in a cleft stick. They were obliged by law to provide an education service, and yet they could not do so without money from the national government. Most authorities complied with the Secretary of State's request, but some delayed, hoping for a change of government. They were not disappointed. In 1970, a Conservative government was elected and the new Secretary of State withdrew the circular, and again left the question of comprehensive schools to be decided by the local authorities themselves.

Most issues of basic policy are decided by the national government, so that the whole country is treated in roughly the same way. Is it right that the question of education should be left to the local authority, with the result that widely differing systems exist side by side, and that children in some areas are much better served than those in other areas? Should the members of the local community be given more or less freedom to decide what type of services should be provided in their area?

LOCAL GROUPS

Political action at the local level is not confined to the official party organisations. There are many people who believe that the local communities should be given more power to direct their own affairs, but that the present system of local government is not a suitable way of doing

this. There is plenty of evidence to suggest that people in general take little interest in local politics; polling at local elections is very low – people do not seem to be bothered about voting; frequently the names of local councillors are quite unknown in the district they serve, and very often people do not even know which party has a majority on the council. Local councillors have to have a fair amount of spare time, or money, so that they can afford to take time off work. The mayor or chairman of the council may be a local businessman or a housewife with a lot of experience of committee work.

These people, it is claimed, have little in common with ordinary working people, and often do not understand their needs. The decisions they are faced with could easily be made by anyone with a little commonsense, and do not require the expert knowledge that is needed by a politician at Westminster. There is no *real* reason why everyone should not have the chance to participate in local government.

The failure of some councils to deal properly with local needs has stimulated the growth of unofficial political groups whose aim is to involve ordinary people more actively with the government of their area. The London borough of Kensington and Chelsea is a case in point. The extreme contrast between the rich, fashionable end of the borough, towards Chelsea and South Kensington, and the depressed and overcrowded district of North Kensington where the residents live in some of the worst housing conditions in the country, must to some extent be due to the inactivity of the local council. Other London boroughs have similar housing problems, yet many of these councils have managed to put into effect vigorous schemes for redevelopment and rehousing. The apparent lack of interest of the Kensington council in past years has caused a number of groups to mount their own attack on first the housing problem, then the lack of children's play-space, conditions in local schools, and the local welfare services. Local action has taken the form of squatting in empty houses, demonstrations against the lack of play space and suggestions as to remedies, some of which the council has been glad to accept. The building of a new flyover, Westway, through the middle of the area, hardly improved the environment, but protests by local groups of residents led to the rehousing of families who would otherwise have been left living almost on top of the motorway. Plans were also submitted, which the council accepted, for turning the space under the flyover into children's play areas rather than the car parks which the council architects at first suggested.

Local interest in politics resulted in 1971 in the election of an unofficial council in the Golbourne area of North Kensington. This council has no official powers at all, and can only act as another pressure group on the official council, and yet the local people's interest in the unofficial council was so great that more than twice as many turned out to vote in the unofficial election as in the official election.

It is possible that ordinary individuals will be encouraged to take a more active interest in local affairs through the activity of local groups such as these. To many people the local council is remote, and the chance to take direct action on the issues that most concern them has been welcomed. It may be that the system of local government will in the end be forced to change to allow this sort of participation by all residents.

Political change

In looking at political systems, we have so far only considered the possibility of change within the system. When we have a general election, we have a choice between Conservative and

Labour, and some people would say that this is really no choice at all. When an election is held in the USSR, the voters have to choose between one Communist and another. They too are limited to choice within the system. There is no way in which we can organise matters so that people can choose between systems, say between our system of representative democracy, and the soviet system. Yet political systems do change. How do they change? What are the processes by which one *type* of government is replaced by another?

Leaders of a revolution often have charismatic personalities. Che Guevara, one of the leaders of the Cuban revolution, had a great popular following. Even in Britain young people stuck up posters with his picture on them, and painted his name on walls or across their T-shirts.

REVOLUTION

One obvious method of changing the system is through revolution. A revolution involves the overthrow not only of the government, but of all political institutions. The old order is replaced by a completely new way of doing things as well as a completely new set of politicians, within a short space of time.

The twentieth century has seen several such revolutions. In 1917 the old regime in Russia was violently overthrown and replaced by a Communist government dedicated to quite different ideals. It is important not to confuse the methods frequently used by revolutionaries with the revolution itself. In some countries the government is overthrown so often that there is hardly time for it to establish itself before the next upheaval takes place. In such cases we do not usually talk of a revolution because although there has been violence, and violence usually accompanies a revolution, not all violent political action is revolutionary. In countries ruled by a dictator, as is the case in several Latin American states, violence is part of the pattern of government; it is part of the system, and force is the method of effecting a change in government, just as elections are the method in this country.

The overthrow of the old regime in Cuba by Fidel Castro and his Communist guerillas was a genuine revolution, in that the old regime had lasted for many years, and a new system has since been set up which has now survived for some fifteen years. The new system is not at all similar to the old and in that sense too, a true revolution has occurred. The pre-revolutionary government in Cuba was a model of all that is worst in Latin American politics, and indeed many countries still suffer under similar regimes. The country was governed by a dictator notorious for his greed and dishonesty. From the leader to the most minor official, the political system was used as a means of enriching oneself and one's family and friends, and of gaining social prestige. The mass of the people lived in appalling poverty, terrorised by the police, the virtual slaves of the landowning classes, and regularly milked dry by government taxation. That the system persisted for so long was largely due to the support of the United States. Americans owned a large proportion of the major Cuban industry, sugar, the profits from which were never spent in Cuba, but were sent off to the United States, so that the Cuban people never benefited from their work. Cuba was also of strategic military value to the Americans, who had important naval bases on the island. So United States governments, anxious to preserve political stability for the sake of their economic and military interests, gave the Cuban dictators the support they needed to remain in power.

It was clear to all observers that the situation could not go on for ever; a people will only put up with such conditions for so long. A time eventually comes when life is so intolerable for a large number of people that they are willing to risk death itself rather than endure it any longer. It is at such a time that a revolutionary leader can count on the support he needs to bring about a successful COUP.

Fidel Castro is a perfect example of Weber's charismatic leader. From the very start, the revolution was his personal movement. It is called by everyone 'Fidel's revolution'. We have seen that in the USSR as in other Communist countries, the Communist party makes sure that the government is stable and permanent. On the death of Lenin, the Russian revolutionary leader, the party provided Stalin to succeed him. Similarly a new Chinese leader has been found following the death of Mao Tse-tung in modern China. In Cuba, the Communist party does not have this role. The unifying force is Castro himself; he personally controls the direction of the revolutionary movement.

There can be no doubt that the revolution has released the majority of Cubans from a terrible existence. The new government has an impressive record. Output in all areas of production has increased, and new farming methods and industries have been set up. The peasants are obviously better off; they have new houses, better roads, free medical care and free education. Everyone has been encouraged to help in the revolution. In 1961 an illiteracy campaign was launched with the aim of teaching even the oldest peasant to read. Young people and anyone else who had had some education, went into the villages and set up reading classes. In this sort of way the people are made to feel that they too are responsible for the success of the revolution. They are urged to work hard, not to enrich themselves, but as part of a co-operative effort to improve the standard of living of the whole country. How long the enthusiasm lasts remains to be seen; it is possible that as a generation of Cubans grows up which has never known the poverty and injustice of pre-revolutionary days, the young people will be less interested in the revolution and will demand other kinds of reward for their work.

EVOLUTIONARY CHANGE

Political change does not only occur through violent upheaval. There has been no revolution in Britain since the seventeenth century, and yet the political system has changed a great deal during the last two hundred years. Political change may *evolve* – come about gradually – by means of a series of minor changes, which add up, after a long time, to a major change.

READING AND UNDERSTANDING

1. Make a list of some of the property owned by any group, such as your family, youth club or district, of which you are a member. How is this property protected?
2. What is the origin of the word 'politics'?

3 Fill in the blanks in the following paragraph: A political system has to provide the means by which —— are made, and it has to ensure that most people —— the system. Sometimes the —— do not have the support of the —— and so they have to resort to physical —— to enforce the laws.
4 What are the three kinds of authority classified by Max Weber?
5 How may a simple society with no formal political system organise itself?
6 What is the importance of the age group in some simple societies?
7 What do you understand by the word *State*? What is the difference between a simple and a complex State?
8 Explain what the following terms mean: Legislature; Bureaucracy; Judiciary.
9 What effect did the rise of industry and the decline in agriculture have on the power of the landed aristocracy in Britain in the nineteenth century?
10 Which groups of people were in favour of reforming the House of Commons in 1832, and why?
11 What is universal suffrage?
12 What is a life peer? What effect has the introduction of life peers had on the House of Lords?
13 What is a constituency?
14 Describe, as fully as you can, the work of an MP.
15 Which British political party is described as right-wing and which as left-wing?
16 Make a list of some of the ideals that are held by (*a*) the Conservative Party, (*b*) the Labour Party.
17 What is a pressure group? Give examples of two pressure groups and explain their aims.
18 What methods are used by pressure groups to achieve their aims?
19 What do you understand by the *electoral system*? What type of electoral system do we have in Britain? Explain how it works. Explain why, in the example on page 98, Smith was elected on a *minority vote*.
20 Why does the Liberal Party do badly in elections?
21 What do you understand by the word *democracy*? Do you think that we in Britain have a democratic system of government? Give reasons for your views.
22 What is a *totalitarian* state? Give two examples.
23 Make a list of some of the functions of the Communist Party in the USSR.
24 What are the Young Pioneers?
25 What is the Central Committee of the Communist Party of the USSR? How do people become members of the Central Committee?
26 What is a *soviet*?
27 What is *Pravda*? What is the influence of *Pravda*?
28 What are the tasks of the bureaucracy? Why are some bureaucracies larger than others?
29 How does the administration of your school fit into Weber's idea of bureaucracy? Write as full a description as you can.
30 Why is a British cabinet minister so dependent upon the civil servants in his department?
31 What is the difference between statute and common law?
32 What is a code of law? Does Britain have a code of law? Describe the British system.
33 What is a *by-law*?
34 What is the most important service provided by the local authority?
35 In what ways have local councils sometimes failed to deal successfully with their local problems?
36 How might local councils be persuaded to change their policies?
37 Make a list of the ways in which political change may be brought about. What are the advantages and disadvantages of each method?

38 Who held power in Cuba before the revolution? Which foreign country supported the former Cuban government? Why? Who led the Cuban revolution?
39 What changes have come about in Cuban society as a result of the revolution?

POINTS FOR FURTHER DISCUSSION

1 Discuss this sentence: 'The word *thief* has no meaning in a society which has no concept of property.'
2 What are the basic tasks of any political system? What happens when the system fails?
3 What kinds of authority are exercised in your school? Do you respond differently to different types of authority? If so, in what way?
4 Does the House of Lords today have any power?
5 Why are most parliamentary seats won by candidates from one of the three main political parties?
6 What alternative electoral systems are there? What are the advantages and disadvantages of these?
7 Why did the Russians invade Czechoslovakia in 1968? Does any country have the right to send troops into a foreign country? Can you think of any other countries where foreign troops have been sent to support or change the existing government?
8 What is 'red tape'? Can you think of any examples from your own experience? Is 'red tape' a necessary evil?
9 'Promotion depends on merit.' What does this mean? On what other qualities might promotion depend? Make a list, in order of importance, of the qualities you think necessary.
10 Do you think that the question of comprehensive education should be left to the local authority, or should the national government lay down a single policy for the whole country?
11 In general, do people take much interest in local politics? Can you think of any explanation for this?
12 Do you think that young people in this country can help to improve social conditions? In what ways can young people help?
13 Do people in Britain control their own work? How much control do your working friends and relatives have over their work? Who gets the profit from the work they do?

PROJECT WORK

1 Find out as much as you can about the government and ways of life in one of the following countries: China, Cuba, the USSR, Yugoslavia, Spain, Portugal, Tanzania or Nigeria. Look out especially for how the government is chosen and how much control it has over schools, industry and the mass media.
2 Ask your teacher to write for information to two or three pressure groups which are campaigning at present; for example, to the National Council for Civil Liberties, Shelter or Oxfam. Then compare the methods they use in their campaigns. Whom are they trying to influence? Are they successful, in your opinion?
3 Make a study of different types of political protest. You could find out about strikes, demonstrations, marches and revolutionary movements. You might look at political protest in a single country or compare several countries. Historical examples are very useful here.
4 What are the services provided by your local council? What provision is there for the old, the very young, leisure pursuits, essential services and schools? How are these organ-

ised? How does your borough compare with neighbouring boroughs?

5 Write to members of the political parties in your area and invite a speaker to school, and/or arrange a mock election in your class or year; you will need candidates representing the major political parties, and a returning officer to be responsible for the organisation of the voting. You can get information about party programmes and policies from the local offices of the political parties.

USEFUL BOOKS FOR PUPILS

Brandon, R. *Central Government* (Harrap 1975)
Currey, J. *Becoming a Citizen* (Harrap 1975)
Gabriel, P. *British Government* (Social Science series) (Longman 1975)
Harvey, J. *How Britain is Governed* (Macmillan 1975)
Jones, G. *Local Government* (Harrap 1975)
Mitchison, Lois *China in the Twentieth Century* (Oxford University Press 1970)
Ottway, D. *Divided Island* (Heinemann Educational 1976)
Pickering, S. *Twentieth Century Russia* (Oxford University Press 1965)
Savage, K. *Marxism and Communism* (Blond 1965)
Sawyer, R. & White, J. *Care and the Community* (Ginn 1971)
Sorrenson, K. *Separate and Unequal (South Africa)* (Heinemann 1976)
Stuart, J. *The Unequal Third* (Network Social Studies series) (Edward Arnold 1977)

Study Packs:
Study Centre Publications for Teaching Politics; pack of source extracts and commentary:
Background to British Political Institutions
British Constitutional Monarchy
Ask the Candidate
Our Democratic Heritage, a series of tapes by the Central Office of Information:
Cabinet
How a Bill Becomes Law
Available from the Commonwealth Institute; Learning Resources Centre booklets:
Social Change
Communist Societies

USEFUL BOOKS FOR TEACHERS

Blackburn, R. *Ideology in Social Science* (Fontana 1972)
Castles, F., Lewis, P. & Saunders, S. *Questions in Soviet Government and Politics* (Open University Press, Course D333 1 1976)
Giddens, A. *Class Structure in the Advanced Societies* (Hutchinson Educational 1973)
Hanson, A. H. & Wall, M. *Governing Britain* (Fontana 1970)
Kelsall, R. *Politics* (Longman 1974)
Kochan, L. *The Making of Modern Russia* (Penguin 1967)
Mair, L. *Primitive Government* (Penguin 1962)
McKenzie, W. M. *Politics and Social Science* (Penguin 1969)
Sampson, A. *New Anatomy of Britain* (Hodder and Stoughton 1971)
Yglesias, J. *In the Fist of the Revolution* (Penguin 1970)

FILMS

Collective Farm in Central Asia; 20 mins; ILEA 1276
A Visit to the Soviet Union
Part 1 – Women of Russia; 35 mins; Concord Films Council
Part 2 – Farm from Moscow; 35 mins; Concord Films Council
Lenin's Revolution; 20 mins; ILEA 1951
Stalin's Revolution; 20 mins; ILEA 1952
Children in China; 19 mins; ILEA 798
One Way to Change the World (Cuba 1968); 25 mins; Concord Films Council
A Private Decision (US electoral system); 29 mins; Guild Sound & Vision Ltd
China in the Modern World; EAV 12kF469
Russia in the Modern World; EAV
Co-operative Store; 16 mins; Central Film Library
It's a Battleground (pupil's participation in secondary school); 40 mins; Concord Films Council

5 Social Stratification

We introduced the term SOCIAL STRATIFICATION in the section on the Aztecs, and said then that the Aztec society was divided into groups according to occupation. Some groups were considered of more importance than others, because some jobs required more skill, more imagination, more education and more money. Thus the society was layered or *stratified*, and a hierarchy formed, with the mass of slaves and peasants at the bottom, and the Emperor at the top, supported by the warriors, priests and landowners.

Not all societies are divided in this way. Although in each band of hunters and gatherers there will be a man respected because he takes decisions for the group, and individuals who have prestige on account of their skill at hunting, their good looks or their strength, these people do not form distinct groups and they receive no more than the prestige accorded to any member of a group if he or she excels at some important activity, or is lucky enough to look specially attractive. Neither do we find systems of grouping people among herding societies. It is only when the division of labour becomes greater, in a farming society, that permanent labels can be attached to groups of people which are in some way related to their occupation and social position.

SLAVERY

Early civilisations, such as those of Greece, Rome and Egypt, depended for many of their achievements on large numbers of slaves. A task as gigantic as that of building the pyramids would today be undertaken with the use of a tremendous amount of mechanical equipment. Expensive cranes and earth-shifting machinery would be driven by a few skilled men. The Egyptians relied on manpower equipped with very simple tools; enormous blocks of stone were shifted with great effort by teams of slaves

People are not only put into groups according to their jobs. In most societies people are also stratified according to their sex. In Britain today many women feel that they are unfairly classed as inferior to men.

Slaves were forced to work without payment. Sometimes slave-owners did not even bother to feed their slaves properly because it was so cheap to replace those that died.

pushing and pulling on ropes. Obviously no one would choose to perform such tasks, and the slaves were given no choice. They were forced to work by law. The state recognised the existence of separate groups of slaves and free men, and passed laws to protect the power of the free over the non-free.

Another example of slavery is that of nineteenth-century America. Africans were captured or tricked by slave-traders in their native lands and shipped across the Atlantic in appalling conditions to work in the southern states of the USA and in the West Indies. They were used mainly on large-scale enterprises such as sugar plantations. The owners could produce more sugar per acre on large than on small farms, and the slave dealers provided them with the necessary labour. The fact that the slaves received no wages and cost the owner only their initial price and upkeep meant that the owners could become richer than if they had had to hire labour.

The basic similarity between the early civilisations and this more recent example is that the society is divided into two basic groups, the slaves and a property-owning plutocracy (i.e. a very rich ruling group) which lives on slave labour.

ESTATES

A rather different system of dividing society existed in the feudal states of medieval Europe. There were three broad groups or estates, the nobility, the clergy and the common people, which corresponded to three basic roles; the nobility led armies, were magistrates and administrators; the clergy looked after the spiritual and moral welfare of the people and maintained communication with God; and the common people provided labour on the farms, in crafts such as metalworking, pottery and boot-making, and acted as servants to the wealthy. Again, it is important to notice that the state recognised the existence of the three estates by making laws which set out the rights and duties of each. It even went so far as to lay down different penalties for the same crime committed by members of different estates.

The estate system was the basis of the political system. The nobility were the rulers, who held their power from the king. Each noble would be given some land by the king on condition that he performed certain duties. He would have to see that law and order were maintained on his land, and if the king needed an army he would have to provide armed soldiers, the number depending on the size of his territory.

CASTE

The Indian caste system was also based on occupation: priests, warriors, traders and labourers. But each caste was far more than an occupational group. It had different customs and traditions, and the individual was rooted firmly in his own caste. He would be extremely unlikely to change caste, either through marriage or change of occupation. The caste system was also the basis of the religious and political systems. Power and authority were exercised by those born into a high caste, and there was no question of this being threatened by a member of a lower caste.

Social mobility

One of the most important features of the caste system was its rigidity, i.e. it was almost impossible for people to change from one caste to another. The term used by sociologists to describe movement from one social position to another is SOCIAL MOBILITY. Social mobility was also very restricted in medieval Europe. If you were born a serf, you could never become a noble. The only way in which a commoner could

UNIVERSITY COLLEGE,
LIVERPOOL.

TO WORKING-MEN.

A COMPETITION WILL BE HELD NEXT OCTOBER
FOR
EIGHT STUDENTSHIPS,
OF THE VALUE OF £5 EACH.

The object of these Studentships is to provide those who gain them with a sum of money sufficient to defray the Fees for attendance at Lectures and the cost of all books necessary for pursuing a course of study in the Evening Classes of the College.

CONDITIONS OF THE COMPETITION.

1.—The Competition will be limited to such men as earn their living by manual labour (working foremen to be understood as included).†

2.—The Scholarships to be held for ONE YEAR. But former winners of them to be allowed to enter again for the present Competition.

3.—Holders of the Scholarships to attend TWO COURSES OF EVENING LECTURES in University College, throughout the year (each course once a week), one of which must be either Political Economy or Political Philosophy.

4.—The subjects of Examination in October, 1892, will be the Outlines of Political Economy, the Outlines of English History since 1688, and English Composition. Books:—Candidates are recommended to read in History:—Green's short History of the English People, or Bright's School History of England. In Political Economy:—Mill's Political Economy, or F. A. Walker's Brief Political Economy. Candidates are also required to bring to the Competition a short Essay of their own unaided composition (not exceeding five pages foolscap) on the subject: "How far does the Poor Law assist the Deserving Poor?" Weight will be attached to this in awarding the Scholarships.

5.—The Examination will consist of written answers to questions, and will last for three hours.

PLACE OF EXAMINATION: University College, Ashton Street.
TIME " " Saturday, October 1st, at 7 o'clock p.m.

Candidates must send their names to the REGISTRAR, University College, Liverpool, not later than Saturday, September 24th.

† In event of any difficulty arising as to whether a Candidate comes under this description the decision of the Principal of the College to be final.

T. DOBB & Co., Printers, 229, Brownlow Hill, Liverpool.

rise in society was by joining the Church. Priests were forbidden to marry, so many priests and monks were recruited from among the common people. Once in the Church, a commoner could in theory rise to the position of abbot or bishop, but in practice these powerful men were almost always members of the nobility. The younger sons of the aristocracy frequently went into the Church, since only one son, the eldest, could inherit his father's title and lands. So there was some movement upwards in the social scale, as commoners became monks and priests, and some movement downwards, as the sons of the nobility also joined the Church.

SOCIAL MOBILITY AND SOCIAL CHANGE

If the groups in society are so rigidly divided that it is very difficult for individuals to move from one group to another, then the speed at which the society can change is hindered. Social change depends on people having new ideas and putting them into practice. In a changing society the old ideas and old social groupings are no longer relevant. New patterns of behaviour are adopted, and traditional customs die. The more people are allowed to say what they think, and use their abilities, the more flexible the system of social stratification, and the

One way of breaking down rigid barriers between groups is to give everyone the same opportunity for education. In Britain in the nineteenth century only the men had the opportunity of going to university. Today far too few children have the chance of a nursery education before starting school.

greater the possibility of social change. Farming societies with very rigid caste or estate systems found it difficult to change into industrial societies. In England, however, the medieval estate system had become almost unrecognisable by the end of the eighteenth century and development into an industrial society occurred earlier than in other countries where the old social differences remained.

INDUSTRIALISATION

The industrial revolution in Britain drastically upset the social order. The landowners were no longer the richest and most powerful group; their place was taken by those with the biggest stake in industry – the owners of money and machines. The bulk of the common people were no longer agricultural labourers living in tiny villages ruled by custom and by the local aristocracy. New towns grew up, inhabited by factory workers in daily contact with more of their fellow men than a farming peasant might meet in a year. The feudal system was gradually replaced by a new system of social stratification in England. Even the names 'nobility' and 'commons' could not be used for the new groups of industrial society.

KARL MARX

It was the German sociologist and economist Karl Marx (1818–1883) who, with a fellow writer, Friedrich Engels, worked out a theory of social stratification to fit the new situation. He used the word 'class' to describe the new social groups, and said that there are basically two classes, the capitalists who own the factories, mines and mills, and the working people who own nothing and are employed by the capitalists. He called the capitalists the BOURGEOISIE, and the workers the PROLETARIATE. He said that the bourgeoisie exploit the proletariate because they

Karl Marx.

force them to work for very low wages, while they themselves get rich on the profits. Sooner or later, however, the situation must come to an end. The working people will no longer put up with exploitation, and will revolt against the capitalists and the state. In the new state that emerges after the revolution, the proletariate will be in control; factories will be publicly owned, and co-operatively run and no one's labour will be exploited. The workers will form the government and everyone will have certain basic rights, such as the right to education and the right to work. This state will be a SOCIALIST state. In the end, however, even this government would disappear, for people who live without exploitation will not need such big networks of social control as we now have. We have thousands of laws, many police courts and prisons. Our social order, based on competition and inequality, will be replaced by one built on sharing and justice. This ideal world, where people act for the good of the whole society rather than for themselves, is the state of COMMUNISM.

In the nineteenth century the difference in the way of life of the rich and the poor was very obvious.

Here is part of what Marx and Engels wrote in their booklet, *The Communist Manifesto*, in 1848:

The history of all hitherto existing society is the history of class struggles.

Freeman and slave, patrician and plebian, lord and serf, guild-master and journeyman, in a word, oppressor and oppressed, stood in constant opposition to one another, carried on an uninterrupted, now hidden, now open fight, a fight that each time ended, either in a revolutionary reconstitution of society at large, or in the common ruin of the contending classes.

In the earlier epochs of history we find almost everywhere a complicated arrangement of society into various orders. . . . In ancient Rome we have patricians, knights, plebians, slaves; in almost all of these classes, again, subordinate gradations.

The modern bourgeois society that has sprouted from the ruins of feudal society has not done away with the class antagonism. It has but established new classes, new conditions of oppressions, new forms of struggle in the place of the old ones.

Our epoch, the epoch of the bourgeoisie, possesses, however, this distinctive feature: it has simplified the class antagonisms. Society as a whole is more and more splitting up into two great hostile camps directly facing each other: Bourgeoisie and Proletariat.

Class in Britain

Marx's description of social stratification in nineteenth-century Britain was very accurate, and his idea of class is still crucial in both sociology and politics. But his views cause furious argument and later writers have greatly modified them. Some say his work is the most useful we have. Others reject it, often because he had little to say about the people who are neither capitalist owners nor industrial workers. In between these two groups are many who are either in the service sector (see p. 38) like hairdressers, postmen and dustmen, or in the professions like doctors, nurses and lawyers. Marx stressed only two classes, and the picture is somewhat confused by the growth of numbers of people who seem to be somewhere in the middle. In Britain today there are roughly as many office workers, teachers, shop assistants and so on as there are workers in the manufacturing sector.

Today it is not easy to see where one class begins and the other ends. Some of the worst hardships of the proletariate and the worst excesses of the bourgeoisie have been mended. At present ownership of factories, machinery and land is in the hands of a very few people in Britain. Another division disliked by Marx, between people working mostly with their hands and those working mostly with their minds, also remains. Despite this, sociologists usually divide society into a number of classes. There are several variations on the theme; the *census* of basic information on the population of Britain uses a method called the Registrar-General's classification. Methods like this one lose Marx's focus on ownership, and sort people into similar groups of jobs, also called occupations.

The Registrar-General's Scale

Showing percentage of population of Great Britain in each class

		Percentage of population
Class I	Professional	4
Class II	Intermediate	18
Class III	Skilled manual	49
Class IV	Semi-skilled manual	21
Class V	Unskilled manual	8
		100%

Source: *1971 Census*

CLASS AND OCCUPATION

A person's occupation in our economic system determines his income. Unless he is an owner, his earnings depend on two factors: whether he has special skills which the society values and which are in short supply, such as the skills of a doctor, and whether he can bargain with his employers and force them to raise his wages or salary. His bargaining power may rest on a threat to stop work unless he gets what he wants, and in most cases this is only effective if all the employees get together and act as a group.

The amount of money earned affects every aspect of people's lives. Income can be used to buy goods – food, clothes, a washing machine; and services – holidays, education for children, an evening at the cinema. A man's or woman's job affects family life, leisure activities, the type of education received by the children, religion, voting and most other aspects of everyday life. A sociologist studying class will therefore look at all these issues in an attempt to understand the relation of behaviour to class position.

The Hall-Jones Scale

Class 1 Professional and high administrative
2 Managerial and executive
3 Inspectional, supervisory and other non-manual, higher grade
4 Inspectional, supervisory and other non-manual, lower grade
5 Skilled manual and routine grades of non-manual
6 Semi-skilled manual
7 Unskilled manual

The Hall-Jones scale of social class was worked out by two sociologists in the early 1950s. It is an expanded version of the Registrar-General's scale, which was developed in the 1920s.

What do the words *manual* and *non-manual* mean?

Name as many jobs as you can which fall into each category.

How are jobs in each category different? How are they alike? Are the differences more important than the similarities?

CLASS AND STATUS

A person may be labelled according to his class, and this is very useful to government departments and to sociologists in general. We all tend to label people, however, and we do not necessarily use the definition of class used by social scientists. We tend to rank people and give some higher prestige than others. We respect some and not others, and we in turn hope that other people will respect us. In other words, we are all striving for STATUS.

A person's social status describes his or her standing in society. Different societies give status on the basis of different factors. Some societies stress the importance of age, others of sex. In some societies skin colour can be a vital factor dividing different groups. In Britain we take a number of things into account; we tend to judge people according to their occupation, but we also consider other characteristics. Consciously or unconsciously, we react to a people's dress and speech, and the colour of their skin. We value intelligence and education, so a Cambridge graduate is accorded a certain respect. Where people live, what kind of car they drive, whether their children go to independent schools, even the way they hold their knife and fork and the words they use, are all signs of upper class social status in our society. Big cars, a villa in St Tropez and a mink coat are STATUS SYMBOLS. They are taken as outward signs of status, and people anxious to improve their status are correspondingly anxious to acquire such status symbols.

'Keeping up with the Joneses' is a common expression used to describe a striving for higher status, by individuals or families. But work groups attempt to improve or maintain their social standing as well. Sometimes they succeed and sometimes they fail. When one group is given a pay rise many other groups press for a rise which would keep the differences between the groups the same. Otherwise the first group might catch up with or even pass the rest, whose status would therefore fall.

A sociologist, D. Lockwood, has made a study of a work group which has lost status over the last hundred years. In his book, *The Black-Coated Worker*, he describes the work and status situations of the clerical worker in the mid-nineteenth century as compared with today, and shows how this occupational group has suffered a loss in status. In the middle of the nineteenth century clerks were a highly respected, well-paid and well-educated group, enjoying middle-class status. Clerical work is non-manual and was accorded higher status than manual jobs. By the beginning of the twentieth century, however, clerks were no longer in such a privileged, exclusive position. The services sector of em-

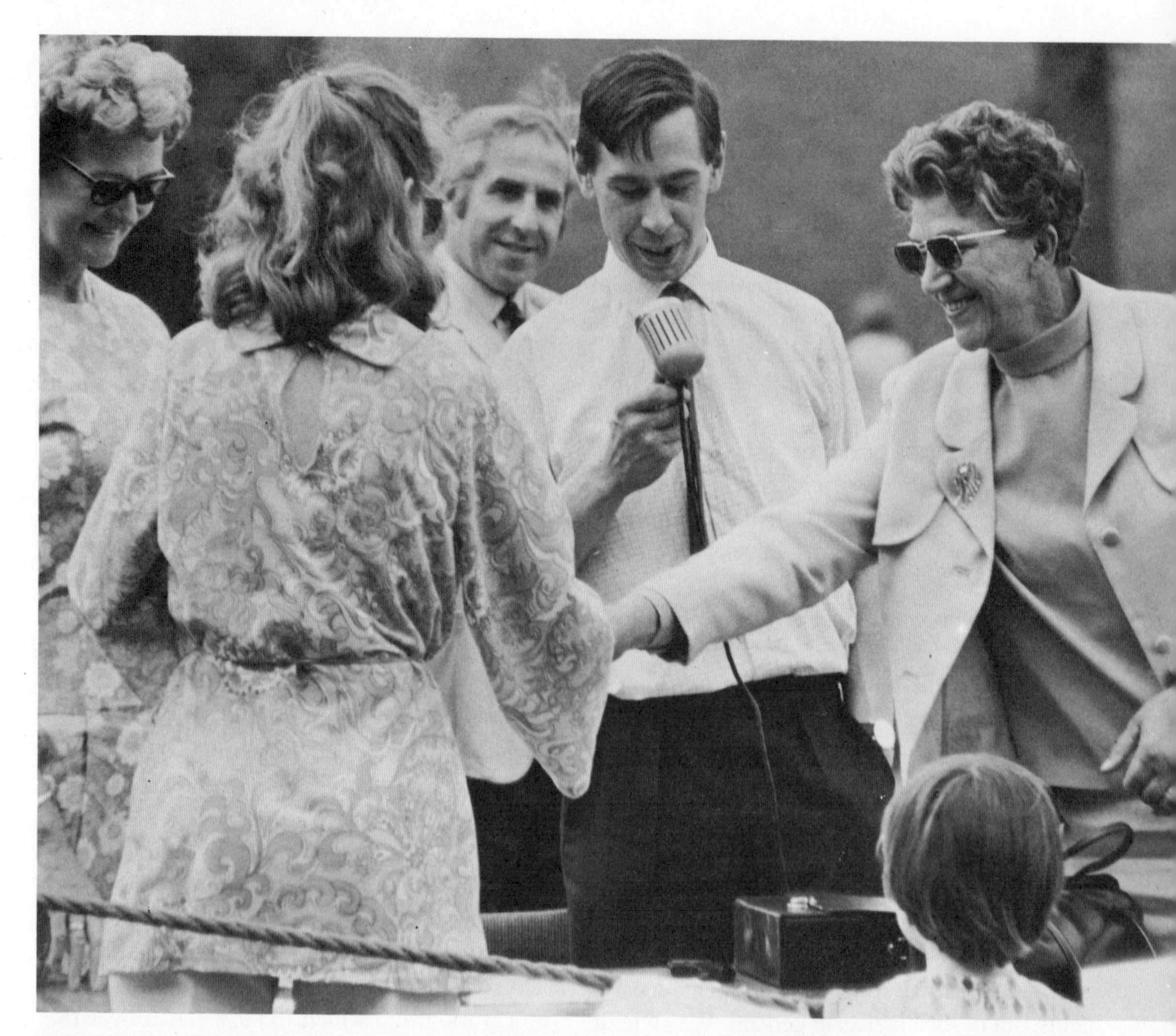

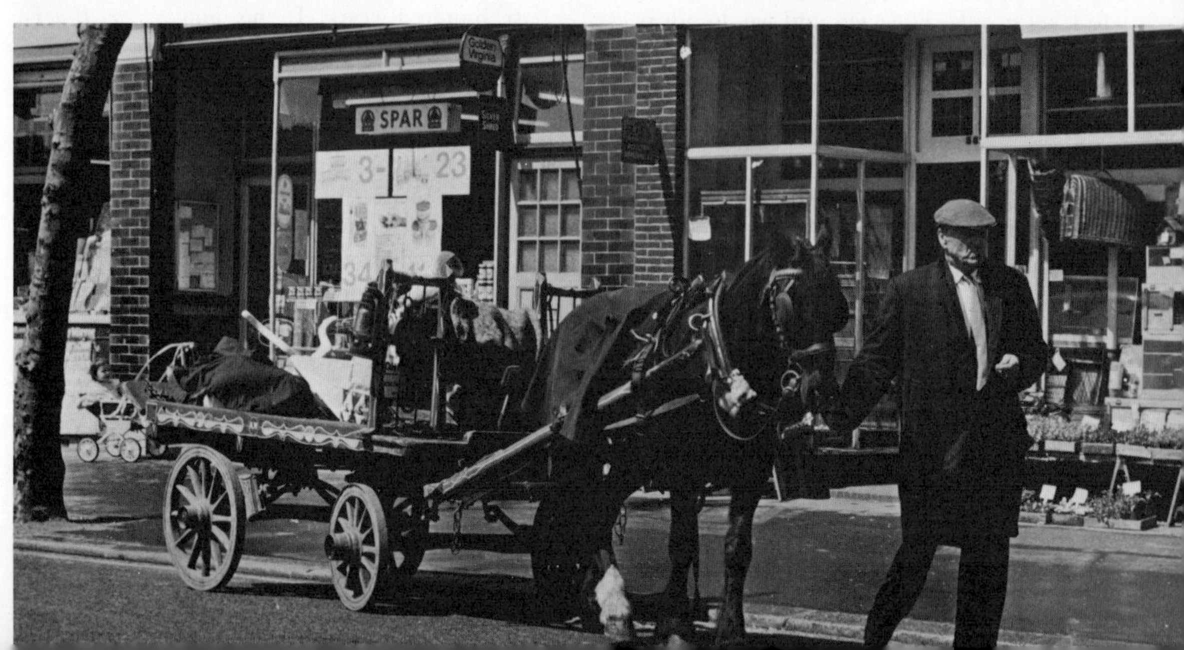
Golden Virginia
SPAR

We are surrounded by indications of people's status. Some indications are more obvious than others.

ployment had grown considerably with the result that:

(*a*) there were now many more clerks and many more offices. Clerical work was open to far more people than previously because of the great demand for office workers, and because compulsory education ensured that the basic skills of literacy were enjoyed by a greater proportion of the society,

(*b*) factory workers and other manual workers had improved their pay and working conditions, so that the gap between manual and non-manual work was no longer so great,

(*c*) the kind of work done in offices was becoming more routine,

(*d*) many middle-class people who would have been prepared to become clerical workers fifty years before were now becoming lawyers, teachers and doctors; these expanding professions had still higher status than that of the clerk.

The result we see today is that although clerical work is still considered a 'respectable' white-collar occupation, clerks have considerably lower status than they would have had in the nineteenth century. It is no longer considered an exclusively middle-class job, and is very much on the borderline between the middle and working classes.

CLASS AND POLITICS

In the other systems of social stratification which we have discussed, the members of the highest caste or estate are the political rulers. Their position is established by law, and they pass on their status as leaders, governors and magistrates to their children. In an industrial society there is no law which says that the rulers must be members of the upper classes. In Britain, politicians, judges and top civil servants may come from any class. This is part of the theory of democratic government. In reality, however, they are likely to come from the middle and upper classes.

According to Marx the rulers of industrial society, the really powerful people who influence major political decisions, are the owners of industrial enterprises. He claimed that the business of elections, parliament, political parties, hides the truth about political and economic power and keeps working people content in the false belief that they have control over government. Actually decisions are taken by, and in the interests of, the capitalists and land-owning aristocracy. Social reform is simply a means of forestalling revolution by the proletariate. Its aim is to help the system by which the upper class, the bourgeoisie, exploits the proletariate. Reforms which gave the workers the vote had no real effect on the distribution of power. Marxists (people who agree with Marx's theories) hold that the power of the rich over the poor is as great today as it was in the middle of the nineteenth century when Marx was writing.

The most powerful people in our society are:
Cabinet Ministers
Heads of the Civil Service
Directors of industry and commerce
Directors of banks
Military leaders
Judges

The educational background of an individual is probably the best single indicator of his social class origins. The table on page 130 shows the educational background of people in top positions in the post-war period (after 1945). It is clear from this table that the government and other ruling groups include mainly members of the middle and upper classes. Figure 32 shows the educational background of MPs and Cabinet ministers in the period 1918 to 1955.

Another way of studying the influence of class in British politics is by looking at the way in which people from different social classes vote. It is generally thought that on the whole, the middle class vote Conservative, while the working class vote Labour. While this is broadly true, studies have found that there are quite a large number of working-class people who vote Conservative, and that in fact, about half the supporters of the Conservative Party are working class. The table on p. 129 shows the proportion of votes cast for the main parties by people of different social backgrounds.

Recently, sociologists have begun to wonder if, as working-class people improve their standard of living, more would turn away from the Labour Party, and vote Conservative. It has been suggested that as the working class achieves a 'middle-class' standard of living, other middle-class patterns of behaviour (such as voting Conservative) will also be adopted.

To test this theory, a study was made by a group of sociologists into the voting patterns of several hundred AFFLUENT WORKERS living in Luton. They found that, far from abandoning support for the Labour Party as their standard of living improved, these workers adhered even more strongly to the Labour Party. When asked for their reasons for continuing to vote Labour, the workers answered that they believed the Labour Party to be the one which could do most to improve the standard of living of the ordinary working man. The table on p. 129 shows the voting intentions of some of the workers studied.

The Conservative Shadow Cabinet in 1970. Most of these people became members of the Conservative Government after the 1970 General Election.

Voting intention (1960s)

	Lab.	*Cons.*	*Lib.*	*Uncertain*	*Abstain*
Husband's earnings less than £18	79%	12%	5%	0%	3%
Husband's earnings £18–£21	74%	11%	7%	3%	4%
Husband's earnings £21 or more	73%	17%	10%	0%	0%

From Goldthorpe *et al.*, *The Affluent Worker: Political Attitudes & Behaviour*

1 What does the word '*abstain*' mean?
2 Which group of workers shows the greatest tendency to vote Conservative?
3 Which group shows the greatest tendency to vote Labour?
4 Do the figures show a strong tendency for voting patterns to change as people earn more money?

Social class related to voting behaviour

Social Class *% Voting*	1, 2, 3	4	5	6, 7
Conservative	66	80	28	17
Labour	23	16	66	80
Liberal	11	4	6	3
Total	100	100	100	100

From *How People Vote* by M. Benny, A. P. Gray, and R. H. Pear (R.K.P. 1956).

1 What occupations are included in social classes 1 and 2?
2 What occupations are included in social class 4? You will find the answers in the table on page 125.
3 What percentage of voters in classes 6 and 7 voted Conservative?
4 In which social class did the greatest percentage of voters support Labour?
5 What *general conclusions* can you draw about patterns of class and voting behaviour?

The educational background of people in top positions in the post-war period. Adapted from Guttsman, The British Political Elite

	Labour government, 1951	*Conservative government,* 1951	*Conservative government,* 1960	*Heads of the Civil Service,* 1950–1955	*Leaders of industry,* 1950/1955	*Directors of largest banks,* 1958	*Army leaders,* 1958	*Judiciary,* 1953
Aristocrats	3	14	15		3			
Working-class	30	1	1		1			
Etonians	5	24	17	3	8	50		
Harrow, Winchester, Rugby, Marlborough	5	16	10	11	8	33		
All public schools	23	52	48		29			36
Sandhurst, Dartmouth, Woolwich		1			1	8	21	
Grammar schools	16	8	18		15			
State secondary schools							4	8
Elementary schools only	22				1	2		
Oxford or Cambridge	23	40	46	50	22	83		
Other universities	8	3	3	15	8	14		

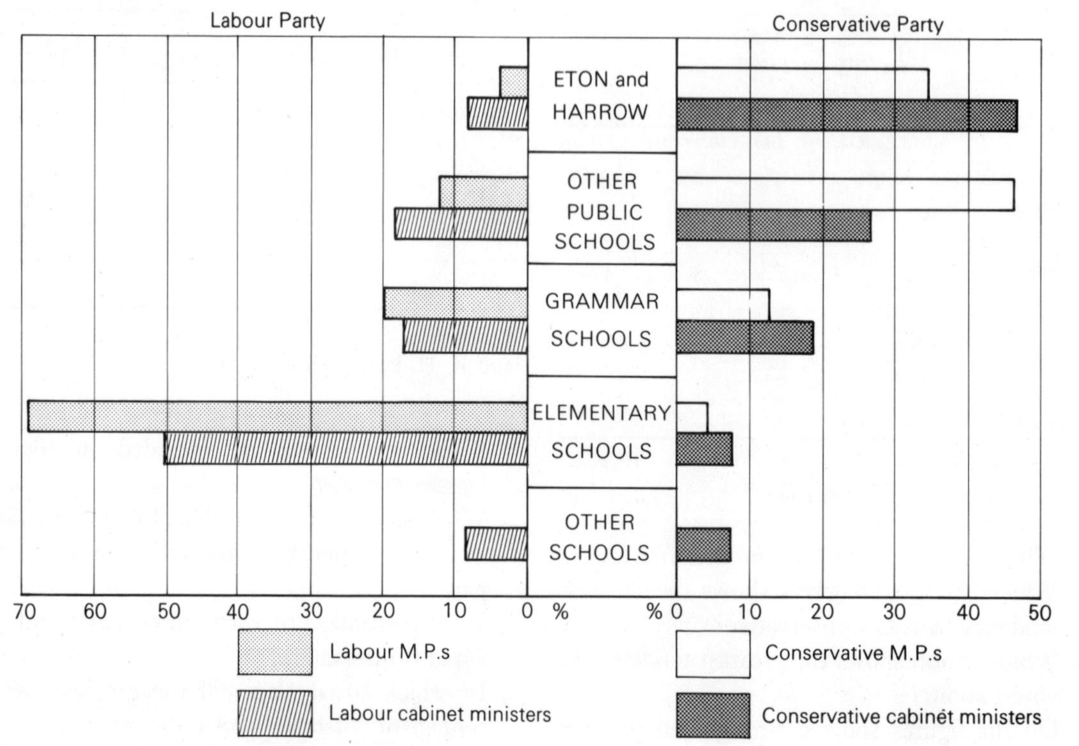

Fig 32 Educational background of M.P.s and Cabinet Ministers 1918–1955. From Guttsman: The British Political Elite.

READING AND UNDERSTANDING

1 In what ways did early civilisations such as those of Greece and Rome depend on slave labour?
2 In which British colonies were slaves used during the eighteenth and early nineteenth centuries, and how were they used?
3 What were the three *estates* of medieval Europe? What were the roles of the different estates?
4 How did the law recognise the difference between the estates?
5 What were the major *castes* of traditional Indian society? Why do we say that the caste system was very rigid?
6 What do sociologists mean by *social mobility*?
7 How could a commoner improve his social position in medieval England?
8 Who was Karl Marx?
9 What were the names given by Marx to the two major groups in industrial society?
10 How does the communist state differ from the socialist state?
11 What did Marx think would happen to the middle class? What has, in fact, happened in Britain?
12 How does the Registrar-General classify the population of this country?
13 What are two important factors which determine the size of a man's income?
14 What aspects of a man's life will the sociologist consider when he is making a study of social class?
15 What does the word *status* mean?
16 Make a list of the factors on which status is accorded in Britain.
17 What is a *status symbol*?
18 What, according to Lockwood, has happened to the status of clerks since the nineteenth century? What explanation does he give for this?
19 Make a list of the most influential groups of people in Britain today.
20 What was the educational background of most (*a*) Conservative ministers, (*b*) Labour ministers in the early 1950s?
21 Is it true that all working-class people vote Labour?
22 What theory was the study of affluent workers in Luton trying to test? What conclusions did the sociologists reach?

POINTS FOR FURTHER DISCUSSION

1 Why does a rigid system of social stratification hinder social change?
2 What did Marx mean by *class antagonism*? Does it exist in Britain today, in your opinion?
3 To what extent does the ordinary person in Britain today have any control over important national decisions?
4 Why do you suppose some working-class people vote Labour and others vote Conservative? Do you agree with the generalisation that on the whole most middle-class people vote Conservative, while most working-class people vote Labour?
5 Is Britain becoming a more classless society?
6 Is there any point in discussing the question of class?

PROJECT WORK

1 Collect a number of advertisements from different newspapers, magazines and periodicals. In groups, or alone, compare the advertisements. Look particularly at the products or services advertised and where they are advertised, and decide on the kind of appeal the advertisements are making. Do they include any status symbols? Are the products luxury goods, and, if so, are they advertised in a so-called 'quality' paper or a 'popular' paper?
2 Compare the living conditions and way of life of different groups in Britain with those of

the same types of groups in another country. Are there differences in the way of life of the old and the young, the rich and the poor, men and women? You could also compare these groups in Britain today with the same groups a hundred years ago.

USEFUL BOOKS FOR PUPILS

Ashton, E. T. *People and Power* (Ginn 1969)
Kent, G. *Poverty* (Batsford 1968)
Orwell, G. *The Road to Wigan Pier* (Penguin 1971)
Ryder, J. *Jobs, Class and Status* (Methuen Educational 1977)
Sorrenson, K. *Separate and Unequal* (Heinemann 1977)
Thomas, M. *People in Need* (Nelson 1972)
Thompson, J. *Sociology for Schools* Book I (Hutchinson 1973)

USEFUL BOOKS FOR TEACHERS

Blowers, A., Braham, P. & Woollacott, J. *The Importance of Social Inequality* (Open University Press, Course D 302 1–2 1976)
Blowers, A. & Thompson G. *Inequalities, Conflict and Change* (Open University Press, Course D302 1976)
Bottomore, T. B. *Classes in Modern Society* (Allen & Unwin 1965)
Bottomore, T. B. *Elites and Society* (Penguin 1964)
Byers, J. & Nolan, P. *Inequality: India and China Compared 1950–1970* (Open University Press, Course D302 25–28 1976)
Central Statistical Office, *Social Trends* (HMSO 1975)
CIS Crisis series *Black South Africa Explodes* (1977)
Coates, K. & Silburn, R. *Poverty: The Forgotten Englishmen* (Penguin 1973)
Douglas, J. W. B. *The Home and the School* (MacGibbon & Kee 1964)
Floud, J. E., Halsey, A. H. & Martin, F. M. *Social Class and Educational Opportunity* (Heinemann 1961)
Glass, D. V. *Social Mobility in Britain* (Routledge & Kegan Paul 1954)
Jackson, B. & Marsden, D. *Education and the Working Class* (Penguin 1962)
Kelsall, R. *Stratification* (Longman 1974)
Open University, *Patterns of Inequality* (Open University Press, Course D302 1–34 1976)
Open University, Sociological Perspective Block 3, Units 9–11 *Stratification and Social Class* (Open University Press, Course D283 1973)
Parkin, F. *Class Inequality and Political Order* (Paladin 1972)
Raynor, J. *The Middle Class* (Longman 1969)
Rose, G. *The Working Class* (Longman 1968)
Salaman G. & Weeks, D. *Stratification and Social Class* (Open University Press, Course D283 9–11 1972)
Stanworth, P. & Giddens, A. *Elites and Power in British Society* (Cambridge University Press 1974)
Townsend, P. *The Concept of Poverty* (Penguin 1971)
Turok, B. *Inequality as State Policy: The South African Case* (Open University Press, Course D302 17–18 1976)
Westergaard, V. & Resler, H. *Class in Capitalist Society* (Heinemann 1975)
Willmott, P. & Young, M. *Family and Kinship in East London* (Penguin 1965)
Young, M. & Willmott, P. *Family and Class in a London Suburb* (Routledge & Kegan Paul 1960)

FILMS

Not in Our Class, Dear; 30 mins; Concord Films Council
What about the Workers? (I and II); 18 mins each; ILEA 1705 and ILEA 1706
Seven Up; 30 mins; Concord Films Council
Seven Plus Seven; 60 mins; Concord Films Council
Our Generation; 35 mins; Save the Children Fund
It's Like This, Doctor; 40 mins; Concord Film Services 1969 and ILEA 2227/8
Man as a Social Animal; Audio-Visual Publications 3515
Wealth and Poverty; 40 mins; EAV EVTF 002
Ideas of Karl Marx; 80 mins; EAV 92TF14

6 Socialisation

Most human beings are surrounded by other people with whom they talk and laugh, sing and dance, share a house, play and work. From the smallest group to the largest crowd other people are there and they matter. A man alone on a desert island has no one to share a joke with or to fight. It would not be noticed if he were happy or sad, silent or shouting because no one would be there to notice.

Usually the people around us are in groups. A boy and girl friend are a group of two. In everyday language this group is called 'a couple' but in social science we have a technical word for groups of two – 'a dyad'. 'Two's company but three's a crowd' – no couple wants a gooseberry around! But there are many other types of groups we could belong to. Most of us grow up in families, sometimes with all our relatives living very near to us. We belong to teaching groups or tutor groups in school, to work groups later on, and to youth clubs, or churches, trade unions or football clubs, fan clubs or political parties.

Some of these groups are particularly important to the way people behave and think. We shall see in a later section that a child who grew up with wolves only learned to behave and think like a wolf. We say that she was SOCIALISED into being a wolf. Socialisation is a process of learning in which children and adults take on the feelings and attitudes and ways of behaving in the society around them. The process never really stops because we continue to change our thoughts and our behaviour until we die, so long as there are people around us to influence us in everything we do.

In this section we shall look more closely at the groups involved in socialisation, especially the family and the school. We shall also look at television, newspapers and radio because in the twentieth century they have an effect on our lives which is entirely new.

Three friends chat, exchanging attitudes and opinions. Socialisation continues throughout life.

The family

From the chapter on the Eskimos we have seen that families may be either *nuclear* or *extended*. In many parts of the world changes are occurring in family life, but the family in one form or another continues to be important in almost all societies. In this chapter we shall look at the rules surrounding marriage and the setting up of new families; the importance of the family in caring for children; the roles played by members of the family in Britain; the economic aspects of family life; and roles and role change in families in other societies.

THE SETTING UP OF A NEW FAMILY – MARRIAGE RULES

Marriage rules have developed in most societies so that all the members of the society will know that a new family has been created. The rules and customs vary a lot from one society to another. An example from the Nuer shows this clearly.

The Nuer were a cattle herding group of people who lived in North East Africa. The exact area is shaded on the map, and is called The Sudan. The Nuer way of life is undergoing change now, although some Nuer still follow the traditional ways. This account relates to the period before the Second World War. The Nuer led a rough and difficult life for they had to find food and water for the cattle on which their livelihood depended. Upon the ownership and care of cattle the Nuer's whole life was built. Marriage and family life, work and leisure, language, songs and dances, art and religion were all related to the basic fact that they depended upon their cattle.

Cattle were owned by families. The head of the household might dispose of the herd as he wished and he would own roughly as many

Members of a nuclear family.

cattle as he had members in his family. As each son reached adulthood he would be given some cows from the herd and would choose a wife from a neighbouring village. He would pay cattle to the wife's father in return for a wife who would bear him children. If a girl in the family wanted to marry, her father would receive cattle in payment for her and the herd would be restored to its original size. The brothers all lived close to each other so that the herd could be looked after by all of them and was not split up by one brother moving away. It was the daughters who moved away when they married. This payment for wives is called BRIDEWEALTH. (How does it differ from a DOWRY?)

The Nuer lived in extended families with the small nuclear families living next door to each other. If they did not do this the herd would be split up and would not survive. When any member of the extended family received cattle, the cattle were immediately shared out not only among close nuclear relatives but among all the members of an extended family. Similarly if a man had to exchange cattle for a bride he would not be able to afford the cost on his own, so his relatives would all help him. Sometimes a bride might cost twenty to forty head of cattle.

Once a child was born to a newly married couple, relatives on both sides would try to be at peace with each other because the child and the payment of cattle created a close bond. Any quarrels were likely to be settled quickly between groups who were related as closely as this.

Among the Nuer a woman might be married to the spirit of a dead man and although she might have children of a real flesh and blood man, they might be treated as the children of the dead man, and inherit the dead man's wealth and high rank. A woman who could not have any children could be married to a 'wife' and act as 'father' to the children of the 'wife'.

In this case it was not the REAL father who mattered but the spirit or person who acted as the SOCIAL father.

It can be seen that marriage was helping the children of the family by providing them with inheritance or security; this is the reason for the importance which is given to marriage rules in many societies. Because marriage rules are so different all over the world it is hard to make one simple definition of the word marriage, but often it is defined as 'a union between a woman and in most cases a man in which the woman's children are regarded as legitimate and in which the union is approved of by the society'.

MARRIAGES OF MORE THAN TWO PEOPLE

Usually in the west one man is allowed only one wife. This is called MONOGAMY. However some societies allow marriage between more than two people. This is called POLYGAMY. There are two sorts of polygamy:

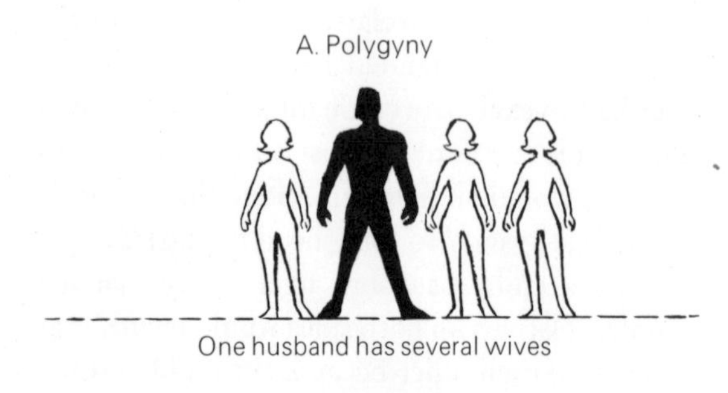

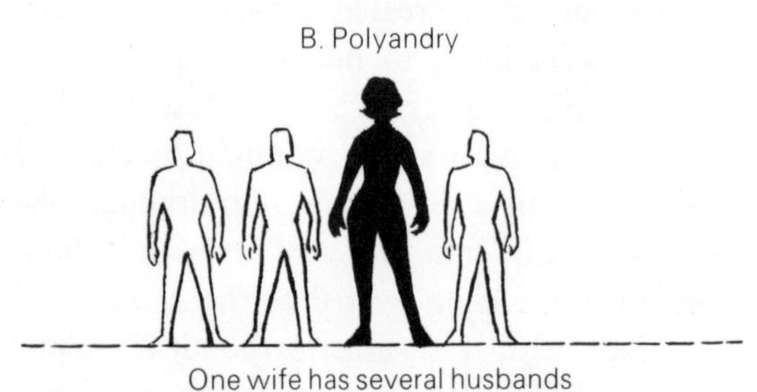

Figure 33

DIVORCE IN BRITAIN

In Britain, a minority of marriages do not last and here we shall look briefly at the break-up of families.

Several hundred years ago, divorce was possible only by an Act of Parliament and only the upper classes could afford the procedure. In the nineteenth century the procedure was transferred to the law courts, but it was still very expensive. Working-class and middle-class people could rarely afford divorce until 1949 when legal aid was started. People whose marriages had broken down were then, for the first time, able to afford to end them legally in Court and since that date many marriages already broken in the home have been ended by divorce. Sometimes it appears that there is a high divorce rate in Britain so the statistics have to be looked at very carefully. Some important points must be made.

1 One-third of couples getting divorced have been married over twenty years and their children are grown up. Many divorces therefore do not involve small children.
2 People live longer these days so married couples have to put up with their partner for longer than they did a hundred years ago. This puts more strain on the marriage so we would expect more divorces.
3 Most divorced people (seventy out of every hundred) re-marry so divorce has enabled them to free themselves from their wrong first choice.
4 The fact that divorce is possible does not cause people's marriages to break up. It makes it possible to free people from marriages which are already broken.
5 Only seven out of every hundred British couples get divorced. The other ninety-three couples stay married.

Since the Divorce Reform Act of 1969 the only reason for sueing for divorce is 'irretrievable breakdown of the marriage'. This means that the marriage is broken and cannot be mended. Neither husband nor wife is made to feel guilty or to take the blame. It is recognised that it takes two people either to make or to break a marriage. Irretrievable breakdown can be caused by one or more of the following situations:

(*a*) one partner commits adultery and the other wants a divorce
(*b*) one partner finds it impossible to live with the other because of his or her behaviour, e.g. physical or mental cruelty
(*c*) one partner has been deserted for two years
(*d*) the couple have lived apart for two years and both want a divorce
(*e*) the couple have lived apart for five years and one of them wants a divorce.

People have very many different opinions on the moral issues involved in divorce. The social scientist takes a careful look at the statistics and tries to make sure that people do not exaggerate them. It is not the job of the social scientist to say which of the moral issues are right or wrong.

NEW FAMILIES

Through marriage a person starts a new family. Here is a diagram showing that each individual can belong to two nuclear families.

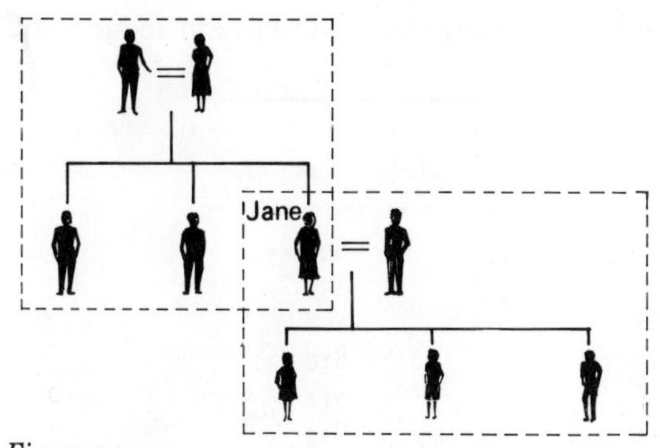

Figure 34

The first family is Jane's original nuclear family into which she was born. The second family is Jane's new nuclear family of marriage. Obviously the new family does not exist unless Jane has children of her own. In this diagram how many daughters and sons does she have?

FAMILY SIZE

In Britain, the average size of families has been decreasing steadily since the late nineteenth century, as shown on the next chart.

Year of marriage	*Number of children in the nuclear family*
1860	6
1880	5
1890	4
1920	3
1930	2
1950	2

Figures from: Kelsall *Population* and Marsh *The Changing Social Structure of England and Wales.*

There are several reasons for the fall in nuclear family size. The most important one is that the upper classes and middle classes began to realise that with rising prices in the late nineteenth century they could no longer afford to support so many children at a high standard of living. They began to think that birth control was useful and morally right and to use the methods available to them at that time. Today couples have more methods available, especially new methods like 'the pill' but these were not used by the couples of the early twentieth century. The working classes began to accept birth control later than the rest of society and until very recently their family size was slightly larger than that of other families. Today family size varies slightly according to social class. This chart, using the Registrar-General's classification, shows that people in social class 1 have slightly larger families, and so do people in social class 5. (Registrar-General's classification, see p. 124). The reasons are different in each case. Can you think of the reasons?

	Social class	*Number of children in the nuclear family in 1961*
1	Professional workers	1·69
2	Employers and managers in large organisations	1·81
3	Junior non-manual	1·20
	Skilled manual	1·36
4	Semi-skilled	1·47
5	Unskilled	1·74

Figures from Kelsall, *Population* p. 56.
The families have not finished having all their children.
The wives were married when they were 20–24.

ROLES WITHIN THE NUCLEAR FAMILY IN BRITAIN

In Britain the most usual form of the family is the nuclear family, but some people have members of their extended family living within a short travelling distance. Over the past hundred years there have been great changes in the roles played by the members of the nuclear family and in particular the part played by the wife and mother.

One hundred years ago the upper class wife was seen only as an ornament in her household. All her property belonged to her husband, who had the authority in the house, and who could even forbid her seeing her children if he chose to do so. The wife was not expected or allowed to go to work, and her children were looked after by a nanny, so that she had nothing to do all day but entertain her friends and her husband's guests. In other words she led a life of enforced leisure. Some upper class women were unfortunate enough not to be able to find husbands (because more male babies died than female babies, and many males were killed in the wars). These women had no choice but to become the maiden aunts of the households. Middle class wives were in a similar position to upper class wives, but for wives in the working class, life was very different. Some working class wives had to work to help with the money shortage in the home. Long hours were spent working in the fields in country areas or in the factories in the cities.

Many of these wives had to work even when pregnant, and went straight back to work after giving birth, when the older daughters or relatives would look after the babies. Life in the working class was tough. Houses were overcrowded and lacked sanitation; epidemics of cholera and smallpox, diphtheria and typhoid were common and killed many people. Children slept many to a room, often sharing their parents' room, food was scarce and hours at work were long. Under these conditions men and women only expected to live to about forty.

		Sex ratios	
Year	*Females*	*Males under 45*	*Males 45 and over*
1901	1,000	955	866
1931	1,000	949	852
1951	1,000	1,008	808
1961	1,000	1,027	810
1971	1,000	1,038	811
1974	1,000	1,041	811

Source: *Social Trends No. 6* 1975

Wives and mothers at work (1971 Census figures)

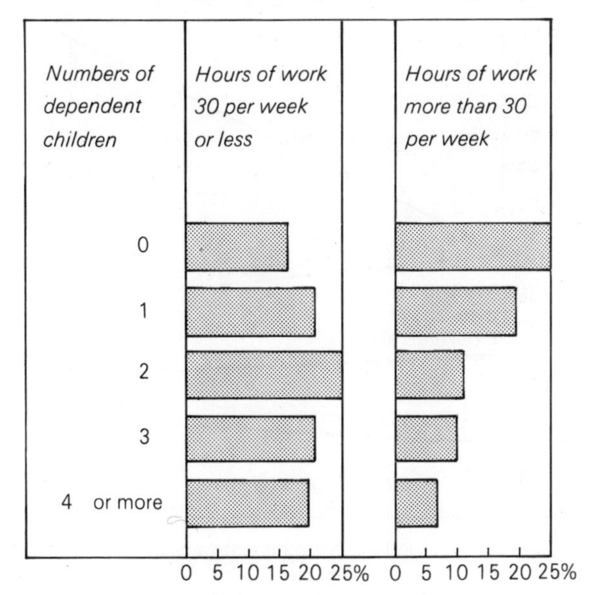

Source: *Social Trends* 1976

Many children died because medical care and food were scarce and the housing conditions were so bad. Their mothers, worn out by years of childbirth, nursing, overwork and hardship, were old by the time they were thirty. Many of the roles played by women have changed considerably since the nineteenth century.

Figure 35 This is a role diagram for a woman today. Are there more roles which you could add to this diagram?

Women's work roles

In the 1970s many women go out to work when they are married. Upper and middle class women are now allowed to work or encouraged to do so, and working class wives are freed from the great poverty of hundred years ago although we know that poverty still exists in Britain (see chapter 2).

The following chart shows that there are more women workers in the labour force today and that more of them are married:

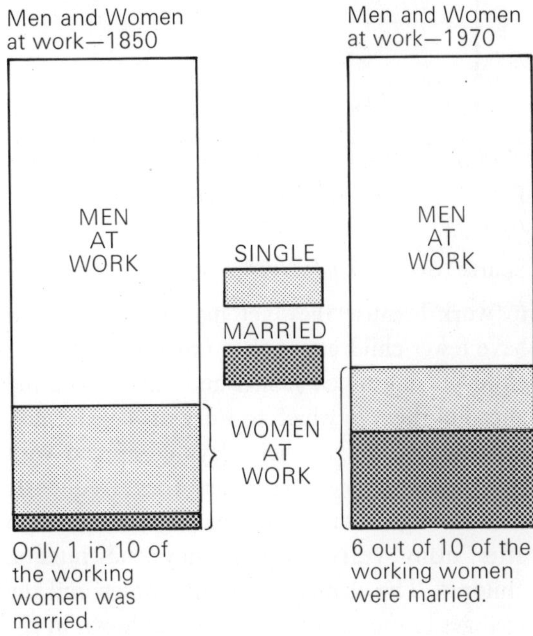

Figure 36

In a book by G. Routh,* figures are given showing the type of work done by men and by women in 1959.

Since 1951 many more married women have gone out to work. There was nearly full employment, a wider choice of jobs, better educational opportunity, an increased demand for highly qualified people, and therefore more married women were needed at work. They are able to go

**Occupation and Pay in Great Britain* 1906–60 C.U.P. 1965.

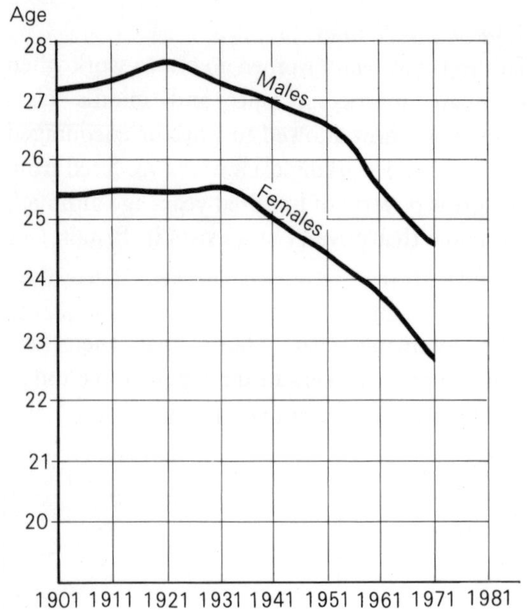

Figure 37 *Changes in average age of first marriage 1901–73*

Source: *Social Trends No. 6* 1975

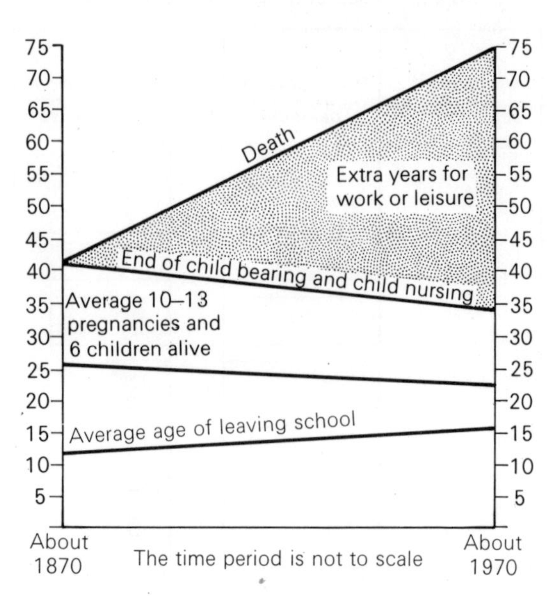

Figure 38 Women's changed living-pattern.

to work because they get married earlier and have fewer children, so they finish their days of child-nursing much sooner and have a long life ahead of them in which to work or have leisure. Women live longer these days compared with the nineteenth century when they frequently died young from disease or from exhaustion after many years of pregnancy and nursing children. The changing lives of women and the changes in the age of marriage are shown in the diagrams above.

ECONOMIC ASPECTS OF FAMILY LIFE

If a mother goes out to work then she is playing an important economic role in her family, whether she lives just with her nuclear family or whether granny also lives with her, extending the family .

In simple societies like the Eskimos, the Bushmen and the Indian village, the family, either in nuclear or extended form, works together to produce goods. Survival is only possible if each member of the family co-operates with the others to get the work done.

In Britain the situation is different. Although some families in the country and in cities work together in a shop, small business, farm, or tiny factory which they own, in most families the members do different work. In cities, the father's job is usually away from home and other members of the family cannot help him with it. The mother often looks after the children when they are small and then goes to work when they are older. The family is an economic unit in the sense that the members earn money which goes into the 'family fund' and from which they pay for rent (or mortgage if they are buying their flat or house), food, fuel and lighting, furniture, clothes, entertainment and other expenses. But the family is not an economic unit in the same sense as the Eskimo family is, for it does not actually *make* what it needs.

In 1976, total consumer expenditure was divided:

Housing	13·1%
Fuel, light, power	5·5%
Food	24·8%
Alcohol	5·1%
Tobacco	3·6%
Clothing and footwear	8·7%
Household goods	15·0%
Transport and vehicles	13·8%
Services	9·9%
Miscellaneous	0·5%

Source: *Annual Abstract of Statistics* 1976

In many nuclear families where there is a working wife the husband's role has changed considerably. The husband and wife may make joint decisions on family matters. Both may take turns in caring for the children, and in sharing the household tasks. They may do the shopping together and act as equal partners in many aspects of their marriage. Sometimes the married couple have a joint savings account, know exactly what the other one earns, and own or rent their house in their joint names.

Copy and complete the following chart.

FAMILY IN AN INDUSTRIAL SOCIETY	FAMILY IN A NON-INDUSTRIAL SOCIETY
Items used and made entirely at home	
Items used and made partly at home	
Items used at home but made elsewhere and bought by the family	

ROLES WITHIN THE EXTENDED FAMILY IN BRITAIN

Although the nuclear family is the most common in Britain today, some people live in the same house as their extended family or in separate houses but very close by. Usually it will be the woman in such a family who stays near her relatives. The husband is likely to move with the wife to live near her relatives. This situation is most common in old established parts of large cities, and also in mining and fishing areas where there is only one choice of job for the menfolk. In some families like this the roles of husband and wife have changed less over the years than in the nuclear families just discussed. For example the men would regard 'caring for the children' as 'woman's work' with which by tradition they do not help.

Two examples are often mentioned when the extended family is being described. The first is Bethnal Green in East London and the second includes mining towns like those in Yorkshire.

In Bethnal Green a few years ago people knew those around them very well. Many nuclear families had grandparents, aunts and uncles living within five minutes' walk, or even nearer. Some people had these relatives living in the same house so they lived with their extended family. A married woman spent her days looking after the children of pre-school age, visiting her mother, her sisters and other relatives. Generations of families would live, work and spend their leisure time together. Often the men of the extended family would congregate at the pub in the evening and frequently they were accompanied by wives and sisters-in-law. When some families had to be rehoused on to an estate several miles away many wives were distressed at the loneliness when this company and friendship had gone.

Within the family the day to day activities were clearly divided into women's and men's roles. This is very similar to the miners' lives described by Henriques and Slaughter in the book *Coal is our Life*. Young children are taught

Grandparents often play an important part in the socialisation of children.

the roles which they will perform when they grow up, with male and female roles more clearly divided than among other working class and middle class nuclear families. Boys are not expected to help at home because men would think this was sissy. The tough dangerous life in the mines excludes women and this has an effect on home life and leisure. Teen-age boys meet as a gang and adult men meet in the pub, club and betting office. Girls remain closely attached to their female relatives and friends before and during marriage, and the whole running of the house is women's work. The men's leisure may include sports such as cricket and rugby which are seen as strong and energetic like their work. Women do not accompany their husbands to the pub.

If men help with the children at all it is more likely that they will take an interest in their sons, e.g. by taking them to the cinema or to the park. When people get old this division of roles sometimes decreases. Older women are seen in the pubs and grandfathers visit their daughters and daughters-in-law to play with the small children. This occurs even more often if the grandmother has died.

In the middle class it is more unusual for extended families to live close to each other, but they keep in touch by letters, phone calls and visits in the car. In a book called *Middle Class Families* by Colin Bell written in 1968, several examples are given. Some middle-class parents will pay for their married daughters to have a home help when the grandchildren are born. Others will buy expensive gifts like bicycles and swings for their grandchildren. Married couples may ask their parents for loans to buy a car and to help with the deposit on a house. The extended family is therefore very important in the middle class but in a different way from traditional working-class areas like Bethnal Green and the mining towns.

A traditional marriage ceremony in the Palace of Weddings, Lugansk.

ROLES AND ROLE – CHANGE IN FAMILIES IN OTHER SOCIETIES

Four examples can be described which show a very different situation from that in Britain.

Russia

After the revolution in 1917, the leaders wanted to change everything in the society so that none of the traditional ways remained to hinder the new life. The family in old Russia had been very important in maintaining the old traditions so it was decided to change completely the style of family life. Marriages were no longer arranged and people did not have to register their marriages, so if couples were living together for any length of time this was regarded as a legal marriage. Divorce was made very easy, the couple having only to sign a divorce form, and abortion was legal.

Many advantages arose from these changes, e.g. sex was freed from superstition and people could talk openly and frankly with each other about their relationships. Children had more rights and freedom and women were equal to men in all ways. However there were also many problems which had not been foreseen. In some cases girls found themselves abandoned if they became pregnant for the man could easily move away. In other cases close-knit families found it difficult to get used to the new idea that the family was not important. Other problems also arose because not enough babies were being born in the society. This was made worse by the high abortion rate, and by 1937 the population was 13 million below what had been expected, so there were not enough adult workers. Some husbands and wives were forcibly separated if one of them was moved from an area of unemployment to a place where work was available. In some areas young people had no emotional ties at all and this led to crime and delinquency. Therefore by the late 1930s the leaders began to think again. They decided that perhaps the family had been broken down too much, and it became the policy of the state once again to strengthen the family ties. Marriage was considered to be important and divorce was made not only harder but almost impossible due to the high charges which were introduced. In 1944 it became necessary to register all marriages in a registry office. Many people thought that abortion should remain legal because of the badly overcrowded housing conditions, but the government disagreed. Children were encouraged to obey their parents and their freedom was now restricted.

Therefore in the Russia of the 1970s the situation within the family is much more like the situation in Britain. The family is seen as a strong, stable and important unit of society. Opinions vary in both Britain and Russia as to the importance of the family.

Yunusat Musaev and his family listen to Madjuda Ahemdova talking about the elections to the Supreme Soviet of the Uzbek S.S.R.

Samoa. Mulliner Village on the island of Upolu.

A Samoan girl in national costume breaks open a coconut.

Samoa

Samoa is a non-industrial island in the Pacific Ocean where people live more simply than in Britain and the society combines ways of life which include hunting and gathering, herding and farming. Samoa is changing rather quickly in the 1970s with the introduction of formal education, so that the way of life described here is becoming out of date. The following account is adapted from the study of Samoa in the 1930s and 1940s by the anthropologist, Margaret Mead.

A Samoan village was made up of about thirty to forty households, each of which was presided over by a headman called a *matai*. In the village assembly each matai had his place, and represented the members of his household. These households included all the people who lived for any length of time under the authority and protection of a particular matai. The households varied from those which included only the biological family consisting of parents and children, to those of fifteen and twenty people who were all related to the matai or to his wife by blood, marriage or adoption, but who often had little close relationship to one another. The adopted members of a household were usually, but not always, distant relatives.

Today Samoan life is changing. This is the local bus in Tutuila Island; it has a thatched roof made of coconut leaves.

Within the household, disciplinary authority depended entirely on age. The newest baby born into a household was below every other individual and his position did not improve until a younger child appeared upon the scene. At adolescence a girl stood in the middle with as many individuals who must obey her as there were persons whom she must obey.

Relatives in other households also played a role in children's lives. Any older relative had a right to demand personal service from younger relatives, a right to criticise their conduct and to interfere in their affairs. So a little girl might escape down to the beach to bathe only to be met by an older cousin who set her washing clothes or caring for a baby. However there were some compensations. A child of three could wander safely and come to no harm, could be sure of finding food and drink, a sheet to wrap herself up for the night, a kind hand to dry casual tears. Any small children who were missing when night fell were simply 'sought among their kinsfolk', and a baby whose mother had gone inland to work on the plantation was passed from hand to hand for the length of the visit. A relative was regarded as someone upon whom one had many claims and to whom one owed many duties. From a relative one could demand food, clothing, and shelter, or assistance in a quarrel. Refusal of such a kindness branded one as stingy and lacking in human kindness, the virtue the Samoans rated most highly.

So the needs and duties of the larger relationship group cut across the life of the household. One day the wife's relatives would come to spend a month or borrow a fine mat; the next day the husband's; the third a niece who was a valued worker in the household might be called home by the illness of her father. Very seldom

The Samoans are friendly. Here on Raiatea Island they wear traditional costume while entertaining visitors with dancing and singing.

did all of even the small children of a biological family live in one household.

Work was divided up according to the age, strength and sex of the people. The women stuffed the pigs for roasting and did the less strenuous cooking jobs, and the men did the heavy work of cooking like cutting up the carcasses, and cutting up the coconuts which the boys and women had gathered. Girls and women had to be able to tell when the food in the oven of heated stones was ready for eating. Men did the skilled and tough deep sea fishing, often handling the canoes in storms and rough weather. Women and girls would look for jelly fish, crabs and other small fish along the edges of the reef. It was this reef fishing which the small boys learned at a very early age as a preparation for deep sea fishing when they grew up.

The strong young women worked in the plantations, weeding, transplanting, gathering and carrying the food. When a girl was old enough and strong enough to do this she stopped being a baby minder and was considered grown up. Now, too, she was taught to weave by the old women, who did the bulk of the weaving, making dark cloth from the bark of the paper-mulberry plant which was grown in the plantations.

The old men made thread by spinning together the fibres of the coconut. They then used this to make fishing nets and fishing lines, to sew parts of canoes together, and to make into rope for lashing together timbers, etc., for house-building.

Tasks were given to people according to their abilities and to a large extent this depended on their age. In general a task was given up because someone younger had become skilled enough to do it, and not because it was beneath the older persons' dignity.

The Eskimos

A team of anthropologists visited the Netsilik Eskimos during the early 1960s. The Eskimos were asked to act out or 'reconstruct' their old way of life so that it could be filmed in detail, never to be forgotten by future generations.

But for some Eskimos disaster followed the white man into their territory. Many Eskimos died from tuberculosis and other diseases, brought by the newcomers. With the use of guns, too many caribou were killed and the herds were depleted, leading to food shortages. Their old skills are useless in a world of machines. They have lost their old jobs but many Eskimos have not yet found anything satisfactory to replace the wonders and fears of hunting on the ice and tundra. Schools have been built for children who were not used to sitting at desks and houses have been built for families who were used to a nomadic way of life.

In a confusing world the old division of labour into male and female roles is no longer meaningful. The mass media bring continuous jangling noise into a world used only to the wide open spaces filled with the sound of human

For many centuries kayaks have been very important to Eskimos. Although they are now being replaced by larger vessels with motors, they are still used, particularly in the remoter areas, for travelling and hunting.

A party in an igloo in Canada.

Modern forms of transport have brought many changes. An Eskimo family poses in front of an aeroplane.

Christianshaab, Greenland, viewed from the inner part of the fjord.

Canada's modern Eskimos: here workers are seen glazing fish.

Eskimo children on Kulusuk Island, Greenland. The modern village is in the background.

voices, dogs barking, storms raging and ice cracking. Perhaps most important of all to the Eskimo is his feeling of being cheated out of the land which he believed to belong to him, his father before him, and his grandfather before that. Some Eskimos fill the vacuum in life with vandalism, promiscuous behaviour, crime and alcoholism. The name given to the meeting of two very different societies is CULTURE CONTACT.

At first, it nearly destroyed the whole of Eskimo society. Very recently, however, some Eskimo groups have begun co-operative communities, with the help of grants from the government. For example Pelly Bay, Canada, see *Canada and the Canadians* by George Woodcock. The Eskimo co-operative runs fish and handicraft marketing services, a fur-trading post, a bakery, a laundry, rubbish collection and fuel oil services. There is also a coffee shop and a tourist office. Such co-operatives may give back to the Eskimos independence and pride. They combine some of the traditions of the Arctic with modern machinery and development of the economy. The world is changing very quickly and the future generations of Eskimos will have to decide whether they will stay in the Arctic settlements or move to towns further south.

Children in kibbutzim leave their parents each night and sleep in Children's Houses, which are split into age groups.

Israel

One of the greatest changes in Israel since it became a State has been the development of co-operative villages of smallholders and collective farms. Both of these are based mainly on agriculture but there are important differences in the family life of the members of the villages.

The Moshav Ovdim is the name given to villages of farming families where each family works for itself on a smallholding but shares some of the machinery with the rest of the village and co-operates in buying and selling and in running the affairs of the community through the council. There are about 350 such villages including about 124,000 people.

The kibbutz (plural: kibbutzim) is the name given to a type of farming village where the members are divided into working men and women, their old parents, their young children and teenagers. A kibbutz couple lives in a single room which acts as a bedroom/living-room. The meals are eaten in a communal dining-room and the children are reared separately by nannies in children's houses. The working men are usually employed in agriculture but they also do work like building, factory work and

A view of the Kibbutz Yoyvata.

plumbing and other jobs needed by a community which provides everything for itself. The working women usually run the transport services, kitchens and laundries. They also teach and do the secretarial work.

Everything is done for the community as a whole and not for individual families. The produce of the fields provides income from which each member of the community gets food, clothing and other necessities of life. The children eat, sleep and spend most of their time in the children's houses and their parents are not responsible for their physical or social upbringing. As the children get older they move with their age group from one children's house to another so the kibbutz acts like a large extended family. Children know and visit their parents and call them father and mother. The parents' idea is that they are entrusting their children into special care to be brought up according to the rules with which the parents have agreed.

After high school the boys and girls live in separate rooms. They are not encouraged to have sexual relationships but if they wish to they are allowed. Those who want to live together permanently apply for a double room

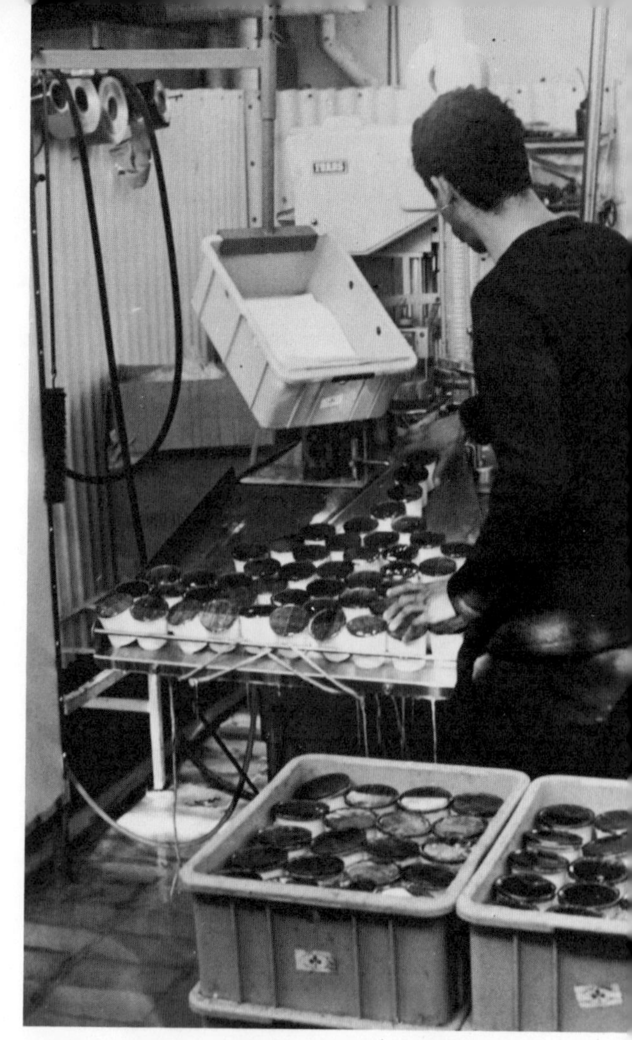

Yotvata Kibbutz – inside the dairy.

The kitchen in Ammiad Kibbutz, Upper Galilee.

A group of young kibbutz workers eat in the communal dining-room. Military training is a part of the daily life and after their meal they will discuss the theoretical military problem sketched on the board behind them.

and they usually marry on the birth of their first child, for the laws of the State put illegitimate children at a disadvantage. Their marriage is based on the physical and strong psychological need for one person. It is this long-term security and companionship which separates married couples from short-term couples. Women retain their original name and belong to the kibbutz in their own right. All members of a kibbutz are free to leave when they wish.

In 1964 B. Bettleheim visited a kibbutz of three hundred people formed by East European Jews in 1932. Some of his impressions are written in the book *The Children of the Dream.* He suggests that children are very secure and never suffer from neglect or from quarrelling parents or broken homes. There is a decrease in mental illness and delinquency, and there is no drug dependence. The old are secure and cared for. However he also suggests that although women are freed from child-rearing, they are mainly involved in housework, e.g. tasks like cooking, sewing and laundry, so their role is still traditional. Children seemed to be weaned early and were sometimes left alone at night, and criticism was made of the strain put on adolescents in mixed dormitories.

Some critics of the kibbutz system suggest that children may become so used to the security of the community that they become slow to take responsibility as individuals. Research on this and other aspects of communal living is being started by Professor Abrams in Britain where there are several communes scattered throughout the country. Some like the kibbutz include old and young people, whilst others are composed of one age group only. Very few are agricultural. Some are religious whilst others are based on non-religious principles.

In the meantime about 90,000 people share kibbutz life in Israel. Some of the young people may leave in the future to to go college and into the armed forces. Whether they return will depend on how this change affects their attitudes to life on a kibbutz.

. . . his emotional needs are love and affection . . . his physical needs are food, shelter and warmth. This modern Eskimo mother is from Greenland.

Caring for children

Because the human baby takes so many years to reach adulthood he must be cared for by adults who are in close contact with him. His physical needs are food, shelter and warmth (for which he needs clothes in our society because it is too cold to do without them). His emotional needs are love and affection. He must learn which things are important, the correct thing to say and which actions are right and wrong. Thus the older people around him are teaching him the VALUES he will hold when he grows up. He also has to learn SKILLS. The most basic skills are movement and speech.

DEPRIVED OR ISOLATED CHILDREN

There are several examples of children who have suffered very severe deprivation. We cannot know for certain that these are completely true cases, but they are interesting to think about.

Kamala

The story of Kamala tells about a child deprived of any contact with human beings. She was thought to have been born to an Indian family earlier this century. When she was a baby playing out in the garden near her parents' remote home, she was stolen by a she-wolf who carried her away (the wolf probably clutched her clothes in its teeth). People searched for Kamala but no one found her. Probably she survived by suckling the mother wolf as the cubs did, until she could fend for herself.

Years later, a story spread around the village of a ghost-like creature prowling with the wolf pack at night. Terrified villagers told the local pastor, who investigated the situation. He found that, instead of a ghost, there was a girl with long filthy matted hair. She ran on all fours and snarled, baring her teeth. When she was captured she crouched in the corner of the yard into which she was locked and howled to the moon.

She was led to the orphanage. And at the orphanage it took Kamala many months, and it took much thoughtful, gentle, patient handling on the part of the minister and his wife, before Kamala was able to change from animal to human ways.

But gradually she learned to like daytime better than night. Gradually she learned to kneel at the table (it was difficult at first for her to stand or even kneel as her knees were very stiff) and to eat the same kind of food that others did. She learned to trust the people at the orphanage. She realised that she was not going to be ill-treated. She was estimated to be eight years old. She learned to accept cooked meat, and to refuse to eat raw dead animals. She began to stop howling and to become friendly. Over a period of years, she gradually came to walk upright and to use muscles that she had never used before. By imitating the humans with whom she was now in close contact, she learned a few words of the Indian language and began to wear clothes.

Kamala died at eighteen or nineteen. She died of an illness but one can hazard the guess that the strain of the change had been too great. But she had made a bridge between the animal life of the wolf pack and human life, based on language, skills, and affection.

(Adapted from Gesell, *Wolf Child and Human Child*)

Kamala's experiences can be compared with those of Anna and Isabelle. These cases are adapted from the detailed accounts by Kingsley Davis who saw both of the children.

Anna

Anna was illegitimate and her grandfather disapproved so much of her mother's behaviour that he had Anna kept in an upstairs room. She was only given just enough attention to keep her alive. When she was found at the age of six, her clothes and bedding were filthy and she could not talk or walk or do anything that showed intelligence. All she did was to lie quietly without responding to anything around her. How she survived at all is a mystery for she was deprived of almost all contact with human beings, including love and affection, and the sound of the human voice.

Anna died four and a half years after she was found. She had not received skilled help, but she had learned a few words, and she walked well although she was clumsy when she ran. She could follow simple instructions, build bricks and play with her doll. It is possible that she was feeble minded but it is hard to tell how far she would have progressed if she had not died and if she had had skilled adults helping her. Hers is an example of very extreme isolation and deprivation.

Isabelle

Her case is very similar to Anna's, for she was isolated because she was illegitimate, and she was found at the same age and at approximately the same time. However she had spent most of her time with her mother in a dark room and therefore she had more contact than Anna had with another person. Her mother was deaf and dumb so they could only communicate by gestures and Isabelle had no one to imitate in order to learn to talk. When she was found she could not walk properly or talk or respond to other human beings. She was very hostile and frightened. She was thought to be feeble minded but those in charge of her decided to train her in a systematic way. Very skilfully, they taught her to speak, read, count and respond normally. Once she could talk, she made very rapid progress and entered school and took part in all the activities as normally as other children. By the age of eight and a half she was normal, which means that she made up for her six lost years in the short time of two and a half years.

Isabelle had been deprived like Anna and Kamala but she had some human love and affection (from her mother) and had skilful help when she was found so she was able to adapt more quickly to human society than either of the other two girls.

Copy the following chart and use it to compare Kamala, Anna and Isabelle.

	Kamala	*Anna*	*Isabelle*
Success in learning to walk			
Communication with human beings			
Adaptation to human company			
Ability to give and receive affection			
Length of life			

What do we find about the needs of children from these comparisons? The experiences of these children show what the needs of children are and that their development is hindered if those needs are not satisfied.

NORMAL DEVELOPMENT

As a baby grows he begins to respond to other people in many different ways, and gradually realises that he is a separate person. He has to develop in both mind and body. The physical growth of the body continues until the age of about eighteen, and is known as MATURATION. The development of the mind is called mental growth and goes on at the same time as physical growth.

LANGUAGE is one of the skills a child must learn if he is to communicate with other humans. Recent work by scientists shows that many animals communicate in quite a complicated way. Baboons, for example, are now thought to use twenty-two different sounds as well as body movements and facial expressions. Humans differ from animals in their very complicated, highly developed use of language.

This chart shows language development in a group of American children

	Age in years and months (from Smith, M. E., *Child Welfare Study Centre in Iowa*)												
	0–8 *mths*	0–10 *mths*	1 *yr*	1 *yr* 3 *mths*	1 *yr* 6 *mths*	1 *yr* 9 *mths*	2 *yrs*	2 *yrs* 6 *mths*	3 *yrs*	3 *yrs* 6 *mths*	4 *yrs*	4 *yrs* 6 *mths*	5 *yrs*
Words used	0	1	3	19	22	118	272	446	896	1,222	1,540	1,870	2,072
					Nouns, verbs and adjectives are used. Very short sentences are made			Language grows more complicated. Sentences become longer and are joined together					

Statistics from *The Psychological Development of the Child*, P. H. Mussen (Prentice-Hall), p. 42.

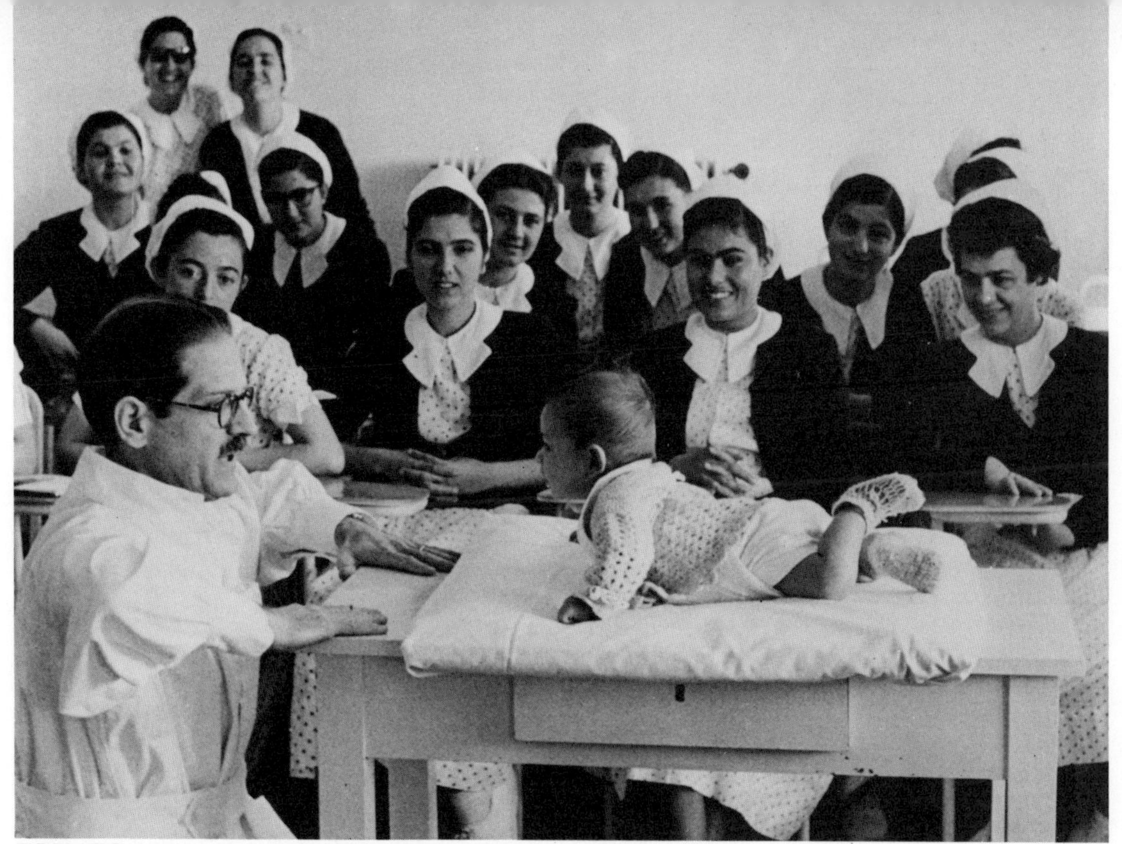

A Greek doctor demonstrates to a class of nurses what a normal contented baby's responses should be.

Figure 39 *Babies develop at different rates.*

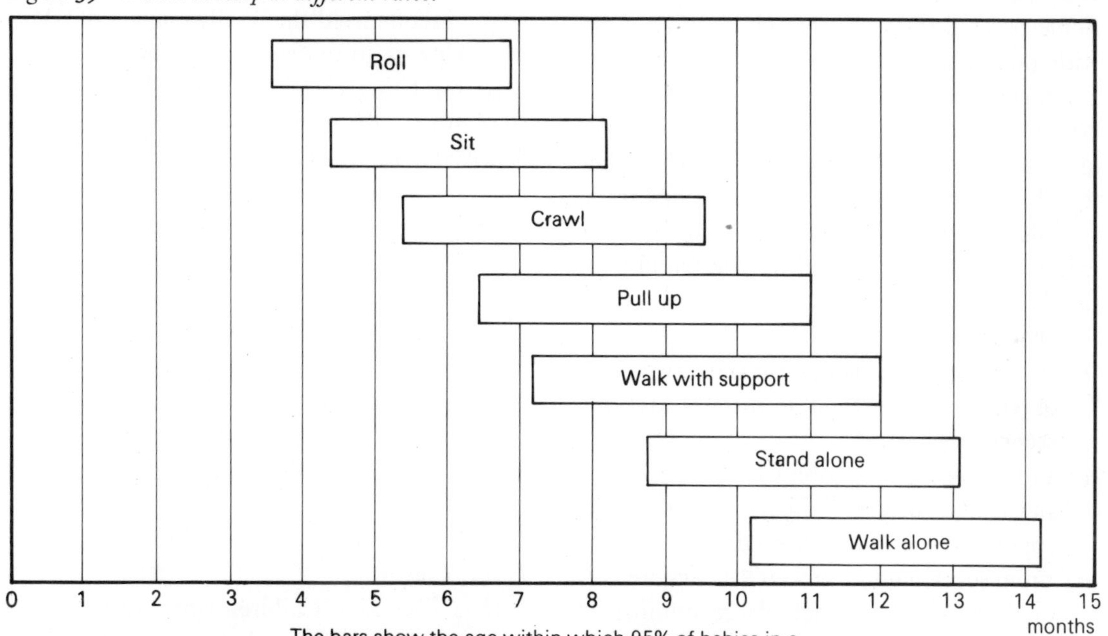

The bars show the age within which 95% of babies in a well-baby clinic (in the USA) achieved these actions (from Hilgard: Introduction to Psychology p. 71, Methuen)

Emotional development
In the early part of the chart below the baby can only use sounds and facial expressions. One of the first signs that a baby is learning to respond to others is his smile when he sees a face. At first it does not matter whether the face belongs to a stranger or to someone he knows. He will even smile at a mask, so long as it bobs around near to him. An American study noted the percentage of babies at various ages who would smile at a strange human face.

Age of babies	*Percentage smiling at a strange human face*
0–20 days	0
21 days–2 months	2
2 months–6 months	98
6 months–12 months	3

(From Hilgard, *Introduction to Psychology*)

Why do children smile at anyone after they are two months old? When do they begin to choose whom to smile at? Why do they do this? Some psychologists say that children are born with the ability to cry but that the ability to laugh comes only as they grow older. Children cry to gain attention or sympathy, and they learn to hold back tears sometimes when they feel like crying. One psychologist kept careful records of the expression of emotion by sixty infants in a hospital in Canada. He found that:

(*a*) At birth babies show no emotion except general excitement.
(*b*) By three months babies can show two types of emotion. The first is distress and the second is pleasure.
(*c*) From five months babies are able to show anger and disgust which, at this stage, appear to be different from distress.
(*d*) From seven months onwards babies are able to show an increasingly large number of emotions including fear, very intense pleasure (elation) and affection.

Babies are thought to develop these emotions by INSTINCT but later they LEARN when to show emotion, what effect the emotions will have, and how to express all that they are feeling.

Harlow's experiment
In 1959 an American psychologist called H. F. Harlow did a series of experiments to investigate the behaviour of monkeys. In one experiment two artificial mother monkeys were made, one of wire and one of cuddly terry towelling. Each one had a body, head, face and breasts from which the baby monkey could suck milk.

The young monkey preferred to cling to the soft cuddly model mother, which was a source of security to the young monkey. Even when the wire model mother gave more food, the baby monkey liked the cuddly mother better. Using the cuddly mother as a base, the young monkey was willing to explore objects around him. If he was very frightened he would show fewer signs of fear if he could be reassured by contact with the soft mother. This experiment shows that young infants need the bodily contact of adults and helps us to understand the human baby's need for being carried and fondled and kept close to a mother or mother-substitute. Children deprived of this contact and security may experience a slowing up or other damage to their emotional development.

CHILD CARE OUTSIDE THE FAMILY IN BRITAIN

Child care today outside the family is divided between local councils and famous voluntary societies like the NSPCC and the Dr Barnado's Homes.

Local councils

1834 *Poor Law* Children who had no family had only the workhouse to go to.

1889–1908 There were several Acts relating

to neglected children or to ill treatment or those in moral danger.

1933 *Children and Young Persons Act* Parents who neglected children could be taken to court. Children 'in need of care or protection' could be removed from home.

1945 *Curtis Committee* People were worried that children in foster homes were not being properly looked after. This led to a big inquiry being made. The idea of foster homes continued to grow providing they were closely supervised.

1948 *Children's Act* Local Councils had to have a CHILDREN'S OFFICER and a CHILDREN'S DEPARTMENT to provide foster homes and children's homes. The Act said that local councils should work closely with the NSPCC.

1952 *Children and Young Persons' Act* This Act stated that children should be looked after in families wherever possible. Keeping the family together and the prevention of distress were thought to be important.

1963 *Children and Young Persons' Act* This Act increased the powers of the local councils to take action to prevent or remove any conditions that might lead to delinquency or to the need for child care outside the home.

1968 The idea developed that the health, welfare and children's services should be grouped together in a FAMILY SERVICE in the local council.

Education

In simple societies children learn their adult roles through play and imitating the older members of their families. Among the Bushmen, from an early age children become accustomed to life in the Kalahari desert, and as they grow older they can take more responsibility, and play a greater role in the work of the family.

In this chapter we shall look at education within the family both in Britain and in simple societies. We shall look at education in schools and other special institutions in Britain, and also consider the future of education in forty or fifty years' time, when adults may be spending very little time at work and so have to occupy themselves during long periods of leisure time.

Children are always learning, whether at school, in the home, or playing with their friends. In a simple society, where there are

A nursery class in Tokyo. Do you think there should be more nursery schools in this country?

A farm school in Kenya. These boys will learn about hygiene and improved farming methods as well as being taught to read and write.

Formal education – an infant classroom in Japan.

fewer jobs and fewer skills, all that a child learns as he grows is taught to him by his family and friends. Whenever learning takes place outside school, it is called INFORMAL EDUCATION. Education in the classroom is called FORMAL EDUCATION.

INSTINCT AND LEARNING

Although some behaviour may be INSTINCTIVE a great deal may be the result of LEARNING, and this learning can be either conscious or unconscious.

We do not have to learn to blink or swallow or to move our hand quickly from something very hot. But we do have to learn which things are hot so that we can avoid them in the first place. Several studies of animal behaviour show that both instinct and learning may be important to young animals. Psychologists are now trying to see if the animal studies can help them to understand the behaviour of human babies.

Do kittens learn to kill mice or does it come 'naturally' by instinct?

One psychologist studied the behaviour of kittens which had been brought up in different ways.

Group 1 The kittens were brought up together with a mouse or rat.

Group 2 The kittens were brought up alone after weaning.

Group 3 The kittens were brought up with their mothers and they saw their mothers kill a mouse or rat every few days.

Of those brought up with a mouse or rat three out of eighteen killed an animal but none killed an animal with which it had been brought up.

Of those brought up alone nine out of eighteen killed animals.

Of those who had seen their mothers killing, eighteen out of twenty-four were killers.

Did the kittens learn to kill when they were brought up without their mothers? How would you explain the behaviour of the kittens?

How do ducklings find out how they should behave?

Another psychologist has done work with baby ducklings. When they are hatched they go through a critical time when they must see an adult duck (usually the mother). They follow the thing which they see in this time and if by some chance they see a human, or a moving cardboard box instead of an adult duck, then they instinctively follow the human or the box. Only by following the adult duck can they learn the way ducks should behave and grow up to be 'proper' adult ducks themselves.

Do the ducklings find out by (*a*) instinct alone, (*b*) learning alone, or (*c*) both?

Do human babies attach themselves to adults in this way? What happens to human babies who find themselves with no adult to imitate and learn from? (Look back to page 154 to help you.)

SAMOA – AN EXAMPLE OF INFORMAL EDUCATION

Until a Samoan child was five years old its education was very simple. Children had to learn to stay out of the sun, never to hinder a woman who was weaving, and never to go near the kava bowl or the kava cup. They had to be careful of fire and knives, and respect adults by not speaking to them unless they were sitting down.

Children learned discipline by having to care for their younger brothers and sisters. Just at the age when a child begins to get naughty it was given the responsibility of looking after an even younger child so it was too busy to get into mischief. The main job facing little girls was baby-minding and they continued to do this until they were strong enough to be of more use working on the plantations or carrying food to the village. At about the same age the adolescent girls were taught to weave and to cook in the oven of heated stones. Weaving was complicated to learn for there were many techniques and the finished articles were beautiful. Baskets were made by plaiting palm leaves and bending the ribs of the leaves to form the rim. Fans were either simple weaves of two strands or highly skilled complicated patterns which only the older women had the skill to make. The hardest items to make were mats e.g. common floor mats, bed mats and the beautiful thin fine mats which took almost two years to make and were part of the girl's dowry. The pandanus leaves had to be soaked and dried then shredded and scraped until they became long thin white strands only one-tenth of an inch thick. These strands were woven into complex patterns and great skill was required. The final mats were as soft and pliable as linen sheets in Britain.

Mulberry trees provided the bark from which cloth was made. It had to be peeled and scraped, then beaten very thin. Only the older women were skilled enough to make the patterns by freehand drawing or using a pattern board. Unless a girl could prove that she was skilled in all these tasks her chances of marriage were spoiled, but after the first stages of learning the girl was allowed a lot of leisure time for the next few years. She knew she would marry eventually for everyone did, so she forgot this for the next three or four years and spent her time in fleeting love affairs, joining the men on fishing expeditions and on expeditions in search of weaving materials. These gave her plenty of opportunity for meeting boyfriends.

For the boys, education was different. They were usually freed from baby-minding much earlier than their sisters, and they then played at fishing games, learning to spear fish in the shallow reefs. They might accompany the older

A meeting-house (Falefono) on the island of Manono, the roof stripped for re-thatching.

A modern Samoan house built in traditional style. Notice the television aerial.

A Samoan girl weaves a basket of coconut palm leaves in the traditional way.

boys on fishing trips so long as they made themselves useful by carrying things. They had a much more playful childhood while the girls were busy learning weaving and helping on the plantations. However, at the time when the girl of seventeen was relaxing and enjoying herself the boy of this age had a much harder life. He had already learned to fish, to manage a boat, to plant and collect taro and coconut and to cut the meat from the carcasses. Now he had to join the AUMAGA, which was the group of young men and older men without titles. He had to compete with all the others in this group for he and his friends were now known as the strength of the village. He hoped to become a MATAI and a member of the FONO which is the group of very privileged headmen who might drink kava from the ceremonial cup. He had to learn a trade in order to be a useful member of the village. His choices were house-builder, fisherman, orator or wood-carver. Unless he was skilled at fishing he would have no food gifts to offer a girl friend and his advances would be scorned. He must prepare himself for the responsibility of a wife and household and yet he wished to remain free with more time to enjoy his youth.

A traditional Samoan house, with a toilet over the sea.

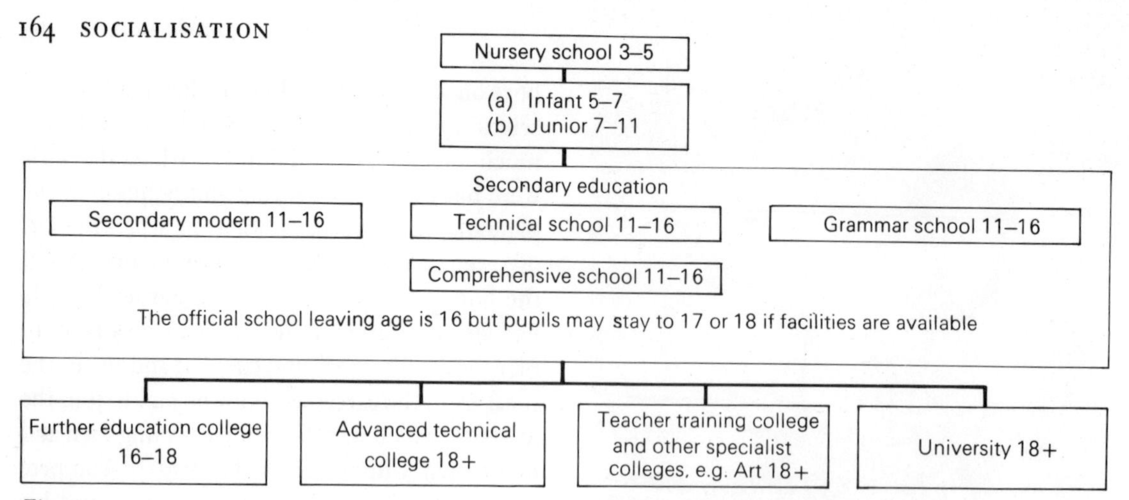

Figure 40

FORMAL EDUCATION – BRITAIN

In Britain the situation is very different. There are so many adult jobs possible for boys and girls that no one family could teach its children enough for them to have a wide choice. Sons sometimes follow in their father's footsteps, but they do not have to do exactly the same job even if they eventually do something similar. In complex societies like Britain, children leave home each day from the age of five to sixteen or over to learn the skills needed for their adult roles. Above is a diagram of the British education system. It shows the formal education which children may receive. FORMAL education may be defined as education in school. INFORMAL education is education which takes place among family and friends.

Nursery Schools

It is hard to find enough nursery school places. The places are either (*a*) in nursery schools where the parents have to pay; or (*b*) in free nursery schools run by the local education authority.

State schools

The chart includes several types of school in the box labelled *secondary education*. The first three were the kinds of schools available after the Education Act in 1944 which for the first time made it compulsory for all pupils including the poorest to stay at school until fifteen years. The type of school attended depended on the marks gained in an examination taken by all children aged eleven. This was called the 11 + examination, and was thought to sort pupils into groups fairly, according to ability. Since 1944 people in Britain have begun to realise that the exam may not be so fair after all. Some children go to poor primary schools where their classes are overcrowded and there are not enough books or pictures or other equipment. They therefore do not have the same chance to gain high marks when they take the 11 + exam. The areas with the worst schools often have very bad housing conditions too. The children cannot sleep properly or find a quiet place to read, paint, draw or write. Often there is nowhere to play so they cannot use their play to help them learn. Even if their parents are very interested in their work they have not the same opportunities for learning. Areas with the worst conditions in which the children go without all these things are called EPAs which stands for EDUCATIONAL PRIORITY AREAS.

Some children are extra lucky. If their parents have a lot of money they are able to buy books,

. . . often there is nowhere to play.

School children visit the National Park at Brecon Beacons. This is informal *education.*

and paper to practice writing and sums. The children often have opportunities to use such things as electric trains, meccano sets, projectors and cine cameras, and may perhaps visit countries abroad and see for themselves the places they learn about in geography and history lessons. Probably they have their own room for undisturbed sleep and for doing school work. These children stand a more than average chance of doing well at school and of passing the 11+ examination.

For these reasons a new kind of secondary school began to be built in the 1950s. It was called a COMPREHENSIVE school (*comprehensive* means *very wide*) because such schools took in a wide range of pupils from all walks of life. This is why in the chart the comprehensive school goes across the other three older types of schools. Because it caters for everyone it is supposed to give pupils a better chance of doing well in secondary education. There is not much new research on comprehensive schools but more is being started. At present the evidence shows that children still do not have equal chances even when they go to comprehensive schools.

Eton in the past – a Public School in 1861.

Private schools

Some children whose parents can afford it travel by a different route through the educational system, until they are eighteen.

Preparatory school 7 to 13
Public school 13 *to* 18

They may then go on to higher education when they are eighteen.

Changes in the state schools

In future years it is possible that there will be changes in the kinds of schools which most of the children in this country attend. Recently a special report known as the Plowden Report suggested that children should leave junior school and go to a middle school when they are eight, and that they should go on to a secondary school not when they are eleven, but when they are thirteen. If these changes took place, the system would look like this

Nursery school 3 to 5
Infant and junior school 5 to 8
Middle school 8 to 13

It is argued that this would give some children who develop later than others a better start in secondary school.

A primary school today.

How many pupils to each teacher?

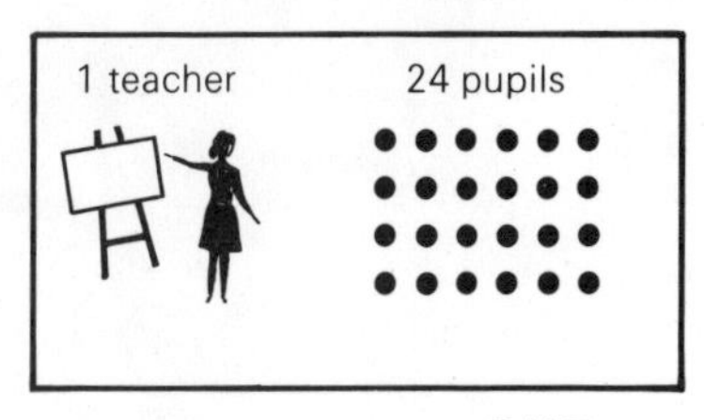

This is the average for all the country

BUT

Many pupils are in overcrowded classrooms in many areas of the country and there may be more than the official maximum that there should be

Infant school

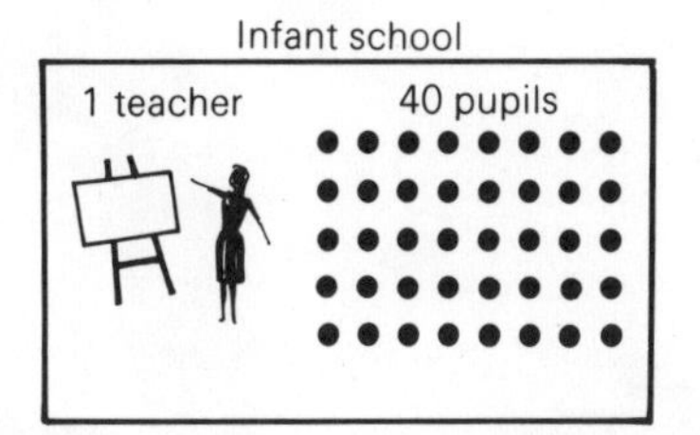

Secondary school

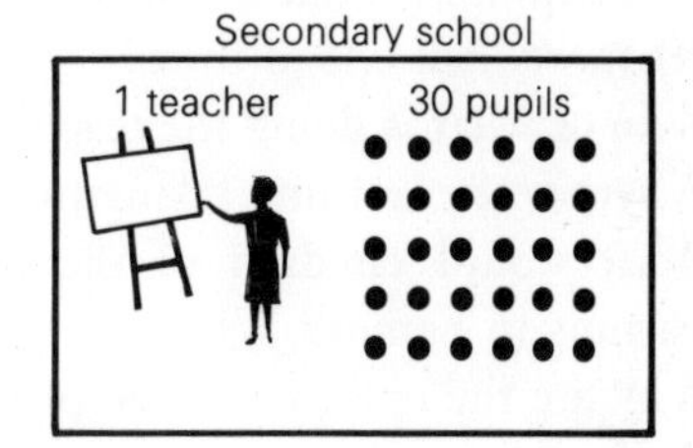

Some pupils are lucky to be in small classes in well-supplied areas of the country

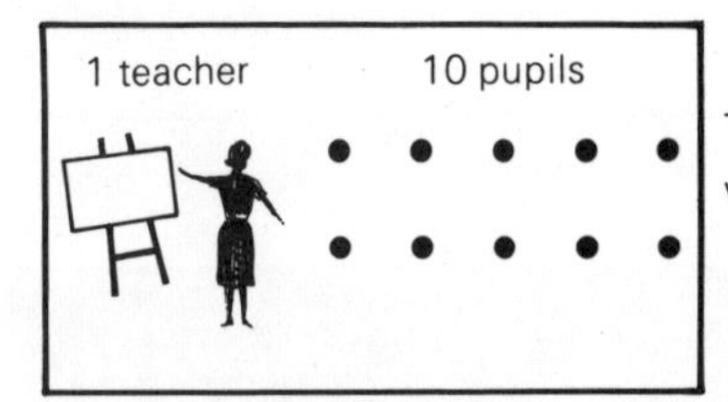

This could be a small sixth form class in a school with enough teachers

Figure 41

Another report, the Crowther Report, suggested that grants should be awarded to families with financial difficulties to enable their children to stay on until the sixth form. At present if a pupil stays on his family has to go without the extra income which he would have earned had he left school and started a job. The grants would help parents to manage without the extra income.

This shows that there is an important difference between teenagers in complex industrial societies like Britain and teenagers in simple societies such as Samoa. Sixteen-year-old Samoan children were almost full working members of their families. They contributed food and goods which the family needed, and they were no longer dependent on their families. In a complex society many fifteen- to eighteen-year-olds do not earn more than a day's money each week, if that, and although physically they are fully adult, they are still dependent on their families for the necessities of life. This may cause conflict in some families where teenagers and parents have different ideas of the roles which they feel should be played.

INFORMAL EDUCATION – BRITAIN

Each of the pictures on the following pages shows children learning something. They are not learning in school. They are learning by informal education. Throughout our life, before school, alongside school and after school, our families and friends are continually teaching us.

Look at each picture and discuss with friends the answers to the questions.

1 Is there one child or a group in the picture?
2 Roughly how old are they?
3 Are the children learning anything? If so, what exactly?
4 Could this be described as
   (*a*) learning a skill
   (*b*) learning behaviour towards others
   (*c*) learning to value something
   (*d*) more than one of these?
5 Who or what is doing the teaching?
6 Where is the learning taking place?
7 What would children of the same age be learning in Samoa? Why?
8 Why are the children in the picture learning this?
9 Are they using anything to help them learn? If so, give details.

Boys in Lima, Peru, play football on waste ground.

Playground, or school – or just a street?

Does playing 'conkers' teach children anything?

EDUCATION FOR ADULTS – BRITAIN

Many people wish to continue their education after they start work. If they go straight to a job which needs special knowledge, as an apprentice or trainee, arrangements may be made for them to attend day-release or block-release courses. The employer allows the trainee to attend classes, probably at a technical college, for one day a week or, in some cases, for a week or more at a time. Or the employer may pay the fees for a young employee to go to evening classes. This type of training, in which the employer plays an important role, is usually, but not always, for young people who have recently left school or college.

But there are other people – who may be any age from school-leavers to old-age pensioners – who decide that they would like to improve their education. As we have seen, people do not have equal chances of doing well at school; and some people who have the best of chances do not use them to the full while they are at school. For these and other reasons people may want to 'go back to school'. Often this is connected with their work: they need some special qualification to fit them for promotion or to enable them to obtain a job which particularly appeals to them. Sometimes it is to improve their social standing, and sometimes it is because they have a 'thirst for knowledge'.

For these people evening classes in technical colleges and schools may offer a solution. Perhaps they just need one 'O' level pass, perhaps they need a special qualification at quite a high level in accountancy or engineering or computer science.

Apart from evening classes, there is now the 'Open University' which teaches to degree level by correspondence, radio and television, with an occasional residential weekend course where students can meet their teachers.

Day-time courses for adults are sometimes held at technical colleges: some of these are attended by housewives and others who do not have regular hours of work. They may be 'refresher' courses in work which the students have done before, to remind them of what they used to know and to bring their knowledge up to date so that they can go back to their old jobs (for instance an ex-secretary may need practice in shorthand and typing and to learn about new office machines). Or they may be 're-training' courses for people who must change their jobs altogether, perhaps because the industry in which they worked has dwindled, or now employs fewer people because of mechanisation, or because they are no longer strong enough to continue with their original type of work.

So starting work does not mean the end of formal education nowadays. Opportunities for 'adult education' are expanding all the time.

EDUCATION FOR LEISURE – BRITAIN

During the sixteenth and seventeenth centuries, when most workers were employed on the land, the average working week was probably about forty hours. By the end of the nineteenth century, as a result of the industrial revolution and because workers were not properly organised, the number of hours worked each week had risen to between seventy and eighty. Now the average number of hours worked has dropped back to about forty a week, due to the efforts of the Trades Unions and the more enlightened attitude of employers who realise that ill or overtired employees cannot do a good day's work. In the future, with improved technology enabling machines to do many of the jobs for which men used to be employed, it is likely that working hours will be fewer still.

Salmon fishing in Argyllshire – the sport of the few. Angling is becoming more popular, but pollution threatens life in river, lake and ocean.

Punts at Oxford. Would you prefer to go out in a motor boat? Which of these leisure-time pursuits is better for the community as a whole? Why?

Women's cricket: a popular sport in Samoa.

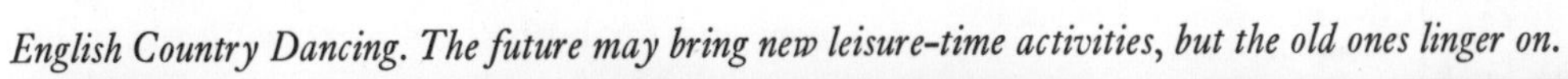

English Country Dancing. The future may bring new leisure-time activities, but the old ones linger on.

There are more cars and motorcycles per head of population. This affects the amount of travel. There were 12 million cars in 1971.

Between 1969 and 1974 real disposable income per head increased by 2·3%.

But leisure costs more than in the 1960s. Inflation is the name we use for price increases.

Whereas in 1966 most people had 2 weeks' paid holiday per year, by 1974 most people were entitled to 3 or 4 weeks per year.

Although the normal basic working week is 40 hours, most people actually work 45 hours. The drop is about 2 hours a week since 1961.

Sources: *Social Trends No. 6* 1975 and *Britain in Figures* (2nd Edition)

Figure 42 Chart showing some of the changes relevant to the time and money available for leisure

All these changes will affect the way people want to spend their leisure time, and therefore schools and colleges will perhaps be educating people not so much for their work, as for the enjoyable use of their leisure.

LEISURE ACTIVITIES IN GENERAL

For the whole population watching television is the largest pastime, according to the Survey 'Planning & Leisure' (see page 226). About one-quarter of all leisure time is spent watching TV. About one-tenth of leisure time is used in crafts and hobbies, such as knitting, woodwork and gardening, and about one-quarter of leisure time is used in outdoor activities which include sports and games and visits to parks and open spaces. Of course, these amounts of time vary according to the weather and time of year, so there are fewer outdoor activities and more TV, crafts and hobbies in the winter time. Women tend to be less interested in active sports than men, and for both sexes marriage leads to less interest in sports and more interest in TV, do-it-yourself hobbies, gardening and crafts. The other main factors are age and the type of work the person does for a living.

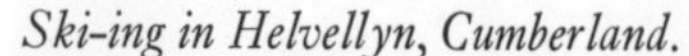

Ski-ing in Helvellyn, Cumberland.

Sailing is increasing in popularity. This is Falmouth, Cornwall.

Many people are thinking of taking up new sports. Grass-ski-ing in the Lake District.

Some schools include horse riding in the timetable. These young people are on a pony trekking holiday in Denbighshire.

Camping at Stonethwaite, Lake District. About one quarter of leisure time is used in outdoor activities, including visits to parks and open spaces.

A school timetable in A.D. 2000 – *perhaps!*

	MONDAY	*TUESDAY*	*WEDNESDAY*	*THURSDAY*	*FRIDAY*
1	English	Mathematics	Drama	?	?
2	Natural Science	Modern Languages	Integrated Humanities	?	?
3	Vocational Guidance	Natural Science	Art or Music	?	?
4	Health Education	Computer Science			
5	Options for Sport	Options for Craft	Options for Sport		
6	Archery	Pottery	Table Tennis		
7	Tennis	Oil painting	Badminton	?	?
	Golf	Toy making	Netball		
	Cricket	Sculpture	Canoeing or Swimming		

The most popular sports and games

1 Swimming in pools
Dancing
2 Table Tennis
Soccer
3 Cricket
Fishing
Tennis
4 Bowls
Golf
Swimming in the sea
(not just on holiday)

In the New Towns where there is a larger proportion of young people, ten-pin bowling is as popular as table tennis. Also, the New Towns are near to the countryside and so fishing is as popular as soccer. Over the whole country swimming, dancing and fishing are popular with all age groups, whilst golf and especially bowls become more popular as people grow older.

In the survey many girls said that they had to give up tennis and netball because there were not enough facilities available to them, and many boys said that either there were not enough facilities or that they had not enough spare time after leaving school, so they had to give up cricket and soccer unwillingly. Many people are thinking of taking up new sports in the future, including golf and fencing, archery and shooting, and it seems that these may become very popular. How does this all affect the timetable of a school?

What other activities and studies could be included? How else could the time periods be blocked? Would any other lessons be integrated? Would they be integrated in other ways? Would driving or flying lessons be included? What facilities would a school need for such a timetable? Would there be a minimum or a maximum number of pupils to make this school possible and pleasant to learn in?

The mass media

WHAT ARE THE MASS MEDIA?

News used to travel slowly when transport was only by foot, horseback or boat. Minstrels travelled round the country with tales and songs about great events, and local news was spread by the town crier. Tradesmen called their wares

Mass media transmit news all over the world.

Drums of this type were used to send messages. They could be heard twenty or thirty miles away.

through the streets or had signs which everyone recognised. Later, when more people could read, broadsheets were circulated. These carried news of wars and the Court, and ballads about heroic deeds or crimes or romances. Sometimes special signals were used to convey news quickly – such as the hilltop bonfires which were to be lit when the Spanish Armada was sighted.

Some of these methods are still used by societies isolated from the modern world, and they may have other methods, such as drum signals, for sending information. But none of these methods allowed messages to be transmitted very far, or very quickly, or to reach very many people.

Mainly through radio, television, magazines and newspapers, most people nowadays receive news very quickly, even from the other side of the world; and advertisers can 'call their wares' right into our homes as well as using newspapers and hoardings to draw our attention to the things they want to sell. To a lesser extent films, gramophone records and tape recordings can be used for the same purposes.

All these methods of communication can reach millions of people over huge areas very,

very quickly, spreading news, information and propaganda, and persuading us to buy certain things or to change our opinions on various matters. These are the MASS MEDIA.

Newspapers

The twentieth century has seen a rapid development of the mass media together with an increase in the education of the population. Raymond Williams in his study of communications shows that whereas in 1850 only one adult in eighty read a daily newspaper, by 1900 this had increased to one adult in five or six and Sunday papers were read by one adult in every three. This trend has continued to the present date.

Here are figures for the present circulation of newspapers:

Below are some suggestions for analysing newspapers.

If you are working with other people in a classroom then you could compare different newspapers printed on the same date. Using your newspaper you could write down the headlines briefly and explain what the main story is about. Each page is divided into a number of columns. To find the total column inches you need first to count the number of columns. Then measure with a ruler the number of inches in each column. Finally you need to know the number of pages in the whole paper, e.g. total column inches = 8 (columns) × 20 (inches per column) × 20 (pages) = 3200.

Next you can measure with a ruler the number of inches of (*a*) news (both for Britain and abroad), (*b*) sport and entertainment (*c*) advertising (both classified and display), and (*d*) the

Daily newspapers	*Date of first issue*	*Average circulation October–March* 1976–7 (to nearest thousand)
The Times	1785	311,000
The Daily Telegraph	1855	1,304,000
The Guardian	1821	300,000
Daily Express	1900	2,556,000
Daily Mail	1896	1,800,000
The Sun	1964	3,739,000
Morning Star	1966	39,000
Daily Mirror	1903	3,832,000
Financial Times	1888	176,000
		14,057,000
Sunday newspapers		
The Observer	1791	656,000
The Sunday Times	1822	1,414,000
The Sunday Telegraph	1961	812,000
News of the World	1843	5,114,000
The People	1881	4,191,000
Sunday Express	1918	3,407,000
Sunday Mirror	1963	4,351,000
		19,945,000

Figures: *Britain – an official handbook*, 1977.

Newspaper	Total column inches	% British news	% Foreign news	% Sport	% Enterta-inment	% Class. adverts	% Display adverts	% Pictures	% Head-lines	Outline of Main Story
The Times										
The Daily Telegraph										
The Guardian										
Daily Mirror										
Daily Express										
Daily Mail										
The Sun										
The Morning Star										
Daily Sketch										
Financial Times										
Local Paper										
Evening Paper										

Figure 43

number of inches of pictures and headlines. When all this is finished you will be able to copy and complete the chart on this page and to compare the different newspapers by answering the questions. Your teacher will be able to help to work out the percentages, which are necessary for comparing papers of different sizes.

Here are some questions to think about.

1 Which papers have the most foreign news?
2 Which papers have the least foreign news?
3 Which papers have large pictures and headlines?
4 Which papers have many display advertisements?
5 Which papers have many classified advertisements?
6 What differences are there in the reporting of the main story?
7 Some of the papers are known as the 'popular' newspapers. Which ones are they? Why do they appeal to so many people?
8 Should all the papers report the same proportion of foreign news and British news? Why do you think that they do not do this?
9 If you were going to advertise a new brand of tea, coffee or chocolate, which papers would you choose to advertise in and why?
10 Suppose that you were a travel agent specialising in luxury cruises. Where would you advertise and why?

Thinking about advertising

This is now a good time to compare display advertisements from newspapers and magazines. You could work in groups, in pairs or on your own. Begin by choosing two or more display advertisements which interest you and think hard about the following points:

1 What is the advertisement trying to sell?
2 What kind of picture is it, e.g.
   (*a*) does it include a glamorous 'sexy' model?
   (*b*) does it show a family?
   (*c*) is there a beautiful view?
   or (*d*) has it something different from (*a*), (*b*), or (*c*)?
3 Do you think this advertisement would be likely to persuade you to buy the product?
4 Might other people be persuaded to buy the product after seeing this advertisement?
5 Why do you think the advertisers have used this particular way of persuading and not another way?
6 Does the advertisement tell you the price of the product?
7 Is the advertisement cheating people in your opinion?

Thinking about television
The first regular TV programmes began in 1936. Broadcasting on radio and TV is controlled by Acts of Parliament. The BBC was set up as a public corporation in 1927 and the IBA began after the Television Act was passed in Parliament in 1954. At present about sixteen million TV licences are bought each year. A licence is still required for a TV set, although licences are no longer necessary for radios. BBC 1 is allowed about 55 hours per week and so is IBA. Extra time is allowed for special educational, political and religious programmes. BBC 2 is allowed about 30 hours per week. The number of hours allowed is changed from time to time. At present there are discussions about extending the viewing time and introducing new channels such as TV 4. It is possible that in the future many more TV channels will become available, but not everyone hopes that this will happen.

Figure 44 (*a*) *A display advertisement.*

Pram for sale £10 or nearest offer. Navy and white. Good Condition. Write Box 271.

Figure 44 (*b*) *A classified advertisement.*

Have you ever wondered why there are no advertisements on BBC television? The reason lies in the methods by which the BBC and IBA are allowed to finance their programmes.

Paying for television
Money received 1976/77

£213 million from licences £57 million grant from government £1·6 million from sale of *Radio Times* after paying for the costs of production £3·5 million from Open University	BBC 1 BBC 2

Source: *BBC Handbook* 1977

£210 million from advertising after payment of £42 million levy to the government £15 million from television companies for renting programme time	IBA

Source: *Guide to Independent TV and Local Radio* IBA 1977

It can be seen that some money is received from sale of the *Radio Times.* Copy the following chart and use the *Radio Times* and *TV Times* to help you to complete it.

We have probably all laughed at these chimps, but how effective are they in persuading us to drink a particular brand of tea?

Time	*BBC 1*	*BBC 2*	*ITV*
10–11 a.m.			
11–12 noon			
12–1 p.m.			
1–2 p.m.			
2–3 p.m.			
3–4 p.m.			
4–5 p.m.			
5–6 p.m.			
6–7 p.m.			
7–8 p.m.			
8–9 p.m.			
9–10 p.m.			
10–11 p.m.			
11–midnight			

In each box of the chart you should fill in the type of programme being shown e.g.

(*a*) Political programmes
(*b*) News
(*c*) Documentaries
(*d*) Quiz and Panel Games
(*e*) Children's programmes
(*f*) Pop music
(*g*) Serious and classical plays
(*h*) Comedies
(*i*) Films
(*j*) Travel programmes
(*k*) Crime and thrillers
(*l*) Sport
(*m*) Ballet
(*n*) Educational programmes e.g. school broadcasts, Open University.

Do you think that any of the programmes should be given more time? Are there any which you would leave out completely? Why would you do so? How much time do you think should be given to programmes watched by minority groups e.g. ballet programmes?

DOING SURVEYS

A different type of survey can also be done. You could choose a particular weekday or a Saturday or Sunday and ask your friends how many hours they watched on that day and at what times. The figures could be used to make a bar graph to show the peak viewing hours e.g.

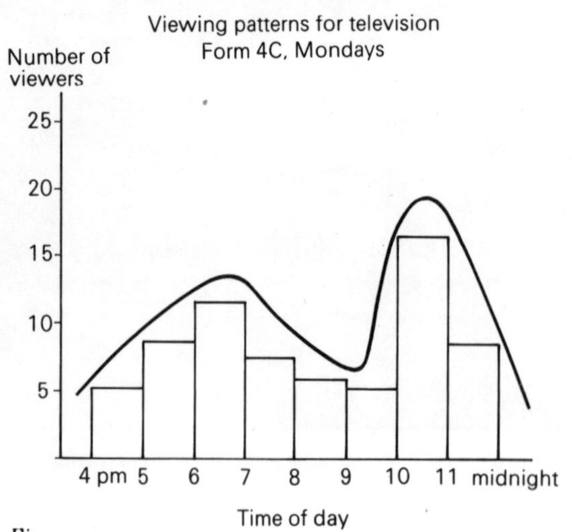

Figure 45

What are the peak viewing hours for your group? Is there one peak or are there two peak times? How would Saturday viewing compare with a weekday? Your survey would be a SAMPLE SURVEY but your results would not necessarily be the same as for the whole country. Can you think of all the ways in which your sample is different from a sample taken from everyone in Britain? A sample which does not represent the whole population is called a BIASED SAMPLE. Sociologists find it more useful to take a sample which represents the whole population, i.e. it has the same *proportions* of old and young, male and female, rich and poor, northerners and southerners as there are in the whole of Britain. This kind of sample is called a RANDOM SAMPLE and from it we can work out what the whole population wants to watch, or to buy, or how everyone thinks, feels and behaves.

THE CONTROL OF THE MASS MEDIA

When we ask people what they like to watch on television we receive many different replies. Similarly people choose different newspapers and magazines according to what appeals to their taste. Some people think that television, newspapers and other parts of the mass media should be very strictly controlled. Although there are several different daily and Sunday papers, they are under the control of only three or four large companies and this has led some people to criticise the power of the press. A large block of the shares for each paper is held by one individual or the members of one family. Some people argue that the control of papers should be in the hands of the government who should decide what is to be printed while others suggest that the newspapers should remain as

Figure 46

they are, free from governmental control. These arguments are closely linked with those for and against CENSORSHIP. Censorship means putting restrictions on the publication of news and entertainment for the benefit of the public. A simple way of phrasing this is to say that censorship means 'cutting bits out'. On all the mass media there are some restrictions – publication of information under the Official Secrets Act is forbidden and so is publication of harmful stories (called *slander* if the facts are spoken, or *libel* if they are written) about an individual. However, beyond these special situations opinions vary greatly as to what should be allowed for publication. There are some restrictions on the portrayal of sex and of violence in photographs and illustrations, and also on the way such matters are described in words.

Ideas and attitudes are constantly changing and what was forbidden for publication last year may be allowed now. The chart on page 180 shows the way in which the British Board of Film Censors classifies films for the cinema. The government reserves the right to withdraw or modify parts of radio and TV programmes but this right is hardly ever used in practice. The IBA has published a *Code of Violence* for television and this is altered from time to time.

We are still finding out about the effects of television on the viewers and some interesting results were found by Hilda Himmelweit in her study of Television and the Child in the early 1950s. Here are a few examples:

1 Children viewed on average about two hours per day.
2 Children were affected by violence if it seemed real, especially if guns or knives were used, but were not frightened if the violence was in the form of cartoons.
3 The conclusion was that television was not likely to cause aggressive behaviour unless the children watching were already emotionally disturbed.
4 Television viewing tended to reduce the number of visits to the cinema and the amount of listening to the radio. Comic reading also decreased but children tended to read more books as a result of viewing television.
5 Sex scenes on television had very little impact upon the children, especially the younger ones who reacted more to violent scenes than to sex ones.
6 For the average child the viewing took second place to outdoor play or social activities.

How many different television programmes can you think of which contained scenes likely to frighten children or embarrass adults? You and your friends will probably disagree about the effects which particular scenes might have on the viewers.

Here is a list of arguments for and against censorship. You will probably find that you agree with some of them but disagree with others. Can you add to the list of arguments? Can you expand the details for the arguments which are already listed? Censorship means cutting bits out of TV programmes, books or films if, for example, they are too violent or too sexy.

The case for censorship

Some situations in books or films might frighten or upset people, especially children.
Some situations might embarrass people.
Children and adults might copy undesirable behaviour, e.g. some children have tried to imitate Batman by jumping off high places to try and fly.

The case against censorship

People who do not want to read about or look at certain situations need not do so.
People enjoy violent or sexy bits in books and films and would be disappointed if those were left out.
Censorship involves a few people imposing their ideas on others by limiting what they may see or hear.

READING AND UNDERSTANDING

1 Why are marriage rules made in many societies?
2 Is monogamy the only possible form of marriage?
3 How many nuclear families did Jane belong to? Give reasons.
4 What has happened to family size in Britain? Give reasons.
5 What are some of the most important needs of children if they are to grow up properly?
6 Why were some upper class women unable to find husbands in the late nineteenth century?
7 Why would you expect most women to marry in Britain today?
8 What have been the main changes in women's roles in the family?
9 What kind of jobs are done by most working women?
10 (*a*) What is happening to the average age of marriage?
(*b*) What effects might this change have upon family life?
11 In what kind of areas would you expect to find traditional extended families?
12 How do the roles within some traditional extended families differ from the nuclear family today?
13 What have been the main changes in Russian family life since the revolution?
14 How was work divided up in Samoan families?
15 What is 'Culture Contact'? How has it affected the Eskimos in the twentieth century?
16 What is a kibbutz? Give details.
17 Upon what grounds may a British couple end their marriage?
18 Do many British marriages break up?
19 What is the difference between formal and informal education?
20 Why has the 11+ exam been abolished in many areas?
21 (*a*) What are comprehensive schools and what are they trying to achieve?
(*b*) Do they always succeed in doing these things?
22 Explain what a Middle School is.
23 What kind of problems might face a teenager in Britain but not a teenager in Samoa?
24 What might happen to the hours of work and of leisure in the future?
25 Why have the mass media developed quickly in the twentieth century?
26 When did television begin?
27 How do the BBC and the IBA get most of their money?
28 What is a 'sample survey'?
29 What does censorship mean?
30 Who controls the newspapers?
31 How much restriction is there on the mass media in Britain at the present time?

POINTS FOR FURTHER DISCUSSION

1 How do you think family roles will change in Britain in the future?
2 Is the family really necessary?
3 How useful is the idea of a Family Service run by local councils? What other suggestions have you for improving the help given to families who need it?
4 How will different price increases affect the spending of different families, e.g. housewives with 2 children on £15 per week; housewives with 2 children on £35 per week; old age pensioners living alone; managers of large firms on £8000 per year.
5 In what ways is life in a wolf pack similar to life in human society? How important were these similarities for Kamala's survival?

6 Should all children have the chance to go to nursery school? What might be the advantages to (*a*) the children and (*b*) the parents of compulsory nursery education?
7 What are the arguments for and against the introduction of comprehensive schooling all over the country?
8 Discuss the advantages of day-release and think about the possible problems that might arise if every school leaver was made to attend day-release classes.
9 The minimum school-leaving age has been raised from twelve in 1870, to fifteen in 1944 and sixteen in 1972. Should it, and could it be raised yet again? Why do you think sixteen is now considered to be the lowest age at which pupils should leave school?
10 Some girls and boys take it for granted that they learn together at school. Others are used to single-sex schools. What are the disadvantages and advantages of mixed and single sex schools?
11 *Education for a girl is not really important because she will not be the main breadwinner in her future family*. How true is this statement? Are attitudes to female education changing? If so in what ways and for what reasons? To what extent should girls hope for and get equal opportunity in the education system?
12 What programmes do you think should be included if new television channels are created?
13 What are the arguments for and against the extension of viewing hours on television?
14 How much censorship should there be of television programmes?
15 Would you like to see more or less government control over the newspapers?
16 Do you think that advertisements persuade people to buy things they do not want? If so, what could be done about this?

PROJECT WORK

1 *Fiction or fact?*
If you are familiar with the following books try to work out what kinds of roles were played by the leading men and women. Did they find their roles easy? Were they playing traditional roles or not?
   Any book in *The Forsyte Saga* by John Galsworthy
   Jane Eyre by Charlotte Bronte
   Pride and Prejudice by Jane Austen
Perhaps you have seen films of these and other stories set in the nineteenth or early twentieth centuries in Britain. If so, discuss with friends whether the films illustrate some of the points made in this chapter.
2 As a class or group, write to (*a*) Dr Barnardo's, or (*b*) the NSPCC, or (*c*) The Pre-School Play Groups Association, or (*d*) United Nations Childrens Fund (UNICEF) asking for information about their work. What kind of help do these organisations give to children? Why is the help necessary? What else could or should be done?
3 Collect newspaper cuttings showing situations of conflict, or success and happiness within families. What kind of images do the papers give of family life? Do they paint a true picture? Do they exaggerate facts or make them into fiction? Are there any examples of children like Kamala or Isabelle? If so, what happened to the children?
4 Read *Kate and Emma* by Monica Dickens. This book is a paperback. What had happened to each of these girls? Did they have any children? If so, were the children deprived or ill treated? Why had each girl's situation developed in the way it did? What help could each one have been given?
5 As a class or group write to the National Council for the Unmarried Mother and her Child (NCUMC) for information about its

work. What is the extent of illegitimacy in Britain today? What are the needs of unmarried mothers? What help can they be given? Is any help being given? If so, is it enough? What disadvantages or advantages might be experienced by the child of an unmarried mother?

6 Carry out surveys of your teaching group on the following topics:
   1 The number of children in the nuclear family
   2 Where the members of your extended family live
   3 Where, in particular, your mother's parents live.

   Use the statistics you collect to make bar graphs or cake diagrams. Use the diagrams to work out (*a*) whether most of the class live with their nuclear or extended family; (*b*) whether the area is one with strong kinship ties; (*c*) whether the area is MATRI-LOCAL. This means that the women of the family tend to live near each other.

7 Construct kinship diagrams of your own extended family, and use them to find out how family size has changed over the last hundred years;
   or, choose any family you have read about and do the same;
   or, make up your own family tree imagining yourself as the founder of the family in 1850. Choose names for the family members, and think about the average family size in each generation.

8 Make a model of a Nuer village showing where each of the families lives. Use the model to show the movement of people and cattle in the Bridewealth system.

9 Find as many examples as you can (by asking teachers and other pupils) of societies where there is or was a dowry system in operation. Use encyclopaedias to help you.

10 Construct kinship diagrams of the head of each Nuer village. As in all societies there are, among the Nuer, rules regarding who may not marry whom, and who may not have intercourse with whom. In some prayer books for the Church of England these rules are written down for Britain. Find a copy of these rules and compare them with the rules among the Nuer given on page 135. Although incest rules become moral rules in many societies, they often start from a desire to protect the property of the kinship group. Which property is being protected among the Nuer? Why does it need to be protected?

The Nuer Marriage Rules (for project 10)
Marriage is *not* permitted between:
(*a*) People of the same clan.
(*b*) Close natural kinsfolk, e.g. mother/son, grandmother/grandson, two close cousins, father/daughter, grandfather/granddaughter, uncles/nieces, aunts/nephews, brothers/sisters.
(*c*) People who are related on their father's or mother's side for up to six generations.

Also
(*d*) A man may only marry his wife's sister if his first wife has died childless.
(*e*) A man may not marry the daughter of any of his own age-friends because she is regarded as his own daughter. This is a special condition known as the age-set. A man must marry within his own age-set.
(*f*) A man may not marry any woman who is of the same lineage as his mother because of his special relationship with his mother.

11 Find out more about education in simple societies. Use your school library or local library and the book lists in the earlier chapters on pre-literate societies to help you.

12 Look ahead to the chapters on Population and World Co-operation. Some children in other societies do not get much formal education. What difficulties are these children likely to have when they grow up? What is being done at present to help with this world problem?

13 What would school be like for boys and girls in Russia or Israel? Use the books and addresses at the end of the chapter to help you find out.

14 The Common Market has several International Schools. What are the aims of these schools, who learns there and what do they learn?

15 Do a detailed study of a small child that you know. What age is the child? What has he learned so far in his life? Who has he learned from? Has he had any things as well as people to help him learn? Has there been anything to hinder his learning? Could he have been helped more than he has; if so, what ways could you suggest of helping him?

16 What local facilities exist for further education for both work and leisure? Make a detailed study of these and write comments on how satisfactory you think the facilities are.

17 Find out more about teenagers and their peer groups (friends of the same age). What do they learn from their friendship within the group? How do they spend their leisure time? What do they believe in? How many are on drugs and for what reasons? What do they spend their money on? What conflicts and satisfactions do they find in family life? You could investigate many more parts of the lives of teenagers and make up your own surveys. Use articles from teenage magazines to help you with this project. Some of the books listed at the end of this and other chapters will also be useful.

18 Make a model or plan of a school in the year 2000. What do you think it will look like? What will the pupils wear? What rules will the school have? What will the pupils learn and why? Who will teach in the school?

19 Find out about the IBA *Code of Violence for Television* from the reference section of your local library. Are there any programmes or parts of programmes which seem to break the code? Do you think the code should be changed at all? If so, in what ways would you like to see it changed?

20 From the books on the reading list, find out the amount of money which the newspapers make from advertising. Do you think that there is an over-emphasis on advertising in the press?

21 Look at several magazines for teenagers. Analyse the kind of advertisements which are in the magazines. Why have they been included rather than other types of advertisements? Are there any magazines in which the majority of the space is advertisements with other reading matter in the minority?

22 Find out the cost of advertising on television. Does it differ according to the time of day? If so, when is it the most expensive? What are the reasons for the high costs at certain times?

23 Find out about the different careers which people might follow in the mass media. There are several books in public libraries which will help with this project.

24 Use encyclopaedias and the reference book list to find out details of the growth of the mass media, e.g.
When was the first satellite transmission?
When did radio begin?
How was colour television invented?
How many books are published each year?
What proportion of the population use public libraries?

USEFUL BOOKS FOR PUPILS

Adams, C. & Laurikietis, R. *The Gender Trap: A closer look at sex roles* books I, II & III (Virago 1975, 1976)

Baker, C. *Talking About the Mass Media* (Wayland 1973)

Blishen, E. *The School That I'd Like* (Penguin 1969)

Bostock, E. *Talking About Women* (Wayland 1973)

Bostock, E. *Talking About Family* (Wayland 1973)

Bourne, R. & McArthur, B. *The Struggle for Education* (a pictorial history) (Schoolmasters Publishing Co. 1970)

Cook, N. *Family and Kinship* (Social Studies series) (Blandford 1974)

Cootes, R. *The Family* (Social Science studies) (Longman 1974)

Daniel, S. & McGuire, P. (eds) *The Paint House – Words from an East End Gang* (Penguin 1970)

Dickinson, S. *Leisure* (Social Science Studies) (Longman 1976)

Douglas, M. *Man in Society* (Macdonald 1974)

Dunthorn, J. *Heredity and Environment* (Social Studies series) (Blandford 1974)

Foot, P. W. R. *The Child in the Twentieth Century* (Cassell 1968)

Foster, J. *From 0–5: The Pre-school Years* (Checkpoint series 8) (Edward Arnold 1975)

Hanson, W. J. *Family Life* (Enquiries) (Longman 1975)

Hanson, W. J. *Learning* (Enquiries) (Longman 1974)

Hastie, T. *Home Life* (Past into Present series) (Batsford 1970)

Holmes, R. *Mass Media and their Social Effects* (Blandford 1975)

Hudson, K. *The Place of Women in Society* (Ginn 1970)

Hurman, A. *As Others See Us* (Edward Arnold 1977)

Jackdaw, 49 *Women in Revolt; The Fight for Emancipation* (Jonathan Cape)

Learmonth, J. *Communicators* (Nelson 1970)

Mathias, P. *Groups and Communities* (Enquiries) (Longman 1974)

Mead, M. *Coming of Age in Samoa*, chs 2, 3, 4 (Penguin 1971)

Moore, K. *Women* (Past into Present series) (Batsford 1970)

O'Donnell, A. *Education and Society* (Social Science studies), (Longman 1975)

Ryder, J. *The Family* (Methuen Education 1976)

Schoolboys of Barbiana *Letter To A Teacher* (Penguin 1970)

Schools Council/Nuffield Humanities Project *Education* (Heinemann 1970)

Silver, H. *Children, Schools and Society* (Methuen Education 1976)

Sommer, P. *Information* (Harrap 1972)

Thompson, J. *Sociology for Schools* Books I and II (Hutchinson 1973)

Townsend, S. *Talking About Education* (Wayland 1974)

West, G. et al. *Looking at Marriage* (Nelson 1975)

USEFUL BOOKS FOR TEACHERS

Barker, D. L. & Allen, S. *Sexual Divisions and Society* (Tavistock 1976)

Barker, D. L. & Allen, S. *Dependence and Exploitation in Work and Marriage* (Longman 1976)

Bettleheim, B. *The Children of the Dream* (Paladin 1971)

Brown, H. et al. *Socialisation* (Open University Press, Course D100 6–9 1971)

Brown, E. (ed.) *Children and Television* (Collier-Macmillan 1976)

CIS Crisis series, *Women Under Attack* (1976)

Dale, I. R. *The Culture of the School* (Open University Press, Course E282 3–4 1972)

Dale, R. & Esland, G. *Schooling and Capitalism* (Routledge & Kegan Paul 1976)

Douglas, J. W. B. *The Home and the School* (MacGibbon & Kee 1964)

Esland, G. *The Construction of Reality* (Open University Press, Course E282 1–2 1972)

Esland, G., Dale, I. R. & Sadler, J. *The Social Organization of Teaching and Learning* (Open University Press, Course E282 5–8 1972)

Evans-Pritchard, E. E. *The Nuer* (Clarendon Press 1968)

Frankenburg, R. *Communities in Britain* (Penguin 1970)

Gavron, H. *The Captive Wife* (Penguin 1970)

Golding, P. *The Mass Media* (Longman 1974)

Halloran, J. *The Effects of Television* (Panther 1970)

Illich, I. *Deschooling Society* (Calder 1971)

Keddie, N. (ed.) *Tinker, Tailor: Myth of Cultural Deprivation* (Penguin 1975)

Kohl, H. *The Open Classroom* (Methuen 1973)

Oakley, A. *Sociology of the Housewife* (Robertson 1974)
Oakley, A. *Sex, Gender and Society* (Smith 1972)
Open University, *School and Society* (Open University Press, Course E282 1–17 1972)

Open University, *Urban Education* (Open University Press, Course E351 1–5 1974)
Ryder, S. & Silver, H. *Modern English Society* (Methuen 1970)
Silver, H. *Equal Opportunity in Education* (Methuen 1973)
Treasure Chest for Teachers (National Union of Teachers Annual Publication)
UNESCO Mass Communication Reports (HMSO)
United Nations Association
UNESCO World Surveys on Education (HMSO)
Whitty, G. & Young, M. *Explorations in the Politics of School Knowledge* (Nafferton Books 1976)
Williams, R. *Communications* (Penguin 1970)
Young, M. & Whitty, G. *Society, State and Schooling* (Nafferton Books 1976)
Young, M. & Willmott, P. *The Symmetrical Family* (Penguin 1975)
Zaretsky, E. *Family, Capitalism and Personal Life* (Pluto Press 1976)

In addition to the organisations mentioned in the project work, useful information is contained in the Family Welfare Association's *Guide to the Social Services* which is published annually. See also list of organisations at end of book.

USEFUL BOOKS FOR PUPILS AND TEACHERS

Connexions series (a) *Break for Commercials* (b) *Behind the Scenes* (Penguin Education 1970) (c) *For Better, For Worse* (d) *His and Hers* (Penguin Education 1971)
Huggett, W. *The Newspapers* (Heinemann 1968)

FILMS

Unmarried Mothers; 30 mins; Concord Films Council (made for *This Week*, Rediffusion)
Born Losers (family in poverty); 25 mins; Concord Films Council (*World in Action* series, Granada)
A Threat or a Promise (human rights, poverty and family life): 10 mins; Concord Films Council
Our World is Yours (problems of the disabled); 25 mins; Guild Sound & Vision Ltd
Women of Israel (includes life in a kibbutz); Israel Government Tourist Office 300 11430, also Guild Sound & Vision Ltd
Children of Japan; 11 mins; b/w; Rank 207011 and ILEA 1456
China Under Communism; 22 mins; ILEA 507
Patterns of Learning (primary); 30 mins; free; Central Film Library UK 2671
Children's Playground in Europe; 19 mins; Centra Film Library V622
School Life in Japan; (Japan Information Centre); 20 mins; colour; ILEA 1243
Thursday's Children (teaching deaf children); 22 mins; b/w; ILEA 72
Seven Up; 30 mins; Concord Films Council
Seven Plus Seven; 60 mins; Concord Films Council
Comprehensive Education (education for the future); Concord Films Council and ILEA 498
The Shrinking World (growth of the mass media; part 17 of 20-part series on History 1917–67); 20 mins; BBC TV Enterprises and ILEA 1963
Comprehensive Education; 10 mins; Concord/ILEA 369
A New School of Thought; Pupil Participation in Decision Making within Schools; 25 mins; Concord Films Services
Summerhill; Concord Film Services
Twenty-One – sequel to Seven Up and Seven Plus Seven; 60 mins; (*World in Action* series, Granada); Concord Film Services
Family of Man; 50 mins; ILEA 2131–4, 2136
Conversation with a Single Parent; 30 mins; (*World in Action* series, Granada); ILEA 2419
John; 45 mins; ILEA 225
What Shall We do With Gran?; 50 mins; ILEA 2338
How Do Children Think?; 30 mins; ILEA 1664
Further Glimpse of Joey; 27 mins; ILEA 329
The Emancipation of Women; Slide Centre Ltd AUC 118
Male/Female; Changing Life Styles; 60 mins; EAV 99TF041
Many good films are available from the Save the Children Fund and the Japanese Information Office.

7 Social Control

People's behaviour is controlled by their social environment in many more ways than they realise. In every group of people there are rules to regulate human behaviour and it is often possible to notice that people behave in similar ways from day to day. These ways of behaving are called NORMS. In this chapter we shall look at many of the methods of controlling people's behaviour including the rules which regulate small groups of people and CUSTOMS or TRADITIONS which regulate people in different parts of society. We shall also look at the control of people's lives by PUBLIC OPINION and LAW.

Jersey's 'Battle of the Flowers' has developed into a procession of elaborate floats, all decorated with real flowers.

The traditional Easter Parade, once held in Hyde Park, has become an annual event in Battersea Park, London, since it was first held there in 1951 at the time of the Festival of Britain.

These school children from Lima, Peru, are playing marbles. Would they need rules?

Scouts are an example of a group that has grown large from small beginnings.

Rules among small groups of people

Whenever groups of people meet regularly they develop their own rules. Consider a family's routine for breakfast in the morning. Do all the members have the same timetable each morning? Is there a rota for the bathroom? Does the same person cook breakfast each day? Does each member of the family eat the same thing that day? Do the members leave the house together? Do they each leave at a regular time each day?

Imagine three friends sharing a flat. What kinds of rules might be developed? What might happen if one of the friends did not stick to the rules that had been made? Some groups have grown large from small beginnings, e.g. some clubs and associations, some schools and sports teams. Some of the voluntary associations, e.g. Oxfam, Shelter and the NSPCC started with a small group of interested people and with few rules, and they gradually grew until many rules and much paper-work were involved. An interesting piece of work is to collect information about one of these associations and to study its history and growth. The addresses are at the back of this book. Another interesting study is the growth of the organisation of trade unions and of political parties during the last hundred years.

The following chart shows how the number of rules increases and the rules become more complicated as the size of a group grows.

TYPE OF GROUP	RULES
Nuclear Family *Figure 47* No rules written down.	Breakfast is usually at 7.30 a.m. Dad leaves at 7.50 a.m. Jimmy leaves for school at 8.15 a.m. Sally leaves for Nursery Class with Mum at 9.00 a.m. Jimmy is allowed out in the evening until 11 p.m. Jimmy is allowed to do a paper-round to increase his pocket money. Dad and Mum go shopping together on Friday evenings. Jimmy looks after Sally while they are out, then goes round to see Sarah, his girl friend.
School *Figure 48* 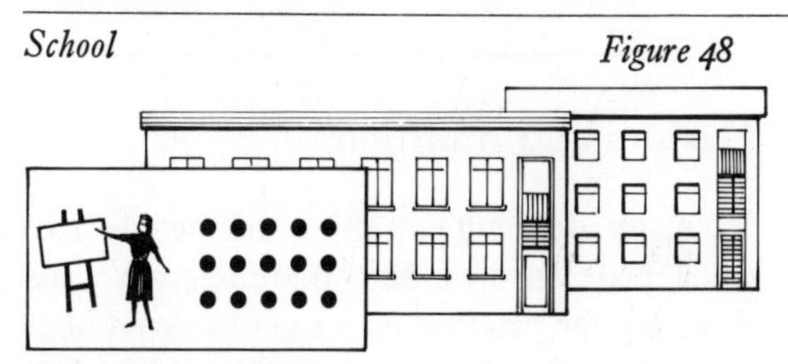 Some written rules. Some rules not written down.	Do not run in the corridors. Only prefects may use the lifts. No smoking in school. 4th years may bring sandwiches. 1st years are not allowed out at lunch time. Everyone must wear uniform except the 6th years. There will be seven lessons in a day. Pupils should register at 8.50 a.m. and 1.40 p.m. The School Council will meet on the first Thursday of each month.
Trades Unions *Figure 49* Many written rules. Some rules not written down. 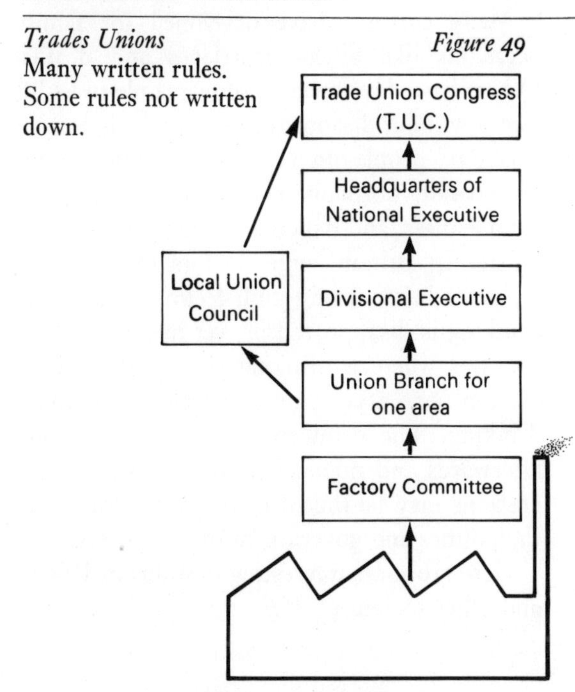 	Members must pay subscriptions. Members in arrears will not receive benefits. 6 weeks arrears may mean that a member may not become a union official. 13 weeks arrears means that a member may not vote on any issue (e.g. in the Transport & General Workers' Union). Delegates from factories may attend meetings of the branch. Delegates from branches may attend divisional (i.e. regional) meetings. Delegates from regions (divisions) may attend executive council meetings. Executive Council may send representatives to the TUC. The TUC may support the Labour Party with funds. The Trade Union must be registered on the Government Register. Workers are represented by Shop Stewards when discussing pay with the boss. Shop stewards may not call official strikes without the permission of the National Executive. Trade Union officials in the Union are to be paid by the Union, but the Shop Steward is an unpaid spokesman elected by his fellow workers. This ruling was new under the Industrial Relations Act 1971.

Other Groups – a few examples

1 A group of ten friends of the same age who are planning a holiday.
2 A boy and a girl who are friends. (Any group of only two people is called a dyad).
3 Members of an extended family living near one another.
4 A large office.
5 A local council.
6 The House of Commons.
7 The United Nations.
8 The US Federation in 'Star Trek'.
9 A criminal gang planning a jewel theft.
10 A football fan club.

What kinds of rules would each of these groups have?
Would the rules be written down, or never written down, or both sorts?
How might the rules have been developed, and why are they necessary?
Which rules might need to be changed some time?

New Year Lion Dance performed by Chinese in Hong Kong. Grotesque masks of various types have been worn for ritual purposes over thousands of years in many parts of the world. Think of reasons for their widespread use.

Custom and tradition

In many different societies the people have developed customs and traditions. Whether these are for pleasure or for very solemn occasions, they may have a great effect on the lives of the people.

Many customs have developed for family occasions like births, marriages and deaths. Others have developed to allow people to let off steam without disapproval. At carnivals and on feast days people often behave in public in ways that would normally not be allowed e.g. by drunkenness, and dancing in the streets to loud music. In Britain some doctors say that the alcoholic has a strong guilt feeling because his drinking is disapproved of, yet in some simple societies where a drinking revelry is held by custom once a year, no one feels guilty about drinking. The drunkenness is forgotten soon afterwards and no alcohol addicts exist. Other customs may be linked to religious ideas or to the politics and government of the society.

Here are some interesting customs in Britain and other societies.

An old custom re-enacted. Burial of a Viking Chieftain at the Peel Viking Festival, Isle of Man, 1966.

Present-day Eskimos keep some of the old customs. This is the Drum Dance at Kap Dan in Greenland.

CUSTOMS CONNECTED WITH BIRTHS, MARRIAGES AND DEATHS

In some rural areas of Sweden and Britain it used to be the custom for a girl to become pregnant before she married so that she and her fiancé would be sure of their ability to produce children to help on the farm. But it was an equally strong custom that no such girl was left as an unmarried mother, for the whole neighbourhood would bring pressure to bear on the couple to ensure that all parts of this 'rule' were carried out. This type of action was both common and allowed, but is not usually practised today. A recent report from the National Council for the Unmarried Mother and her Child (NCUMC) shows 8·6% of all births are illegitimate in Britain today.

Year	*Total births (to nearest thousand)*	*% Illegitimate*
1918	663,000	6·26
1919	692,000	6·05
1920–24	815,000	4·41
1925–29	673,000	4·36
1935	599,000	4·19
1940	590,000	4·34
1942	652,000	5·60
1944	751,000	7·34
1945	680,000	9·33
1950	697,000	5·06
1955	668,000	4·66
1958	740,000	4·88
1960	785,000	5·44
1965	863,000	7·67
1966	850,000	7·89
1968	819,000	8·52
1970	784,000	8·25
1973	750,345	8·60

A fishing festival in Northern Nigeria, 1959.

The illegitimacy rate was decreasing until the 1950s, except for a sudden increase to a record level in 1944–1945. Sociologists say that this was probably due to couples being prevented from marrying by the war.

In the 1950s a rise in the illegitimacy rate began in London and the South. The increase appeared in other cities, then in smaller towns and finally in rural areas.

Sociologists do not agree about the causes. Part of the rise may be due to migration of people from the country to the cities. Another cause may be the spread of new patterns of behaviour from the cities into the rural areas via the mass media.

It is generally agreed that there is less stigma attached to illegitimacy these days. In other words, it is not frowned upon in the same way as fifty years ago. In large cities today the social pressures on a pregnant single girl do not force her to marry. This is one reason why the illegitimacy rate appears to be greater in cities. Ideas about marriage have changed, and it is recognised that a forced marriage may be a very unhappy one and that this may harm the adults and the child.

Some sociologists would argue that there is more intercourse outside marriage, particularly among young people who are caught between many pressures. Some teenagers find that their friends are married with children whilst they themselves are still at school and they resent being treated as children. However the Schofield Report *The Sexual Behaviour of Young People* shows that only a minority of teenagers have regular sexual relationships. Sociologists also disagree about the impact of modern contraceptives like the 'pill'. Some say that the availability of the pill does lead to more intercourse whilst others say that it makes very little difference.

There is growing concern for the future of illegitimate children. Adoption is a possible solution but not necessarily the best one. Many people feel that an illegitimate child is best kept with its mother and that far more help should be given to her. She needs somewhere to live, someone to care for the child while she works during the day, and support and friendship while she plays a very difficult role. At present illegitimate children are at a disadvantage in British society. Attitudes towards the children

In Britain the bride traditionally wears white. How old is this custom? Other cultures have different traditions.
(a) Hindu wedding in the West Indies. By tradition the bridegroom wears pink and the bride's face is hidden by a flower-strewn veil.
(b) Japanese wedding.

An English custom: formal dress is worn at this wedding.

and their mothers are changing but facilities are not being provided to help the mother to cope.

Many customs surround the marriage of a couple including that of choosing bridesmaids. In some areas the bride's friends or relatives are usually chosen whilst in others the bride has to choose bridesmaids from both sides of the family. A bride may meet conflict if she does not understand or follow the correct rules.

Funerals have many associated traditions, e.g. the curtains may be drawn even in the day-time in the relatives' houses; a feast may be provided after the occasion both to provide nourishment for those who have travelled a distance to the funeral and to provide a release of tension for those most closely linked with the dead person.

At Abbotts Ann in Hampshire a crown of paper roses used to be hung in the church if a young woman of good reputation died. The roses were carried at the funeral and then hung permanently in the church, with the name, age and funeral date of the young person. Every year a special service is held on the last Sunday in August at Eyam in Derbyshire to commemorate the self-sacrifice of the villagers who died of plague in 1665–1666 by isolating themselves in their village rather than spreading the fearful disease to the rest of the district.

There are many other customs which could be mentioned. How many do you know? What other customs connected with birth, marriage or death in other European societies have you heard about?

Celebrating November 5th with fireworks and bonfires has become a national custom even though most people know little about the political and religious struggles which gave rise to the Gunpowder Plot.

CUSTOMS LINKED TO NATIONAL FESTIVALS

Examples of special customs could be given for New Year's Day, Shrove Tuesday, Whit Monday, Easter and Christmas. How many can you think of? May Day celebrations began in England in ancient times and may have been fertility rites in honour of the sun god. The old festivities were lively affairs with much drinking, dancing and promiscuity. Today the remains of these customs are mild in comparison. Almost every town and village had a maypole and London had several. A few still stand in remoter places, and at Ickwell in Bedfordshire a May Queen is crowned each year on the village green and there are colourful complicated dances around the seventy-foot maypole. On 5 November many families celebrate Guy Fawkes' unsuccessful attempt at blowing up the Houses of Parliament, and arguments rage these days about the dangers of fireworks. Some Sussex towns and villages have their own special celebrations. Rye has a 'Rye Fawkes', when a visiting personality comes to light the bonfire, and sometimes a boat is burned. In Kent at Edenbridge three brass bands help in a torchlight procession with decorated floats.

In the spring many coastal and rural areas have adapted old pagan customs into Christian ones and on Plough Monday some villagers have a ceremonial blessing of the ploughs, whilst in fishing villages the nets and even the sea are blessed.

CUSTOMS WHICH DEVELOPED AS GOVERNMENT BECAME MORE COMPLICATED

In areas of London and other cities it is not usual to find many old customs concerning the Local Councils. However in Hungerford in Berkshire there is an annual celebration when the council officers are elected. They are called Tythingmen or Tutti-men, and on the day of election they carry a pole with a bouquet of spring flowers and a real orange at the top. They visit each house followed by a man with a sack of oranges. He wears a top hat and is called the Orange Scrambler. Each local person receives an orange. The men must pay with a penny and the women with a kiss. No one however shy may escape, as the Tutti-men carry a ladder to reach even the most out-of-the-way window! Any extra oranges are thrown to the children who scramble to get one.

In London a Lord Mayor is elected annually on Michaelmas Day (29 September) in the Guildhall. He takes office on the second Saturday in November with a ceremony known as the Lord Mayor's Show. He drives in a coach drawn by six horses from his official house (The Mansion House) to the Royal Courts of Justice in the Strand, where he is received by the Lord Chief Justice as representative of the Queen. All the guard of honour and attendants wear bright ceremonial robes, and the procession is a mile long. Thousands of people watch this procession, which dates from 1215 in the reign of King John.

Public opinion

We have now seen that families, schools and other groups have rules which control the behaviour of their members, and that people often fit in with the customs and traditions of their area. Their behaviour is also partly controlled by public opinion because they want others to think well of them.

The way in which this affects people's behaviour is seen clearly in the influence of fashion. Mini, midi and maxi skirts; trousers with and without turnups; single and double breasted jackets; pointed, oval and square toes come and go continually, and most people do not ignore these fashion changes, though some adapt to them more quickly than others. They are all obeying a type of rule. Why do they do this? Do people's ideas really change, or is it just that they do not want to appear frumpish? Do people really dress to please only themselves or to have the approval of their friends and to improve their status?

In issues of nationwide importance public opinion also plays its part. Juries may be told not to read the newspapers in case they allow public opinion to influence their judgment. Similarly public sympathy for or against political prisoners may have an effect on the sentence they receive.

During the spring and summer of 1971 discussions raged back and forth amongst the British public on the question of Britain's entry into the Common Market. Very few citizens clearly understood the complex issues involved (see page 47), although fact sheets were published by the government and available free from Post Offices. Many people based their opinions on either side on very little evidence or knowledge, and some of the newspapers exaggerated some points and left out others entirely.

Carnivals provide an opportunity for gaiety and 'letting off steam'.
(*a*) *A beautiful headdress made of beads and feathers, worn by a competitor in the Trinidad carnival.*

(b) These men in Trinidad wear grotesque heads and carry rattles. Can you think of an ancient custom which they may be carrying on, though it is now done just for fun?

Many carnivals, now staged mainly as tourist attractions, are based on ancient religious festivals or pagan rites.

(a) The carnival queen holds a sceptre – a symbol of her status.

(b) Carnival procession, St Vincent.

Law

If people do not follow the fashion trends, or attend the blessing of a plough or the Lord Mayor's Show, no one will take them to court or accuse them of crime. However, there are some rules which do have penalties attached if they are broken. These are the rules known as LAW.

LAW IN SIMPLE SOCIETIES

Look back to page 134 on the Nuer. Cattle meant everything to the Nuer. A Nuer man might be nick-named after his favourite ox and he would fight to protect his cows. The last thing he wanted to do was to give his cows and oxen away, but sometimes he had to.

If a man injured another man he paid cattle in compensation. If he speared someone from a nearby village the spear would be sent to the wounded man's relatives who would treat it magically to prevent the wound being fatal. They also sent a sheep for sacrifice to appease the spirits.

The easiest feuds to settle were between close neighbours because any split would endanger the close co-operation needed if the herd were to survive. If a close neighbour had been killed cattle were quickly paid in compensation and it was pointed out to the ghosts that as cattle had been paid the man's death should not be avenged. If it had been avenged the feud between close neighbours would continue and soon no one would be left alive.

It was a different matter if the injured or killed person was more distant. The feud was then harder to settle and might result in war, with neighbouring villages helping each other out against the enemy.

Most of these feuds between distant people arose over cattle being stolen and a Nuer man would fight to defend his cattle (his property) and to plunder other people's cattle. The Nuer did not have courts or any official way of settling disputes.

Sometimes they might refer a dispute to a Leopard Skin Chief. This was a man with high status and a leader in the ritual performances. However, the disputing parties did not have to abide by his decisions as they would in a court. His main role was to get the disputing people talking and to agree on right and wrong. The judgement belonged to the people, and was not dictated by the chief. The parties would go on talking until agreement was reached.

The Nuer way of life was very simple, but life in the villages in India was more complicated. Bisipara is the name of a very remote Indian village, miles away from the modern cities of India. In Bisipara there are members of many of the Indian castes. For example there are high priests, merchants, farmers, and people who make things such as pots and baskets. If the village is to exist in peace and harmony everyone must perform his own task and not hinder others performing theirs. This is especially the case when members of different farming families must work together in the fields. If one man's supply of water were cut off by another man then the crop would be ruined and the people would starve.

Similarly when there is public work to do like repairing the temple, the paths, or the irrigation channels, then if one man does not pull his weight and do his share he is hindering and perhaps even endangering the lives of others.

In Bisipara the changes occurring in the Indian cities have not yet had much effect. Life is still continuing as it has for hundreds of years. Many parts of India are in a similar situation and poverty, illiteracy (inability to read) and hunger are widespread. In many villages life is still very close to survival level and in this respect life in Indian villages is similar to the struggle for survival among herding people like the Nuer and the Lapps, and hunters like the Eskimos and Bushmen.

But there are differences too. Among the Nuer there were no official means of settling quarrels: there is no court. In Bisipara there is a court made up of the leaders of families of the village. The court is presided over by the head-man of the village, and the schoolmaster (if there is one) will keep a record of the cases; the law is mainly handed down by word of mouth. The court is called the PANCHAYAT, which translated literally means 'court of five men'.

Where a man has damaged his neighbour's crops, or has some other private dispute between himself and his neighbour, or when the village is outraged about a public issue (like a man refusing to repair the irrigation channels), then the case may be brought for discussion before the court. The cases may go on for days in the same way as a discussion among the Nuer over a dispute was carried on at great length. In the Panchayat there are no judges or lawyers, but merely ordinary villagers who give some of their time to hearing the cases. Anyone found guilty can be punished by a fine (paid to the court) or by paying compensation to the victim. In serious cases the punishment is OSTRACISM. This means that no one will help the man or talk to him. No one will feed his cattle or sell him goods. His relatives will not call at his house or attend the wedding of his daughter, nor attend baptisms or funerals with him.

In such a small society everyone will know of his punishment and take part in helping to punish him. If anyone broke the ostracism rule it would not work properly, and therefore it is important that if ostracism is decided on as the punishment, everyone must agree that it is just and agree to help make it work. It is for this reason that the decisions of the Panchayat must be unanimous, and must satisfy everyone in the village.

If a very unpleasant decision has to be made then the case may be referred to the gods. The disputing parties may take an oath in the temple and whoever first falls ill afterwards is thought to have lied. Or they may undergo 'trial by ordeal' when whoever emerges worst is thought to be guilty. In a situation like this the gods are thought to have given the verdict and the villagers are released from the unpleasant task of doing so.

Bisipara is a small isolated village where people are related to each other within their own castes, and people meet each other all the time. They may meet on social occasions such as births, marriages and deaths, at festivals and dances, in trade and in all aspects of work. For this reason all grievances are thoroughly aired so that they do not disturb the harmony and economic co-operation necessary for survival.

LAW IN CITIES AND IN COMPLEX SOCIETIES

In the Indian village the law is passed down by word of mouth from one court judge to the next. This type of law is known as COMMON LAW. Some British law which has been handed down in the law courts from judge to judge is this type of law. However in industrial societies like Britain, and in the larger cities of non-industrial societies, such as India, the situation becomes much more complicated. The law is written down and is decided in the first place by the Government, not the judges. This type of law is known as STATUTE LAW and it is written in books known as statute books. Examples of statute law in Britain are (*a*) the Divorce Reform Act 1969, (*b*) the Children and Young Persons Act 1969, (*c*) the New Towns Acts of which there have been several since 1945, (*d*) The Industrial Relations Act 1971, (*e*) Misuse of Drugs Act 1971.

The following chart shows how one of these Acts of Parliament becomes law.

A daily event in London: Changing the Guard. Originally a military necessity, it has become a tourist attraction.

1	Before an Act becomes law it is called a BILL. The Government or a private MP introduces it into the House of Commons
2	*First Reading* The bill is printed and read
3	*Second Reading* The bill is debated in the House of Commons
4	*Committee Stage* The bill is sent to a special committee who discuss it and make suggestions for changes (amendments)
5	*Report Stage* Another large debate takes place. The bill may be rejected or sent back to the committee again
6	*Third Reading* This is the last reading in the House of Commons. The bill is then sent to the House of Lords
7	*The House of Lords* The bill is discussed three times and can be sent to committee between discussions
8	*The Queen (or King) signs the bill* The bill is now an Act of Parliament and what has been written in it becomes statute law.

'Beating the Bounds' at the Tower of London. In many places beating the bounds was carried out, usually once a year, when a party of local dignitaries travelled round the perimeter of the parish concerned. Nowadays this is done in a very few places just for ceremonial purposes. Could there have been a practical reason for the custom originally?

Another way of dividing legal rules is into those which deal with private matters and those which deal with matters of public concern. These types are given technical names.

1 Legal rules concerning private matters are called CIVIL LAW and these cases are tried in CIVIL COURTS, e.g. divorce, claims for damages, disputes about wills.

2 Legal rules concerning public issues are called CRIMINAL LAW and these cases are tried in CRIMINAL COURTS. Criminal cases can be grouped in several ways, e.g.

(*a*) Crimes against property, crimes against people and crimes against the nation.

or (*b*) Non–indictable cases tried without a jury; indictable cases tried with a jury.

or (*c*) Petty (small) crimes; very serious crimes.

Some criminal statistics

Male offenders (1975)			
		Under 17	115,000
1,799,000	Total	17–21	265,000
		Over 21	1,419,000
(Figures to nearest thousand)			

Female offenders (1975)			
		Under 17	11,900
189,900	Total	17–21	21,400
		Over 21	156,600
(Figures to nearest hundred)			

Source: *Annual Abstract of Statistics* 1976

People in Prison (1974)			
		New Prisoners	
	Total 40,900	Total	28,100
Under 3 years sentence	38,900	Male	27,000
3 years or longer	2,000	Female	1,100
(All figures to the nearest hundred)			

Source: *Annual Abstract of Statistics* 1976

Dealing with those found guilty

There are many changes taking place in the law courts, prisons, and places to which young offenders under seventeen can be sent.

CRIMINAL COURTS–BRITAIN

HOUSE OF LORDS
In rare cases a final judgement is given by the Law Lords.

COURT OF APPEAL
A person found guilty in a lower court may be allowed to appeal to this court against conviction and/or sentence.

CROWN COURTS
These were established in 1971 to replace Assize Courts and Quarter Sessions. They have a judge and jury and are organised in six areas in Britain. Serious cases may be tried here for the first hearing or referred from a Magistrates' Court.

MAGISTRATES' COURTS
Magistrates are trained but are usually unpaid. There is no jury and there may be one or several magistrates.

One of the most famous parts of the Crown Court, the Old Bailey or central criminal court.

Persons found guilty in Magistrates' Courts or Crown Courts
1973

	Number	*Percentage*
Total	259,278	100
Absolute discharge	2,108	0·8
Conditional discharge	23,854	9·2
Probation	23,829	9·2
Fine	145,931	56·3
Detention centre	4,661	1·8
Borstal training	5,383	2·1
Suspended sentence	20,836	8·0
Imprisonment	26,664	10·3
Attendance centre	216	0·1
Other sentence or order	5,796	2·2

Source: *Annual Abstract* 1974

The problem with collecting statistics is that those who are doing the counting have to decide before they begin on the kinds of groups or 'categories' that they are going to count. Look at the statistics on page 205 and discuss with your friends (*a*) who would be likely to collect statistics on 'crime', (*b*) how you would count someone who had wounded and robbed an old man, (*c*) in what different ways you could change the list of categories and what effect that might have on the statistics.

Under the Children and Young Persons Act 1969, young offenders can be brought before Juvenile Courts, which can make three kinds of decisions if the offender is found guilty. (These are in addition to sending the offender to a Detention Centre or a Borstal.)

(*a*) The Court can bind over the parents or guardians to try to force them to take more care of the young person and to have more control over him.

(*b*) The Court can place the young person under supervision, which is a form of probation.

(*c*) The Court can order the young person to be taken into care by the local authority. The local authority can then place the young person in a Community Home or place him with an adult who is considered suitable.

1 *Community Homes*

Community Homes is the new name for Approved Schools, Remand Homes and Probation Hostels. Where new Community Homes are needed, the speed with which they are built will depend on the amount of money which is available and on joint planning by local authorities and voluntary organisation.

The Children and Young Persons Act also proposed that in the future the 'age of criminal responsibility' should be raised to fourteen. At present anyone over ten years old is considered capable of committing a criminal act, but in the future, of those aged between 10 and 14 only those who are accused of murder or manslaughter will be brought to trial. This raises many issues, particularly about how to deal with young people who do things which, if they were older, would

A policewoman takes the oath before giving evidence.

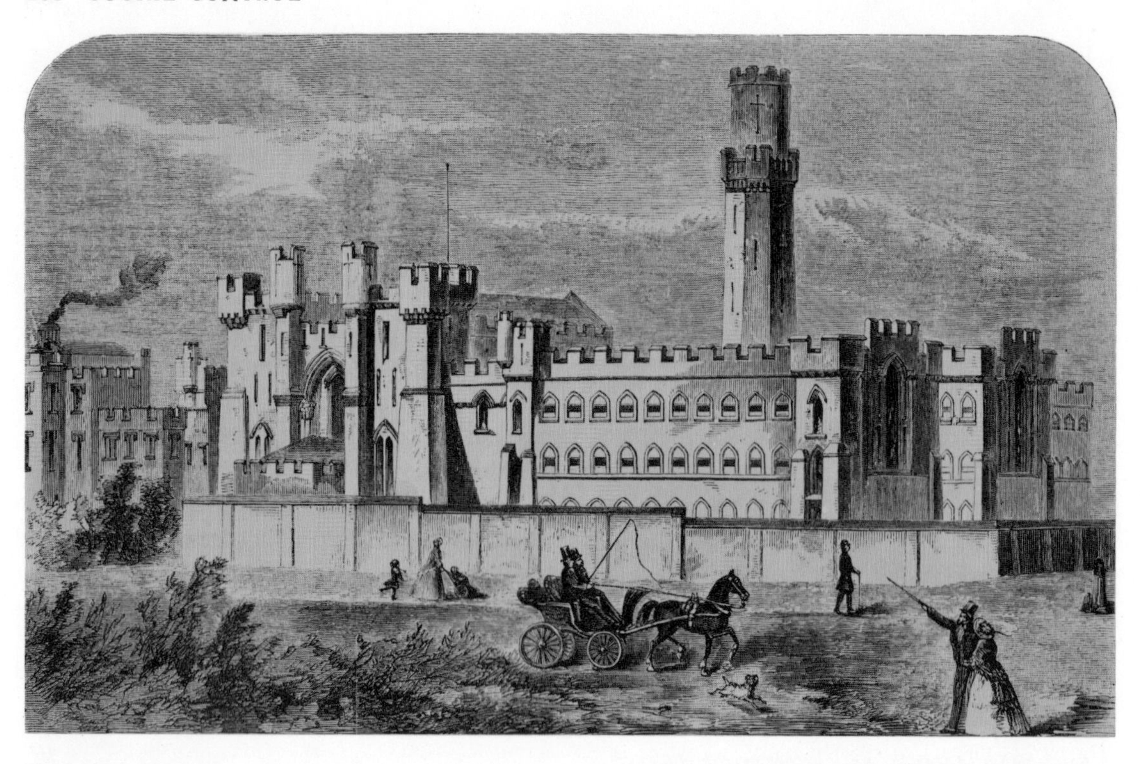

Too many old prisons are still in use. These two pictures are of Holloway, the women's prison in North London. When it was built in the middle of the last century it stood in open country; now it is in a built-up area. But many improvements have been made inside the prison, particularly in the sections used for long-term prisoners.

be criminal acts. For instance, should there be special courts, and if so should the Police be allowed to give evidence?

Borstals and Detention Centres were not dealt with by the 1969 Act of Parliament. The next section outlines a few details about them.

2 *Borstals* *Age:* 15–21 *years old*
Stay: 6 *months* to 2 *years*

These are run by the Home Office because they are really prisons for young people. Usually these are not first offenders. The discipline is strict. The young offenders learn a trade and the aim is that they should use their stay constructively so that they can return to an occupation on leaving.

3 *Detention Centres* *Age:* 15–21 *years old*
Stay: 3 *to* 6 *months*

Here the aim is a 'short sharp shock' to deter the first offender from committing more crime. The control is brisk and firm. The main emphasis is very hard work without soft comfortable conditions.

4 *Prisons*

The court may send an offender over twenty-one years of age to an adult prison. Many of these are old buildings dating from the nineteenth century and conditions in some are appalling. The idea which has developed in the last twenty years is that prisons should not just act as places of punishment. Instead the idea is that prisons should reform the prisoner and prepare him for a non-criminal role in the society when he leaves. Many older prisons are now thought to make prisoners worse, because they resent the conditions and the treatment they receive. This has led to new OPEN PRISONS being built. The emphasis is on training, there are fewer restrictions, rooms are more pleasant, and a greater variety of activity is allowed in recreation time.

Statistics on those who return to prison, 1974

	Males	*Females*
With 1 previous sentence	4,000	108
With 2 previous sentences	3,369	52
With 3 previous sentences	2,551	31
With 4–5 previous sentences	3,114	37
With 6–10 previous sentences	2,937	23
Over 10 previous sentences	1,582	6
Totals	17,553	257

Source: *Annual Abstract of Statistics* 1976

Some people continually return to crime and in some cases people have been known to commit petty crimes with the hope of being caught. Those who habitually return to crime are known as RECIDIVISTS and some of them are thought to be so used to prison life that they regard prison as home and when they are freed they desire to return. Such people are said to be 'institutionalised'. In other words they are totally adapted to prison, which is a kind of institution.

Recently there has been a growing concern about prisoners serving long sentences, e.g. of ten years or more. This includes people serving life sentences for murder. There is too little evidence on the conditions under which such prisoners live, although some letters smuggled from prisons (e.g. those which appeared in the *Guardian* during June 1971) suggest that prisoners may experience solitary confinement, mental strain and physical deprivation, and that the sentence is felt to be a slow tortuous death in place of a short quick one.

There is always controversy about dealing with offenders. On one hand we know more about the social pressures upon criminals, why they commit crimes, and the effects upon them of imprisonment. On the other hand, we desire to protect society, particularly from violent criminals. Some sociologists argue that sweeping social reform is the only way of decreasing

Police trainees at the Metropolitan Police Training School in Hendon learn about Court procedure and the rules of evidence.

crime, which they say is highest where poverty and high-density city dwellings exist together. In any case, there is a cost in terms of money and of people's freedom when individuals are put in prison. Below are some statistics on the money involved.

What is crime?

An action which is thought to be deviant or criminal in one period of history might not be considered criminal at a different historical time. From one society to another opinions vary as to which actions are considered 'criminal'. A good example is children at work. In the nineteenth century factory owners, mill owners and other employers could make children work long hours for very little money. In the early nineteenth century a factory owner could buy orphans and put them to work, some on day shift and some on night shift. It was not 'against

Expenditure on prisons 1969–1970 (*Annual Abstract of Statistics* 1971)

(Year ending 31 March 1970)

General administration and staff	35,361,000
Inmate maintenance	4,853,000
Building maintenance	2,087,000
New buildings	8,738,000
Cost of materials for manufacturing (prison workshops, etc.)	3,217,000
Other costs	3,608,000
Total	£57,864,000

the law', in other words it was not 'criminal'. Today that action would be criminal because there is a law which tries to stop employers from making children work and there is a law which tries to force parents to send children to school.

Another example is that in some societies a person who is hungry is allowed to take whatever food he needs from someone else's garden. It is not thought of as theft as food is not private property. In Britain food is private property and people who take food from shops, markets or gardens are considered to have done a criminal action, even if they, or their relatives, are very hungry. Many actions that attack private property are thought to be criminal in our society, in which a few people own nearly all the property (land, food, clothing and furniture, factories, stocks and shares, flats, tenements and many other examples).

Whenever we think about a law we could ask:

Who is being helped most by that law?

Who is being made into a criminal by that law?

Which people or groups of people decided to make that law?

You could choose a law that seems to you and your teaching group to be interesting and try to answer those questions. If you look in the newspapers you could find out which new laws are being debated or put forward, and which old laws are in the process of being changed, and why. Does the new law make someone into a criminal who would not be a criminal as the law stands now?

Here are some points to consider:

1 What is it about child labour that makes people in twentieth-century Britain decide that it is a crime?
2 Here are two incidents: (*a*) Two men have an argument in the street and one hits the other with his walking stick; (*b*) A pupil 'cheeks' the teacher and is hit three times with a cane. Does the law call it a crime for one person to hit another in both these cases? Do you think the two cases should be treated differently?
3 An eleven-year-old boy breaks into a house and steals money and jewellery. Is he considered a criminal under the law? Do you agree with the law?
4 Often employers disregard safety laws and, as a result, workers in their factories are injured or suffer industrial injury. Very few of these employers are prosecuted. Why do you think they get away with their actions? Should their actions be regarded as criminal or not?
5 In some countries it is considered a crime to oppose the government. Can you think of any countries which have such laws? Why do they have them? What do you think of such laws?

READING AND UNDERSTANDING

1 What are 'norms'?
2 Why do larger organisations have more written rules?
3 What kinds of behaviour are controlled by customs or traditions?
4 Why are there more illegitimate births now than there were in the 1950s?
5 In what ways can public opinion affect people's behaviour?
6 What part did cows play in disputes among the Nuer?
7 What did the Leopard Skin Chief do?
8 How does law in Bisipara differ from law among the Nuer?
9 What are (*a*) the Panchayat, (*b*) ostracism?
10 What is the difference between common law and statute law?

POINTS FOR FURTHER DISCUSSION

1 How did life in the Indian village compare with other simple societies, e.g. how much economic security was there (*a*) among the Nuer, (*b*) in the Indian village? Did everyone

A well at Hope, Derbyshire, decorated with flowers for the annual 'Well Dressing' ceremony. Find out whether any unusual ceremony is still carried out near where you live and try to trace the original reason for it.

in the Indian village have to grow his own food? If not, why not? Give examples.

How much specialisation was there (*a*) among the Nuer, (*b*) in the Indian village?

The Leopard Skin Chief played several roles. Who played these roles in the Indian village?

2 Using the chart below, discuss the amount of choice in the roles open to a British man and woman compared with an Indian man and woman.

Figure 50

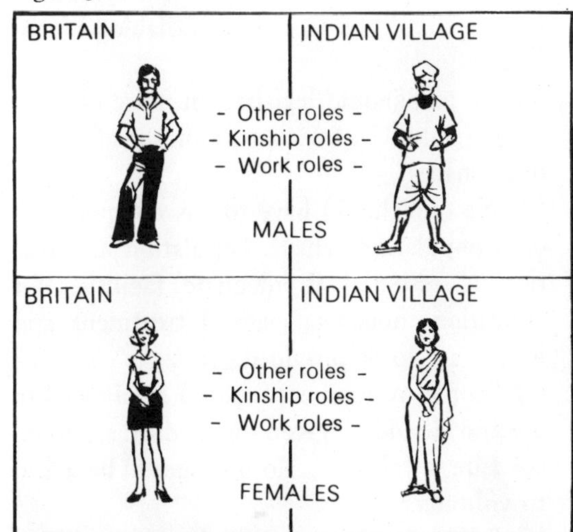

3 Look at the following figures on crime. Draw bar graphs to illustrate these figures.

What conclusions do you draw about (*a*) minor offences, (*b*) serious offences? In view of your conclusions do you think that the newspapers and TV exaggerate the problem of violent and serious crime?

Indictable offences (1974)	
Murder, manslaughter and infanticide	400
Wounding and assault	32,000
Sexual offences	7,000
Robbery	3,000
Burglary	64,000
Theft and handling stolen goods	204,000
Fraud and forgery	18,000
Criminal damage	36,000

Non-indictable offences (1974)	
Assault	12,000
Drunkenness	98,000
Motoring offences	1,173,000
Motor vehicle licences	85,000
Wireless and telegraphy offences	34,000

Source: *Social Trends No. 6* 1975

4 In 1818 there was so much concern about juvenile delinquency that a society was formed especially to study it and to see what could be done to improve the situation. Bearing this in mind, how would you compare crime then and now? Do the facts support the popular ideas that people commit more crimes these days? Are young people worse now in this respect than they were 100 years ago?

May Day is celebrated in many parts of the world. This picture was taken in the Isles of Scilly. The primitive origin of May Day may have been the celebration of the Spring equinox combined with fertility rites to ensure a good harvest.

It shall not be deemed unfair dismissal if a worker is dismissed after a strike	Wear crinolines and be in the trend
	Stealing is punishable by fines or imprisonment
Trespassers will be prosecuted	Do not eat in the classroom
Only one wife allowed at a time	Drive on the left
	Work in silence in the library
Manufacturers of drugs must be on the government register	Come and see the Well Dressings
	A person may vote at 18
Children under 16 should not be sold cigarettes	

5 Which of the above are (*a*) rules for small groups of people, (*b*) customs, (*c*) rules of public opinion, (*d*) legal rules? Make up your own 'rule box' including examples of all the different kinds of rule. Which rules would you like to see changed? Give reasons.

6 Life without rules: In industrial twentieth-century Britain there are thousands of rules of all kinds affecting people's lives. Some we would not miss but without others there would be chaos. Our attitudes and values will make us decide which are essential and which are not. Try to decide which rules are necessary for humans to live in large communities. Robinson Crusoe would need fewer rules than, for example, the whole of Greater London with ten million people.

People often disagree with one another about important subjects, and some have very extreme views on one side or the other of an argument. Here are various views, some unusually extreme; discuss these and try to examine the values and attitudes which affect your own opinions.

(*a*) Birth control drugs should be put into drinking water supplies so that anyone who wants a child should have to seek medical help. Married couples should have to get permission cards from the government if they wish to increase world population by having children. Birth control is a matter for personal choice and no one should interfere.

(*b*) Drugs should be controlled by law. Drug taking is a matter for individual choice. Heroin should be as widely available as nicotine.

(*c*) No one should legislate on noise control. People should be free to use radios in all public open spaces.

(*d*) No one should have to answer questions on a population census. Population information is essential if adequate facilities for education, housing, medical treatment and leisure are to be provided.

(*e*) People over seventy should be allowed to die and should be given the medical aid to do so. Life is valuable. No one should be asked to volunteer to die.

(*f*) Education in nursery schools should be compulsory for all children after the age of three. Children should not have to start school until they are seven years old.

(*g*) Every firm should have to provide a crèche for the pre-school children of working mothers. Women should not be encouraged to go out to work while their children are very young.

PROJECT WORK

1 Collect several local and national newspapers. Cut out all news items concerning crimes. Sort the cuttings into groups according to the type of crime. Look up 'Crime' and 'Criminal' in encyclopaedias and compare the way

crimes are classified there with the way that you have classified them.

2 Find out more about
   (*a*) why people commit crimes
   (*b*) the procedure from arrest to trial
   (*c*) the work of the law courts
   (*d*) the work of the police
   (*e*) the probation service.

Teachers can obtain useful information from the following organisations:

Scotland Yard
The Police Federation
The Metropolitan Police Recruitment Centre
The Home Office
The Central Office of Information
The Probation Service.

USEFUL BOOKS FOR PUPILS

Behan, B. *Borstal Boy* (Hutchinson 1967; also in Corgi paperback)
Bulwer, P. *Law and Society* (Social Studies series) (Blandford 1975)
Connexions series, (a) *The Law-breakers* (Penguin Education 1969) (b) *Violence* (Penguin Education 1970)
Forbes, T. & Sommer, P. *The Law* (Harrap 1972)
Hurman, A. *As Others See Us* (Edward Arnold 1977)
Marland, M. (ed.) *Z Cars Scripts* (Imprint series) (Longman 1968)
Roshier, R. *Crime and Punishment* (Social Science series) (Longman 1976)
Sillitoe, A. *The Loneliness of the Long Distance Runner* (Star Books 1975)
Solzhenitsyn, A. *One Day in the Life of Ivan Denisovich* (Penguin 1970)

USEFUL BOOKS FOR TEACHERS

Becker, H. *Outsiders* (Free Press, June 1966)
Christian, R. *Old English Customs* (Country Life 1966)
Cohen, S. *Images of Deviance* (Penguin 1971)
Cohen, S. & Taylor, L. *Psychological Survival* (Penguin 1973)
Douglas, M. et al. *Man in Society* (Macdonald 1964)
Taylor, I. et al. *New Criminology* (Routledge & Kegan Paul 1973)

FILMS

Out of Harm's Way (prisoners in a new prison); 30 mins; b/w; Concord Films Council
Inside:
   1 Men in Prison; 2 Women in Prison; 3 Young Offenders (Detention Centres); 32 mins each; b/w; British Film Institute
The Lawyers (legal profession in England and Wales); 83 mins; Central Film Library u/c 1969
It's Just Our Job (the police force); ILEA 831
Sentence of the Court (young offenders – originally part of BBC TV for Schools programme *Scene*); 30 mins; b/w; BBC TV Enterprises
Last Bus, forerunner to Sentence of the Court; 30 mins; BBC *Scene* programme; BBC TV Enterprises
The Law of the Land; a series of filmstrips; 20 mins each, distributed by the Law Society

8 The Urban Environment

We use the word *environment* to mean our surroundings. As we have seen in the chapters on socialisation, our surroundings often include important people. The closest are our family and friends. But our environment also includes the place in which we live and the *things* as well as the *people*. This chapter looks in more detail at our physical surroundings – the houses, the streets, the towns, and the countryside. In the chapter on population we see that people create rubbish, dirt and noise. Pollution and the physical environment are continually in the news

Perhaps in 100 years' time people will look back, amazed that anyone could survive in such conditions.

because we have only a short time left in which to limit population growth and to clean up the mess which we are making of the land.

In the nineteenth and twentieth centuries there has been a great increase in the number of people in the world and in the building of towns and cities for them to live in. The growth of towns and cities is called urbanisation from the word 'urban' which means 'town'. Perhaps in one hundred years' time we shall look back at the dirt and overcrowding in our cities, amazed that people could survive in such conditions. On the other hand, if we do not plan more pleasant places to live in we may not survive at all. This is why this chapter is called 'The Urban Environment'.

Figure 51

Housing

During the nineteenth century the number of people in Britain increased from 10·5 millions to 33 millions. Since then the population has increased to its present level of 55 millions. Many of these people live in large cities as shown on the map.

People need houses. During the nineteenth century many houses were built as cheaply and quickly as possible for the growing numbers of town dwellers. Sewers and fresh water were often not provided and the houses quickly developed into slums. Gradually public health became such a problem in the towns and cities that government action was necessary. In 1868 the Towns Act allowed local councils to begin to clear the slums but this was not compulsory until the Public Health Act of 1875. Clean water and proper sewers had to be provided by the local authorities and they had the power to clear the slums. Little was done in most towns, and, although in London 28,000 slum houses were demolished, hundreds were still standing at the beginning of the twentieth century.

As soon as transport developed and the middle classes could travel easily to work in the towns and cities they moved to houses on the outskirts leaving the working classes in the central areas. One of the problems of the towns and cities is that as fast as old houses are pulled down others have deteriorated and then they also need clearing. In the 1970s we are still trying to cope with the problems inherited from the past. Slum housing still exists and the overall shortage of housing in the cities is very high.

HOUSEHOLDS

There are not enough dwellings for all the existing households. A household is a group of people who regularly eat meals together and sleep in the same dwelling. Here are some examples of different households:

(*a*) a nuclear family with several young children
(*b*) a husband and wife with two unmarried adult children
(*c*) a nuclear family with a lodger, e.g. a student, who pays for his food and his rent
(*d*) three friends sharing a flat
(*e*) a man and woman living together
(*f*) an old person living alone

How many more examples can you think of?

These households have different housing needs. They need different sized dwellings to live in and different facilities such as garages, pram sheds, gardens and somewhere to hang the washing.

There are not enough dwellings to keep up with the number of people needing them. Also the dwellings are in the wrong places, or are too expensive. Some landlords will not rent to people with children.

People move to cities to find work. If there are not enough houses then the people have to share and this leads to overcrowding. Overcrowding can be of two main types. The first type is found where one large family lives in a dwelling which is too small. The second type is found where two or more smaller families have to share a dwelling and thus there are too many people for the number of rooms. The second type is called MULTIPLE OCCUPATION.

ADEQUATE HOUSING

Let us look at an extended family (Figure 52 below). We can imagine that Peter's extended family is quite lucky and that all the members have an ideal housing situation.

In the detached house there are four bedrooms, a lounge and a dining-room and also a garage, greenhouse and shed. In the semi-detached house there are three bedrooms, a lounge and a dining-room and also a garage. In the terraced house there are two bedrooms, a lounge and a dining-room. The flat has two bedrooms, a lounge and a dining-room, and also a pram shed and garage. In each dwelling there is a bathroom and toilet, and a kitchen which is large enough to hold a table for eating breakfast.

Therefore each part of Peter's extended family has somewhere adequate to sleep and to eat. There are enough communal rooms and other facilities to make life comfortable. Peter's own nuclear family have a spare bedroom which may also be used as a study or a workroom.

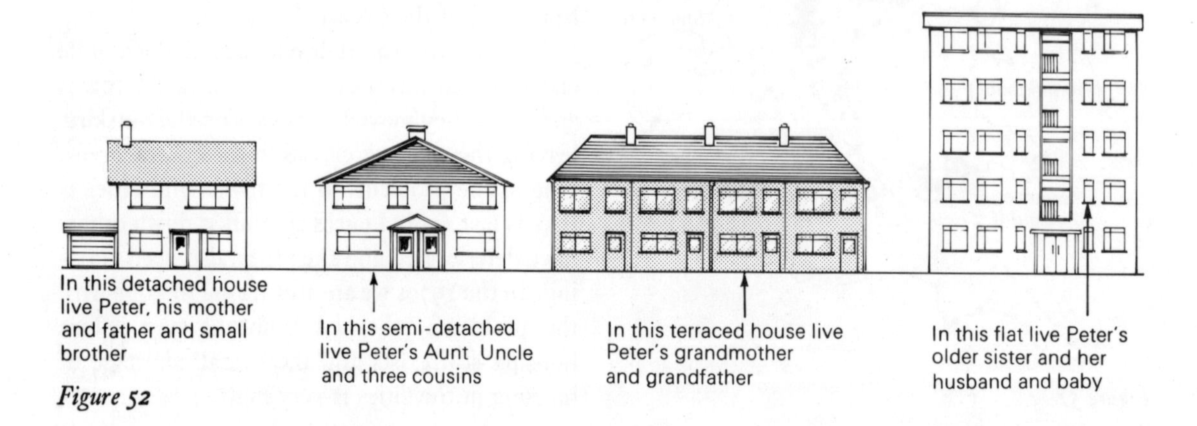

Figure 52

Low-density housing in Basingstoke, Hampshire.

Adequate housing? New Addington, Croydon, Surrey.

Every great city has its slums, and in many places they are far worse than in Britain. Here, in Belem, Brazil, more than a thousand children live in 'stilt city' where lights, pure water and modern sanitation are unknown.

INADEQUATE AND OFFICIALLY OVERCROWDED HOUSING

Not all families are so fortunate. We have already seen that many have to live in slum houses. There are also thousands in TWILIGHT AREAS which are areas that still have some sound housing, but the rest of the housing is beginning to decay, and the area could become a slum in the future.

What does it really mean to live in inadequate or slum housing? Where is most of this type of housing? Which facilities are lacking? It is hard to measure the true amount of overcrowding. One measurement which is often used is the number of rooms compared with the number of people. If there are more than one and a half people per room the family is officially overcrowded. In the 1966 census of population a kitchen was counted as a room if it could be used for eating in. Each married couple and single adult was to have a separate bedroom, and only children of the same sex were to share. Using these measurements it was found that 390,000 families with 1,420,000 children were overcrowded. But many families living in very cramped conditions were not officially overcrowded.

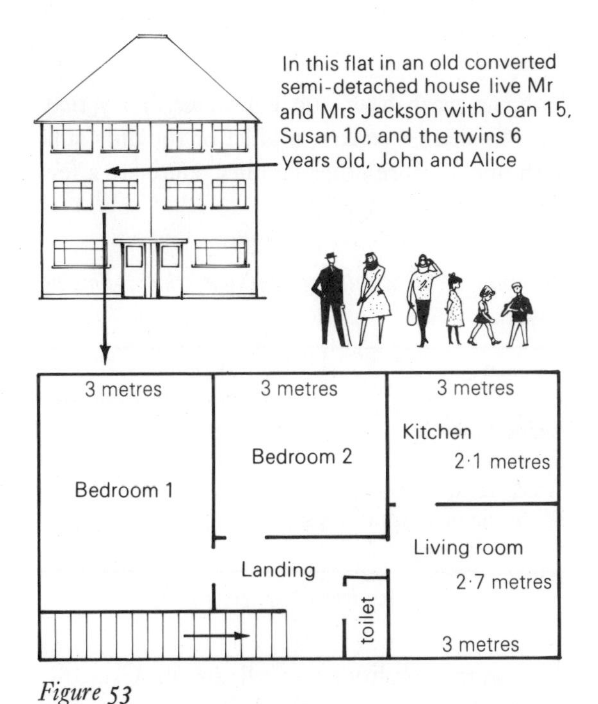

Figure 53

The family in Fig 53 has no privacy. The rooms are small. Joan and Susan have nowhere to do their homework. John and Alice have only a cramped space to play in. Mrs Jackson keeps the place spotless. There is no garden, or shed for large toys or bikes. The front door opens on to the pavement. The house is in a road behind the shopping centre which is crowded at peak times. The flat has no bath but it has its own cooker and toilet. This family is officially living in adequate housing, because there are no more than one and a half persons per room. No account is taken of the size of rooms in the government census. From the point of view of the government, families like the Jacksons do not have a housing problem. There are so many in much worse conditions that their problems are considered small by comparison.

Official overcrowding – this family sleeps, eats and lives in one room.

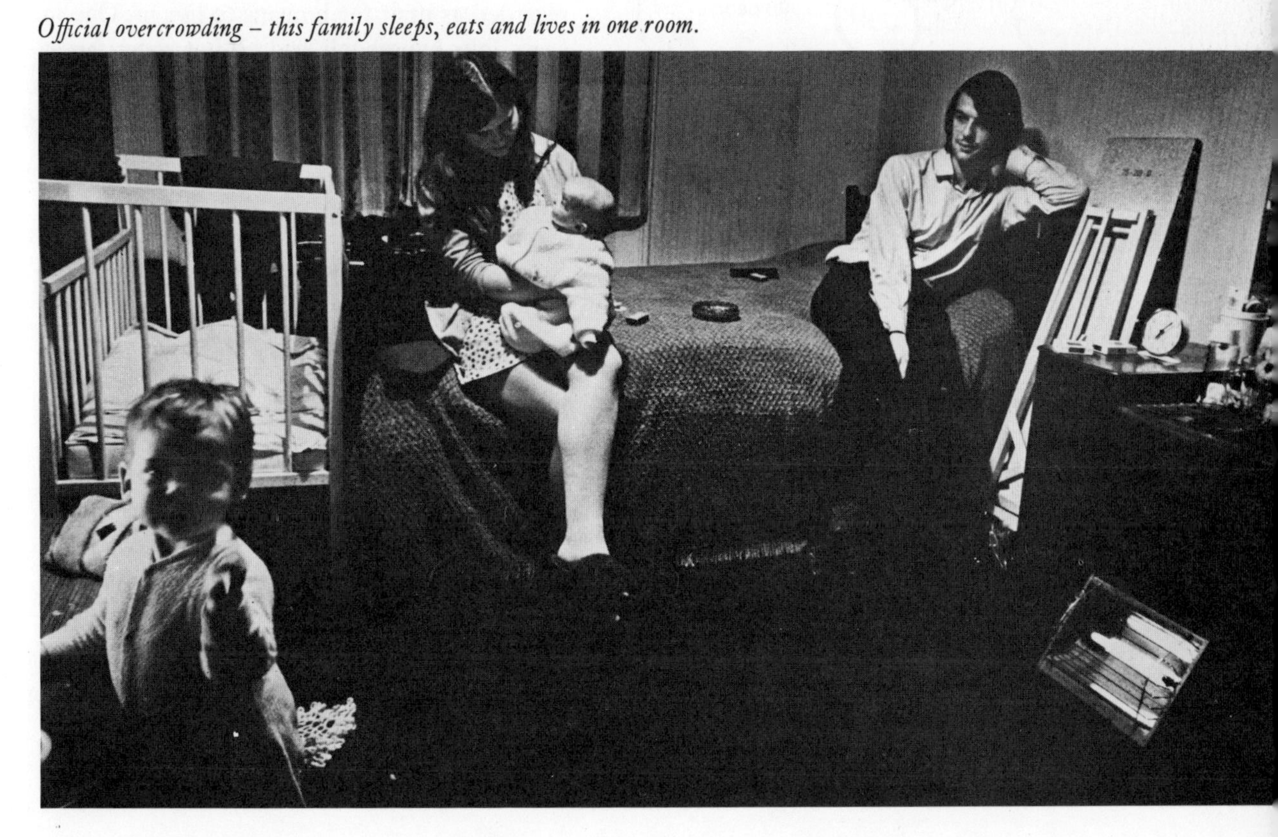

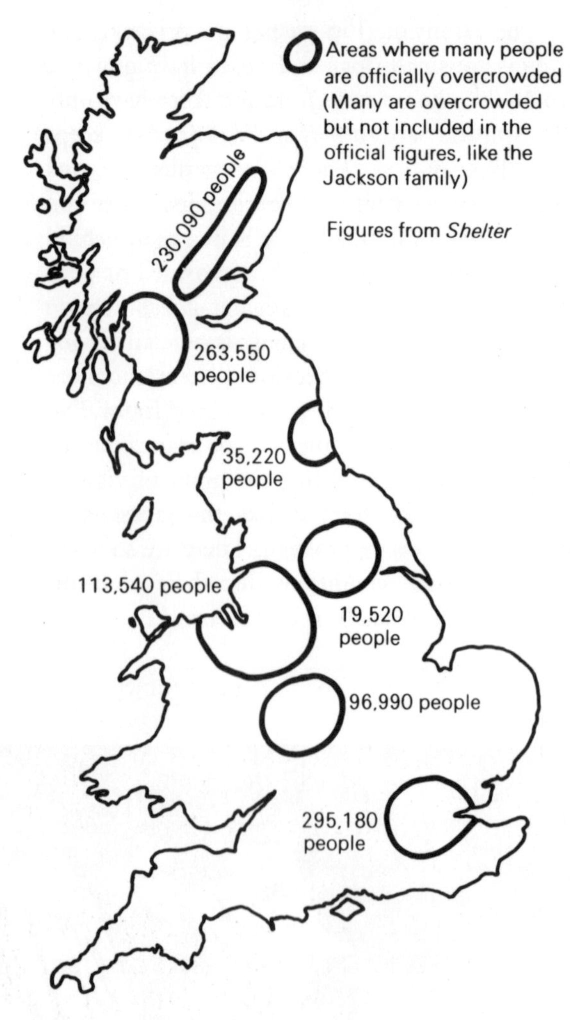

Figure 54

Figure 54 is a map of housing in Britain. This time the people who are officially overcrowded are included on the map. The others are left out. The families on the map have more than one and a half people for each room in the dwelling.

In some of the most overcrowded areas one-tenth to one-fifth of the people are in very cramped conditions.

For many families the above figures do not mean very much. What really matters to them is that they may have no inside toilet, no fixed bath, no wash basin, no hot water. They may have to share a cooker, a toilet or the only sink with one or more other families. Here are a few figures:

Percentage of dwellings without the following items:

	S. E. Lancashire	*West Midlands*
Inside toilet	28·2	23·0
Fixed bath	17·5	12·3
Wash basin	21·7	19·2
With one or more of these items lacking	29·1	27·4

(Figures from *Shelter*, 1971).

The worst conditions of all are in Glasgow. Nearly half (41%) of the housing was below standard in 1966, and 20% of dwellings were regarded as unfit for humans to live in. One in every four households had no hot water tap at all, and hundreds of families were sharing sinks and cookers with other families.

THE EFFECTS OF BAD HOUSING

What kinds of effects do these conditions have on the family life of the people?

Even the most stable person can break down under constant stress and strain. Lack of privacy, tiredness from poor sleeping conditions, boredom from lack of play space for children and recreation facilities for adults, and irritability from continual disturbance by other family members all add together to create mental and physical suffering in children and in adults. In a good environment most people—even those who have unstable personalities—manage to cope with their problems. But faced with dirt, lack of space, noise, poor schools, overcrowding and low wages the strains are too great and people cannot cope.

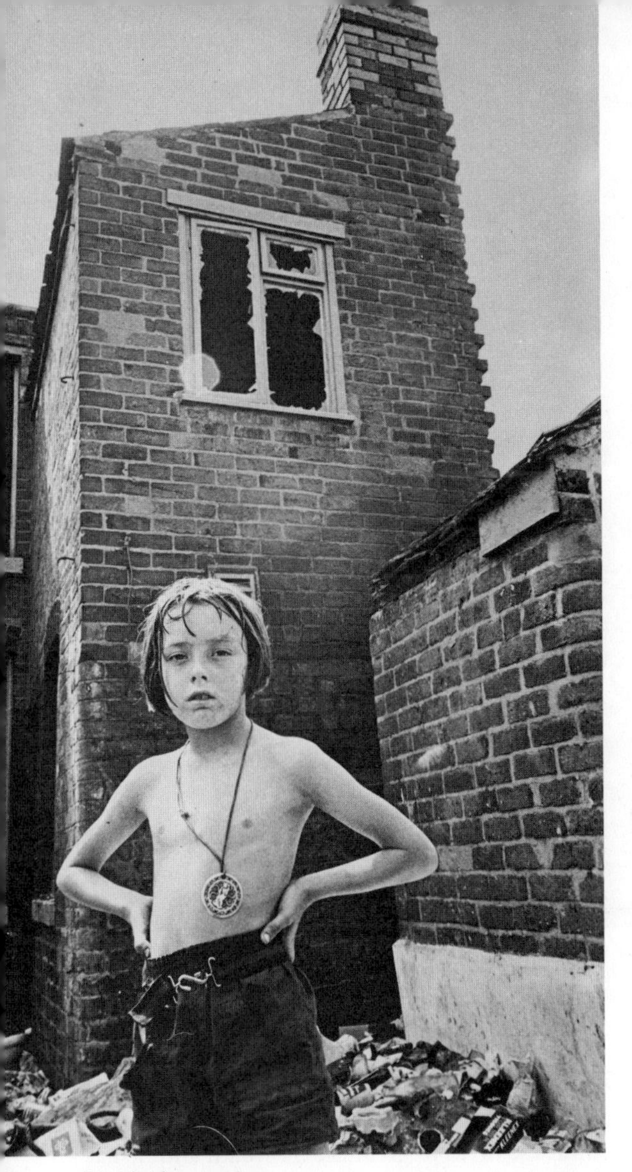

Birmingham 1969.

Sometimes conditions are so bad that a dwelling is no longer fit for children and then the family may break up if it cannot find anywhere else to live as a group. Sometimes the children have to go and live with relatives; sometimes they have to go to children's homes or foster homes. In the year ending March 1970 nearly 6,000 children were separated from their parents because of housing difficulties. Many other children live with their families in temporary hostels where conditions frequently lead to unhappiness.

Children living in bad housing have nowhere to do their homework, nowhere to read quietly, nowhere to play, inadequate lighting and heating and nowhere to sleep restfully. Many have to share beds in noisy rooms and so they sleep badly and are too tired to work in school or to enjoy their leisure. They cannot achieve the success they are capable of in either primary or secondary school. No matter how clever a child is he cannot do as well as he would like if he has bad housing that hinders him.

Mr and Mrs Jackson are living in overcrowded conditions, but at least they have a roof over their heads. Mr and Mrs Peters, on the other hand, have nowhere at all of their own because when their first baby arrived they had to move from their furnished flat and could find nowhere else. They are some of the 20,000 people living in temporary accommodation provided by the local council until the council can rehouse them or they can find somewhere by themselves.

In 1969 nearly 22,000 people asked to go into temporary accommodation provided by local councils. Only 5,500 could be fitted in and the rest had to be turned away. Nearly all the people asking for help had been evicted legally or illegally by their landlords. In London six out of ten of the people were British or Irish and four out of ten were Commonwealth immigrants. The situation was worst in London where almost half of the people needing help lived.

WHO CAN HELP?

Shelter is a charity which tries to rescue people in very bad housing situations. It was set up in December 1966 and tries to tell people the facts about housing and about the misery which bad housing causes. It tries to show how people can help in the work of voluntary HOUSING ASSOCIATIONS and it tries to raise at least £1 million per year for this purpose.

Even the most stable person can break down under constant stress.

A housing association may be formed by a group of people who care about the housing situation in a particular area. They may receive money from Shelter and can then borrow between five times and eight times as much from local councils. The money is used to buy up old but sound houses, to change them quickly into clean flats and then to rent them at moderate or low rents to people who are desperate for somewhere to live. Here are some typical examples of families who have been rehoused.

Mr and Mrs S. lived in Notting Hill in one room 3.7 x 3 metres in size, for which they paid £3.50 a week. They shared the bathroom and w.c. with six other people and even the cooker and sink, which were on the landing, had to be shared with other people. The place was dirty and their little boy was ill. Now that they have a decent place to live in the boy is a different child. He loves to go in the new bath and he has somewhere to play and a quiet place to sleep. Mr and Mrs S. think it is wonderful to have two rooms, a kitchen and bathroom – and no bugs!

John was a little boy whose health became worse and worse when he lived with his mother, father and sister in one room. When he was five he was taken to a children's home because the one room was so damp. His family was rehoused in 1969 and John was able to return to his family.

Mr and Mrs N. have four children. The little boys are aged five and three and share a single bed. The girl, who is fourteen, and a boy of twelve have to share another single bed, while

This little boy has learnt to concentrate, but can a child do his best in bad housing conditions?

their mother and father have a mattress on the floor. They keep themselves clean but are terribly overcrowded. There is no bathroom and they share a toilet with three other families. They badly need somewhere else to live.

Shelter exists to deal with emergencies but the real problem can only be solved over a long period by the government and local councils. They provide money out of rates and taxes for building new dwellings and improving or converting old houses, and are responsible for clearing slum areas. Their problem is to find enough money to do all this when they have so many other things to spend on. Private builders also provide dwellings but they want to make a profit and must balance the costs of building materials, land and labour against the money obtained from selling the houses. When there is a shortage of anything the prices go up. At the moment there is a great shortage of land and privately-built houses are quickly becoming much too expensive for ordinary working people to hope to buy their own home. But somehow the housing problem must be overcome, otherwise there will be a growing number of people living in unhealthy and miserable conditions, particularly in our big cities.

Town and country planning

Look again at the first map in this chapter. The regions with a very dense population are really regions where several towns have grown together so that most of the countryside in between is swallowed up. These regions are called CONURBATIONS. (The word comes from 'con' meaning with and 'urban' meaning town. Conurbation means an area 'with lots of towns' with hardly any space in between.) Here are the sizes of the populations in several conurbations:

(To nearest million)

Conurbations	*1971 Census Figures*
Greater London	7·5 m
West Midlands	2·4 m
Merseyside	0·8 m
S. E. Lancashire	2·4 m
West Yorkshire	1·7 m
Central Clydeside	1·7 m

Statistics from *Annual Abstract* 1974

Find the main towns in each conurbation from the first map, and if you wish, copy and label your own map and include the size of each conurbation. The conurbations have other problems beside the housing situation. Pollution of the air, roads and water by traffic noise, dirt, fumes and smells; congestion in narrow roads and in shopping centres; high travelling costs and long daily commuting time; high rates and rents for industry as well as houses: these are just a few of the problems. There are many advantages too. City children who visit the country may complain of the lack of theatres, cinemas, dance halls, cafes and discotheques. They may dislike the lack of shelter when it rains or the long walking distances from place to place. Country-lovers think that the wide open spaces and peace and quiet are marvellous, and they may dislike the throb of the city with its hustle and bustle.

There are several ways of combining the advantages of both kinds of environment so that people may enjoy both the facilities of towns and the beauty and peace of the country. All these ideas are related to the growth of the idea of planning the physical environment so that people may develop all parts of their personality and their social lives.

Sometimes people's environments are planned without concern for their wishes and their needs. In a book called *The Pre-School Years* by W. Van der Eyken, there are many comments on the limitations on small children who live high above ground level in blocks of flats. The flats may be modern, dry and warm and have plenty of room, but the children are prisoners inside them. They cannot be let out alone and so have no one to play with and nowhere to play. They may not make a lot of noise and are not allowed to keep pets. They rarely see trees or flowers, or run around on grass. Sometimes planners have ideas about what they think people want, but unless they *ask* people they may be providing quite the wrong things. For this reason some plans have developed after surveys have been done asking people if they mind living in flats, how near they would like to be to shops and schools, stations and buses, and what recreational facilities they would like for themselves and their children. Towns and cities and conurbations are for leisure as well as working, eating and sleeping.

In 1969 a government social survey was published which gave an account of people's leisure activities over the whole country, and also in special areas like New Towns and large cities. The survey was called 'Planning for Leisure'.

THE NEW TOWNS

The New Towns have been created since 1946 under the New Towns Act. There are twenty-four New Towns planned or built (as shown on the map) where people from overcrowded cities and conurbations can be rehoused. A variety of industries and services are available to provide employment so that very few New Towns dwellers need to commute to the cities each day. Some New Towns are created where there is already a growing industry, e.g. Corby in Northants, or in an area where there is plenty of work but where the housing in the area needs improvement, e.g. Cwmbran in a mining valley in Monmouthshire.

People who live in New Towns tend to be young married couples with children. Nearly all of them have a whole house or a maisonette or flat with a private garden, and about two thirds own a car. In London there are more people in the older age groups. Only one-third of households have a whole house or other accommodation with its own garden, and just less than half of the households have a car.

PEOPLE AND LEISURE

It was found in the survey that many factors have an effect upon the way people spend their leisure, e.g. their ages and income, where they live and what kind of dwelling they live in, whether they have a car and the kind of education they had. Nearly all households (about 90%) had a television when the survey was done.

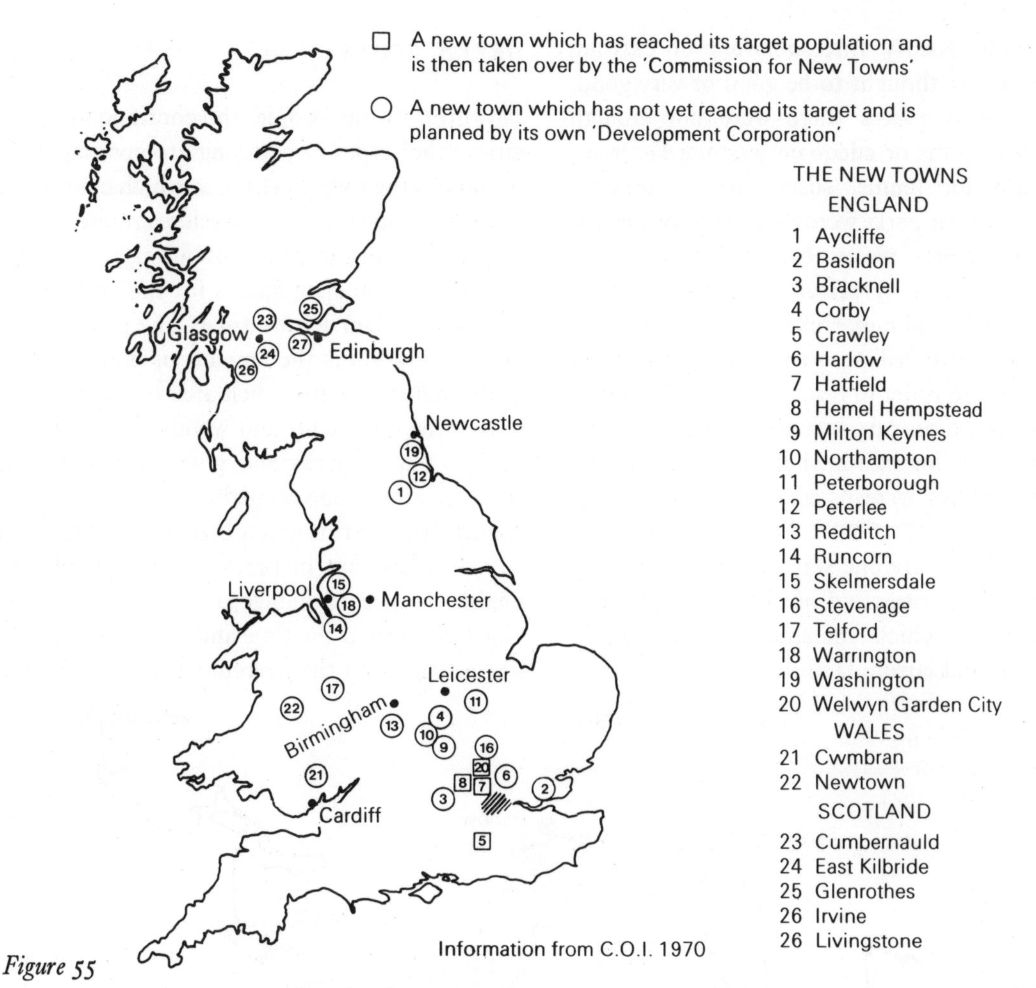

Figure 55

In the survey people were asked general questions about leisure, and detailed questions about outdoor activities and sports. The survey was trying to link people's wishes and needs with the planning of the physical environment. Everywhere people said they would like a garden of their own, and this was especially true for Londoners because so few of them had gardens. Many people wanted to see more grass and trees around them and said that they would like more parks and open spaces. In London many mothers wanted more playgrounds for younger children, and in the New Towns the greatest concern was for more swimming pools and paddling pools for children to use.

Near their homes all the people wanted to have shops and parks and many wanted indoor sports centres. At the top of the list older women put shops, younger women put theatres and parks, and young single men put indoor sports centres. The sports and games facilities were mainly provided by local councils, but private clubs and social clubs in factories and other places of employment also provided recreation such as table tennis, fencing, archery, shooting, badminton and squash. Works clubs mainly provided soccer, cricket and table tennis.

The actual sports chosen varied from place to place and are mentioned in the chapter on

Education. Nearly three-quarters of existing facilities were thought to be good or very good, but in many places there were not enough changing rooms or adequate washing facilities, especially for tennis, soccer and swimming. Many more car parks were thought to be needed near the sports places because most of the players travelled by private transport, such as cars, scooters and motorbikes. When people had cars they were willing to travel further away from home in order to reach the sports facilities. Those who took part in water sports travelled furthest, e.g. for half an hour or more, whilst tennis facilities were usually only ten minutes away.

New Towns are one way of coping with the overspill from cities and of planning a physical environment which includes housing, work, education and leisure facilities.

GREEN BELTS

However, for the people who continue to live in cities other types of planning are possible. One of these is the GREEN BELT idea which consists of a wide expanse of countryside around cities, separating them from neighbouring towns, and providing wide open spaces for the city people to enjoy in their leisure time. The government deliberately limits the amount of building that is allowed in the green belt area but it does not have to be only fields and woods. Part of it can be laid out as parks and golf courses so that sports facilities are available within the open area. In theory this green belt is available to all city dwellers, but in practice some people are unable to take advantage of the facilities provided because of the time and money needed to travel to it from the overcrowded centre of the

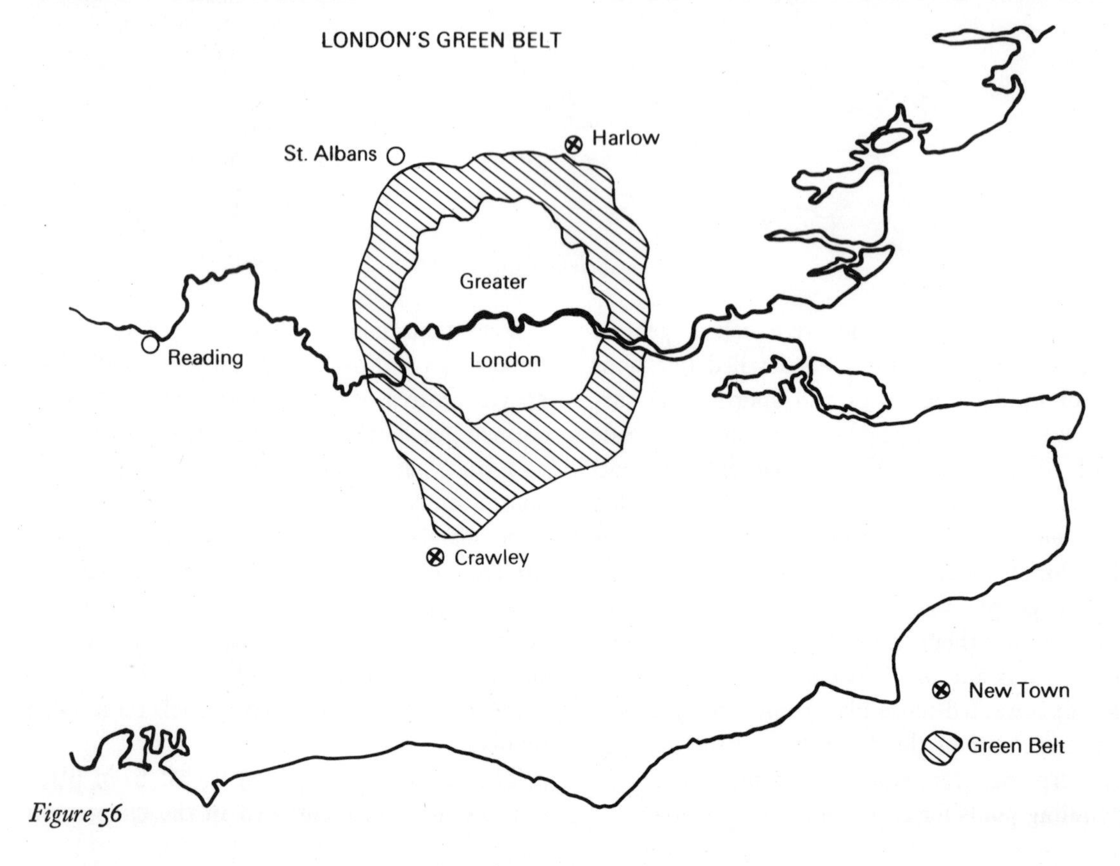

Figure 56

city. Many people from the suburbs travel into the central area daily to work. In the London conurbation some people in the suburbs spend an hour or more each way getting to and from work. Others may commute from towns and villages outside the green belt, e.g. from Brighton, Dartford, Gravesend, Southend or Reading; their travelling time each day may be three, four or even five hours. This raises the question of the amount of real leisure time people have after travelling, eating and sleeping.

Some people have more choice than others of where to live and to work. Much depends on the person's social background, his education and the work available in the area in which he was brought up. In recent years unemployment in some areas of Britain has increased. The reasons for this are outlined in pages 70–71. Some of these areas have been called DEVELOPMENT DISTRICTS where Government grants have encouraged businessmen to start new industries and provide more jobs. Even so many people have left to seek work elsewhere. Most have moved to the Midlands or S.E. England, pulled by the amount of work available. This is called the 'S.E. drift' and has increased the overcrowding in these areas. As a result planning on a large scale is urgently needed in the S.E. where there is a congestion problem, and in the Development Districts where the problem is one of an ageing or unemployed population.

PLANNING, CONSERVATION AND POLLUTION

In the twentieth century we have begun to realise that our surroundings are better if they

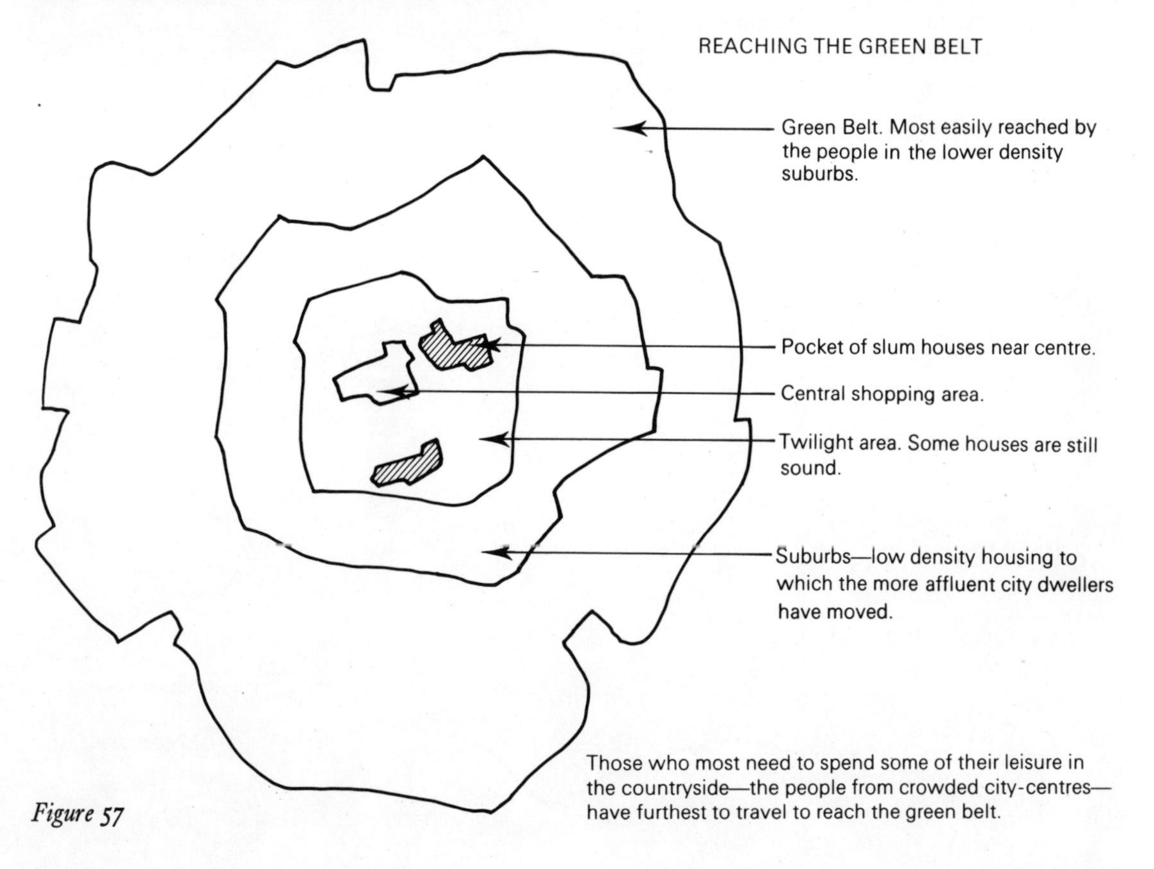

Figure 57

consist of well-planned towns, beautiful buildings and unspoiled fields, woods and sea-shores. We have also realised that if this is to be possible we must have strict controls on pollution. A start has been made. Pollution is a very familiar word to many people these days, but we have a long way to go before Britain becomes 'a green and pleasant land' again.

As a society we have spoiled lovely views by criss-crossing them with telegraph posts, and hiding them with large road signs and posters and advertisements. We need roads and houses, shops and factories, but if we are to enjoy our physical environment these will have to be planned so that they add to the beauty instead of spoiling it.

Under the Town & Country Planning Acts local planning authorities are able to limit the number of display advertisements, e.g. posters and hoardings, in case they become unsafe or unsightly, and to control the development of new mines and quarries in order to try and prevent them spoiling the countryside.

Unspoiled countryside: the Roman Wall at Housesteads, Northumberland.

We have begun to realise that it is necessary to have strict controls on pollution.

Lake District National Park. Is litter a greater menace in the countryside than where people live?

National Parks in England and Wales.

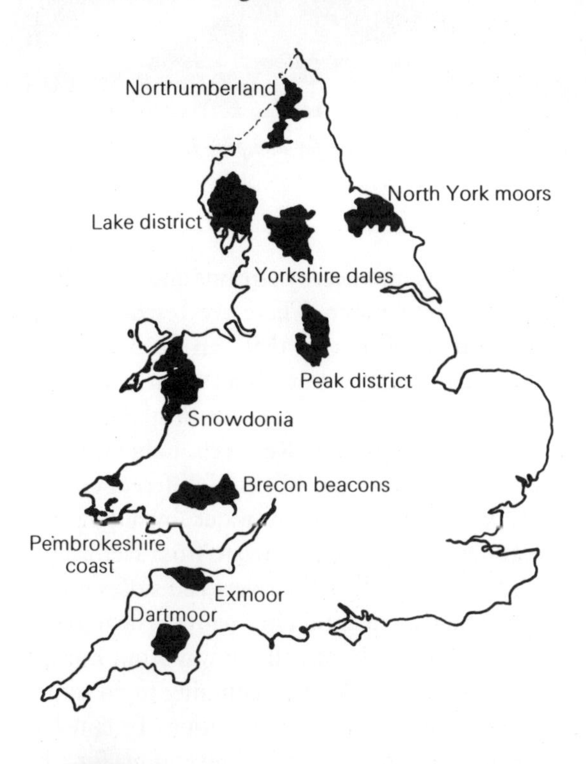

Many voluntary societies exist to try and protect the countryside. The National Trust was founded in 1895 and owns and cares for large stretches of beautiful scenery. At the present time it has begun a campaign called 'Enterprise Neptune' to preserve 900 miles of coastline, some of which is in danger of being ruined by buildings or sea-shore pollution.

In 1949 an Act of Parliament was passed which began the formation of National Parks. Ten of these have already been established as shown on the map. They cover over 5,000 square miles (nearly 13,000 square kilometres – about one-tenth of the land in Britain) and they exist in order to keep the scenery as naturally beautiful as possible and to provide and improve leisure facilities. As individuals we can play our part by not leaving litter. Humans and animals have been hurt by pieces of broken glass left in fields or outdoor swimming baths, and farm animals have died after eating plastic bags left by picnickers. Beaches and woods have been dirtied by rubbish of all sorts, from abandoned cars and old mattresses to paper and banana skins.

Getting rid of rubbish is becoming more and more of a problem. Is there any excuse for dumping it at the roadside like this?

One of the biggest problems for a complex industrial society with many people living in towns is getting rid of rubbish. Some rubbish can be burned or crushed, but even so the ashes and the non-burnable waste have to be put somewhere. Some local councils use old quarries and mines as rubbish tips, gradually filling in the holes until the countryside is level again. In other places huge mounds of rubbish pile up and we must ask ourselves what kind of mess we are making for future generations to look at. Sometimes the rubbish can be dangerous as well as horrible to look at. We have been slow to realise the need for laws to control the dumping of dangerous chemicals like cyanide, which is poisonous and can easily be washed from the rubbish tips into nearby streams and from there into drinking water. There are restrictions on the kind of chemicals that can be discharged from factories into our rivers from which the water boards have to take our drinking water. The Water Pollution Research Laboratory at Stevenage studies the effects of different chemicals in the pollution of water including the treatment of sewage and waste from factories.

The sea as well as the rivers can suffer pollution. The *Ra* expedition in a papyrus boat found oil pollution of the sea all the way from Europe to the Americas. We are beginning to do something about this kind of pollution. Britain has joined the International Convention for the Prevention of Pollution of the Sea by Oil, which

A tanker goes aground on the Goodwin Sands. Detergent sprays help to disperse the oil washed up on our beaches. But is this an adequate answer to pollution of the sea?

began its work in 1958. There are now many regulations which restrict the dumping of oil at sea within fifty or sometimes a hundred miles of coastlines and for large areas of certain oceans.

In some instances the very things which cause pollution are also wasting our resources. This is especially true of many of the elaborate packings in which foods, cosmetics and other items such as drinks are now sold. People may just throw disposable bottles in the dustbin and think no more about them, but hundreds of thousands of bottles a day are involved, which all have to go somewhere; and at the same time raw materials and fuel are being used to replace them.

Not only bottles but many other products could be 'recycled', that is be cleaned and re-used or the materials from which they are made (paper and metal for instance) could be used again for some other product. In these ways resources could be conserved and pollution could be reduced at the same time.

READING AND UNDERSTANDING

1 How is population growth in Britain linked with the present housing situation?
2 (*a*) What is a household?
  (*b*) Do all households have the same housing needs?
3 What kinds of overcrowding can occur and what causes overcrowding?

4 (*a*) What is the official measure of overcrowding?
   (*b*) How useful is it?
5 Why don't the Jacksons count as being overcrowded?
6 Which areas suffer the most serious overcrowding?
7 What effects does bad housing have on family life?
8 What does Shelter do to help those in bad housing conditions?
9 What is a conurbation?
10 Explain what is meant by (*a*) New Town and (*b*) Green Belt.
11 What kinds of problems can occur in cities, besides poor housing?
12 Explain the meaning of 'Development District'.

POINTS FOR FURTHER DISCUSSION

1 What are some of the items on which the government must spend money? Look back to pages 48–56 to give you ideas. Which items do you think are most important? Is it easy for a government to decide what to spend money on?
2 *Town or Country?* Discuss the advantages and disadvantages of living in each type of area.

PROJECT WORK

1 Do a survey on different types of roads in your area. Which types of houses are found there? How old are the houses? Are they in good condition?
2 Ask your teacher to write to the local council for statistics on housing in your area. Draw bar graphs and cake diagrams to show
   (*a*) the income of the householders
   (*b*) whether the houses are rented or owned by the people living there
   (*c*) whether any of the houses are in multiple occupation.
3 Read *Cathy Come Home* by Jeremy Sandford. Why did Cathy's housing problem arise? What happened to Cathy? How could Cathy have been helped?
4 Collect all the news cuttings about housing from the local papers. Do the news cuttings tell of any families with housing problems? Do any tell of council housing plans? Will any other building plans affect the housing in the area?
5 Some people suggest that a 'green wedge' is a better idea than a green belt. Find out more details about green wedges and write comments on their usefulness.
6 Make a map of your area to show
   (*a*) parks and open places
   (*b*) main roads and bus routes
   (*c*) shops
   (*d*) entertainment facilities
   (*e*) areas of low or high density housing.
   From this map what are your conclusions about town and country planning in your area? Would you re-plan in any way? If so, how would you do it? What reasons would you give for your changes?
7 Find out how to buy a house. You will come across the following words:
   estate agent solicitor surveyor
   building society mortgage owner-occupation
   freehold deposit leasehold
   interest
   Find out the meaning of each of these technical terms and write an account in detail of all the things you would have to do from the time you decided you wanted somewhere of your own to the time when you moved in. Many of the books on the reference list have sections on this project, and also you can get information from Shelter which publishes a special booklet on house purchase, and from the Building Societies Association. The addresses are at the back of the book.
8 What kinds of cities will we have in the

future? Use Jackdaw number 80 to give you some ideas, then try to design your own city, e.g. a Sea City or a Plug-in City or a Tower City. What facilities will you provide? How will you get rid of waste products? Where will people work?

USEFUL BOOKS FOR PUPILS AND TEACHERS

Butterworth, E. & Weir, D. *Sociology of Modern Britain* (Fontana 1975)
Butterworth, E. & Weir, D. *Social Problems of Modern Britain* (Fontana 1975)
Connexions series *Shelter: Environments and Human Needs* (Penguin Education 1974)
Church, D. & Ford, B. *People in Towns* (In Focus Books) (Nelson)
GLC *London: Facts and Figures* (published annually by GLC) Free copy available from County Hall
GLC *Housing in London* (published annually by GLC) Free copy available from County Hall
Goodley, B. *Where You're At* (Human Space Stage One) (Penguin 1976)
Holme, R. & Perry, G. *Quality of Life* (Social Studies series) (Blandford 1976)
Jackdaw, 80 *Man and Towns* (Jonathan Cape)
Mackillop, A. *Talking About the Environment* (Wayland 1973)
Pahl, R. *Patterns of Urban Life* (Longman 1970)
Pahl, R. *Readings in Urban Sociology* (Pergamon 1968)
Potter, M. & Potter, A. *Houses* (John Murray 1973)
Smith, M. *Guide to Housing* (Housing Centre Trust 1971)
Thompson, J. *Sociology for Schools* Book 1 (Hutchinson 1973)
Ward, G. *Utopia* (Human Space Stage One) (Penguin 1976)
Wilson, D. *'I know it was the place's fault'* (Oliphant 1970)
Wright, D. *Survival* (Human Space Stage One) (Penguin 1976)

USEFUL BOOKS FOR TEACHERS

Attenborough, K., Porteous, A., Cannell, J. & Sparkes, J. *The Built Environment* (Open University Press, Course DT201 15–18 1973)
Hamnett, C. *Inequalities in Housing* (Open University Press, Course DI302 11 1976)
Knox, F., Clarke, B. & Blowers, A. *Planning and the City* (Open University Press, Course DT201 27–29 1973)
Sarre, P. et al. *The Future City* (Open University Press, Course DT201 31–33 1973)
Thomas, R. & Cresswell, P. *The New Town Idea* (Open University Press, Course DT201 26 1973)
Thomas, R. & Peacock, R. *Housing* (Open University Press, Course DT291 4 1975)

Several of the books listed after the chapter on population are also relevant to pollution and conservation.

Teachers can obtain useful information from the Countryside Commission and the Town and Country Planning Association, in addition to those mentioned in the project list.

FILMS

Slum Housing (Gorbals in Glasgow); 30 mins; b/w; (from *This Week*, Rediffusion); Concord Films Council
Somewhere Decent to Live (Housing problem in London); 27 mins; GLC Housing Department
New Towns (Scotland); 19 mins; colour; Scottish Central Film Library 2 DCY 3 567
Lewis Mumford; six films on the city (based on his book *The City in History*); Concord Films Council
Automania 2000 (cartoon about the take-over of cities by cars); 10 mins; colour; Rank
Who Cares for England? (need for planning for unspoilt countryside); 20 mins; colour; Guild Sound & Vision Ltd
Shadow of Progress (pollution; conservation); PFB 1970
Clean Air; 21 mins; Shell-Mex & BP and ILEA 954
Our Generation (family life and bad housing); approx. 30 mins; colour; Save the Children Fund
St Ann's (based on Coates and Silburn: *Poverty: The Forgotten Englishmen*) 45 mins; Concord Film Services or Shelter

9 Society and the Problems of the Individual

Introduction

In this section we look at two important problems in our society. The first of these is drug dependence and the second is alcoholism. It might seem that these are the concern of the individuals involved; but sometimes there are many people with the same private problem, which may itself arise because of the social conditions in which they live. When this happens the trouble becomes a public concern as well as a private concern. We say it is a *social* problem.

It is not always easy to decide whether a problem is public as well as private, social as well as individual. Sometimes the rest of society does not know or care about individuals and their problems. People may be isolated, lonely, ill or afraid without anyone else being aware of this, or paying attention to their difficulties. Many old people are in this situation and so are many of the young who come to large cities in search of work and friendship. These people may find work but no friendship so that they have to return each evening to a lonely bed-sitter. There are other people, too, who are very unhappy because of real or imagined difficulties. Among these lonely and unhappy people some will look for an answer in suicide or attempted suicide, which is now understood to be a desperate appeal for help.

It is to help the lonely, the afraid and the desperate that Chad Varah founded an organisation known as the Samaritans. A person in need of someone to talk to can telephone the Samaritans (the number of the local branch is easily found in the telephone directory) and can tell his troubles to a sympathetic listener who will help the caller to sort out his problems without criticising him or blaming him. The Samaritans cannot offer money. They do offer something which cannot be measured in economic terms – a friendly ear which will listen and the company of another human being who cares.

. . . now, oh dear, how shocking the thought is
They makes the gin from aquafortis;
They do it on purpose folks' lives to shorten
And tickets it up at two-pence a quartern.
– *ballad*

We could study many different problems in this chapter. We have chosen two: drug 'dependence' because it is in the news so much and is often wrongly linked only with 'young people; and alcoholism because it is 'a hidden problem', like suicide, which society is very slow to understand.

Drugs

A drug is a chemical which can kill pain or change the mood or state of mind of the person who takes it. In 1964 the World Health Organisation made a suggestion that people who could not manage without drugs should no longer be called 'addicts' but 'drug dependents'.

It is amusing to think of ladies drinking numerous cups of tea as being drug dependents, but in fact tea contains *caffeine*, a drug which used to be thought dangerous in Britain. Caffeine is also found in coffee, cocoa and chocolate, and is an acceptable drug in Britain today. Alcohol and nicotine (in tobacco) are the other two drugs which are legal in most situations.

However there are other drugs which are legal only on doctors' prescriptions. These are sometimes grouped into (*a*) dangerous or non-dangerous drugs or (*b*) hard or soft drugs; but neither of these groupings is satisfactory because it is hard to decide which drugs should be put in which groups and which drugs are the most dangerous. The drugs included in this chapter are grouped according to their effects and their origin, i.e. whether they are man-made or from plants such as poppies, coca plant and hemp.

Group	*Drugs included in group*
Opiates	Opium, Morphine, Heroin
Cannabis	Marijuana, Hashish
LSD	Lysergic Acid Diethylamide only
Cocaine	Cocaine only
Amphetamines	Benzedrine, Methedines, etc.
Barbiturates	Many varieties e.g. Veronal, Luminal, Nembutal

THE DRUGS LANGUAGE

Many drugs have nick-names and there is a whole language of slang used in the drugs world. Here are some examples:

There are several technical words and phrases which have a special meaning in the drug scene:

Tolerance. This means that a person needs more and more of the drug to get the same effect.

Physical dependence. This means that the person's body actually needs the drug and cannot manage without it. It is quite different from the feeling in the person's mind that he needs the drug. Drugs which have this *physical* effect include heroin and barbiturates.

Psychological dependence. This means that the person *thinks* he must have the drug. His body may actually need it, or not need it at all. The point is that he goes on craving for it because he thinks he needs it. This craving can be so strong that he finds it difficult to give up the drug. Heroin, amphetamines, LSD, cannabis and barbiturates may have this psychological effect.

Hallucination. A hallucination is like a strange dream but it occurs while the person is awake. A person sees, hears and feels different things around him when he is on certain types of drugs, e.g. LSD and cannabis.

Heroin	H, horse
Cannabis	Pot, marijuana, weed, grass, charge
Hashish	Pot, hash
LSD	Acid, sugar, zen, chief
Cocaine	C, coke, snow, charlie
Cocaine and Heroin	Speedball, H & C
Methedrine	Meths, speed
Barbiturates	Sleepers, goof balls
Barbiturates and Amphetamines	Purple hearts, French blues
An injection, e.g. of heroin	Fix
Pleasant feeling whilst on a drug	Buzz, high
Person who sells drugs on the black market	Pusher
Person dependent on drugs, especially heroin	Junkie
To be arrested	To be busted

An opium den in the East End of London, around 1880.

TYPES OF DRUGS

Type	*Origin*	*Medical use and non-medical misuse*
OPIATES opium morphine heroin Used as capsules, tablets and ampoules. May be dissolved and injected, either into a vein (mainlining) or under the skin (skin-popping).	 poppy juice from opium from morphine	*In hospitals* – These are used as pain killers. *When misused* – They reduce tension, ease fears and relieve worry. Nausea and vomiting can occur. Use of dirty needles can cause liver and skin infections and tetanus. In the long run, loss of appetite and of energy occurs with constipation sometimes, and the possibility of death by overdose. Users may die of malnutrition and disease because they have no desire to eat or keep themselves clean.
CANNABIS marijuana hashish Marijuana is a greenish-grey herb and hashish is a blackish-brown resin. Usually smoked and smells like burning leaves.	From the Indian hemp plant, either the leaves and flowers (marijuana), or the sticky resin (hashish).	This is *not* usually used by doctors. *When misused* – The effect depends on the dose, personality and mood and expectations of the user, and the environment in which it is used. Usually tiredness disappears, and the user feels aware of things and is happy. Hallucinations may occur which are either pleasant or horrible. The long-term effects are not known and much more research is needed. We do not know if lack of energy and lung damage will occur. We do not know how many pot users also use other drugs, nor how many go on to take heroin.

TYPES OF DRUGS

Type	*Origin*	*Medical use and non-medical misuse*
LSD Abbreviation for lysergic acid diethylamide. Colourless, odourless tasteless liquid. Taken in tablets, capsules or on a sugar lump or blotting paper.	A chemical originally found in the fungus that grows on the rye plant, now made synthetically.	*In hospitals* – It may be used in the treatment of psychological illnesses. *When misused* – Like cannabis the effect depends on mood, expectations and previous experience. Users are said to be on a 'trip'. The main effect is hallucinations in which colours change, shapes change, still objects appear to move, sounds become distorted, and the sense of time is lost. Sometimes these are pleasant effects but the 'horrors' can occur when users are depressed, tearful, and dizzy. To a person having a 'bad trip' sounds and visions can be terrifying and the user may believe friends are ganging up on him. In the long run anxiety and mental changes may occur, and 'trips' can recur days or months after the last dose. The proportion of bad trips experienced by users is not known and more research is needed on the genetic effects.
COCAINE	From the coca plant grown principally in S. America.	*In hospitals* – It used to be used as an anaesthetic by dentists and surgeons. Modern anaesthetics are artificial varieties of cocaine that are less dangerous. *When misused* – It produces excitement and elation. The user feels confident he can do whatever he tries. Sometimes the user has hallucinations such as that people are going to attack him or that ants are crawling on his skin.

On a 'trip': in the grip of LSD.

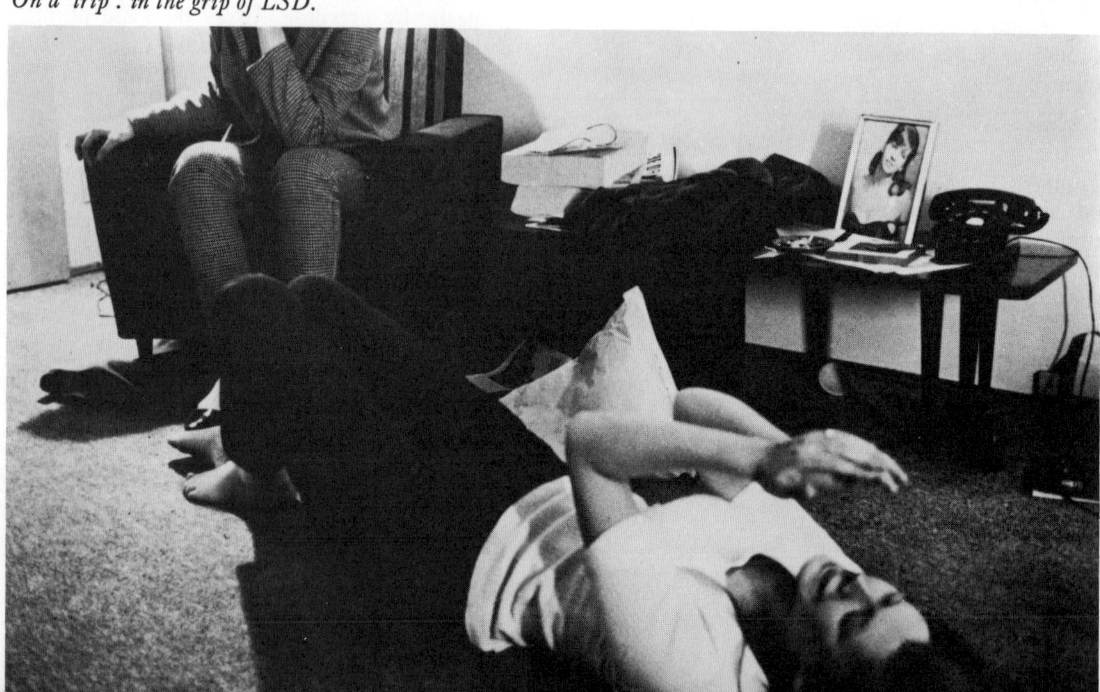

A nightmare world. Drugs may make everything look larger than life, but dreams are by no means always pleasant.

TYPES OF DRUGS

Type	*Origin*	*Medical use and non-medical misuse*
AMPHETAMINES e.g. benzedrine, dexedrine methedrine.	Man-made chemicals used as stimulants.	*In hospitals* – These are stimulants used to relieve depression and to depress appetite for people who want to slim. *When misused* – They are used to pep up the user and keep him awake and aware for long periods. Larger doses cause very great excitement especially if injected into a vein. In the long run amphetamines can cause mental dependence in which people feel they cannot do without the drug.
BARBITURATES Taken as pills of many colours, shapes and sizes.	Man-made chemicals used as sleeping tablets.	*In hospitals* – They are used to treat sleeplessness (insomnia) and anxiety and epilepsy. They are tranquillisers and sedatives. *When misused* – The user feels less anxious, less tense and more relaxed. After a while the user feels sleepy and if large doses are taken the user may stagger around as if he is drunk. Children may mistake these pills for sweets and users may die of overdose by mistake or on purpose. Their effects are heightened if they are taken with alchohol. People who have taken an overdose need immediate hospital treatment, artificial respiration and a stomach pump.

WHAT KIND OF DEPENDENCE?

Drugs	*Dependence and giving up the drug*
OPIATES	Dependence is both physical and psychological and the user soon needs more and more of the drug. Withdrawal symptoms are very unpleasant and include anxiety, running eyes and nose, sweating, twitching muscles, cramp, vomiting and diarrhoea. It is very hard to give up these drugs because of the speed with which dependence occurs and the fear of the withdrawal effects.
CANNABIS	Dependence is thought to be mainly in the mind, i.e. the body is not actually in need of the drug but the mind thinks it is. It is easier to give up than opiates but the user may stay on the drug because he cannot face life without it.
LSD	Dependence is mainly in the mind and many users feel that they really need this drug. However there are no withdrawal symptoms if it is given up, and the body soon learns to do without the drug, even if the mind of the user still feels a need.
COCAINE	In this country cocaine is usually taken with heroin, in the form of speedballs. The user soon needs more and more and the withdrawal effects are painful and unpleasant like those of the opiates.
AMPHETAMINES	A person can think he needs these drugs even if the body does not need them. On withdrawal all the tiredness and weakness and depression, which the drug has hidden, come to the surface and the user suffers complete exhaustion and depression. There are no other withdrawal symptoms.
BARBITURATES	These drugs cause dependence both of body and mind. Withdrawal symptoms are greatest if there is a sudden stop in using the drugs and then they include convulsions, delirium tremens and even death. All withdrawal should be carried out gradually in hospital.

WHY DO PEOPLE TAKE DRUGS?

People who find it hard to cope with life may become dependent on drugs. They may be anxious, insecure, immature, continually depressed, feel unable to make satisfactory relationships with others and so on. Taking drugs becomes a means of escape, and unless the person is helped with the basic problems then he may not be able to give up drugs, or he may return to the drugs after trying to give them up. The person needs help with the personality problem as well as the drug dependence.

Other people living in desperate social and physical conditions such as great poverty, bad housing, chronic illness or malnutrition, may resort to drugs as their only solution. They may not have any personality problems, but they have living conditions in which no human ought to be forced to live. This is the case in some

The hard-drug user is brought back to reality with a severe jolt when supplies run out.

parts of Britain, and in some countries of the world today. The situation is made harder for these people if drugs are easy to get because it is harder to resist, e.g. in the Far East where heroin addiction is an enormous problem and in S. America where cocaine is available. The 'gin palaces' of nineteenth-century Britain provided for small cost the only relief from poverty and suffering for the working-class poor, who used this type of alcohol as their drug.

Sometimes a person may become friendly with a new group of people and find that they regularly or occasionally use drugs. He may be persuaded to try them because he wishes to fit in with the group. On the other hand he may have joined the group in the first place because he wanted to try the drugs or was already experimenting with drugs and wanted the company of others. Therefore the problems of dependence are not simple to describe or to solve. Many other problems must be solved jointly with the drugs situation.

Many drugs, produced to cure illness or relieve pain, are extremely dangerous if misused.

There is no typical drug dependent

Miss A. Aged 17. She started taking blues at parties whilst at school. She continues to take them now that she has left.

Miss B. Aged 22. She took pep pills whilst doing finals. She became dependent but is trying to give them up.

Mr C. Aged 24. He smoked pot with friends whilst playing in a pop group. He thought he needed pot to give him confidence. He still smokes the drug occasionally and has been persuaded to try other drugs including heroin.

Mrs D. Aged 31. She became fat and depressed after her two babies were born, and asked the doctor for slimming tablets. Now she feels that she cannot do without amphetamines ('Mother's little helpers') because they stop her feeling depressed.

Mr E. Aged 45. He started as a social drinker with friends, but was unlucky in attempts to make girl friends and took to spirits (e.g. whisky) to help him gain confidence. Now he is dependent on alcohol and takes sleeping pills too.

Mrs F. Aged 60. She is arthritic and is on pain-killing drugs. She also needs sleeping tablets on which her body has become dependent. She feels that she must have them or she cannot face life.

What do you think will happen to each of these people in the future? Could they withdraw from their drugs? How could each one be helped?

THE PRESENT LAW ON DRUGS

In 1971 the Misuse of Drugs Act was passed.

1 Cannabis and heroin were put in different groups, and drugs were divided into three categories of danger with different penalties attached to each.

2 LSD was considered as dangerous as heroin and put in the same group. Maximum penalties were increased from 2 to 7 years with the possibility of unlimited fine.

3 Pushers and addicts were considered separately. The penalty for pushing (trafficking in) heroin was increased from 10 years and £1,000 fine to 14 years and unlimited fines. Tighter controls were placed on doctors prescribing the drugs and authority was given to the government to deal with new drugs if and when a problem arose.

HEROIN DEPENDENTS

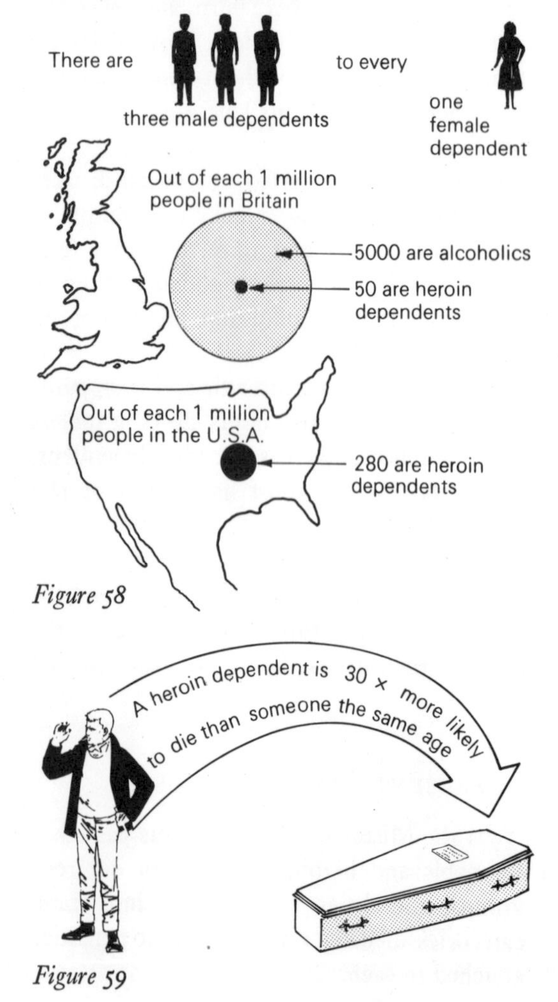

Figure 58

Figure 59

Beautiful but dangerous – pods of the opium poppy.

DRUGS IN BRITAIN. HOW MANY DEPENDENTS?

The Home Office has been collecting statistics since the 1930s and has figures on the number of known opiate and cannabis dependents. Figures are also estimated for amphetamines and barbiturates, but for all drugs the real numbers may well be twice the estimated or known figures.

Opiates and cocaine

From April 1968 all heroin and cocaine addicts who were registered at treatment centres had to be notified to the government. Between 1947 and 1959 about 400 heroin dependents were known and they had mainly become dependent after being prescribed the drug as a pain-killing medicine. However since 1959 cases have been increasing and there were nearly 2,000 by July 1968.

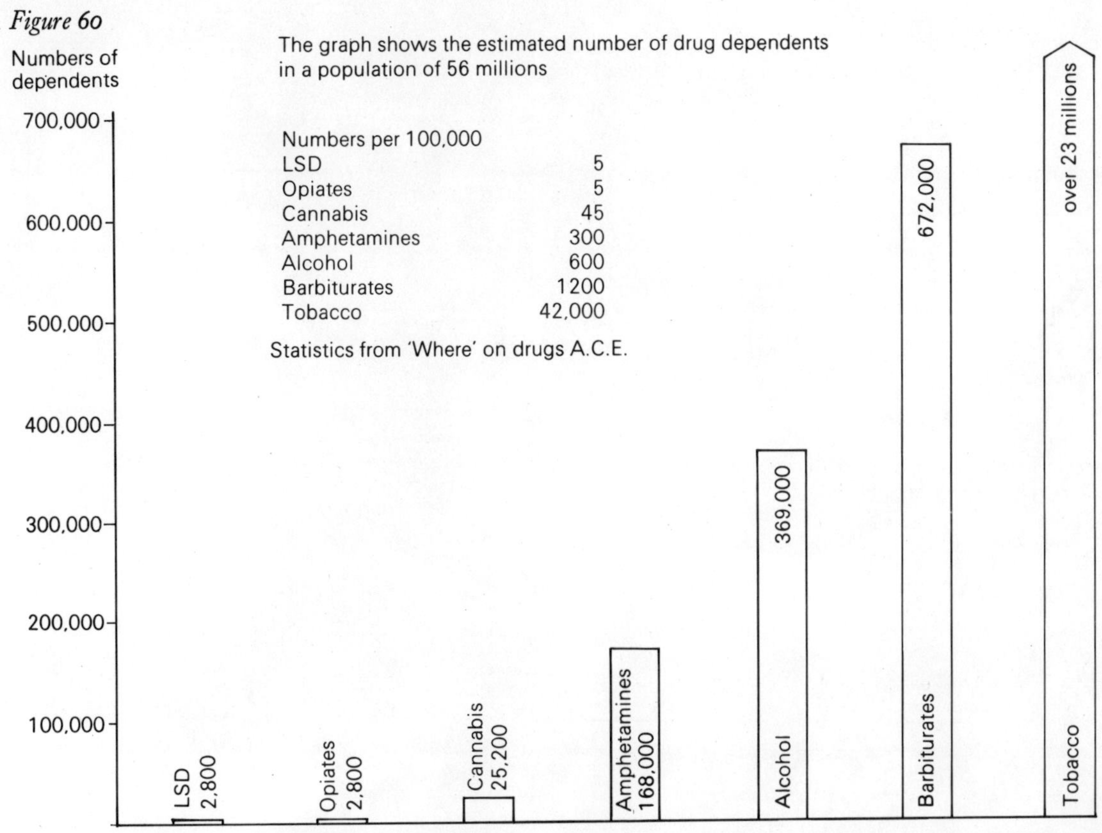

Figure 60

1965–1966		
Under 20 yrs.	↑	by 127%
20–34 yrs.	↑	by 61%
35–49 yrs.	↑	by 21%
Over 50 yrs.	↓	by 2%

Table showing the percentage change, in age groups, of those addicted to opiates and cocaine.

Cannabis

The Wootton Report, published in January 1969 after an enquiry into the use of cannabis in Britain, said that it was very hard to measure how many dependents there were. The number could be anywhere between 30,000 and 300,000. Much more research is needed. The report suggested that cannabis should not be under the same laws as heroin, and that the pushers should be dealt with more strongly than those using or merely possessing the drug. It was thought that the drug should be available on prescription for use in treatment, and that police powers of arrest and search should be reviewed. Between two-thirds and three-quarters of all drugs offences are for cannabis. The proportion depends on whether the total offences are taken as those relating to dangerous drugs only or for all types of drugs. Most offenders had no previous convictions but nearly one-fifth were imprisoned for this first offence and the report suggested that penalties imposed were too severe, especially as the amounts of cannabis involved were small. Cannabis does not in itself make people more liable to commit crimes but it is often taken by people who are already likely to lead a life of crime for social and personal reasons.

Cannabis dependence does not necessarily lead to heroin dependence, but some people use both drugs out of a desire to escape from life.

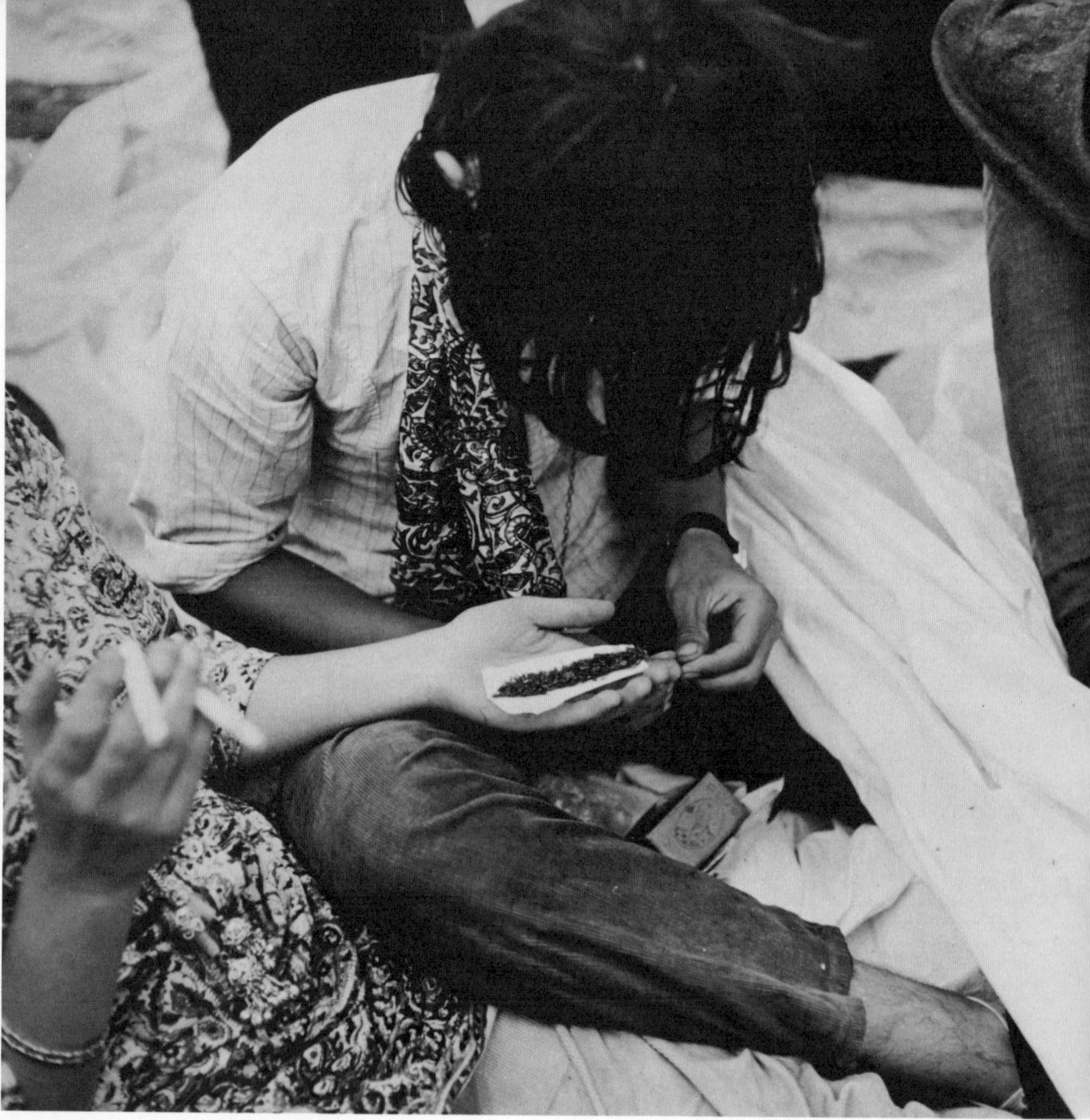

Rotterdam Pop Festival, 1970 – making a reefer.

There are very many cannabis users but far fewer heroin users. From the numbers it looks as if most cannabis users do not go on to heroin, or use it at the same time. Also nearly all heroin addicts are in London but people all over the country take cannabis, and they do not seem to be changing into heroin addicts in these places. For all these reasons the Wootton Report asked for new ideas on cannabis so that it might be controlled differently from heroin.

Amphetamines – are they the future problem?
These are often stolen from chemists, surgeries and chemical factories, split into small parcels and sent from London all over the country via the black market. Young people may come into contact with them as pep pills and blues at parties. A dependent can lose interest in his job, steal to get money for more of the drug and become delinquent and isolated from society. Bad cases can arise where the user gets the

An attendant prepares a pipe of opium for a customer – a den in Bangkok, Siam.

horrors and attacks of panic, confusion and fear and he may need urgent treatment in a pyschiatric hospital. At present there is less international control of these drugs than of the opiates, cannabis or cocaine. In the past over-prescribing by doctors has led to increased numbers of dependents, but people who are at school or have just started work and do not know about these drugs or their risks are the most likely to become dependent if they once get involved. Amphetamines do not necessarily lead to heroin or other hard drugs. The point is that they themselves can be dangerous if misused and suffering can be avoided only by those who really understand the danger.

THE WORLD DRUGS SITUATION

Many countries import and export drugs legally for use in hospitals and by doctors. There are many international agreements which control this kind of manufacture and use, although there is alarm at present about the lack of control over amphetamines and LSD.

However, the real world alarm is linked with the growing amount of misuse of drugs, the illegal growing and manufacture of drugs and the increase in trafficking in illegal drugs on an international level. Concern has increased to such an extent that in 1970 the Economic and Social Council of the United Nations held a special session to discuss the problem. On 2 October 1970, the Commission on Narcotic Drugs recommended the setting up of a United Nations Fund for Drug Abuse Control. This has been started and the fund had £2 million initially which increased to £5 million in 1971. Three main problems are to be tackled by this fund. The first is to find better means of controlling drug traffic so that illegal traffic can be stamped out. The second is to end the growing of crops which produce drugs and this means finding something else to put in their place, e.g. wheat instead of cannabis so that the people still have work on the land. The third is to improve the economic and social conditions of people in various parts of the world so that they do not need drugs as an escape, and to treat and help those who are already dependent on drugs.

Area	*Problems and possible solutions*		
	Opiates	*Cannabis*	*Other*
AFRICA	These are a very small problem.	This is a large problem, but traffic is mainly inside Africa between states. Some goes to Europe.	
AMERICAS	Heroin is increasing rapidly, from Europe which acts as half way house.	Cannabis is increasing rapidly, including Jamaica and S. America. Approx. 15% students in N. America have tried cannabis. It comes partly from Europe.	Cocaine is increasing. It is very high in Peru and Bolivia where it is made. Amphetamines are a new and increasing problem in N. America and Canada.
NEAR & MIDDLE EAST	Opium is grown, so many people can get it. The area is an important centre of supply and traffic to Europe and USA. There are thought to be organised gangs of smugglers	Cannabis is grown, so many can get it. Also supplied to Europe and USA.	
EUROPE	Heroin is increasing.	Cannabis is increasing. It is the commonest of the drugs in Britain.	There is increasing fear of amphetamines and LSD especially in Sweden but also in other European countries.
FAR EAST	The Opium poppy is grown on a large scale so many people become dependent. Trafficking is widespread to the rest of the world.	Cannabis is also high in Far East. Thailand and Burma are used as routes but are trying to control production, to raise the economic and social standards and to replace cannabis by wheat growing rather than cause unemployment.	
	India has very tight controls on opium.	India is concerned with the extent of traffic in cannabis and cannabis is exported illicitly from Pakistan.	
	Vietnam has much illegal opium.	Vietnam has much illegal cannabis. Soldiers on leave have taken it to Australia.	
	Hong Kong and Singapore have a large opium problem.	Cannabis is still high in Singapore.	
	Japan had 19% fewer prosecutions for all drug offences between 1966 and 1967, but in spite of strict measures there is traffic in heroin from Hong Kong, opium from Thailand and Burma, cannabis from Singapore and Vietnam.		

Area	Problems and possible solutions		
	Opiates	*Cannabis*	*Other*
OCEANIA	There is no great opiates problem.	In Australia cannabis is increasing.	
	In New Zealand drugs are closely controlled and trafficking is not a great problem although thefts from surgeries and chemical factories create an illegal supply.		
RUSSIA	In the Narcotics Bulletin of the UN in 1971 the Russian spokesman on drugs said that there was hardly any problem in the USSR. The state controlled all production although some illegal opium and cannabis was known to be grown. There were no heroin cases or cocaine dependents except for those who had become addicted whilst on prescription. The persuading of others to use drugs was severely punished especially if the other person was under age. LSD was banned in 1967. Although LSD and amphetamines were causing grave concern elsewhere there appeared to be no problem in the USSR. It was claimed that this was a result of the favourable social and economic conditions in Russia.		

Alcohol

WHAT IS ALCOHOLISM?

The alcohol which is in drinks is a chemical called ethyl alcohol. Distilled spirits have about 40% alcohol and include drinks such as whisky, gin, rum and brandy. Beer has about 5% and wine has from 12–20% alcohol.

We live in a society where it is customary to drink and teetotallers are few and far between. Over a drink we can enjoy the company of friends, discuss business affairs and negotiate bargains. Strangers feel that they can relax and talk together if alcohol is provided. People drink for social reasons as well as to get pleasurable effects from the drink. Why then is alcohol a 'problem'? How big a problem is it?

Several different degrees of drinking can be found. Most people drink moderately and a few may from time to time get drunk. These are called 'social drinkers'. Others drink much more and this can be seen from the frequency with which they become drunk and from the effects of drink on their bodies and on their lives. These are called 'excessive drinkers' and they may or may not need medical care. Others will go on to become entirely dependent upon alcohol. These are 'alcoholics' in the true medical sense of the word. Most of them reach a stage in which their brains and bodies are harmed by alcohol even when they are not drinking. This stage is called 'chronic alcoholism'.

It is estimated that about 33 million people are social drinkers in Britain and that just over one in every one hundred of these are suffering from some degree of alcoholism. The figure could be between 330,000 and 450,000. Most of the alcoholics are not the 'down and outs' whom we read about in the newspapers. These are only a tiny minority (about three in every one hundred) of all those who are alcoholics.

An alcoholic is not a person with weak will power as used to be thought in the past. He is a person who is allergic to alcohol and will always be allergic, so the only way for him to recover and to lead a normal life is to avoid alcohol altogether. Apart from this there is no known medical cure. Doctors now realise that an alcoholic is suffering from an illness, and needs help. However, many are not helped either because they do not seek help or, if they do, their problems are not properly understood or there are no facilities, such as treatment centres, available to help them. What can happen to alcoholics? The World Health Organisation has estimated

Public House in London, 1870. Do you think children should be allowed in pubs?

that there are 350,000 alcoholics in Britain, and that a quarter of these have damage to the brain and the body. Alcohol causes both physical and mental dependence and the withdrawal symptoms can vary from the 'shakes' to delirium tremens (tremors and hallucinations), and the alcoholic may experience fits. Death can sometimes result from withdrawal illnesses. Alcohol can damage nearly every part of the body but the most common and serious damage is cirrhosis of the liver, peptic ulcers, tuberculosis of the lungs and damage to the heart and the brain. Many heavy drinkers are trying to escape from pressing social and personal problems but the severe drinking makes the problems worse and alcoholics often lose their jobs and have upset family lives. There may also be neglect or ill-treatment of children.

Alcoholism has been described as the 'lonely disease' because so few people understand the causes or the suffering of alcoholism.

Those who are not treated sometimes end up in prison, and some may regard prison as a place of refuge. But this is a useless treatment. There is a need to help alcoholics understand the different ways of recovering so that they do not end up either in the gutter or the jail. Many alcoholics kill themselves, and in 1961 an article in the *British Medical Journal* suggested that the rate of suicide was between seventy-six and eighty-six times as high for alcoholics as for males of the same age not on alcohol. Drunken drivers cause much harm to other road users, both in cars and on foot, in Britain. In *New Scientist* in 1958 it was estimated that five hundred deaths and two to three thousand serious accidents could be prevented each year if there were no drunken drivers.

Down-and-out winos and meths drinkers in London. Such social outcasts are only a tiny minority of the alcoholics in Britain.

WHAT CAN BE DONE TO HELP ALCOHOLICS?

Kessel and Walton in their paperback on alcoholism suggest a need for much more help under the National Health Service. Most alcoholics do not seek help from doctors and many doctors do not want to treat alcoholism as a disease. An alcoholic usually gets treatment only if the alcohol has caused other diseases. Many patients in British hospitals are in fact alcoholics, but their condition has not been recognised so they are not treated for their alcoholism. Some doctors believe that they have no alcoholics in their area, but there are probably quite a number. The point is that the alcoholics either have not been seen by a doctor or the alcoholism has not been diagnosed. There is therefore a large 'hidden' problem.

Another solution to the problem is for the public to know and understand the causes of this lonely disease. This is one of the aims of the

Undertakers would have less work if there were fewer drunken drivers – and so would hospitals.

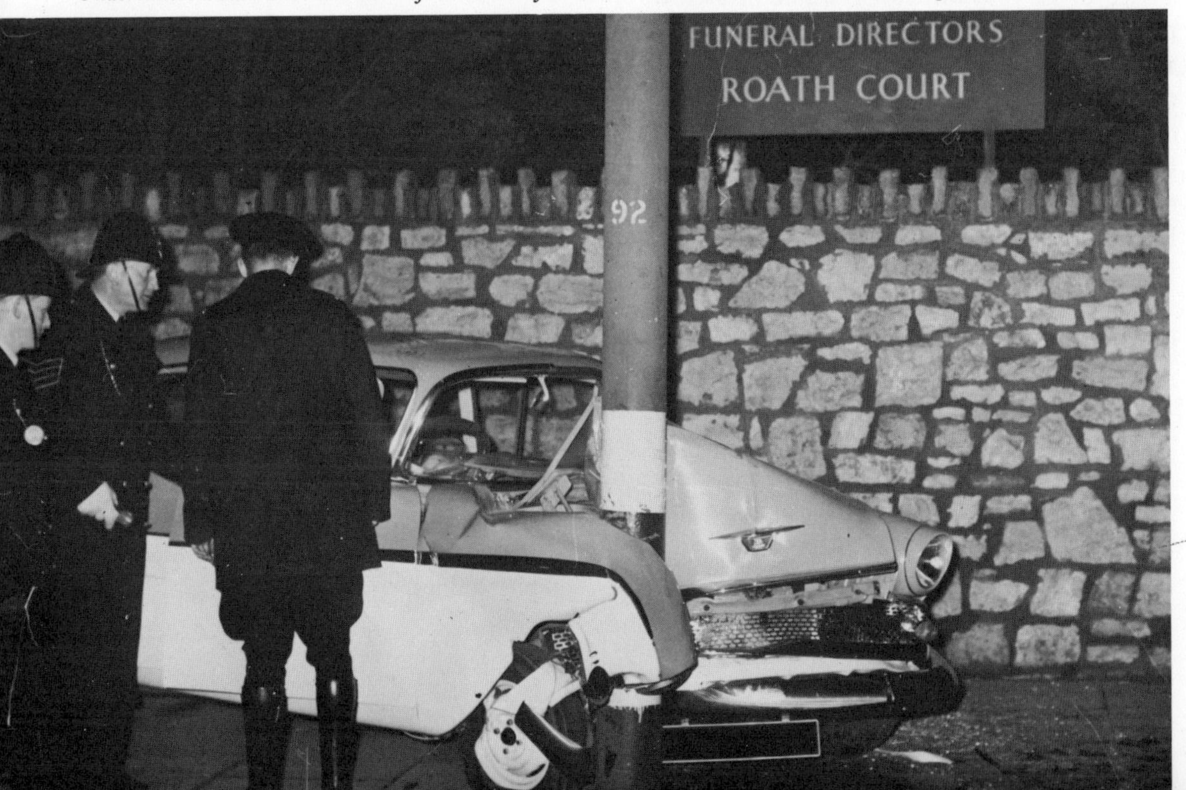

National Council on Alcoholism which was founded as a voluntary health organisation under the Charities Act of 1960. It aims to provide Regional Information Centres in Britain which will give advice and information to alcoholics and their friends and families. It tries to encourage research into alcoholism in industry, for it is estimated that over £40 m is lost to industry each year through days off due to excessive drinking. It also campaigns for better treatment facilities for alcoholics because there is a wide gap between the number of sufferers and the amount of help which is available to them.

Another association which exists to help alcoholics is known as Alcoholics Anonymous. A person who wishes to recover from alcoholism contacts the association and meets other members, all of whom are known only by their first names. The members are able to help the newcomer by discussing his difficulties with him and telling him of their own personal experiences. Members have found that only by abstaining from all drink can they hope to recover and they know from experience that punishment or advice 'to use your will power' would be useless in helping the new member, because his body is allergic to the alcohol which he feels compelled to drink. Therefore by befriending him they offer him the support of a strong group of people who understand his problems. There are over two hundred groups of this association in England and Wales.

READING AND UNDERSTANDING

1 What is caffeine?
2 How could different drugs be put into groups?
3 What is the difference between physical and psychological dependence?
4 Are hallucinations always pleasant?
5 Describe the use and effects of any two types of drugs.
6 Which drugs are hardest to give up once the user is dependent?
7 What was a 'gin palace'?
8 What are the main points of the 1971 Drugs Act?
9 There are 2,000 heroin dependents in Britain and *perhaps* 200,000 cannabis dependents and 200,000 amphetamine dependents.
(*a*) are the numbers accurate?
(*b*) are the numbers increasing; if so, say in what way?
10 Which is the larger problem (*a*) heroin (*b*) alcohol?
11 How does the heroin problem compare in Britain and America?
12 What was the Wootton Report?
13 Where do amphetamines come from? Who uses them? What are the risks?
14 Why has the UN Fund for Drug Abuse Control been started?
15 Where do supplies of (*a*) heroin, (*b*) cannabis, (*c*) cocaine come from? Find and label the actual countries on a world map.

POINTS FOR FURTHER DISCUSSION

1 Why is it said that 'there is no typical drug dependent'?
2 What could parents, teachers, friends and the mass media do to help young people avoid dependence on drugs?
3 Some dependents have personality problems. Will they be able to give up their drug dependence?
4 An old lady is on barbiturates. Should she continue to be supplied with them if she thinks she needs them?
5 Why might doctors be concerned that some of their colleagues are over-prescribing amphetamines?

6 Which of the reasons for drug taking on pages 242 and 243 are psychological and which are social? Why do you think we divide the reasons up in this way?
7 What should be the role of the police in the drugs scene?
8 Should the police be allowed to search without a warrant? What are the arguments for and against this?
9 Should the supply and use of cannabis be legalised? What are the reasons for and against such a change in the law?
10 What are your reactions to the 1971 legislation on the manufacture and use of drugs? Discuss your reasons carefully.
11 Can the USSR really be so sure that it has no drug dependents?
12 Why do you think that LSD and the amphetamines are causing world-wide concern?
13 Why do you think that Thailand and Burma are managing to lessen the cannabis problem?

PROJECT WORK

1 Find out more details about the harmful effects of the different types of drugs, by reading the books on the list and by reading newspapers.
2 Collect statements and articles from the mass media on the drug situation in Britain. Do the articles give a true picture or do they exaggerate some aspects of the situation and leave out others?
3 Carry out a survey on the attitudes of your friends and relatives to the drugs situation. Present the information you collect in the form of diagrams and try to write down the conclusion you draw from the survey.
4 Find out more about the link between drugs and crime. Use the reference books to help you.
5 Ask your teacher to write for information to the different societies that help alcoholics. Find out as much as you can about the reasons for alcoholism, and the solutions to the problem of alcoholism in Britain.

USEFUL BOOKS FOR PUPILS AND TEACHERS

Becker, H. S. *Outsiders* (Free Press, NY 1950)
BMA Family Doctor Booklets, e.g. *Behind the Drug Scene; Pot or Not*
Connexions series, *Out of Your Mind* (Penguin Education 1970)
Cresswell, P. *Suicide and Crime* (Open University Press (teachers only), Course D291 6 1975)
Hanson, W. J. *Drugs* (Enquiries) (Longman 1974)
HMSO, *Misuse of Drugs Act*, 1971
Kessel, N. & Watson, J. *Alcoholism* (Pelican Original 1965)
Laurie, P. *Drugs* (Penguin 1967)
Lingeman, R. R. *Drugs from A–Z, A Dictionary* (Allen Lane 1970)
McAlhone, B (ed.) *Where on Drugs* (Advisory Centre for Education 1970)
Sandford, J. *Down and Out in London* (New English Library 1972)
Schofield, M. *The Strange Case of Pot* (Penguin 1971)
Solomon, D. (ed.) *The Marijuana Papers* (Panther 1972)
UN Organisation, Narcotics Bulletins (UN library-teachers only)
Wyatt, J. *Talking About Drugs* (Wayland 1973)
Young, J. *The Drugtakers* (Paladin 1971)

FILMS

Smoking and You; 11 mins; colour; ILEA 531
Gale is Dead (Drug addiction – made for *Man Alive* series); 50 mins; b/w; Concord Film Services
Is There a Problem?: 40 mins; ILEA 2391
Experience; 40 mins; ILEA 2392
Why Drugs?; 40 mins; ILEA 2393

10 Population and its Problems

This chapter and the next are related to each other. First we look at some of the world problems which are linked with population growth and secondly we examine co-operation between different societies in the world.

In the twentieth century we have had two major wars which split the world in conflict. But we have also seen the first attempts by human beings to help each other irrespective of race or nationality.

In the chapter on the urban environment we said that although some action is being taken to combat pollution in this country we have a long way to go before Britain is 'a green and pleasant land' to live in, and that planning is needed to protect our environment. Here we are looking at planning on a much bigger scale.

The World's Population

The world's population is now increasing by about 65 million people per year. If this rate of increase continues, then by the year 2000 there will be twice as many people in the world as there are now.

A table of figures shows that this is a 'new' world situation which has only developed in the last two hundred years.

The world's population

(UN figures)	
Birth of Christ	200–300 million
1650	500 million
1850	1,000 million
1950	2,500 million
1960	2,990 million
1968	3,483 million
2000 (UN estimate)	7,000 million

Never before has mankind seen such a rapid population growth. The reasons for it lie in the combined effects of an increased birth rate and a lower death rate.

A consequence of the population explosion? Holiday-makers on the Exeter By-pass.

(1) *Birth rate*
= number of babies born each year to every 1,000 adults in the society;
and
(2) *Death rate*
= number of deaths each year out of every 1,000 people in the society.

In Britain one hundred years ago the death rate began to fall owing to improved sanitation, the development of clean water supplies and the use of vaccination against 'killer' diseases like smallpox. At that time the birth rate remained very high and so the population increased quickly. From about 1870 onwards people began to accept the use of the existing methods of birth control and later on new methods of contraception were introduced. The birth rate fell and the population began to rise at a slower pace.

In simple societies both the birth rate and death rate are high so population does not increase, but in the complex developing societies today there has been a drop in the death rate while the birth rate is still high and population is therefore increasing quickly.

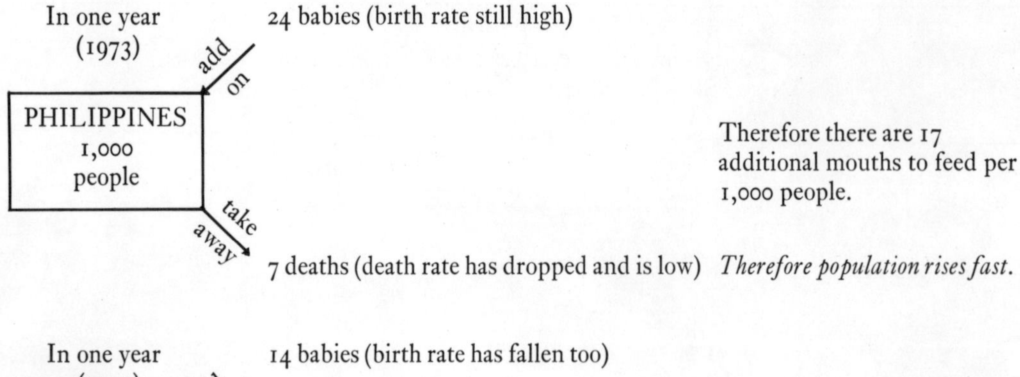

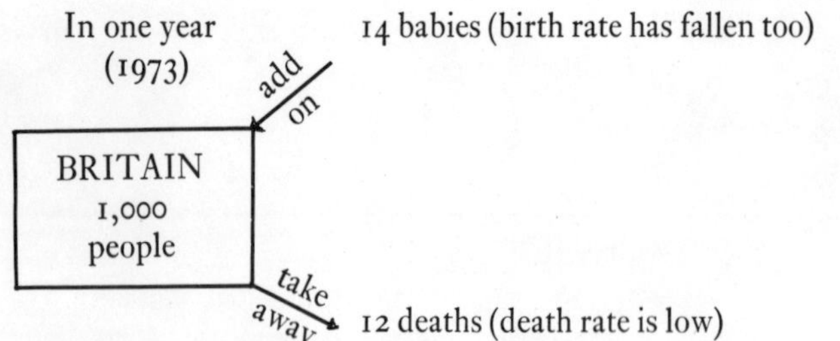

Therefore there are 2
additional mouths to feed per
1,000 people.

Therefore population rises but not so fast.

Figures from *Social Trends No. 6* 1975

Problems caused by population growth

The present world population growth is causing many problems and is making some existing problems worse. The four main problems are:

1 *Hunger*
There are too many mouths to feed in many areas of the world and the present methods of farming cannot cope with the increased need for food.

2 *Disease*
Although the death rates of many societies have fallen sharply, there are still too many sick people and not enough medicine or qualified staff to cure them. Some of the diseases are caused by hunger whilst others are made worse when people are weak from lack of food.

3 *Lack of education*
Where there are too many people there are often not enough teachers and not enough equipment. The problems in some areas of Britain have been discussed in earlier chapters. These problems are small compared with the vast shortages or the total lack of educational opportunities in many developing countries of the world. The name given to this problem where people cannot read or write is ILLITERACY.

4 *Pollution*
People produce waste products both natural and synthetic. Where a society's population is increasing, the control of and disposal of waste becomes a major problem. Unless population is checked soon future generations may face not only hunger, disease and illiteracy but also a world full of rubbish, dirt and poison.

These four problems exist in different degrees in different parts of the world. Look carefully at the following chart, parts of which are left blank. Copy and complete it after discussing how to fill it in. Check that you know where each country is on a world map.

	Advanced industrial societies	*Developing societies*
	e.g. Common Market Countries, USSR, USA, Canada, Australia, New Zealand, Japan	e.g. India, Malaysia, Africa, S. America
Birth rate	Low	High
Death rate	Low	Low
Population increase	Slow	Fast
Malnutrition	?	?
Under-nourishment	?	?
Disease	?	?
Illiteracy	?	?
Air pollution	?	?
Water pollution	?	?
Waste bottles and tins	?	?
Food production	?	?
Income per head	?	?

Each of these problems will be studied here in detail.

HUNGER

All human beings, no matter what race or society they belong to, have basic needs for certain types of food; these are carbohydrates, fats, proteins, vitamins and minerals. Each of these types can be found in a wide variety of foods (although no single food contains every one). Each is essential because it supports the cells of the body in the daily battle for survival.

These basic needs can be met by eating some

(*a*) milk and dairy products (providing fats, proteins and vitamins, calcium and other minerals), and

(*b*) meat, fish, poultry and eggs, nuts (providing proteins, fats and vitamins), and

(*c*) grains and starchy vegetables such as peas, beans and potatoes (providing carbohydrates, vitamins and some protein), and

(*d*) fruits and green vegetables (providing vitamins and minerals, some protein and carbohydrates).

However, in the developing countries where population growth is fastest most of the people's food is mainly of group (*c*) and so the people are getting mainly carbohydrates but very little protein, vitamins and minerals needed for repairing body tissues and for growth. In many parts of the world meat, fish, poultry and eggs are scarce and their cost puts them out of reach of the families who are hungry. Similarly the hungry millions of the world cannot afford fruit and vegetables, or cannot get them because they live in remote districts to which these foods cannot be easily or cheaply transported.

There are two technical words which are used when discussing hunger. The first word is UNDERNUTRITION which means not enough calories in the food. (A calorie is the measure of energy provided by the food.) The second word is MALNUTRITION, which means that the food is not the right type even though the calorie value is high.

Undernutrition

The amount of energy in calories that a person needs from food depends on age, weight, sex, physical activity and environment. In many developing societies people do not get the calories they need and many are slowly starving to death. Between 300 million and 500 million people in the world today are not getting enough food to keep them alive and healthy. Because of the complicated machinery and methods used in food production in industrial societies there are fewer very hungry people. Also, scientists in industrial countries have studied the reasons for, and learnt how to prevent, soil erosion. Many of these countries have temperate climates which do not change quickly from extreme heat to extreme cold, and where the rainfall is steady and can be predicted. Fertilisers can be manufactured and pesticides developed to control the pests which attack crops. In Britain the agricultural revolution began *before* the rapid rise of population. The increasing population of the nineteenth century did not strain the food resources to the same extent as in the developing countries today.

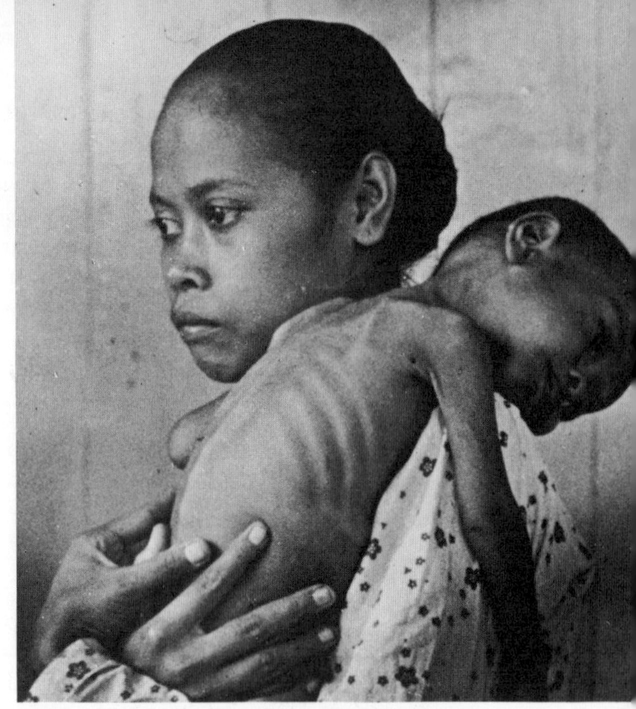

Toddlers need a balanced diet to fight off disease. Malnutrition lets the enemies in. A worried Indonesian mother with her baby.

Malnutrition

The best source of protein is animal protein from meat, fish, poultry and eggs. The following chart compares the animal protein consumed in different parts of the world.

	Animal protein grams per day (to nearest five) per person
Europe	50
N. America	65
Oceania	65
Far East	10
Near East	15
Africa	15
Latin America	20

Figures from Ehrlich and Ehrlich p. 71

This child had kwashiorkor but is beginning to recover after four days on a high-protein diet.

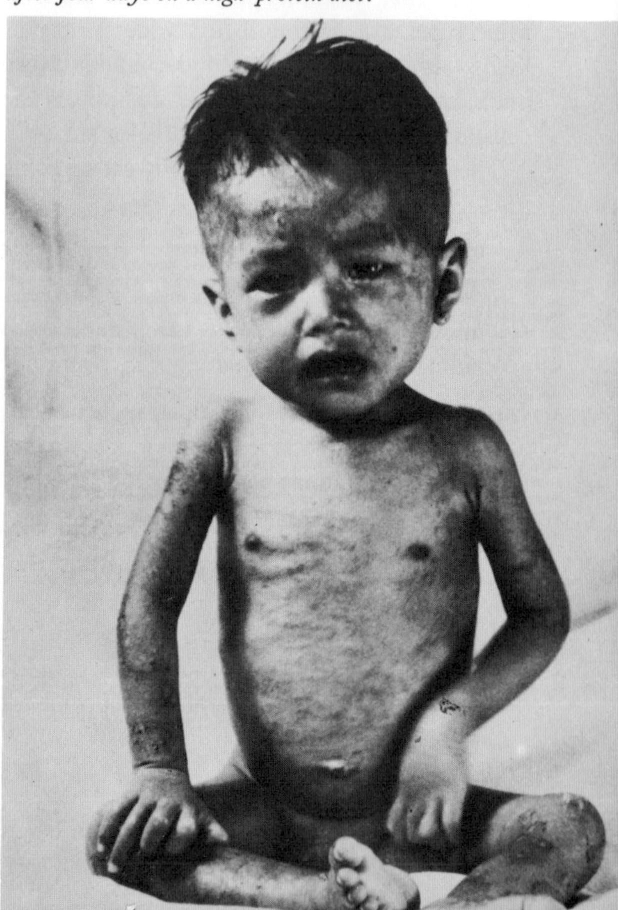

In many developing countries people have to get most of their energy (calories) from cereals, starchy roots and sugar. These foods are not rich in vitamins or minerals or animal proteins so the people lack these things in their diet. In

Britain not many families live only on cereals, potatoes and sugar, but in developing countries nearly two-thirds of families have to depend on starchy foods and nearly all of these families are suffering from malnutrition.

DISEASE

This problem is closely linked with hunger. Lack of food, or of certain types of food, will cause DEFICIENCY DISEASES. These are of several types, the symptoms varying according to the type of food missing from the diet:

Kwashiorkor: this is due to lack of protein and is especially common among young children who after being weaned have only starchy foods to eat. The arms and legs waste away, the skin discolours and may peel off, and the stomach distends due to fluid being stored in the tissues. There may also be diarrhoea and anaemia. If there is no treatment death may occur, but treatment with high protein fluid can cure this disease if given in time.

Marasmus: this is similar to kwashiorkor except for lack of a skin rash. The cause is a lack of all types of food – general undernourishment, and the cure is the same as for kwashiorkor.

Other diseases

In addition to the diseases caused by food deficiencies, there are many diseases caused by viruses and bacteria which are harder to resist if a person is already weak through hunger. The death rate from pneumonia and measles is greatly increased if people are weak, and a poor diet hinders the recovery of the 500 million people who suffer from the terrible eye disease called trachoma. In many countries the population increase has caused a strain on water supplies, and dirty water can lead to cholera, bilharzia and typhoid.

Vitamin deficiency diseases

Disease	*Vitamin lacking*	*Areas of world*	*Results*
Beri-beri	Vitamin B	Far East	Wasting and paralysis of limbs
Pellagra	Vitamin B	Among maize-eating peoples	Diarrhoea Mental illness Skin diseases
Avitaminosis	Vitamin A	Children in S. America, Far East	Blindness
Rickets	Vitamin D	Many developing countries	Deformities of the bones

Mineral deficiency diseases

Disease	*Mineral lacking*	*Areas of world*	*Results*
Nutritional anaemia	Iron	Especially affects pregnant women and young children in many countries	Can cause death in childbirth. General weakness
Goitre	Iodine	200 m people in many countries	Abnormally low mental and physical growth

FACTS AND FIGURES ON WORLD HEALTH

Facts and Figures on World Health

	Population	People per doctor	People per hospital bed
Britain	56 m	770	110
USSR	255 m	340	90
USA	214 m	610	150
Japan	111 m	870	80
India	599 m	4,160	1,620
Kenya	13·4m	16,300	760
Cameroon	6·4m	26,220	480

UN Demographic Year Book and *WHO Annual Statistics* 1973–6 *Vol. 3*

Whenever over-population leads to crowded housing conditions the increase of sewage problems and rubbish disposal can create a breeding ground for lice, typhus-carrying fleas and disease-bearing rats.

The weakness caused by hunger and disease has an effect on the length of life of people in different parts of the world. A child born in India between 1941–1950 could only expect to live thirty-two years. In 1970 this situation had changed considerably, but the Indian child could still only expect to live fifty years as compared with seventy years or more for a British child.

Sakeneh looks a normal, lively child in this picture, but a year earlier she was taken to a home in Iran suffering badly from malnutrition.

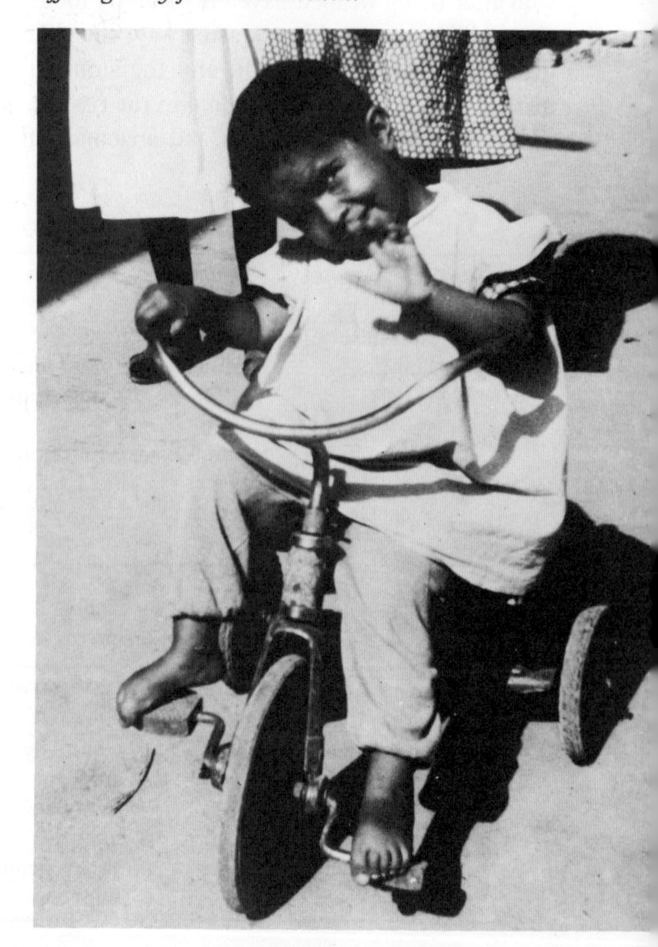

Education

Over half of the world's population is under twenty years of age, and the proportion is increasing because fewer babies die in the first year of life. Some countries still have high birth rates and very many babies are born each year. Nearly half of the world's children of school age (five to fourteen) do not go to school, and many who do can only go for a short time.

The world map shows the percentage of illiterate people compared with the population of different areas in 1960. The figures are from UNESCO. Without formal education people

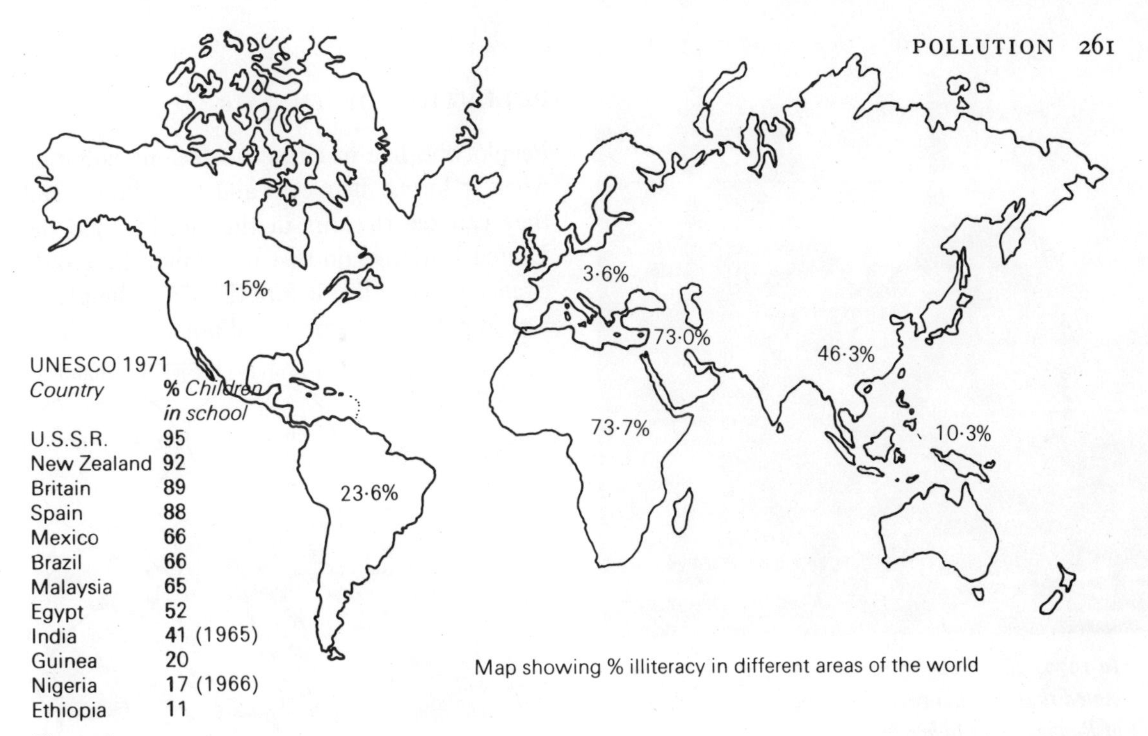

UNESCO 1971

Country	*% Children in school*
U.S.S.R.	95
New Zealand	92
Britain	89
Spain	88
Mexico	66
Brazil	66
Malaysia	65
Egypt	52
India	41 (1965)
Guinea	20
Nigeria	17 (1966)
Ethiopia	11

Figure 61

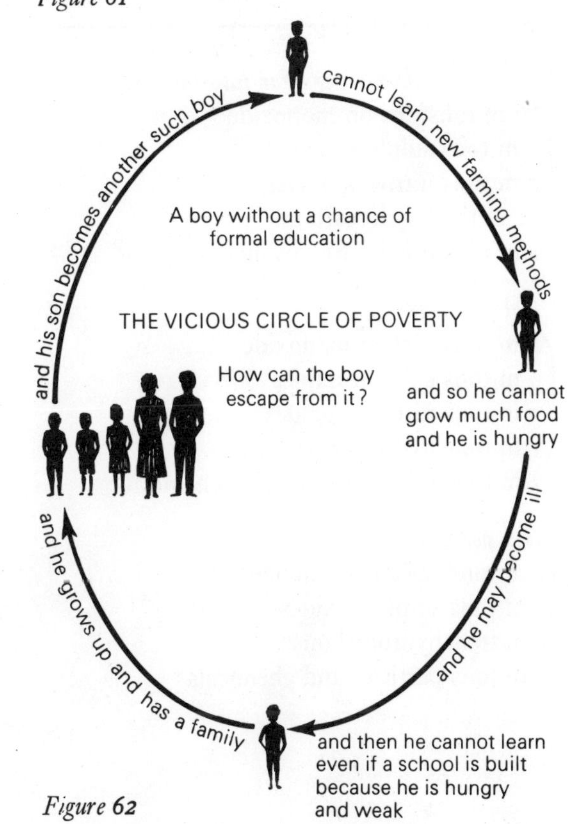

Figure 62

cannot learn about nutrition, new farming methods, the use and repair of machinery, the use of new seeds, fertilisers and prevention of soil erosion. Their whole life is centred around the desperate struggle to survive from day to day, and the children cannot escape from this circle of poverty, hunger and disease because they do not know how. Birth control may be forbidden by religion, or methods available may be unacceptable, and so the families cannot escape from the situation of having too many mouths to feed.

Therefore the problem of education is closely linked with the problems of hunger and disease.

Pollution

People produce waste. Too many people produce so much waste that getting rid of it becomes a world-wide problem. Today the population explosion causes pollution of the air we breathe, the water we drink and the food we eat.

In 1970, when this picture was taken, it was estimated that it would cost £5,000,000 to make the air of Rawmarsh fit to breathe.

POLLUTION OF THE AIR

People who live in cities can feel air pollution when it burns their eyes and their lungs, and they can see the dirt in the air. In 1968 the United Nations said that man might have only twenty years to live before the air of the planet was so polluted that it would not support life.

The three wise monkeys on the theme of pollution

Drink no water

Eat no food

Breathe no air

Figure 63

Late 1960s – USA per year into the air.

66 m tons carbon monoxide
1 m tons sulphur oxides
6 m tons nitrogen oxides
12 m tons hydrocarbons
1 m tons other particles including lead

USA per year

2 m tons carbon monoxide
9 m tons sulphur oxides
3 m tons nitrogen oxides
1 m tons hydrocarbons
3 m tons other particles and chemicals

USA per year

2 m tons carbon monoxide
3 m tons sulphur oxides
1 m tons hydrocarbons
1 m tons particles and chemicals

Figure 64 How is the air polluted?
(From Ehrlich and Ehrlich *Population, Resources and Environment*)

In England the overall rate of air pollution is higher than for the USA.

Who are the main sufferers?

Figure 65 On Friday, December 5, 1952, the fog and smoke over London turned into smog. *About 4,000 people died due to air pollution.*

The polluted River Tyne near Newcastle.

Figure 66 In this traffic jam some drivers and passengers may experience acute carbon monoxide poisoning. The symptoms are headache, loss of vision, nausea, abdominal pain and lack of co-ordination in the muscles. Carbon monoxide attacks the blood so that it cannot do its work of carrying oxygen. This may cause disastrous strain on people with heart or lung diseases.

POLLUTION OF WATER

In complex industrial societies water is purified before it is distributed. It is carefully filtered and chlorine is added to kill bacteria and viruses, so that it may safely be drunk straight from the tap. This is what we have come to expect, but in some cities in America there is alarm at present because the water is not purified properly and liver disease is spreading from one area to another, possibly through infected water supplies. As population grows the treatment of sewage may not be good enough and so rivers and reservoirs become polluted, with the result that it is more and more difficult to provide safe water supplies.

At the same time the industries which have attracted the increased population to the area are themselves spreading. Factories discharge large quantities of lead, detergents, sulphuric acid, phenols, ether, benzene, ammonia and other chemicals into the streams, rivers and lakes and along seashores.

As population grows, and industry grows, so there is a need for increased food production. To the water are now added pesticides, herbicides and nitrates from the farms. Like many other chemicals, nitrates can be helpful or harmful. As fertilisers they help to increase the yield of food. However, if they seep into drinking water they can be very harmful, in particular to children and animals.

INSECTICIDES

We cannot see the effects of using insecticides until years after they have been absorbed into human bodies. Recent research shows that concentrations of DDT and other insecticides were higher in the fat of patients who died of softening of the brain, brain haemorrhage, hypertension, cirrhosis of the liver and various types of cancer. DDT has been shown to increase the likelihood of cancer, especially liver cancer, in mice. Will it do the same for humans? It is too early to say.

Another study showed that trout exposed to a certain amount of DDT were completely incapable of learning to avoid electric shocks as compared with fish with no DDT. Their nerve patterns had been destroyed. DDT has been in use since the Second World War, but in recent years its use has been limited in many parts of the world because its dangers are now known.

In the developing societies, DDT is still used to combat insect-carried diseases. The disease is a more urgent problem than the future risk of pollution. American and British breast-fed babies drink about ten times the recommended amount of another insecticide called dieldrin. So here again discoveries which should help to control pests and stop the spread of disease may themselves cause harm if not used with great care.

Complex industrial societies are not the only ones in which food, air and water pollution are taking place. In developing societies more and more fertilisers and insecticides are being used in an attempt to increase food production. Sewage disposal and water supplies may be a very large problem in cities all over the world; and in some areas people may have to drink from the rivers in which they also wash and into which untreated sewage is allowed to flow. Other dangers may arise from air pollution by open fires, and from the difficulty of disposing of rubbish.

DDT can be harmful – but sometimes it is the lesser evil. Here it is being used to control malaria in Burma.

Figure 67 The Pollution of food.

DDT is just one of the insecticides used

A fruit tree is sprayed with DDT

an apple is eaten

humans absorb some in the fruit

A farmer sprays his wheat with insecticide

the insecticide is washed into the ground and into streams

the streams flow to the sea

fish absorb the insecticide then men eat the fish

OTHER KINDS OF POLLUTION

Whenever people are crowded together they produce *rubbish*. There is a problem of getting rid of it in both complex industrial societies and developing societies. Cities in India and Brazil for example have large rubbish problems in the slum areas where the waste dumps act as a breeding ground for rats, cockroaches and flies. If the waste is burned, air pollution is caused. If it is not burned then the rain washes through and pollutes the water supplies. In complex industrial societies there are added problems of

But where does it go after this?

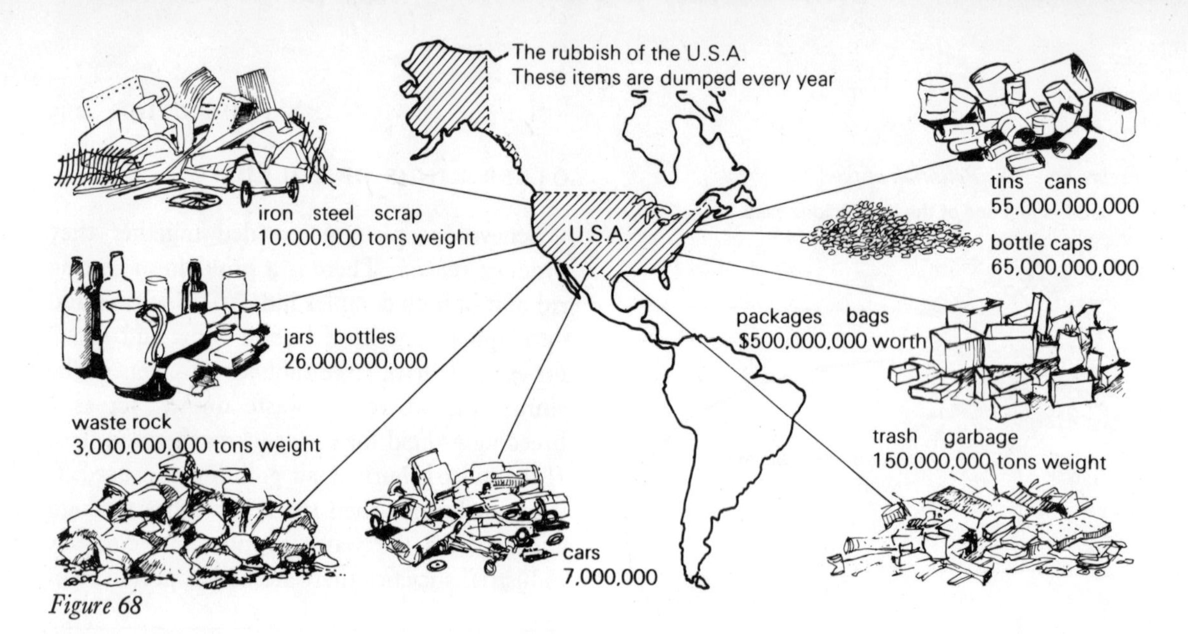

Figure 68

tin cans, bottles, industrial waste and the wrappings and packets in which the large variety of goods are bought. The map of the USA shows the size of these problems. The faster the population grows in any country the greater is the problem of getting rid of waste.

Another problem causing world-wide concern is noise. Some of the effects of noise pollution and the causes are shown in this chart.

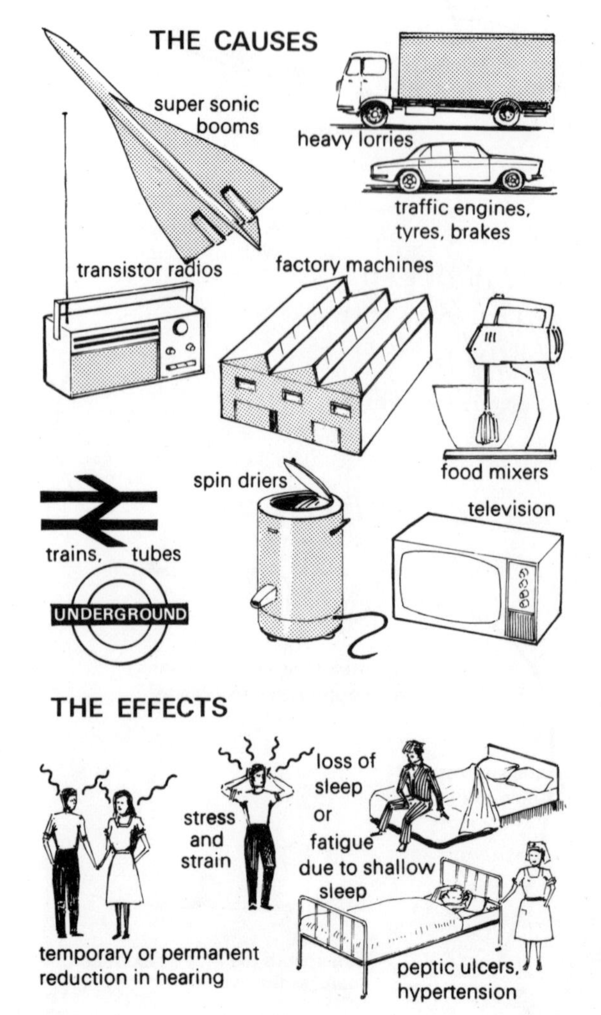

Population, cities and pollution

It is in the large overcrowded sprawling cities that many of the problems of pollution have to be faced. Perhaps the largest problem of all is the deterioration in the physical environment in cities with the overpowering presence of buildings, lack of open spaces, and overcrowding of human beings. These conditions, outlined in detail in the chapter on the urban environment, almost certainly contribute to the increase in mental illness and of crime, which are most noticeable where people are faced with the stress and strain of city life.

Figure 69 Some causes and effects of noise pollution.

In cities, motorways, houses, shops and offices fight for space. This is the freeway, Los Angeles, USA, where pollution from cars is a major problem.

Debris in the disused Rochdale Canal at Ancoats, Manchester.

As population grows, cities grow and pollution of all sorts increases. The question is what can we do *now* to prevent the disaster which will face the world if population continues to increase?

Some answers to this question have been suggested in chapter 8, and the next chapter will examine other possible solutions.

READING AND UNDERSTANDING

1 What is happening to the world's population?
2 (*a*) What is meant by the birth rate and the death rate?
(*b*) How do the birth and death rates compare in Britain today?
3 What are the four main problems that are linked with population growth?
4 What is meant by (*a*) malnutrition (*b*) undernourishment? Give details of their causes.
5 Kwashiorkor, pellagra and rickets have different causes. What are these causes and in what way are they linked with population growth?
6 What diseases can be caused by dirty drinking water?
7 What is illiteracy and why does it exist?

8 What is meant by the 'vicious circle of poverty'?

9 (*a*) In what ways is mankind spoiling his natural environment?
  (*b*) Is the damage very serious?

POINTS FOR FURTHER DISCUSSION

1 Should the developing countries be given aid? If so what kind of aid? Remember that they have very many *people* but little capital equipment.

2 Limiting family size is common in Britain, but it involves some families in moral problems. What kinds of moral problems might arise? Are there any solutions to these?

3 The fall in family size in Britain was due to a change in attitude to birth control, rather than new techniques. Why did this change in attitude come about? See the book list for references.

4 Some governments have schemes for family planning. What kind of schemes do you think governments could put into operation to restrict population growth? Several of the films about India have interesting points for discussion on this theme.

5 Litter is a form of pollution. How polluted is your school or college?

6 Would mass migration solve the population problem? Where could people migrate to?

7 To what extent was it important that Britain had an agricultural revolution *before* industrialisation?

PROJECT WORK

1 Write to Oxfam (Education Section) and the Voluntary Committee on Overseas Aid and Development (VCOAD) for more details about the population situation in the world. It may be necessary for your teacher to write for you or to send all the letters in one envelope.

2 Make tracing paper maps of the world, and on one, colour in the countries with the fastest population increase; on another colour in countries with the highest illiteracy; on another, colour in countries with the greatest malnutrition. Then stick or staple one edge of the maps together so that they lie on top of each other. What do you notice when you look through the top tracing paper?
(Another way of doing this is to use acetate sheets on an overhead projector.)

3 Look at Longman's Oxfam Series and pick out the books which particularly interest you. Make maps, bar graphs, essays and poems to illustrate the information you find out from these books.

4 Collect a series of pictures on the population situation from colour supplements, Oxfam, and VCOAD. Either write your own account of each picture *or* design a questionnaire that you could use on other members of the class to build up a story about each picture.

5 You are a reporter for a Sunday paper. After looking at pictures and films on population write your account for your paper, illustrating it in a way that would be interesting to other members of the class. If several of your friends do this you could publish a newspaper called 'World Population' or you could choose your own title. Remember to rely on the facts, and not in this case on your imagination.

6 It is possible that you have studied birth control in health education or biology lessons. It is beyond the scope of this chapter to include all the details of different methods and also some pupils and teachers wish to leave the detailed study of this subject until later. If you and your teacher feel that this would be a good subject for a project then your teacher should write to the Family Planning Association and ask your local library for a list of references including the *Which?* reports.

USEFUL BOOKS FOR PUPILS

Borgstrom, G. *Too Many* (Macmillan 1972)

Connexions Series, (a) *Fit to Live in?* (b) *Living* (c) *Food Tomorrow* (Penguin Education)

Gordon, S. *World Problems* (World Wide series) (Batsford 1971)

Kent, G. *Poverty* (Past into Present series) (Batsford 1968)

Matthews, B. & P. *Happily Ever After?* (Edward Arnold 1973)

McKenzie, A. *The Hungry World* (Faber 1969)

Oxford Study Sheets:
Disease; Water; Hunger; Malnutrition, etc. (Oxfam Education 1975)

Richards, M. *Population* (Social Science studies) (Longman 1975)

Stuart, J. *The Unequal. Third* (Network Social Science studies) (Edward Arnold 1977)

Tamplin, A. & Gottman, R. *Poisoned Power* (Chatto & Windus 1973)

Thompson, J. *Sociology for Schools* Book 2 (Hutchinson 1973)

USEFUL BOOKS FOR TEACHERS

Arvill, R. *Man and His Environment* (Pelican 1969)

Ehrlich, P. R. & Ehrlich, A. H. *Population, Resources, Environment* (Freeman 1970)

Kelsall, R. K. *Population* (Longman 1967)

Meadows, D. et al. *The Limits to Growth* (Earth Island Ltd 1972)

Mellanby, K. *Pesticides and Pollution* (Fontana 1969)

Ward, B. & Dubos, R. *Only One Earth* (Pelican 1972)

FILMS

The Earth and Mankind; 30 mins each; b/w; Concord Films Council, and ILEA 2036/6/8
1 People By the Billions (population explosion)
2 Man and His Resources (inequality)
3 To Each a Rightful Share (social change)
4–6 also available

The Population Problem; 30 mins each; b/w; Concord Films Council
1 Brazil – The Gathering Millions
2 The European Experience
3 Japan – Answer in the Orient
4 India – Writing on the Sand
5 USA – Seeds of Change
6 The Gift of Choice

The Problem of Refuse Disposal; 16 mins; Gateway 1969 277 D12

The Vicious Spiral (made for Christian Aid – problems of aid and trade); 30 mins; colour; Concord Films Council

Unseen Enemies (man against disease; made with WHO); 32 mins; colour; PFB

Food or Famine; 45 mins; colour; PFB

The Squeeze (the population explosion); 10 mins; b/w; ILEA 412 and Concord Films Council

The Torrey Canyon; 20 mins; Unilever

After the Torrey Canyon; 14 mins; ILEA 886

Human Population and Resources; Audio-Visual Productions 3512

Environmental Pollution and Conservation; Audio-Visual Productions 3513

There are also several Oxfam films now available on hire from Concord Films Council.

11 World Co-operation

'Poverty breeds more poverty.' The problem for the person caught in the vicious circle on page 261 was how to escape from the circle. Poor nations, and poor people in rich nations, are caught up in a day to day fight for survival. They are forced to live a 'hand to mouth' existence and they cannot put enough aside to help them look to their future and to escape from their present situation. It is impossible to break the circle of poverty without help from the outside. The United Nations has been working for almost a quarter of a century to help to improve the quality of life for people all over the world. We shall first look at a brief history of the United Nations (UN) and its different parts, and then we shall look at each of the four problems of the last chapter and see how attempts are being made to overcome these problems.

How the United Nations began

After the First World War many nations co-operated in a Peace Conference in the hope of creating a world organisation that would keep the peace and help to create a better world. The leaders of the nations first met in November 1920 and the assembly was called the League of Nations.

The League's work was linked with that of two other organisations:

(*a*) The *International Labour Organisation* (set up 1919). The ILO brought workers, employers and government representatives together from all over the world to discuss ideas 'for improving the work and welfare of working people'. In particular it helped to protect children at work in factories, mines and plantations. There were 45 ILO member states in 1919.

(*b*) The *World Court* (*International Court of Justice*) which it was hoped would settle disputes between countries. The aim was to have as many viewpoints as possible among the judges so that a fair decision could be made whenever two nations

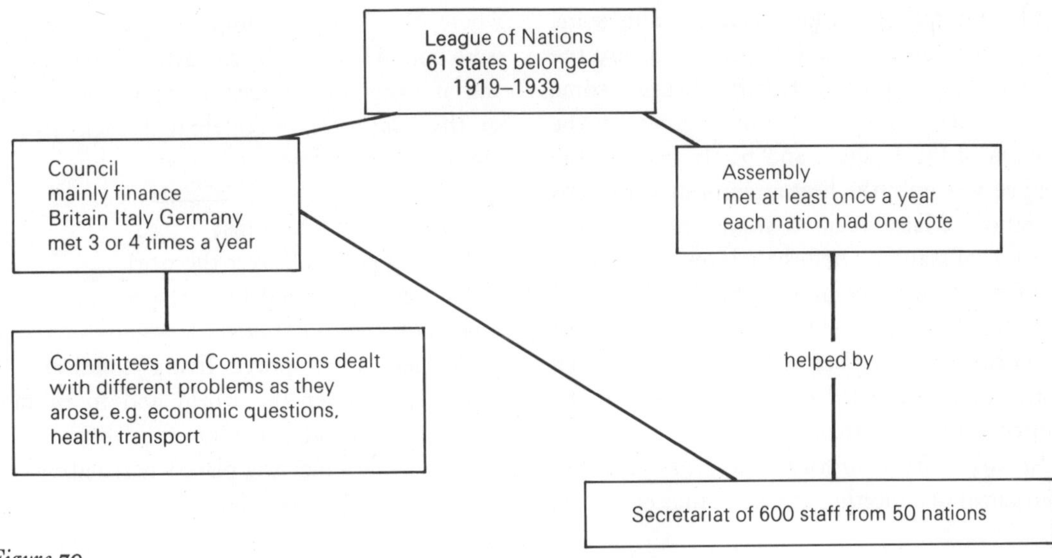

Figure 70

asked the court to settle a dispute, and to achieve this, fifteen judges from countries all over the world were elected. The motto was Law not War, but often the nations of the world neglected to use the court and attempted to settle disputes by other means.

Figure 70 shows how the League worked.

The International Court of Justice in session at The Hague.

The League of Nations succeeded in some ways but in others it failed, partly because the USA was never a member; partly because some nations attacked other nations, ignoring the protests of the League; and partly because the League was only the first attempt at world co-operation. Many nations would not put the interests of mankind before their own individual interests. With the coming of the Second World War the League dissolved, but it had come closer than anything before to co-operation on a world level, and it led to the formation of the United Nations in 1945.

In 1945 fifty countries sent representatives (delegates) to a meeting at San Francisco, USA, where the UN was founded. The members were bound together by a charter or constitution and it came into force on 24 October 1945, so that day is now celebrated each year as United Nations Day.

The UN has four aims:

1 To keep peace all over the world.
2 To develop friendship, respect and equal rights between nations.
3 To help to improve living conditions of people all over the world and to promote human rights and freedom for everyone.
4 To provide a meeting place where nations can discuss all their problems.

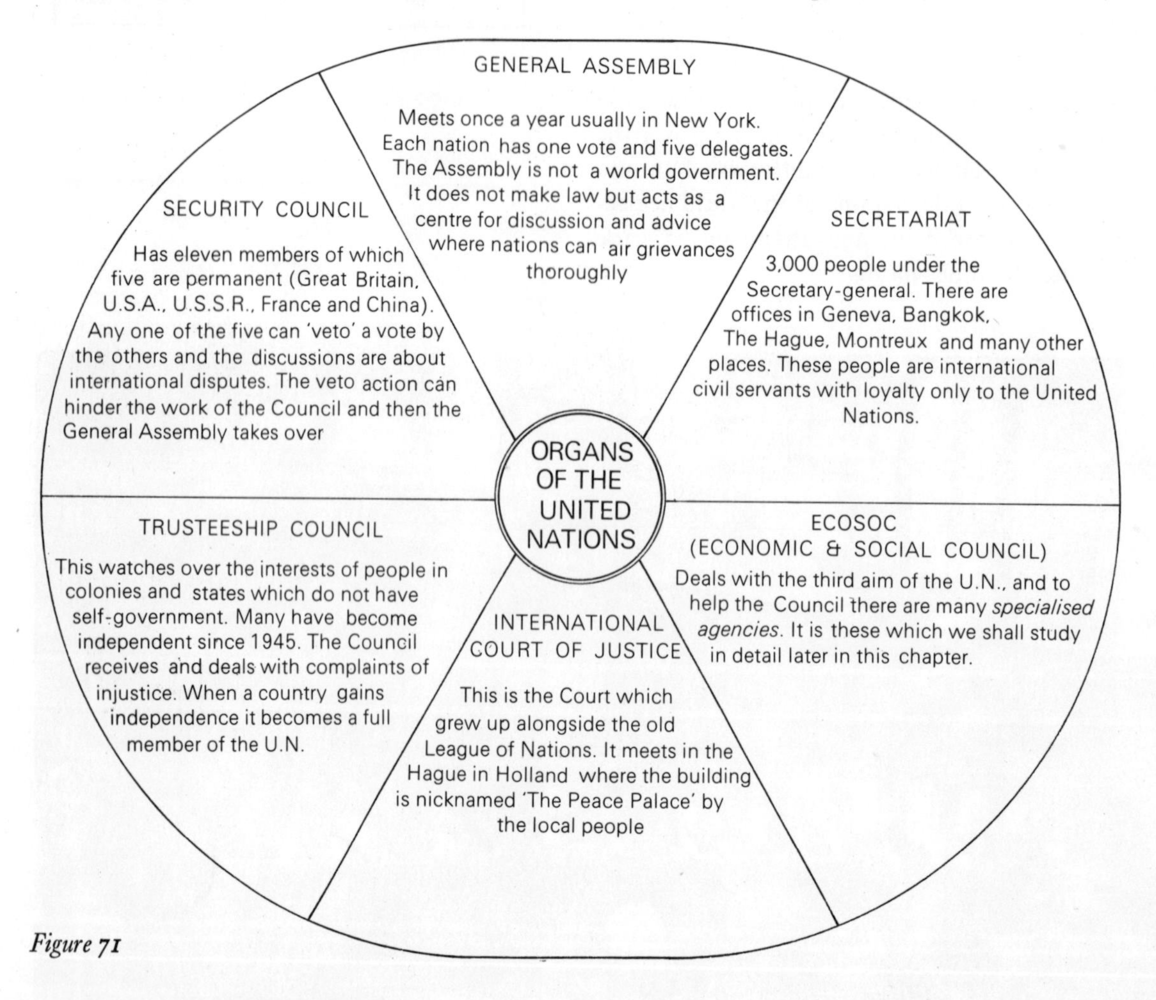

Figure 71

ECOSOC

This is the short name for the Economic and Social Council which deals with questions such as jobs for all, trade, health and education. It also works to secure the rights and freedom of people everywhere. ECOSOC has done a great deal to help the developing societies to overcome the problems of hunger, disease and illiteracy which were examined on pages 256–61.

The specialised agencies are listed below and their work is so varied that it would be impossible to cover all aspects of it here. Instead we shall look at examples of the work done in different parts of the world. Look at the suggestions for project work if you want to find out more.

In Guatemala the people have too few cattle and they cannot afford milk. Malnutrition is common and so a high protein value food has been developed called incaparina. *Research was done at the Institute of Nutrition of Central America and Panama, aided by WHO. These children will not suffer malnutrition because they are drinking* incaparina.

THE WORLD HEALTH ORGANISATION (WHO)

Vital research and projects are going on in many parts of the world to free people from sickness, poverty and hunger.

One of the greatest world health problems is mental health. It fills more hospital beds than cancer, heart diseases and T.B. combined. Many people who are outside hospitals are not well enough to lead normal happy lives. In many countries the old lunatic asylums and mad houses are being rebuilt and changed into open mental hospitals where patients are freer and are treated as needing care and modern medicine, not as animals that should be locked away. The 1959 Mental Health Act in Britain showed a movement towards cure and treatment rather than punishment and scorn for the mentally ill, and it separated the mentally ill from the mentally subnormal. Mental hospitals in Britain are beginning to be kinder places with more knowledge and understanding of the needs of patients.

In this picture from the Philippine Islands the patients are making friends during a game of basket ball. All over the world people are beginning to lose their horror of mental disease and are coming to regard it as curable like other sicknesses.

Johnny was an American boy who never spoke, could not walk, and did not communicate with anyone. Doctors thought this was because he was totally deaf until a therapist saw him when he was six and discovered that he was mentally ill. With her help he is now much more lively, and has started to play with other children.
The WHO helps hundreds of children every year in its campaign against disease of the body and of the mind.

This is an artist's impression of a French recreation centre for mental patients. It has a restaurant, shops, hair-dressers, entertainment halls, libraries and a hospital block.

THE UNITED NATIONS EDUCATIONAL, SCIENTIFIC AND CULTURAL ORGANISATION (UNESCO)

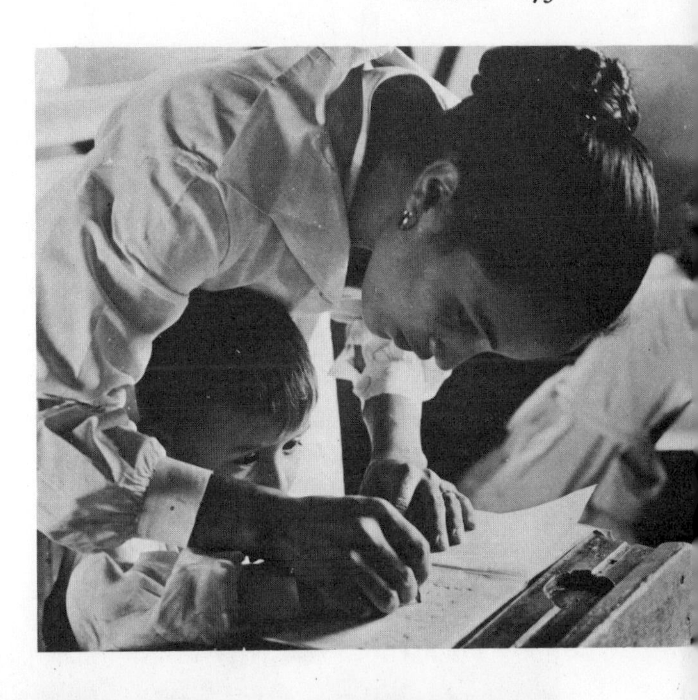

In many countries UNESCO is fighting the illiteracy problem. Seventy-seven children in a primary school in Paraguay have only one teacher. Without this school built by UNESCO in 1958 there would be no teacher at all.

Children and adults learn new methods of agriculture, the use of new types of seeds, and the use of irrigation and fertilisers. The boys here are using the school garden to help them learn about agriculture. They live in the Upper Volta in Africa.

THE FOOD AND AGRICULTURE ORGANISATION (FAO)

This organisation started the Freedom from Hunger campaign in the 1960s. It is especially concerned with the development of new methods of farming in the developing societies so that more food can be grown by the 'hungry millions' of the world.

In this picture the Indians of remote villages high in the Andes are discussing farming methods. This is part of a large plan to improve the social and economic life of the area, and the plan includes schools, health services, social services and clubs.

The World Bank and International Monetary Fund

Development plans to fight hunger, disease and illiteracy need money and other forms of aid.

The World Bank of the United Nations. The proper name is the International Bank for Reconstruction and Development. Sixty-one countries jointly own this bank whose headquarters are in New York. It lends money for many new projects.

A large iron and steel works in India which has been financed by the World Bank. This kind of aid involves complicated capital equipment but it must be remembered that the main needs in developing societies are seeds, fertilisers and irrigation systems for the farms. If there are too many factories in which machines do the work of men then the men may become unemployed. In societies with too many people, the new methods must make use of the men in the population if unemployment is to be avoided. Developing societies need a balance of new factories and new farms which use labour, for that is what they have most of.

A hydro-electric power station in Mexico which provides electricity for farms and for factories, offices and houses in cities. The money for this project was borrowed from the World Bank.

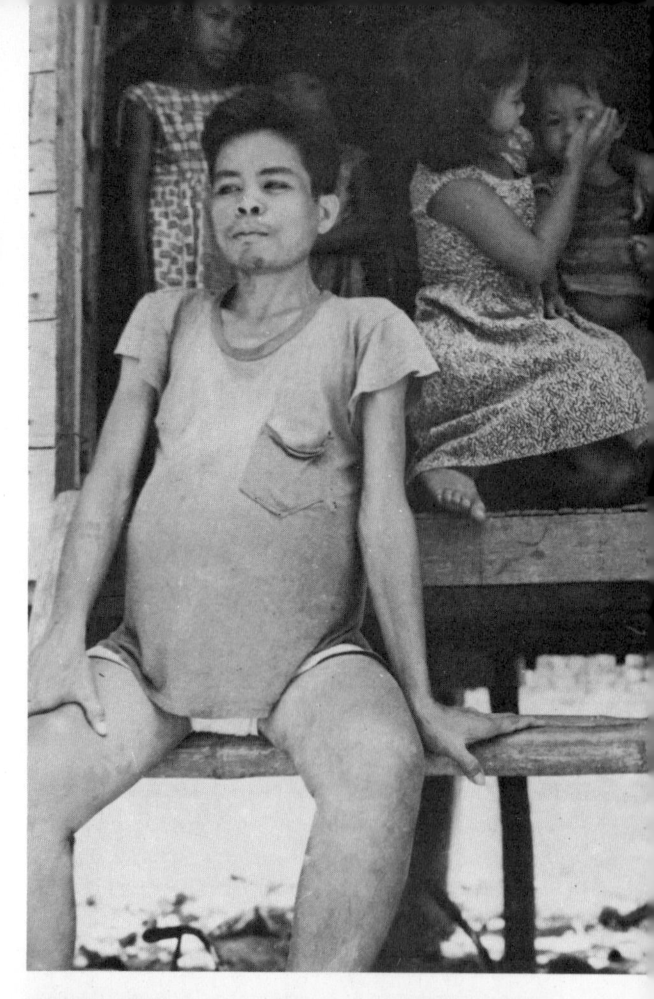

In this picture a dam is being built, paid for by a loan to India from the World Bank. Great care must be taken to ensure that dams do not cause an increase in the water-carried disease bilharziasis. This may happen if the water becomes infected as a result of bad sanitation in nearby towns and villages. It attacks children and young men under twenty-five. Its effects can be seen in this picture taken in the Philippines.

The United Nations Children's Fund (UNICEF)

This began as an emergency fund to help children in times of war and crisis but has become a permanent agency of the UN. The picture illustrates some of UNICEF'S work: The children are from Resistencia, an industrial city of 75,000 people in the cotton growing area of northern Argentina. WHO and UNICEF are jointly providing the money for hospitals, midwifery kits, rural health centres and sanitation systems to help the Argentinian government in its public health programme.

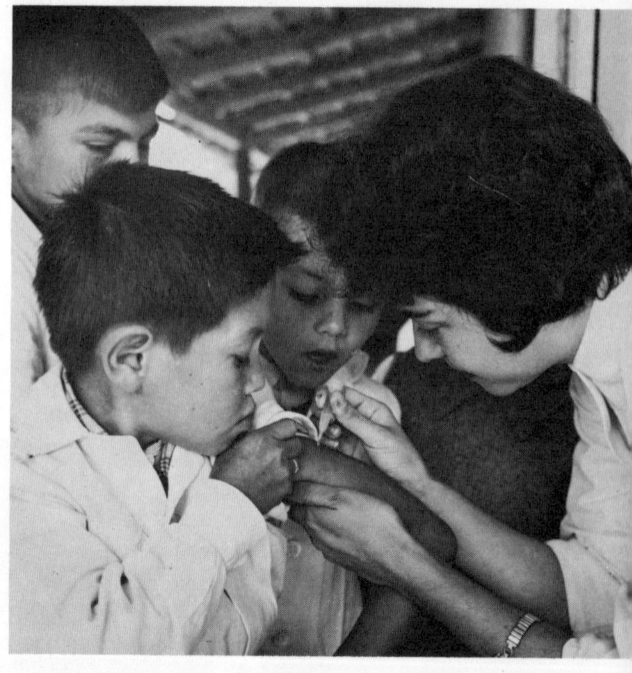

A small boy is vaccinated against smallpox and the others watch, knowing that they will be next.

In French Morocco villagers gather around a travelling UNICEF clinic which will help to cure the children of trachoma.

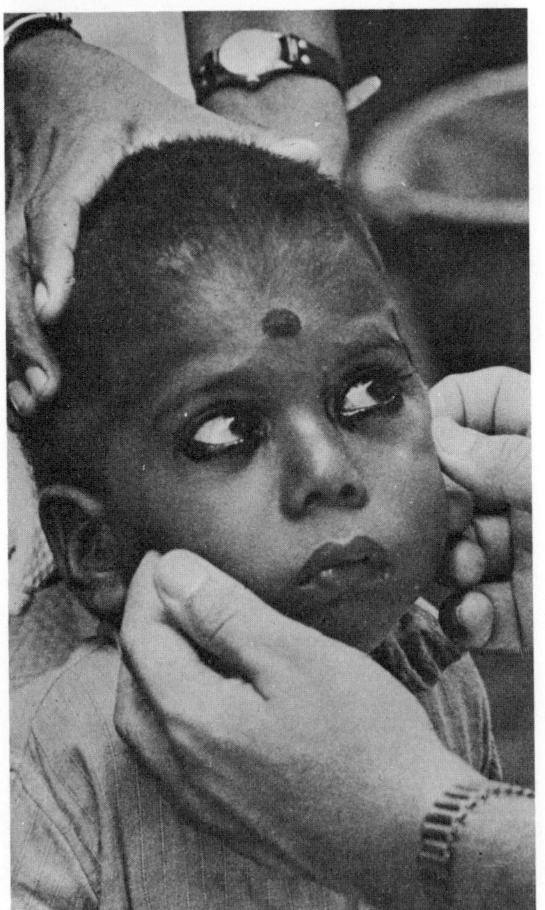

Children are the main sufferers from malaria in Burma. UNICEF is providing the money for DDT which is diluted and used to spray the mosquito-infected areas.

Since 1953 over eight million people have been protected. The use of DDT in the developing societies causes a future pollution problem. The developing societies have to balance the need to control disease against the need to prevent pollution. For this reason a ban on the use of powerful insecticides is resisted by the developing world. This is an example of the difficulty of finding solutions to population and its problems.

Pollution and environment – The Stockholm Conference 1972

In June 1972 many countries of the United Nations met at Stockholm in Sweden to discuss possible world situations to the problems of the environment. Many recommendations were made, particularly concerning pollution of rivers and oceans, and conservation of forests, plant and animal life. We have to wait and see how many of the proposals are put into practice, and whether all the nations involved will be prepared to put the interests of the whole world before their own national interests.

READING AND UNDERSTANDING

1 What was the League of Nations?
2 What are the aims of the UN?
3 What are the main 'organs' of the UN?
4 'ECOSOC'. What does this stand for?
5 (*a*) ECOSOC cannot do all its work on its own. Which agencies help ECOSOC?
(*b*) Give details about the aims of three of these agencies.
6 What is UNICEF and whom is it particularly concerned with helping?
7 What does the World Bank do?

POINTS FOR FURTHER DISCUSSION

1 We have seen that developing countries need aid. This can be either capital-intensive or labour-intensive. Why are both kinds of aid needed, and why is it important to have a balance between the two types?
2 The spread of the disease bilharziasis is a side-effect of improved irrigation. Have you heard of any other harmful effects of men's efforts to improve their environment? How would you try to avoid this sort of thing happening in the future?
3 Why cannot developing countries 'go it alone' and help themselves without help from others?
4 By helping developing countries the advanced industrial societies are really helping themselves. How far and in what ways might this be true?
5 Do you think a united world will ever exist?
6 'The atom bomb is a quicker and cheaper way of solving the population problem.' Is there any sense in this statement? What problems, if any, might be caused if this idea were put into practice?

PROJECT WORK

1 Write to the UN Committee in Britain. They produce a list of pamphlets and books which they publish and also some free reading material. Use the information you collect to find out more about
ILO WHO UNESCO
FAO UNICEF
2 Find out more about the history of the UN. The books on the reading list will help you.
3 Many voluntary organisations like
Save the Children Fund
Oxfam
War on Want
The Salvation Army
are helping in the world population problem. Their work is often linked with the United Nations. Write to them (or ask your teacher to write for you as they receive hundreds of letters each week) and use the information they send to find out
(*a*) how they started
(*b*) what their aims are
(*c*) what kind of work they do
(*d*) how their work is linked with other organisations and the UN.
4 The UNDP (United Nations Development Programme) is part of the work of the UN. It involves many agencies working in close co-operation. Find out from the books in the reading list and the material from Project 1 as much as you can about UNDP.

USEFUL BOOKS FOR PUPILS AND TEACHERS

Bailey, S. D. *The General Assembly of the United Nations* (Praeger, New York 1964)
Beckel, G. E. & Lee, F. *Workshops of the World: the UN Family of Agencies* (Abelard Schuman 1962)
Heater, D. & Owen, G. *World Affairs* (Harrap 1975)
Jackdaw, 100 *The United Nations* (Jonathan Cape)
Larsen, P. *The UN at work throughout the World* (Dent 1970)

Stuart, J. *The Unequal Third* (Network Social Science series) (Edward Arnold 1977)
UN *Office of Public Information* (12th edition 1964)
UN *Your United Nations Official Guide Book* (New York)
Information can also be obtained from the Council for Education in World Citizenship, the United Nations Association and United Nations London Information Centre.

USEFUL BOOKS FOR TEACHERS

Barber, J., Negro, J. & Smith, M. *Politics between States: Conflict and Co-operation* (Open University Press, Course D332 4 1975)

FILMS

Workshop for Peace (remake); 29 mins; Central Film Library v.375
The Philippines; Economic Progress; 10 mins; b/w; EFVA 14X
The Philippines: Social Progress; 10 mins; b/w; EFVA
United Nations Development Programme (mainly in Kenya); Central Film Library v.707
The Children (work of UNICEF); 10 mins; b/w; Concord Films Council
For All the World's Children (UNICEF); 10 mins; b/w; EFVA 85X
Uniting the Nations (History 1917–67 part 20); 20 mins; b/w; BBC Enterprises and ILEA 1966

FILM STRIPS WITH TAPE COMMENTARY (MISCELLANEOUS)

From Concordia Films:
- Tuesdays at Eight (probation)
- From Me to You (adoption)
- House for Sale (the Race Relations Act)
- Time off Their Hands (service of youth)
- Mr. Councillor (local government)
- Youth in Community (community service)
- Tinker, Tailor . . . (juvenile employment)
- One Nation (Community Relations Commission)

From Carwal Audio-Visual-Aids Ltd, PO Box 55, Wallington, Surrey:
- The Family
- Urban Renewal
- Conservation
- Human Groups

ADDRESSES OF PUBLISHERS

Allen (George) & Unwin Ltd,
40 Museum Street, London, WC1
Arnold (Edward) Publishers Ltd,
25 Hill Street, London, W1X 8LL
Arnold (E.J.) & Sons Ltd,
Butterley Street, Leeds, LS10 1AX
AVM Publishing Ltd,
27 Birchington Road, London, NW6

BBC Publications,
35 Marylebone High Street,
London, W1
BPC Publishing Ltd,
St Giles House, 49/50 Poland Street,
London, W1
Blackie & Sons Ltd,
Bishopbriggs, Glasgow, G64 2NZ
Blackwell (Basil) Ltd,
108 Cowley Road, Oxford, OX4 1JF
Blandford Press Ltd,
Link House, West Street, Poole,
Dorset, BH15 1LL
Blond Educational,
PO Box 9, 29 Frogmore,
St Albans, Herts

Cambridge University Press,
Bentley House, PO Box 92,
200 Euston Road, London, NW1 20B
Cape (Jonathan) Ltd,
30 Bedford Square, London, WC1
Cassell & Co. Ltd,
35 Red Lion Square,
London, WC1R 4SG
Collins (William) & Sons Ltd,
144 Cathedral Street, Glasgow, C4

Granada Publishing,
PO Box 9, 29 Frogmore,
St. Albans, Herts

Hamlyn Group,
Astronaut House, Hounslow Road,
Feltham, Middlesex
Harper & Row,
28 Tavistock Street,
London, WC2E 7PN
Hart-Davis (Rupert) Educational
Publications,
PO Box 9, 29 Frogmore, Herts
Heinemann Educational Books Ltd,
48 Charles Street, London, W1
Hodder & Stoughton Ltd,
47 Bedford Square, London, WC1B 3DP
Holmes McDougall Ltd,
137 Leith Walk, Edinburgh, EH6 8NS
Holt Blond Ltd,
Distributed by Hart-Davis Ltd

Hutchinson Publishing Group Ltd,
3 Fitzroy Square, London, W1

Jackdaw Publications,
30 Bedford Square,
London, WC18 3EL

Kingswood Publications,
9 Kingswood Place, London, SE13

Ladybird Books Ltd,
Loughborough, Leics
Longman Group,
Pinnacles, Harlow, Essex

MacDonald & Evans Ltd,
8 John Street, London, W1
Macdonald Educational,
49–50 Poland Street,
London, W1A 2LG
McGraw Hill Publishing Ltd,
McGraw Hill House,
Shoppenhangers Road,
Maidenhead, Berks
Macmillan Publishers Ltd,
Houndmills, Basingstoke,
Hants, RG21 2XS
Methuen & Co. Ltd,
11 New Fetter Lane,
London, EC4P 4EE

Nelson (Thomas) & Sons Ltd,
Lincoln Way, Windmill Road,
Sunbury-on-Thames,
Middlesex, TW16 7HP

Oliver & Boyd,
Croythorn House,
23 Ravelstone Terrace,
Edinburgh, EH4 2TL
Oxford University Press,
Ely House, 37 Dover Street,
London, W1X 4AH

Penguin Books Ltd,
Bath Road, Harmondsworth,
Middlesex
Pergamon Press Ltd,
Headington Hill Hall, Oxford
Perpetua Press,
11 Kendall Place, London, W1
Publishers' Distribution Co-operative,
Biblios Distribution Services Ltd,
Glenside Industrial Estate,
Partridge Green, Horsham, Sussex

Routledge & Kegan Paul,
39 Store Street, London, WC1E 7DD

Scholastic Publications Ltd,
161 Fulham Road, London, SW3
Schoolmaster Publishing Company,
Derbyshire House, Lower Street,
Kettering, Northants

Thames and Hudson Ltd,
30–34 Bloomsbury Street,
London, WC1B 3QP
Third World Publications,
138 Stratford Road,
Birmingham, B11 1AG

University of London Press Ltd,
See Hodder & Stoughton Ltd

Visual Publications,
197 Kensington High Street,
London, W8

Writers' & Readers' Publishing
Co-operative, 9–10 Rupert Street,
London W1

LIST OF ADDRESSES

Advisory Centre for Education,
18 Victoria Park Square,
Bethnal Green, London, E2 9PB

Alcoholics Anonymous,
11 Redcliffe Gardens, London, SW10

All London Teachers Against Racism
and Fascism, 2 Balfour Road,
London, SE24

Amnesty International,
55 Theobalds Road, London, WC1

Anglo-Chinese Educational Institute,
15 Camden High Street,
London, NW1 1NN

Anti-Nazi League,
12 Little Newport Street,
London, WC2

Architectural Press, Ltd,
9 Queen Anne's Gate,
London, SW1H 9BY

Association for the Prevention of
Addiction,
15 King Street, London, WC2

Association for the Teaching of Social
Sciences,
15 Serpentine Road, Harborne,
Birmingham 17

Audio Learning Ltd,
84 Queensway, London, W2

Audio Visual Library Service,
Powdrake Road, Grangemouth,
Stirlingshire, FK2 9VT

Audio-Visual Productions,
15 Temple Sheen Road,
London, SW14 7PY

British Broadcasting Corporation,
Head Office, Broadcasting House,
Portland Place, London, W1

British Film Institute,
81 Dean Street, London, W1

Building Societies Association,
14 Park Street, London, W1

Carwal Audio-Visuals Ltd,
PO Box 55, Wallington, Surrey

Central Film Library,
Government Building,
Bromyard Avenue, London, W3

Central Office of Information,
Hercules House,
Westminster Bridge Road,
London, SE1

Centre for World Development Education,
Parnell House,
25 Wilton Road,
London, SW1V 1JS

Child Poverty Action Group,
1 Macklin Street, London, WC2

Christian Aid,
2 Sloane Gardens, London, SW1

Colour Centre Slides Ltd,
Farnham Royal, Slough, Bucks

Commission for Racial Equality,
Elliot House,
10–12 Arlington Street,
London, SW2

Commonwealth Institute,
Kensington High Street, London, W8

Communist Party,
16 King Street, London, WC2

Community Relations Commission,
15–16 Bedford Street, London, WC2

Community Service Volunteers,
237 Pentonville Road, London, N1 9NS

Concord Films,
201 Felixstowe Road, Ipswich

Concordia Films,
Viking Way, Bar Hill Village,
Cambridge, CB3 8EL

Conservative Party,
32 Smith Square, London, SW1

Consumers' Association,
14 Buckingham Street, London, WC2

Contemporary Films Ltd,
55 Greek Street, London, W1

Council for Education in World Citizenship (CEWC),
93 Albert Embankment,
London, SE1

Counter Information Services (CIS),
9 Poland Street, London, W1

Countryside Commission,
1 Cambridge Gate, Regent's Park,
London, NW1

Cyrenians,
40 Charleville Road, London, W14

Department of Education and Science,
Curzon Street, London, W1

Doctor Barnardo's,
Stepney Causeway, London, E1

EAV Ltd,
Butterley Street, Leeds, LS10 1AX

Educational Film Centre Ltd,
68/70 Wardour Street, London, W1

Educational Foundation for Visual Aids (EFVA),
33 Queen Anne Street,
London, W1

EEC Information Service,
23 Chesham Street, London, SW1

Equal Opportunities Commission,
Commission House,
Grosvenor Hill, London, W1

Family Planning Association,
27 Mortimer Street, London, W1

Family Welfare Association,
Denison House,
296 Vauxhall Bridge Road,
London, SW1

Friends of the Earth,
9 Poland Street, London, W1V 5OH

Gateway Educational Films Ltd,
St Lawrence House, Broad Street,
Bristol, BS1 2HF

Geffrye Museum,
Kingsland Road, London, E2

Gingerbread (One Parent Families),
9 Poland Street, London, W1

Greater London Council (GLC),
General Administrative Offices,
County Hall, London, SE1

Guild Sound and Vision Ltd,
Woodston House, Oundle Road,
Peterborough, SE2 9PZ

Health Education Council,
78 New Oxford Street,
London, WC1A 1AH

Help the Aged,
218 Upper Street, London, N1

Her Majesty's Stationery Office (HMSO),
Atlantic House, Holborn Viaduct,
London, EC1

Home Office,
Whitehall, London, SW1

Howard League for Penal Reform,
125 Kennington Park Road,
London, SE11

Independent Broadcasting Authority (IBA),
70 Brompton Road, London, SW3

Inner London Education Authority (ILEA),
County Hall, London, SE1

Institute for the Study of Drug Dependence,
Chandos House,
2 Queen Anne Street, London, W1

Israel Government Tourist Office,
59 St James's Street, London, SW1

Japanese Embassy Information Centre,
9 Grosvenor Square, London, W1

Jewish National Fund,
Rex House, 4 Regent Street,
London, SW1

Keep Britain Tidy Group,
27 Queen Anne's Gate, London, SW1

Labour Party,
Transport House,
Smith Square, London, W1

The Law Society,
Law Society Hall,
113 Chancery Lane,
London, WC2A 1PL

Learning Resources Centre,
275, Kennington Lane,
London, SE11 5QZ

Liberal Party,
7 Exchange Court, London, WC2

Longman Resources Unit,
9–11 The Shambles, York

Metropolitan Police Recruitment Office,
201 Borough High Street, London, SE1

Micro Slides (Oxford) Ltd,
7 Little Clarendon Street, Oxford

National Association for Mental Health,
39 Queen Anne Street, London, W1

National Association for Multi-Racial Education,
58 Collingbourne Road,
London, W12

National Audio Visual Aids Library,
Paxton Place, Gipsey Hill,
London, SE27

National Children's Home,
85 Highbury Park, London, N5

National Council for Audio Visual Aids
33 Queen Anne Street, London W1

National Council for Civil Liberties,
186 Kings Cross Road, London, WC1

National Council for the Unmarried Mother and her Child (NCUMC),
255 Kentish Town Road,
London, NW5

National Council of Social Service,
26 Bedford Square, London, WC1

National Council on Alcoholism,
212a Shaftesbury Avenue,
London, WC2

National Deaf Children's Society,
31 Gloucester Place, London, W1

National Society for Clean Air,
Field House, Breams Buildings,
London, EC4

National Society for Mentally Handicapped Children Bookshop,
Pembridge Hall,
17 Pembridge Square, London, W2

National Society for the Prevention of Cruelty to Children (NSPCC),
1 Riding House Street, London, W1

National Union of Teachers,
Hamilton House, Mabledon Place,
London, WC1

Nature Conservancy Council,
19/20 Belgrave Square,
London, SW1X 8PY

New Scotland Yard,
Broadway, London, SW1

Open University Educational Enterprises, Ltd,
12 Cofferidge Close, Stony Stratford
Milton Keynes

Oxfam Education,
172 Archway Road, London, N6

Petroleum Films Bureau,
4 Brook Street, London, W1

The Police Federation,
8 Rathbone Place, London, W1

The Pre-School Play Groups Association,
87a Borough High Street, London, SE1

The Probation Service,
1a Walton Street, London, SW3

Race Relations Board,
see Commission for Racial Equality

Radical Education,
86 Eleanor Road, London, E8

Radical Science Journal,
9 Poland Street, London, W1

Rank Film Library,
1 Aintree Road, Brivale, Greenford,
Middlesex

Release,
52 Princedale Road, London, W11

Royal Anthropological Institute,
21 Bedford Square, London, WC1

Salvation Army,
101 Queen Victoria Street,
London, EC4

Save the Children Fund,
29 Queen Anne's Gate, London, SW1

Schools Council General Studies Project,
9/11 The Shambles, York

Science Museum,
South Kensington, London, SW7

Shell-Mex and BP Group,
Head Offices, Shell-Mex House,
The Strand, London, WC2

Shelter,
157 Waterloo Road, London, SE1 8UU

Slide Centre Ltd,
Slide Filmstrip Producers,
11 Bellevue Road, London, SW17

Socialist Teachers Alliance,
89 Meadvale Road, London, W5

Socialist Workers Party,
6 Cotton Gardens, London, E2 8DN

Society for Cultural Relations with the USSR,
118 Tottenham Court Road,
London, W1

Sound Services,
see Guild Sound and Vision Ltd

Spare Rib,
27 Clerkenwell Close, London, EC1

The Stock Exchange,
61 Threadneedle Street, London, EC2

Study Centre Publications,
Burton Chambers,
24 Hamilton Road, Felixstowe,
Suffolk

Teaching London Kids,
79 Ranalds Road, London, N5

Town and Country Planning Association,
The Planning Centre,
28 King Street, Covent Garden,
London, WC2

Trades Union Congress,
Great Russell Street, London, WC1

UNESCO
All publications are dealt with via HMSO. Other information is available from the following United Nations addresses:

United Nations Association,
93 Albert Embankment, London, SE1

United Nations London Information Centre,
14 Stratford Place, London, W1

United Nations Organisation Library,
14–15 Stratford Place, London, W1

UNICEF Educational Material,
Mr W. W. French,
102 Coventry Road, Warwick

Urban Systems Ltd,
Parlane Associates,
192 Chiltern Court, Baker Street,
London, NW1

Voluntary Committee on Overseas Aid and Development (VCOAD),
see Centre for World Development Education

War on Want,
26 The Grove, London, W5

Wires (Women's Information Referral & Inquiry Service),
32a Parliament Street, York

Women's Research and Resources Centre,
27 Clerkenwell Close,
London, EC1

FOR USE WITH THIS BOOK

Especially made for use with this book are four filmstrips containing supplementary data and illustrations.

Titles:
1 The Family
2 Urban Renewal
3 Conservation
4 Human Groups

Produced by: Carwal Audio-Visual Aids Ltd, PO Box 55, Wallington, Surrey

Index